BEYOND GIBRALTAR

Maristella de Panizza Lorch

TBR Books
New York

Copyright © 2020 by Maristella de Panizza Lorch

All rights reserved. No part of this publication may be reproduced, distributed, or transmitted in any form or by any means, without prior written permission.

TBR Books is a program of the Center for the Advancement of Languages, Education, and Communities. We publish researchers and practitioners who seek to engage diverse communities on topics related to education, languages, cultural history, and social initiatives.

    CALEC - TBR Books
    750 Lexington Avenue, 9th floor
    New York, NY 10022
    www.calec.org | contact@calec.org
    www.tbr-books.org | contact@tbr-books.org

Cover Design: Eunjoo Foster

Front Cover Illustration © Gabriel Suchowolski

First published in 2013 by Pegasus Press

ISBN 978-1-947626-26-3 (paperback)
ISBN 978-1-636070-26-1 (hardcover)
ISBN 978-1-636070-25-4 (eBook)

Library of Congress Control Number: 2020947419

Dedication

To E.R.L.

Explorer Of Spaces

Stiller Freund der vielen Fernen
Quiet friend of the many distances

Und wenn dich das Irdische vergass
Zu der stillen Erde sag: Ich rinne.
Zu dem raschen wasser sprich: Ich bin.

And if the earth will have forgotten you,
Tell the quiet earth: I run
To the rapid water say: I am.
(Rilke)

To
The World of our Families

"O frati," dissi, "che per cento milia
perigli siete giunti a l'occidente,
a questa tanto picciola vigilia
de' nostri sensi ch'è del rimanente,
non vogliate negare l'esperienza,
di retro al sol, del mondo sanza gente[...]

Infin che 'l mar fu sopra noi richiuso"
(Dante, Inferno XXVI, 112-142)

"Brothers," I said, "o you, who having crossed
a hundred thousand dangers, reach the west,
to this brief waking-time that still is left
unto your senses, you must not deny
experience of that which lies beyond
the sun, and of the world that is unpeopled. [...]

until the sea again closed over us"

(Transl. Mandelbaum)

We are born with the dead:
see, they return and bring us with them...
Right action is freedom
from past and future also
(T. S. Eliot)

Deciding to remember and what to remember
is how we decide who we are
(Pinsk)

Also by Maristella de Panizza Lorch

OTHER VOLUMES OF THE TRILOGY

Mamma in her Village (2020, first published in 2005);
The Other Shore (2019).

OTHER PUBLICATIONS

Critical edition of Lorenzo Valla's *De Voluntate* (1431-44);
On Pleasure (translation of Lorenzo Valla's *De Voluptate*);
A Defense of Life: Lorenzo Valla's Theory of Pleasure;
*Folly and Insanity in Renaissance Literature (*with Ernesto Grassi);
Ziliolo Ziliolo's *Michaelida* (1431), editor.

In Praise of Beyond Gibraltar

Beyond memory: Fiction and History

Beyond Gibraltar is the second volume of a trilogy that leads us through the 19th and 20th century, from the once Austrian Tyrol via Rome to New York through three generations. The first volume, *Mamma in her Village* (first published by Ruder and Finn Press, NY 2005), is built on memories from stories the author heard from her mother complemented by historical documents of the time. This second volume cannot be classified as any specific 'genre.' If taken literally, according to Maristella Lorch, the work could be considered a kind of memoir by an American of Italian origin who spends her first eighteen years (1920-1940) in her native Tyrol (that became Italian after WWI) and the four years of War (1940-1944) in Rome, where, in 1944, she meets and, in 1945 marries, an American lieutenant of Italian origin. After a year spent with the Allied Military Government (AMG) in Venezia Giulia on the Yugoslav border, the story closes with the protagonist's first four years as a war-bride in the US.

The author rebuilds her story by memory, aided by a diary for the years of the War, by a close dialogue with her sister Bona who had followed her to America, and by historical documents of the period. Her firm intention is indeed to recreate her personal story within a well-defined historical context.

Yet *Beyond Gibraltar* is not a *memoir*. What makes for the richness and originality of the story is the fact that Imagination leads Memory as the author succeeds in transforming her memories into what must be plainly qualified as a "novel." By refusing a linear narrative, Lorch succeeds in building a true 'intrigue' which keeps the reader constantly in suspense as she reinvents the story. The author, whose imagination is rooted in a strong classical and modern culture, is influenced by Homer and Virgil as well as by Pirandello. The novel's two threads of Ariadne are the stories of Dante's Ulysses in the *Divine Comedy* and that of the play *Millionaire Naples* by Eduardo de Filippo-- a powerful classical reference on one hand, and a beautiful expression of modern literature on the other.

As background to Lorch's story, Dante acquires a meaning beyond the role that the *Divine Comedy* occupies in Italian literature and culture from the Middle Ages on. Much of the author's professional life in America has been dedicated to the discovery and clarification of Medieval and Renaissance Italian literature. In fact, while she was writing the present novel, after half a century of teaching at Columbia University, she dedicated time and energy to initiating a vast American public outside the University to the subtleties of the *Divine Comedy*. A character can be a hero, even if condemned to Hell by a deeply Christian author. This is the case of Ulysses who served as a constant inspiration to the author in the gestational years of composition of *Beyond Gibraltar*.

It is well known among specialists that Dante's Ulysses lives in a world which is not that of Homer. As an old man— as he tells Dante who meets him in the deepest Hell, where, transformed into a flame he lives among the "bad advisers"—Ulysses gave in to the urge of abandoning his beloved little Ithaca and facing the Atlantic Ocean beyond Gibraltar. He died along with his old and tired friends, swallowed by the Ocean, after months of navigation, just as he sighted land, an isolated cone-shaped mountain which happened to be the 'Mountain of Purgatory.' In Dante's world, that is in a 'divine' *Comedia*, Ulysses, by crossing Gibraltar, deserved God's punishment. He had broken the law that reserved the crossing of an immense Ocean only to the dead who would repent for their sins on an isolated island before they could be admitted to Paradise. Today, Ulysses can serve as the greatest hero of a 'human' *comedia*.

As Lorch interprets the episode for a general American public, Ulysses becomes, by his very death, the mythical, heroic precursor of a practical and down-to earth Columbus who, by successfully crossing the Ocean, blazed the trail for thousands of emigrants in search of a better life in a "new" world. As protagonist of the present novel, the author willfully follows in the footsteps of her mythical father who, in *Mamma in her Village,* at the dawn of the century, had been exiled by his own father "beyond Gibraltar" as punishment for a sin that was in fact an act of love.

In the footsteps of Columbus and of thousands of emigrants, the protagonist of the present novel can be seen as conquering the original curse connected with the crossing of the Strait by re-establishing, in the reality of her own life, the symbolic, mythological tie between the Old and the New World. It is Dante's human dimension that remains the backdrop for this central volume of the trilogy.

Millionaire Naples by Eduardo de Filippo, a tragicomedy on Naples in the immediate postwar thriving of black-market activities, is equally symbolic but in quite a different way. This particular work, which was a spectacular success in Italy in 1945, enters the author's personal life in two decisive instances. While in Italy and during the long crossing of the Ocean she and her husband consider it as their key to New York City: Times Square becomes, in their mind and plans, the connection between the Old World and the New. When her husband Claude, who had translated the play under de Filippo's supervision and had found a producer in New York ready to sponsor it, unexpectedly fails at the very last moment to have it performed, the defeat weighs heavily on the couple in different ways. After a moment of despair, it becomes for the "war-bride," almost unconsciously, the first incentive to face 'America' on her own, to fight for her own survival and the survival of a family that had rapidly grown from two to five members.

Four years later, in the fall of 1951, by a curious combination of events, *Millionaire Naples* surfaces again. The once 'war-bride' has hardly lived her first week as a young Assistant Professor of Italian at Barnard College, the women's College of Columbia, when she is offered the possibility of co-directing and acting in a special adaptation of the first act of de Filippo's play.

This event sets the stage for one aspect of her future career as promoter of Italian culture on the Columbia campus. It will complement her courses on Dante, Italian poetry, Italian theatre and film besides Renaissance Humanism with her popularity on campus with students as well as colleagues, many of them veterans of the Mediterranean campaign [...].The book closes with the 'revelation' of a name – Edgar R. Lorch – a perfect example that distances *Beyond Gibraltar* from 'Memory' or 'History' and clearly defines its author as a 'novelist.'

Another original aspect of the work is the convergence of personal, family, national, not to say world history, craftily managed through a series of permanent flashbacks and flash-forwards. Thus, Alcide de Gasperi, the future leader of the Italian Christian

Democrats, at the time Secretary of the Vatican Library, becomes the protector of the family and Maristella Lorch's personal supporter in the first steps of her research at the department of Classics at the University of Rome, simply because he had once been helped by her paternal grandfather. Another example of these coincidences is when, during the celebration of a marriage in her husband's family in Schenectady, in February 1951, Lorch meets a Spanish Professor, husband of the bride, who insists she should apply for the position of Italian Professor at Barnard College, thus inviting her to finally enter the much longed-for Columbia gates.

While the author remains the center of the story, a crowd of family members holds the stage around her -- her mother, sisters and brother, her Dalmatian and her German brothers-in-law, the latter a fighter in the 2nd Polish Corps who joins her in New York with a student visa. Over them all reigns, as guardian angel of the family, the shadow of a mythical father whose life in 'America' at the dawn of the century is religiously kept a secret until 1940 when the family decides to leave the mountains for Rome. From the dawn to the middle of the 19th century, through two World Wars, a depression, Fascism, and Liberation through the beginning of the Cold War, History intersects at specific moments with this family that, at the border with Austria, longs for Italy.

It is the composition itself of *Beyond Gibraltar* that makes of an autobiography a *récit d'initiation* on the model of the *Odyssey*. As a modern Ulysses, our heroine leaves her Ithaca, locked in by impenetrable mountains, traveling through the sunny Italian peninsula to reach the very heart of Rome, shortly before the second World War. At 17, in Ostia, near Rome, she finally discovers the sea. At the Liberation of Rome, she meets some Italian-Americans who facilitate her approach to a totally unknown world 'beyond Gibraltar.' Before facing it directly, she is made to experience the strange and dangerous world at the border with communist Yugoslavia. She finally boards a military ship in February 1947 with two *viatica* -- a letter of introduction to the President of Columbia University, Nicholas Murray Butler, and the translation of *Millionaire Naples* -- *viatica* that at first reveal themselves ineffective. Like all heroines of the imagination, Lorch is subjected to several trials, many of which she does not overcome.

It is precisely thanks to this work of literary creation which moves way beyond the Memoir genre that Lorch gives us a precious historical testimony. The relation to history is double -- both direct and indirect. Direct – in that she serves as a witness, when, with her first boyfriend, a Greek graduate in political science from Oxford, she listens to Mussolini in Piazza Venezia in June 1940 declare war on the side of Hitler. Direct also when, in order to hide her men at home, she enters the Resistance. Asked to induce German soldiers to desert, she is finally arrested by the Gestapo shortly before Liberation and is briefly imprisoned.

Her indirect presence runs throughout the whole story. It is a story at first of a small, impoverished, middle-class family during twenty years of Fascism, a regime to which the family is at the start benevolently indifferent but to which it becomes clearly hostile as Mussolini, with increasing gusto, engages in his imperial military enterprises, beginning with the Abyssinian non-declared war. After the declaration of War in 1940, the family, like most Italians, moves, step by step, into a blind, deaf, silent, and desperate opposition. The novel at the same time witnesses the arrival of the first European emigrants in America after the end of World War II. It tells of the force of the American Dream and of life in Greater New York in the mid 20th century. The reader can clearly discover how the step by step acceptance of a 'strange America' is closely connected to the cultural diversities of the Old World.

The interweaving of memory, fiction, and history makes for the attraction of *Beyond Gibraltar*. Through memory the past becomes living present, while the novelistic construction excites the imagination by exploiting to the maximum a real-life story. The story of an individual's life thus becomes a precious historical document on life during the first half of the 20th century, as seen from both sides of the Atlantic Ocean.

—*Recteur Philippe Joutard, Professor of History at the University of Provence and at the Ecole des Hautes Etudes en Sciences Sociales*

Maristella Lorch, who was born in the Alto Adige right after World War I, has written the second vivid book of her trilogy recounting the deep mountain roots of her family in the Alto Adige - the Alpine region that with the stroke of a pen in the 1919 Treaty of Versailles went from being Austrian to Italian - and her own journey to professorship at Columbia University. Maristella's grandmother and mother, each successively widowed, managed to raise their children despite the privations of hunger, roving soldiers, sickness and politics that threatened life during the three decades spanning World War I and II. Woven through both books is the compelling fabric of family and culture; a passion for education as an essential tool of survival; and stories of insistent love and romance against all odds. Above all, Maristella's sensory descriptions take you from rural Italian kitchens to remote Alpine valleys to the bombed-out streets of Rome, ending with the struggle of making a new life with her GI husband in New York City of the 1950s.

—*Alex Belida, Voice of America*

The memories of Maristella Lorch impose themselves on the reader, as they span the period from childhood in the Tyrol in the second half of the 1920's until her maturity in Rome and the beginning of her career at Columbia University in New York to which she moved at the end of World War II after marrying an American officer.

Masterfully written by a close and privileged observer of momentous events, the narrative is fascinating, in how it weaves a succession of personal events into an eager and keen understanding of the feelings of all the characters involved. Their personal experiences, interwoven into the "great" history, are never separated from a pointed, careful, and realistic chronicle of the facts.

In the fresco painted by Maristella Lorch, each episode stands as witness to her tale, enriched by precious literary memories of time, weather, and place, always interwoven in the historical context. It captures the reader's attention with the clarity of its psychological analysis. Moreover, her clear and critical vision of the whole offers more than one opportunity for a re-reading and a reflection on those crucial years for Europe and the whole of humanity.

—*Franco Rocco, Architect*

Acknowledgments

Beyond Gibraltar has been underway for so long that it is impossible for me to thank by name the students, colleagues, relatives and friends who have helped me in various ways, with suggestions, research, criticism, and editorial work. I remember with gratitude my daughter Ingrid who years ago provided very useful notes on an earlier version, as well as financial support. I must limit myself to thanking by name two of my former students who have become good friends, Pellegrino d'Acierno and Ingrid Rossellini, and the two students from the Columbia Undergraduate Scholars Program who processed the manuscript with my revisions, Tiffany Bryant and Thomas de Swardt. My daughter Lavinia, most helpful as usual, remained in the background. My grateful thoughts go foremost to the characters of my story, to all those who allowed me to live again with them as I imagined I had lived once in Bolzano, Merano, Rome, and America. I owe to them the story. I owe the actual crossing to Lieutenant Claude Bové and his family, who are still with me today. I offer warm thanks to the family to which I belonged before the crossing — my mother, my sisters, my brother, and also to my father who, thanks to Mamma, stayed close to us, as a tangible presence, after his untimely death. This was my great supporting family during our odyssey from Bolzano to Merano to Rome.

I cherish especially the only surviving member, my sister Bona, and her New York family.

For Rome I shall always long, not as *caput mundi* but as the final and lasting fulfillment of my European life. Of the family at large, I remember gratefully nephews and cousins who helped me in so many ways.

For information and documents, I wish to thank, among my cousins in Trento, Andreana Froner, Giulietta Manci, and her two daughters, and in Mamma's family, Gina Cristoforetti in Tajo, Dermulo, and Los Angeles.

Among my friends close to me after retirement, my warm thanks go to Countess Maria Fede Caproni, Annalisa Cima, and Gigi Giustina.

For my revival of Bolzano and Merano, I am deeply grateful to Hofrat Inama von Sternegg in Innsbruck who provided precious family documents, and above all to Mary de Rachelwitz. Mary not only made available to me her library and her home in Tirol; she also shared with me, besides her "Dante" and the *Cantos* of her father Ezra Pound, her personal knowledge of the birth-place we had in common, as we happily discovered when we met at Yale University at the presentation of my book, *A Defense of Life*.

I owe thanks to Senator Peterlini for his suggestions and his invaluable publications, to Ambassador Corrias for his friendship and his father's book. For support and research in Bolzano and Trento, I am grateful to Daniela Parisi of the Catholic University of Milan and to Luigi Bonatti of the University of Trento, Luciano Borrelli, Elena Ravelli, and Fabrizio Leonardelli of the Biblioteca Comunale of Trento, Christoph Hartung von Hartunger, historian of Bolzano/Bozen, Hans Feiss, Director of the Landes Archiv in Bolzano. Among my latest supporters I thank my friends of EPIC (Emeriti of Columbia), my colleague and friend Robert Paxton for his contributions on the study of Fascism, and the French historian Philippe Joutard, author of *Histoire et mémoire, conflits et alliance* (Paris, 2013), and his wife Geneviève.

I owe my home at Columbia to The Italian Academy for Advanced Studies in America, whose staff I thank for their gracious hospitality from 1996 to the present. Barnard College shall always remain for me my harbor in America.

I remember gratefully my family, Duncan, Ingrid, Madeleine, Claudia, Lavinia, Donatella, their husbands and children, with special mention of Fiamma and Tristan who, by living so close to me in the autumn of my life, witnessed the story as it grew.

Like *Mamma in her Village, Beyond Gibraltar* owes its very existence to my daughter Lavinia who, after the death of her father, the *ERL* of the story, made its fulfillment one of the top priorities of her own life. She revised as I wrote and kept me going when I gave signs of fatigue. There are no words to express what I owe Lavinia.

Finally, my deepest gratitude goes to Fabrice Jaumont, founder of CALEC, and to Jane Ross, friends and collaborators in an ongoing project of opening up the world through the sharing of cultures and languages.

Table of Contents

Acknowledgments — xiii
Rosengarten — 1
From Villa to Villa — 11
The Dream of Rome — 57
Rome from Villa Moskau — 63
Love and War — 81
Vatican Adventures — 107
A School on the Tiber — 127
War at Potra Metrona — 137
The Germans – The Women's War — 159
The Liberators — 191
Regina Coeli — 205
St. Peter's — 211
Venezia Giulia — 223
Times Square — 261
Montclair — 271
Schenectady — 277
Manhattan — 293
Napoli Milionaria — 299
The Marine Shark — 319
A Baby and Tuberculosis — 333
Rome: Lost and Reconquered — 363
Theater at Barnard — 371
Epilogue — 393
A Personal Note — 395
Chronology — 399
About the Author — 403
About TBR Books — 405
About CALEC — 407

CHAPTER 1

Rosengarten

On the evening of July 13, 1925, Papa and I sat together on a marble bench in our garden. I was five years old. Four years had elapsed almost to the day since Papa and Mamma had pushed me in my carriage across the city of Bolzano and the foaming mountain river Talfer. We went from the bank which Papa directed in front of the cathedral in Waltherplatz, to the green paradise of Gries. For four years, we had been living happily at Villa Soell, in sight of the jagged Dolomite Mountains. Each year, we had celebrated together the birth of a baby. First, beautiful Francesca, then a boy, Neri, as blond as baby Jesus. And, finally, blue-eyed Bona who was now eight months old. I was born in Papa's bank, just opposite the cathedral. But the cathedral did not mean anything to me nor did the bank. What counted for me in July 1925 was Villa Soell, where I had lived for four years as the happiest child in the world.

That evening of July 13, 1925, however, I wasn't happy in our garden and I couldn't figure out why I wasn't. The fleshy petals of the peonies had begun to wither. The air was heavy and the sun lingered high in the sky. The wide garden lay around us, spent, after yet another long heavy day of a scorching summer.

Papa and I were both tired. A dark cloud seemed to hang over us. From bits of conversation I had caught during the past months at home, I gathered that Papa was not well. In spite of it, he never gave up planning. He had recently decided to move the family to Merano, fifteen miles up the Adige Valley from Bolzano. Merano was a more famous *Kurort* or health spa than Gries, a beautiful green enclave, with fruit orchards, vineyards, palm trees, and mimosas, an island in the heart of the looming Alps. Papa was building a villa for us there, so that we could grow up away from the evil influences of a world he did not trust, and live there at least until we were ready to contribute to a "world without war." We children were often left in Gries with Aunt Emma while Mamma accompanied Papa on some of his daily trips to Merano. Mamma would have liked to help him in his business, but he insisted on keeping her out of it.

A few weeks earlier, on a warm day in May, Mamma had taken me with her by train to the village of San Paolo. Once a teacher in Austria, she had recently been asked to teach in an Italian high school. It was a warm day in May. Our little train rolled gently amid blooming fruit trees whose fragrance filled the air, and I felt so privileged to be riding alone with Mamma that I hugged her. She embraced me back, so moved by my action that she couldn't speak; she held me tight, her eyes bright with tears.

Then she whispered to me not to worry, but I really wasn't worried. I was happy. Her plan would turn out well in the end, she said, lowering her voice, but now I must keep our trip to the school in San Paolo a secret, just between us — and never tell Papa. She was preparing herself to go to work — she whispered in my ear as if Papa were around – even though he would have disapproved, because he was ill and his business was going from bad to worse. She loved Papa more than anyone in the world and didn't want to displease him, but the best way to help him and the family was for her to return to teaching, since Italy, which had taken the place of Austria in the Südtyrol where we lived, had finally allowed her to do so. I promised that I would keep the secret.

On that train, she told me in a matter of fact voice that after the Great War (which had almost killed her and Papa), Meran and Bozen, as they were called in German, and Gries, and the whole region of Südtyrol including her village in the Non Valley, were taken away from Austria of which they had been a part for centuries. As one of the victorious nations, Italy claimed them. Now the German-speaking people here worried about what would happen to their language and culture. But that wasn't her problem, she said firmly, because she had been hired to teach in Italian. She was confident that she was a good teacher and she liked to teach. The language in which she would teach did not matter. Politics was of no concern to her. All she cared about was her family.

Then the train conductor came along to chat with her in his thick, heavy German. When he finally left, she was her smiling self. She never mentioned the secret again.

Later, Papa told me more about this in a different way, through one of his stories. In ancient times, he said, some barbarians called *Baiuvari* descended from beyond the Alps through our Adige Valley, which they called "Etch," into the green fertile plains by the sea. Some other barbarians called *Longobardi,* who had settled on those fertile plains and had adopted as a language the Latin of the Romans, pushed the Baiuvari back up the Adige Valley to the village of Salorno not far from where we lived. From then on, those who lived north of Salorno spoke the German of the Baiuvari, which was still the language of the people around us in Gries, including our great friend Herr Trafojer who owned the hotel and Villa Soell. However, the people south of Salorno spoke a Latin dialect which resembled the beautiful Italian we spoke at home. People had lived together peacefully for centuries, each respecting the language of the other, until recently a man called Mussolini took over the government in Italy and imposed Italian on everybody without exception! There wasn't much he could do, Papa added, to help Herr Trafojer and his friends hold on to their German. He had no power to help them since his bank had closed and he was unemployed. That must have been bad for all of us in the family, because he took me on his knee and kissed me tenderly to reassure me that things would be all right even so. We just had to be patient.

I loved Villa Soell as my home, the rooms on the park and the large kitchen where Zia Emma, Mamma's sister — tall, thin, always dressed in black like a nun — cooked delicious meals, holding one of my younger siblings, Neri or Bona, in her arms, while Francesca and I wandered in the park or peeked during Carnival onto the dance hall of the Hotel Trafojer where ladies in colorful dresses danced, holding gentlemen in black. Francesca and I ate dinner at the big round table with Mamma, Papa, and Zia Emma in a room with a huge window facing a mountain that looked like a castle because of its rocky towers. We had to say our prayers before we could touch food as well as before we went to bed. Zia Emma took care of that. I myself couldn't leave Villa Soell mainly for another reason.

Villa Soell was the enchanted castle of Papa's stories. In his library and in our park everything came alive through his stories which gave me the reason for what was around us and how it came to be. So I learned why the mountains turned red at sunset and how the moon got its spots, and I learned the origin of the torrent's foaming water, of the rainbow after storms, of each star in the night sky, and of every corner of our garden including the section that was forbidden to us (the famous Tyrolean vineyard with a big sign that said *Verboten ("Forbidden"),* the first word I learned to read because it bothered me so much.

In that park, under a huge chestnut tree, Papa told me of distant cities that lay beyond our mountains on the shores of a blue sea, especially one called Troy which was now dead, but, at one time, was just as stunning as Rome is today, both as distant from us as the moon. He talked of people, mostly men, who did not believe in Jesus Christ as we do but believed in many gods such as the Sun, the Moon, the Earth, the Sea.

Earlier that July day, my parents had taken me to Merano for the first time, to witness a ceremony which I didn't care for — the laying of the roof of our future home. The best part of the day was our train ride home along the foaming river Adige, among fruit orchards overflowing with pears, apples, peaches, apricots and cherries. The cherries were the best. Their branches brushed against our train. Papa grabbed one branch heavy with fruit, much to Mamma's disapproval, and handed it to me. We spent the rest of the ride happily eating cherries together and making cherry earrings for both Mamma and me.

I could still taste the sweet juice of cherries in my mouth later that evening, as I sat with Papa in the garden listening to the story he was telling. We always sat together in the garden, while Mamma put the younger children to bed. On that evening, Papa led me back to the splendid city of Troy that we both loved. King Laomedon had the powerful walls of his city built by the gods of the sea and the sun, promising as remuneration a pair of winged horses he kept hidden in his stables. It was a tale of broken promises which would have dire consequences for the Trojan King. In the end, Laomedon was forced to sacrifice his own beloved daughter Andromeda in order to save his people from a flood brought on by the angry god of the sea. Andromeda, a willing victim tied to a rock, was about to be devoured by a horrible sea monster, when Mamma called from the balcony. The children were asleep, she said. My time with Papa was up.

In the middle of the night, I heard voices wailing around me. At first, I refused to wake up because I was afraid of what might happen to Andromeda. I felt comfortable in my parents' large bed. When I finally opened my eyes, I saw Papa sitting in his armchair near the bed, his feet in a basin filled with water. Mamma was kneeling near him. Both she and Aunt Emma were reciting a Latin prayer I had never heard before. Then, crying and praying at the same time, they begged God in Italian to have pity on Papa.

"What did Papa do wrong?" I asked. Mamma replied that he was dying.

"Why is he dying," I asked, "if he didn't do anything wrong?"

She didn't answer and I screamed. "Tell me please! Why is he dying?"

Then Papa whispered something to Mamma and she led me to him. He held my hands in his and smiled. I was reassured. He couldn't die if he smiled. Then he turned to Mamma and whispered something like, "Remember your promise ... the children!" While Papa held my hand, Mamma fetched Francesca and Neri from the next room. They refused to open their eyes as he kissed them both. Aunt Emma held Bona in her arms near him. He smiled at her and that made me happy. I stopped crying.

Next day, we children had lunch as usual in the kitchen: boiled meat and potatoes, Papa's favorite meal. Before the meal, Mamma made us recite a prayer for Papa, who, she said, from now on would always be with us, every moment of every day, no matter where we were. Her eyes were dry and her voice so convincing that I never doubted what she said.

"*Requiem aeternam,*" the prayer said, "*dona ei Domine. Lux perpetua luceat ei. Requiescat in pace.* Give him, O Lord, eternal rest. May eternal light shine upon him. May he rest in peace." From that day on, this prayer became the magic formula we invoked during difficult moments of our lives. After the meal, Mamma led me into her bedroom. The shutters were closed to keep out the heat. Papa lay on the bed, dressed in his best suit, but without shoes. His eyes were shut and his hands folded on his chest. Mamma put one of my hands over his.

"He is cold," she said. "He is dead. They will take his body away from us soon." She placed a white rose on his chest and stood there for a long while, silently looking at him. Finally, she bent over him and kissed his forehead.

Then she turned to me and said in a gentle but firm voice: "I found twenty lira in his pocket. From now on, I must work hard and you must help me." She held me tightly.

I learned later that Mamma and Aunt Emma had washed Papa's body early in the morning and dressed him, as they had washed and dressed the body of their father years before in their village.

Two days later, Mamma led us to a window in the long hall overlooking the street. Instead of the red and yellow tramway that we children loved, we saw a long procession of people with a band and a priest.

"That's Papa's funeral," she explained, looking at the procession while breastfeeding Bona. "They are taking his body to a cemetery, but the real Papa is with us right now and he always will be."

§ § §

On a hot day later that summer, Mamma and Aunt Emma led us children away from Villa Soell in Gries to their village, Tajo, in the Valle di Non. Uncle Silvio and Aunt Speranza were at the streetcar station to greet us. Mamma went on alone to prepare for our new life in Merano.

We children were familiar with Mamma's old farmhouse because of our frequent summer visits to Nonna Orsola and Aunt Speranza and Uncle Silvio, and we loved Aunt Speranza as much as she loved us. Nevertheless, when Mamma left us in Tajo after Papa's death, I was desperately lonely, as if both Papa and Mamma had abandoned me in a strange new world.

In the Tajo farmhouse, the four of us children were lodged with Aunt Emma in two rooms carved out of the old hayloft. We slept in two huge beds, on mattresses called *paion* by the farmers. They were made of dry cornstalks. In time, I came to love those rooms and those mattresses, mainly because the fragrance of hay and corn during hot summer nights gave me the feeling of sleeping with the crickets in a field of freshly cut hay. At first, however, the ambience, so different from my home at Villa Soell, contributed to the feeling of abandonment I had had since Papa's sudden death.

One morning, while Mamma was in Merano, I woke up at dawn in the bed I shared with Francesca. The rustling she produced by turning over on the *paion* had awakened me. "When will Mamma be back?" I whispered to her. She shamed me: "Stop whining and sleep!" For some reason, she didn't seem affected in the least by what gave me pain.

I climbed out of my bed and walked to the open window. The chirping of birds and crickets filled the room, mixed with the heavy smell of cow manure from the stable. High up over the roofs of the village, the mansion of Papa's family lifted its stark, heavy body in the light blue sky of a crystal-clear summer dawn. One question caused me anguish, sitting like a stone on my heart. I knew nobody but Mamma could answer it. What did Uncle Silvio mean when he said to us just as we arrived, "This house from now on will be your home!" I desperately longed for Villa Soell, the only home I had ever known. Only Papa could take me back to where I belonged, far away from Mamma's village, behind those mountains that separated me from Mamma and Papa.

Back in bed, I cried until Francesca angrily silenced me again. Then I decided to close my eyes and turn for help to Papa himself with the magic prayer Mamma had taught me the day after he died, when we stood alone in front of him as he lay on his bed all dressed up. From then on, we recited that prayer at every meal and every time we needed help, without knowing what it meant, a "magic" formula to call Papa to us: *"Requiem aeternam dona ei Domine. Lux perpetua luceat ei. Requiescat in pace."*

The magic worked. Papa was near my bed, talking to me softly so as not to bother Francesca in her sleep. As I listened, I forgot about being in Mamma's village desperately wanting to run away from it. I closed my eyes and I was back at Villa Soell on the happiest day of the year, the last Christmas we spent together.

There was great excitement around us. Baby Bona, who slept peacefully in her room in a crib under white veils like Snow White, was about to become a soldier of Christ, Aunt Emma had told me, and Christ himself was about to be born at sunset in a little crib under a tree in Papa's library. I was worried about both babies, Bona and Christ: what could they do as tiny babies, but there was no time that day at Villa Soell to answer my questions. Even Papa was too busy to speak to me. All he told me that morning in church was that "Bona is being baptized" which did not mean anything to me. Our home was full of people talking and laughing. The kitchen table was full of sweets, the door of the library was locked until sunset, after baby Jesus had put up a big Christmas tree and placed many gifts under it.

When the bells rang, I was the first to enter the library; Bona's crib had miraculously made its way in before anyone else. Mamma led Francesca and Neri by the hand. I went on my own, because I wanted some glimpse of the Christ Child before he left the room. I was surprised at the things he could do, this little baby who was younger than Bona.

A huge tree filled most of Papa's library. It reached up to the ceiling, its wide-stretching branches holding burning candles and balls of all colors. I saw silver and gold everywhere, heard the music of angels, smelled burning wax and baked cookies. That divine tree in Papa's library quelled all of my questions except for two: Where was Paradise? And where was Baby Jesus now? Perhaps he was hiding under the white veils in Bona's crib. I had to discover the answers on my own.

As everybody sang and prayed, I stayed alone in my corner, when suddenly my eyes wandered from the big tree to the wide window. Out there in the light blue sky, behind the window, rose a gigantic mountain, rocks piled up on rocks, bizarre forms, crenellated turrets, a sequence of spires and steeples so light and thin it seemed as if they might break like toys in the wind, vertiginous stone castles.

That mountain was burning right before my eyes with lights brighter than those on the tree. It shone with the warm pink of roses in May. Was that mountain Paradise? Why wasn't anybody paying attention to it? Why didn't anybody care? Only Papa, I thought, knew for sure what that mountain was, because he had told me its story one evening at sunset as I sat on his lap in the library. It was winter, and the trees in the garden shivered, naked in the wind.

"That mountain is called Rosengarten because once upon a time, it was a huge garden of roses. Now, we can see the roses only at sunset and sunrise," Papa had explained.

He told me how the king of the dwarves, Laurinus, reigned happily over the Dolomites. Kind and provident, not only to his own dwarves but to all humans, he offered everyone the sight of an immense garden of roses all over his mountain, blooming winter and summer. But one day, some courtiers tried to murder him. Blind with anger, Laurinus pronounced a curse: all rosebushes should disappear from sight throughout the day and night. In his anger, he forgot about sunrise and sunset.

On Christmas Eve, the garden of roses came right into our home. As a favor to the Christ Child, I thought, the generous dwarves had woven silver around our Christmas tree. Mamma, with baby Bona in her arms, was kneeling by the manger. The pink light of the Rosengarten illuminated them and Papa, who held Francesca and Neri on his knees. He waved me over and I joined them in the singing. Then he led me to a corner where my sister and brother were playing with their toys.

Among the toys, there was my gift, *I Monti Pallidi* ("The White Mountains"). I held that book tight to my heart, like a baby. I woke up looking for Papa. He was gone.

In anguish, I slipped out of bed. I tiptoed lightly through the room adjacent to mine, where Aunt Emma slept in a big bed between Neri and Bona, then went down the crooked red marble stairs, afraid that somebody might stop me. At the bottom of the stairs, the door to the kitchen was wide open. Aunt Speranza stood tall and heavy near the crackling fire. The smell of fried potatoes filled my empty stomach. I ran into my aunt's arms and buried my head in her bosom.

"Get me out of here!" I screamed. "Give me back to Mamma!" She cuddled me in her bosom like a baby and caressed my rumpled hair with her rough, calloused hands. I didn't understand a word she said. Eyes shut, I felt the warmth of her hands on my scalp, tasted her warm, salty tears dropping on my face and fell asleep in her arms.

When Mamma came back from Merano, I couldn't hold myself back from attacking her:

"Remember," I screamed at her, "what you promised Papa."

I didn't really know of any promise she had made, but Mamma, appalled by my mention of Papa, burst out crying.

"I know," she said, holding me tight. "I know and I promise I shall never leave you again. I will be near you from now on, always. All through life, you shall be my companion and my help."

CHAPTER 2

From Villa to Villa

PAPA'S VILLA

Merano's curse was its magnificent vineyards. We arrived in Merano in September, when the immense vineyards that encircled the town were weighed down by heavy clusters of purple grapes, each the size of a small plum. Papa's villa, a new small house amid the old vineyards, seemed so insignificant in its newness, smelling of fresh cement and plaster, that at first we children couldn't consider it a home. After a two-year stay in that modest villa, we had to pack and leave. We had never even given it a name. As prisoners of vineyards whose fruit we couldn't touch, we had been transformed from carefree children into a team of efficient workers that Mamma could count on.

The first lesson we learned was to refrain from stretching our hands through the barbed wire that separated our little garden from the wealth surrounding us. To grab a cluster or two of juicy grapes, Mamma informed us, after having slapped Francesca who had been caught red-handed, not only was punishable by law but would ruin our reputation with our Tyrolean neighbors. We'd be taken for run-of-the-mill Italians. Mamma didn't seem to care for the law as much as for a good relationship with the local landowners. As newcomers who spoke Italian at home, we had to be extra careful to respect our hosts and thus be an example to others. Now that we owned our own house, no matter how modest, we should take pride in it.

Having made sure we had the respect of our neighbors, Mamma, supported by the meek, indefatigable Aunt Emma, turned to shaping our relationship with the villa itself, with one another, and with her as the new leader of the pack. Within a week after our arrival, our daily occupations had changed radically. Starting from the very first day, most of our time was spent helping her and Aunt Emma transform the courtyard, which we found filled with rubble from the construction, into a flower and vegetable garden for the next spring.

Although the garden had priority because of the season, attention also had to be given to the house itself, which had to shine in order to be rented out, room by room. As much as I personally resented the idea of renting most of the rooms of the house that was supposed to be our home, I had no good argument to counter Mamma's. We children lived happily day in and day out in spite of the awareness that our survival depended on Mamma's meager salary, and that "creditors" haunted Mamma day and night like a pack of dogs chasing a courageous doe.

I didn't know and didn't want to know who these "creditors" were and why they acted as they did, because Mamma made it clear to me that the creditors were her responsibility, not ours. She was in charge of the war. We had to act as good soldiers and follow orders. The war with the creditors lasted throughout the two years we spent in Papa's villa. It ended not in a defeat, according to Mamma, but in an honorable retreat on our part.

The years we spent in Papa's villa were marked, first, by Mamma's absence from our home. She taught school, trying her best to make ends meet. Although she rushed home between jobs to make sure the household was running as she expected it to, she spent her time after school supervising work at what she called Papa's business, the candy shop, the tobacco store, and the bar of the Opera House.

Although our daily routine for meals and bedtime remained much the same, the household resembled a hotel more than a home. Italian executives rented rooms on the upstairs floors, constantly coming and going, and Aunt Emma rushed in after they left to clean their rooms. One day, Aunt Emma fell while polishing a floor, broke her leg, and had to be taken to the hospital. We children felt her loss so much that Aunt Speranza was called from Mamma's village to stay with us until Aunt Emma could walk again.

Besides Aunt Emma, another member of Mamma's old family lived with us, and he was the cause of great concern and trouble for Mamma. Felice, the teenage son of Mamma's brother Damiano, who had died on the Russian front at the onset of the Great War, led a disorderly life instead of studying and helping as the rest of us did. He built strange gadgets, engaged in dangerous politics, smoked heavily, and hung out with disreputable friends.

We children treasured Felice as the welcome leader in our rare hours of play. He let us ride down a steep hill on his homemade bicycle, much to Mamma's disapproval. He helped us have fun at Christmas, which, after Papa's death, had become an occasion for prayer and mourning for Mamma. On Christmas Eve, while Mamma was out working, he led a procession, dressing us up as saints and devils. He taught us to make up plays in which we made fun of the world around us.

Felice's presence as a lively, creative, older playmate counterbalanced the other, unpleasant aspect of his nature: his hatred for the rich, the upper class, the intellectuals, everything that our family represented, according to him. We were bookworms, he said, living at the expense of the poor workers. A self-proclaimed socialist and proletarian, Felice liked to raise embarrassing political issues related to our financial situation. He told us one evening that Papa's former business partner, a man named Pavinato, an Italian war veteran and the principal cause of our financial disarray, was a hated Fascist, one of the murderers of Matteotti, a socialist hero whom he revered. Since Mussolini was forced to put him in prison, Pavinato never gave Papa the 100,000 lire he owed him, and so Papa died because of Pavinato's dishonesty.

Felice was surprised at the indifference with which we children received the news.

One guest whom Mamma always welcomed warmly was her brother. For weeks at a time, Uncle Silvio took over our dining room, the only room we could use besides the bedroom, where the four of us children slept in Mamma's big bed. "Pray God Silvio may find a wife," Aunt Emma whispered to us as she cleaned up her brother's mess in the morning. One of his mistresses had left in a huff after a stormy night of insults. Uncle Silvio, on the other hand, served an important purpose in our present situation. He was Mamma's chief adviser in her war with the creditors; he was also the generous provider of sacks of wheat flour, potatoes, turnips, and apples for our winter meals. He bought our winter coats and my heavy mountain boots for going to school, as well. I knew for certain that he was obsessed not with women but with apples and pears. Women as candidates for marriage were only a means to an end, the end being a flourishing fruit business that would bring prosperity not only to him and us but to the whole Valle di Non.

In the intervals between one mistress and another, Silvio would spend hours in the dining room discussing apples and creditors with Mamma after she finally returned home, exhausted after a full day's work. I fell asleep to the sound of their familiar exchanges in dialect, as I used to fall asleep at Villa Soell listening to Papa's stories. I disliked Uncle Silvio for a personal reason - he would run after me, lift me up in his arms, and, as a sign of great affection rub my face against his beard. But I accepted him for Mamma's sake, for his generosity, and for his unfailing optimism. He did not believe in bankruptcy, a bad word that was often mentioned in our household.

Finally, God answered our prayers. After two mistresses, one worse than the other, Uncle Silvio got himself a wife. He discovered her in the village of Cloz in the Valle di Non, where he supervised a group of local women who packed large Canada apples and William pears in boxes. They worked hour after hour, late into the night, sitting in huge, cold storerooms. The most independent, intelligent and generous of those women became my beloved Aunt Elvina.

The following May, Mamma took me in our grocer's car to Cloz for Uncle Silvio's wedding. It was a most memorable trip for me not only because I had never been in a car before, but because I vomited continually going and coming. Finally home, as I lay under the bluest sky in our garden, I discovered that the two little blue wedding candies I had been holding tightly in my hand for the whole trip back were miraculously one and the same with the blue sky over my head. To prove it to myself, I put one of those candies in my mouth and sucked it slowly. It tasted like the sky. Francesca, who had grabbed the other, claimed it tasted like a regular candy. We got into a fight and Mamma, called in to arbitrate, declared that Francesca was right.

"A candy is a candy and nothing else," Mamma declared.

"Mine was different from hers!" I replied.

"No," Mamma corrected me. "It is you who are different from Francesca."

§ § §

For many reasons, my first two years in school, which coincided with my two years in Merano, stand out as one of the most enjoyable experiences in my life. School was a place where, undisturbed by guests and relatives, I could quietly learn to read a book, write a letter, and play with numbers. School was also wonderful because it allowed me to enjoy the rare moments of freedom in Mamma's life. She and I would walk to school together twice a day six days a week for ten months a year. We walked along a brook, then through a meadow where cows and goats were pastured. I was afraid of them until Mamma laughingly taught me to let them get close to me.

During our long walks, she told me everything I wanted to know and more about trees, flowers, herbs, stones, and the sky. She knew most of the stars by name and could find my star among millions.

Our path ended at the church of "Maria Trost," whose bells called the German-speaking people to a Mass in which even Latin sounded like German. The school was in the old village of Unter-Mais, or Maia Bassa, the home of Tyrolean farmers. Some Italian workers had appeared recently from the new chemical factory at Sinigo. They were ignored or kept at a distance because they were said to be Fascists.

I liked everything about my school, where Mamma taught and I studied from first to fourth grade, including its new Italian name, Cesare Battisti, which had replaced the name of a famous Austrian educator, much to the regret of the locals. The Italians saw Cesare Battisti as a martyr, the Austrians saw him as a traitor, but I saw him as a friend, because Mamma told me he had been a friend of Papa in Trento before Papa went to Vienna. They were both "rebels," Mamma said. That's why I liked him.

The person I liked best in the sunny spacious building of the school was my teacher, Fräulein Bazzeghin. She sometimes struck our hands with a ruler, but, on December 6, she would save us all from the German-speaking devil who came with Saint Nicholas to punish bad pupils. I wished that instead of punishing us children, the devil would punish the school's principal, Scipione Fabbri, and with him Il Duce, who had sent him from Rome to humiliate Mamma.

Every teacher, Mamma told me, received a grade at the end of the year just as we children did. I knew that Scipione Fabbri never gave Mamma the grade she deserved. In my eyes, Mamma was the best teacher, not only in Austria, but in Italy as well. Deeply hurt by the humiliation inflicted on her by the principal, I refused to sing the Italian national anthem at the daily school assemblies and was punished for it. All I made out of that difficult hymn was the mention of a certain "Scipio" who once upon a time had crowned the head of the goddess Roma. If that Scipione was the same as the principal who came from Rome, well then, I didn't want to have anything to do with Rome, either, nor with Il Duce.

I loved school so much, I hated vacations and illnesses that kept me home. The longest of those periods of illness happened in the spring of my second year. All four of us children got measles, whooping cough, and bronchitis, in quick succession.

Dr. Franceschini, one of Mamma's most valuable friends, having diagnosed Francesca with the measles, told Mamma to put us all in the same room together to "get this over with once and for all." That wasn't difficult anyway, because we lived in one room and slept in one bed. The nightmare ended with the four of us lying on mattresses under the shade of the cherry tree in our garden, exhausted from coughing and too weak to stretch a hand to catch the fruit.

For a whole month before that, we had lain on cots placed around the mahogany dining room table, in complete darkness because measles can blind you. Neri told me one day that Francesca, who had the worst case, was already blind, but when she heard him say that, she hit him on the head with a cushion, which meant she wasn't blind at all.

Whooping cough was by far the worst of these diseases. Mamma and Aunt Emma ran around that table day and night to clean up our vomit. It was while convalescing from those illnesses in our cozy little garden full of flowers that we finally felt at home in Papa's villa.

We were hardly back on our feet when Mamma's war with the creditors came to an end. We often heard her speaking with Uncle Silvio who had rushed down from Tajo to help her. They talked about Count Pompeati and Uncle Cappelletti, her legal advisers, about Pavinato, the Fascist partner of Papa's firm, and Papa's brothers Tullio and Antonio. The Count and Uncle Cappelletti wrote to her and phoned her from Trento, but Uncle Cappelletti, the more helpful of the two, had a heart attack one night at dinner and died. And Aunt Maria, Mamma's sister in Creto who had lent her some money in a hurry, died also while selling medicines in her pharmacy. Papa's businesses failed also, first the bar at the theatre, then the candy store, and finally the tobacco store.

After prayers at dinner one night, Mamma told us that we were indeed fortunate. We are going to avoid bankruptcy, she said. This means that we have to give up much of what we have in this villa and the villa itself, but we'll move to a much better villa in the best part of town which is beyond Grabmaierstrasse. She stressed that word "beyond," which meant north of the road that divided Merano into two sections.

Mamma proceeded then to give us her own personal version of the topography of Merano, a city divided in two by a road, Grabmaierstrasse, that meandered among villas with parks. The people she tutored lived in those villas. She had decided to take us north of that road because there lay the villas and parks of her rich clientele. From now on, she told us, we would be living in a very old villa, like Villa Soell, with a turret overlooking the mountains. The name itself, "Dolomitenblick" or "view of the Dolomites," was, for me at least, a guarantee of future happiness. The last days in Papa's villa were full of excitement. All of us children helped to transport as much as we could into the safe harbor of friends' houses. We had to save as much as possible from the repossessors, who were about to take away everything they could lay their hands on. In the end, Mamma said, less was better than more. When those hateful fellows came, they just put stickers on our furniture and left with a smile.

After prayers on our last evening in our villa, Mamma led us to say good-by to Papa's leather armchair where he had sat when he told me his stories and where he died. It was too heavy to transport, she said. That night, after we were all sound asleep, Felice engaged a sturdy friend of his and silently, without our knowing it, removed Papa's armchair from the villa. That armchair was delivered to us a year later in Villa Dolomitenblick.

Felice no longer lived with us. He had moved to Tajo, where he lived under the whip of Uncle Silvio, whom he hated. At Villa Dolomitenblick, there was hardly room for the six of us: Mamma, Aunt Emma, and the four of us children.

§   §   §

VILLA DOLOMITENBLICK

"*Eins... zwei... drei....*" Frau Spatzier stood, as erect as a general under a cherry tree heavy with fruit, all five feet of her dressed in an impeccable dark green and red Tyrolean uniform. Bona, Neri and I slid down the branches, our faces and hands red from the cherries we had eaten. "*Vier!*" she thundered, spying Francesca, "*vier verdammte Kinder!*" ("Four! Four damned children.") Her gardener and lover Hans, following her orders, made us march to the villa, like prisoners of war. A full moon lit up the scene of the crime.

When Mamma showed up at 10:00 pm, after eighteen hours of work, she found us not in bed but lined up against the wall of our dining room, near the yellow-and-red porcelain stove, ready for execution. How could we commit such a serious crime so soon after we'd arrived in our new paradise?

Only two months had passed since the day Mamma had led us away from Papa's villa to our new home. Villa Dolomitenblick suddenly appeared before us, slightly north of the main dividing line, Grabmaierstrasse. There were vast vineyards north and east, and a few other sparse villas to the south and west, gray and decayed with age. The villa itself was stubbornly dignified in a half--urban, half-rural way, like the elderly lady who owned it when we arrived.

Frau Spatzier had welcomed us roughly, with a series of "*Verboten*" uttered sternly in strongly accented German. Anticipating the arrival of four children of an Italian-speaking family, she had protected her garden with a triple set of heavy barbed wire. The garden included, among flowerbeds and vegetables, two big fig trees and what seemed to us a gigantic cherry tree. All were in full bloom when we first saw them.

We reached the villa itself along a narrow, graveled path. Our quarters on the ground floor consisted of a kitchen, a bathroom, and three rooms, one of which Mamma had wisely sublet before our arrival to a Fräulein Job, the director of the aristocratic Froebel Kindergarten. Understandably, she couldn't stand the sight of children once she came home from work at night, so her room was permanently locked.

In time, we discovered that Mamma's foresight, along with Divine Providence, had saved us all from danger, since Miss Job's room had a balcony that stretched out into the Forbidden Garden, a balcony flanked by two fig trees. Yet since cherries ripen before figs, it was the cherry tree that got us in trouble, because it stood right in front of our kitchen windows.

The night of our crime, we had climbed it and had gorged ourselves on cherries. When Mamma arrived home from her long hours of private tutoring after school, erect in spite of her fatigue, elegant in her black silk uniform complete with a black hat, covered with the veil of widowhood, she patiently listened to an interminable speech by Frau Spatzier, who was explaining our crime in detail. Then, without even looking at us, in a low almost inaudible voice, Mamma declared we were guilty of trespassing and "irremediably" consuming Frau Spatzier's goods.

I admitted my guilt, and, given the impossibility of returning something that had been by then digested, I asked the old lady for forgiveness. Neri followed my example. Bona, only four at the time, was excused. Francesca, however, stood defiantly silent.

Mamma disappeared into our common bedroom and returned seconds later with one of Papa's leather belts. Her face was livid, but her hand did not shake as she pulled Francesca away from the wall and whipped her three times, so strongly that Frau Spatzier intervened to stop her. After the two ladies had separated with courteous words, Mamma ordered me to put the children to bed. Then she fell onto a chair of the dining room with a thump.

"Coward!" Francesca spat at me as I was leading her away. Her legs were bleeding.

When all was quiet in the bedroom, I moved back to the dining room. Mamma sat sobbing, her head in her arms on the table.

"Come to bed, Mamma!" I whispered to her. She quietly followed me like an obedient child.

§ § §

Those happy, carefree years I spent learning with Mamma at Cesare Battisti came to an end at villa Dolomitenblick. I was eight years old, one year earlier than the earliest date usually allowed, when she decided I should start preparing for the admission exam to the Ginnasio Liceo Giosuè Carducci.

"We don't have time to waste," she said, justifying her decision, while I argued in favor of delay.

The ginnasio, an old Benedictine monastery converted into an aristocratic and exclusive educational institution, had filled me with awe during our Friday trips to the marketplace in the center of town. I admired its long, imposing yellow facade, its elegant, slim turret facing the theater, but I had no desire to enter it.

Had I been aware of the length of the program — eight years — I would have to undergo within that building, I would have been as frightened as if I were taking solemn vows.

The selective classical school, called Ginnasio Liceo G. Carducci, was the only route to a university education. During the first five years, we would study Latin and Greek. In the last three years, we would study classical literature in the original, as well as history, sciences, mathematics, philosophy, political science, and art history. This was capped by a month-long final written and oral exam, called the *maturità*, which covered all the subject matters studied at the liceo.

What frightened me at age eight was not what lay ahead of me, for I was totally unaware of it, but the responsibility I now had to assume toward the family. According to Mamma, our future success as a family depended upon my passing that admission exam with a minimum "A-" average.

Mamma's salary supported us only through the middle of the month. The rest came by the will of God, as she put it, which meant by her extra work. In my case, exemption from tuition, which could be obtained with a "B+" average, was a prerequisite for my entering the ginnasio liceo, besides setting the example for my siblings.

I vaguely felt then that the promise Mamma had made to Papa, to send us all to the classical school and then to university, weighed heavily on me. Still heavier for my mother (not for me) was the specter of Papa's haughty family, which we officially visited once a year in their sturdy mansion dominating Mamma's village. Her dream was that some day her children would climb higher than her brother-in-law, Antonio. The only way she could see that happening was to put all four of us through the most elitist schooling available, and that had to be achieved within her meager budget. I accepted the challenge and her strategy in the abstract. Yet when my training for admission to the ginnasio began, the pressure that Mamma suddenly put on me in her tutorials threatened to change my relationship toward her and my whole attitude toward learning. Gone was the freedom of enjoying what I had so far learned from Papa and Mamma. At age eight, learning became for me a means to an end, a passport for success. Mamma trained me like a race horse or an Olympic champion, and at first I rebelled.

"When will you learn the difference between a square and a cube?" Mamma asked me one Sunday morning, during one of her tutorials.

"Never!" I felt like screaming, but I knew better and so kept silent. Mamma then hit me so hard on the head with the cube she held in her hands that I burst into loud sobs. She embraced me, resigned to my deficiency in math.

"You are not made for geometry!" she sighed.

When it came to my training in writing, however, I was eager to cooperate. On Sundays, during the sweetest spring days, I sat patiently for hours on end reading aloud to her from *Il Cappelletti,* an enormous volume dedicated to the heroic wars of Italian independence. Those wars, in Mamma's view, were supposed to be the background for the creative writing section of my exam, a two-hour composition on a theme of the student's choice. Day after day, I patiently wrote and rewrote the essay Mamma had decided I should create. It was the story of a heroic deed by my paternal grandmother, the mythical Baroness known as Nonna Maria, whom I had hardly ever seen. A true Italian patriot, according to Mamma, Siora Maria, as she called her, had once risked her life by closing her mansion to the archduke of Austria, who was passing through her village. She had also created, in a section of her park, the Italian flag with red and white carnations. I could not have cared less for the event, but I wrote an essay on it and learned it by heart, under Mamma's supervision.

When the day of the exam finally came, I sat down in the refectory hall of the Benedictine convent to write my memorized essay. However, the professor in charge, an elderly gentleman, told us to feel free to write a story we liked, perhaps even invent a story. What almost automatically flowed from *my* pen then was not the glorious epic of Nonna Maria that I had memorized under Mamma's supervision, but a short story of my own, a variation on a nursery rhyme Papa used to recite to me at night at Villa Soel in Gries, which began with the refrain, "once upon a time there was a mighty little woman who owned a mighty little house." When I, the first to do so, turned in my single sheet to the old gentleman, he looked surprised at how short my story was, which I had enriched with detailed drawings.

"Why don't you go back to your seat and add something to the story?"

I cut him short, assuring him that was all I intended to write. I was by far the smallest of all the candidates, the tiniest of four girls in a hall full of boys. He glanced through my story and smiled down to me. I smiled back at him. I had never been so happy.

My satisfaction, however, was short-lived. By the time I reached Grabmaierstrasse on my way back to Villa Dolomitenblick, I experienced a vague uneasiness, which soon turned into a painful feeling of guilt. Would I ever make it, with what I had written on my own against Mamma's precise orders, to the A- average that would free her from the burden of my tuition?

After a nightmarish week, we walked together to the ginnasio. The grades were posted on a white sheet against a white wall under an old arched ceiling. I had a B+, Mamma said, which entitled me to half tuition. "You are marvelous!" she cried aloud, tears in her eyes. In front of everybody, she lifted me up high in her arms and kissed me. "I am so proud of you!"

After the apprehensions caused by the entrance exam, my life at the ginnasio and later the liceo moved forward as smoothly as I could have hoped. School became my life. Through the eight years I spent there, girls and boys lived together in the classroom in a joyful community of learning. Girls were always a tiny minority, two or three percent in the first five years (the ginnasio), barely one percent in the last three years (the liceo). Outside the classroom we were kept strictly apart. Learning slowly became for us the tie that united us through the years, long after the Tyrolean political situation and a horrible war broke us apart. In later years in Rome, most of my school mates would write to me from Stalingrad, as soldiers in the German Army, with respect for my different political ideals and choices.

During the long winter, the classroom was heated by a huge porcelain stove, into which we students fed large pieces of fragrant wood as if we were in our own living room. Together, we faced our professors — male and female, all Italians sent up from the peninsula — with awe and, after a while in the liceo, with respectful affection. Our learning experience as a community helped us ignore not only the hard discipline of the school, but the much harder conflict between Tyroleans and Italians that raged, increasingly through the years, outside the walls of our safe domain, and the Fascist oppression of the local German-speaking population. What held us together in Merano were the classics we learned to read in the original. Latin and Greek were the basic subjects throughout, complemented in the upper class by Italian literature (Dante), history, philosophy, mathematics, science, and art history. After Il Duce's concordat with the Pope in 1927, an hour of religion was added to the program.

Though we lived with Fascism, we students did not ever engage in political discussion within the walls of our monastery school. We girls were aware that some of the boys were members of a subversive political organization. In school, however, we were all members of the same family. We read Plato together. At first, we conversed among ourselves sometimes in Italian, sometimes in German. But after some years, Italian prevailed, naturally, without external imposition from outside. It was the language of our professors.

Every Saturday afternoon, Il Duce provided us with entertainment — "il sabato Fascista" ("Fascist Saturday"), which was mostly taken up with athletic games. There were parades on great occasions and films featuring Il Duce himself or Scipio, the ancient Roman hero who conquered Carthage, or the heroic Ben-Hur which made us all cry. Our favorite activities were the athletic competitions, in which we all took part eagerly. Though the shortest of all, I was first in running, fencing and dancing. Mamma carefully screened the Fascist activities to which we were subjected, but there wasn't much she could do to stop us from taking part in them. Soon, like all the other children, we were all made members of the Fascist organization, the Opera Nazionale Balilla.

School had nothing to do with "Fascist Saturday" where the boys called "Balilla" and the girls "piccole Italiane" marched happily through town on national holidays, singing "*Giovinezza, giovinezza, primavera di bellezza*" ("Youth, youth, spring of beauty"), and "*Fischia il sasso, il nome squilla*" ("The stone whistles, the name rings"). The only activity from which Mamma excluded us, much to my personal dismay, were the films. At times, Francesca and I invoked Il Duce's supreme authority or simply attended a movie without her permission — and were later punished for it when Mamma, inevitably, discovered our transgression.

On Sundays, though we were all Catholic and had the Latin Mass in common, the two communities, German and Italian, were divided into two groups — not by the Latin mass but by the language of the Gospel and the sermon that followed it. German was spoken in the cathedral, Italian in the Church of the Holy Ghost. No Tyrolean would attend the Mass of the Italians and vice versa. We would never meet in church. Some churches and convents in Maia Bassa/Untermais eventually became centers of Tyrolean resistance against an increasingly harsh Italian rule. Although Mamma firmly kept us out of the political world, we attended Mass at the Church of the Holy Ghost, which, in itself, was a political act.

§ § §

North of Villa Dolomitenblick, that is Grabmaierstrasse, all the way to the bottom of the mountains, vineyards alternated with villas hidden in splendid parks. One of these parks for a long time had attracted the attention and interest of us children.

Aunt Emma's illness offered us the perfect occasion to stealthily enter it. Our beloved Aunt had been lying for weeks on her makeshift bed in our dining room, too weak even to go to the bathroom without support. A wise old woman whom Mamma had summoned from her village to help us in the emergency had identified the cause of her illness, a huge lump under her armpit. It had been there since she was freed from the cast they put on her to heal her broken hip. The old village woman suggested the lump be treated with poultices of boiled wild herbs which we children were asked to pick from the fields.

While looking for wild herbs on a sunny afternoon in May, we crossed into the park we had eyed for a long time, and, led by a scent, moved silently in single file along a path meandering among trees. Suddenly, at a turn, we were met by three immense pink clouds of flowers we had never seen before. We were all busy grabbing them, when a barking dog frightened us. Our arms filled with pink clouds, we ran as fast as we could toward the fence. Bona was pushed first through the barbed wire, followed by Francesca, then me. Neri crossed with difficulty and, caught by a lady on a horse, revealed the purpose of our visit to her. He came back with her advice: flowers would certainly help the sick woman but calling a doctor was a better solution.

Aunt Emma felt much better that night, enveloped, like images of the virgin Mary in the Assumption, in a pink cloud of wild azaleas. Mamma was also happy and did not ask where we had gotten the flowers. The next day, she called Dr. Franceschini, who told us the big lump was cancer. Unlike tuberculosis, cancer was not contagious, but it was just as bad. There was no cure for it. An operation would serve no purpose, so Aunt Emma was moved to Mamma's village. During summer vacation we saw her wither away, like a leaf in autumn, on a bed in the best room in Mamma's house, the one reserved for special guests. She died in November.

I was told about her death while playing in a recital in the English Women's Convent. I didn't like piano but had been forced to learn it because, Mamma said, it "came to us by birthright." Out of pride, a guest of those noble nuns, I held my tears back while at the concert, but I cried and cried at home.

Even with so many deaths in the family already, Papa's death and the deaths of aunts and uncles who had come to help us, it was Aunt Emma's death that made it real for me, and I couldn't take it, until one night in bed Francesca told me I was stupid to cry. If anybody was a saint, Aunt Emma was. Now we could count on the very best help from Paradise for our daily needs. Had I forgotten that saints perform miracles? All we had to do was pray.

From that moment on, I could feel Aunt Emma's presence in our daily life, like water gurgling under the ice. Francesca and I felt sure she would perform her miracle as soon as she had a chance. We were not surprised when she did.

A few months after her death, Neri came home one afternoon from school with a high fever, choking from a strange sore throat. Dr. Franceschini, summoned urgently, locked Neri and Mamma in our bedroom and called Frau Spatzier who, after Aunt Emma's death, had become a surrogate aunt to us. The doctor entrusted us to her until he could summon Aunt Speranza who arrived, as usual, as fast as she could from Mamma's village.

He explained to us that Neri was suffering from diphtheria, a deadly illness for which there was no remedy, like cancer or angina pectoris, which had caused Papa's death. Like tuberculosis which had recently hit four of our cousins in Papa's family, diphtheria was terribly contagious. We could not approach Mamma and Neri until he said so. All we could do was pray that Neri would be spared, he added, meaning he wasn't at all sure he would be, although he seemed to be sure that Mamma wouldn't contract diphtheria.

We were all shocked. How could God take away Neri, the sweetest of us all? A handsome boy with a mane of blond curls and big brown eyes with long eyelashes, Neri was always ready to laugh and make us laugh. Sitting around the table with Frau Spazier in her kitchen, Francesca counted our many dead, one by one, and wrote their names on a piece of paper with the approximate dates of their deaths. It was then decided by common consent to concentrate on Aunt Emma, who had died most recently and who loved Neri best. We lit a candle, given to us by Frau Spatzier, and prayed with her in her harsh German dialect, as she couldn't speak any Italian, despite our best efforts to teach her.

Aunt Emma accomplished the miracle two weeks later. One evening, while we were all sadly praying in the dining room under the wings of large Aunt Speranza, Dr Franceschini opened the door of Mamma's bedroom and Neri waved to us from her bed, too weak to raise his head from the cushion, but alive!

Yet that was not the end of our troubles. A few months later, when Aunt Speranza was back in her village and we were all, Neri included, busy preparing for the end of the school year, Mamma couldn't get out of bed. Dr. Franceschini, promptly summoned, assured us with a smile that she did not suffer from diphtheria or any other illness. The word he used was *collasso* – a nervous breakdown. Mamma had simply collapsed from too much stress. She needed a rest.

Since Frau Spatzier had fallen ill, Signorina Ines, a lady provided by the doctor, took over the household and ran it like nobody had done before. Ines was beautiful to look at. She dressed in silk and sang and danced around the house as if it were a stage. Too bad, we all thought, her stay was so short. When Mamma was ready to take care of herself, Ines helped us pack for Mamma's village, our refuge during all emergencies. Dr. Franceschini, who saw us off at the train, took me aside.

"Your Mamma is not well," he told me. "Her energy is limited. When she comes back, she must cut her work hours and move into a cheaper apartment, even if her villa lies on the wrong side of

Grabmaierstrasse!" He was well aware of Mamma's stubborn determination to live north of that road, in the residential, German-speaking part of town.

I knew I couldn't persuade Mamma to do anything she didn't want to do, and the last thing she wanted was to leave Villa Dolomitenblick. So, I dismissed the painful thought. Back in her village, Mamma was as happy as a bird in its nest.

§   §   §

Mamma took us to her village every summer until I, at the age of 12, was considered ready to work in the city, that is, to tutor children younger than myself. Summers in Mamma's village were for all of us children the most memorable and joyful experiences of our childhood. The journey itself — approximately thirty miles, crossing mountains and valleys — was an event that took all day. We started out by horse and carriage from Grabmaierstrasse to Merano's railway station, where we boarded a small train that took us to Bolzano (Bozen). There we had to catch "in flight" the express train "Berlin – Rome," which had become a local one hour earlier, when it crossed the Italian border. Mamma, helped by other passengers, literally threw us out of the train at the fourth local station, that is, about half an hour from Bolzano. There we waited, drinking soda water and eating sausages, in the garden of a bar, for a streetcar that would meander through a narrow gorge for an indefinite time, through Mamma's wide valley. We survived the voyage by singing, under Mamma's direction, songs of the Great War. She took turns holding our heads, as we vomited out of the window what we had eaten at the pub.

Tajo was paradise on earth, from the moment our two aunts collected us in their arms at the local streetcar station, whose "chief" was one of Mamma's cousins, and the father of twelve children.

For three months after that epic arrival, we lived not the life of farmers, but that of privileged children under Mamma's supervision. For one hour we visited, in our city clothes, the mansion of our paternal uncle, Antonio — Mamma's *bête noire* — where we were received most cordially by his wife and children. From that moment on, life was sheer pleasure. On a good day, led by Mamma, we would walk to the *spiazzoi*, the dry steppe bordering the forest, where as a child she pastured her goats, to collect mushrooms or snails after the rain. For the rest, we were free to follow our aunts in their daily farm work or play with neighboring children, which we did in the late afternoon for hours on end. As for me, the day of the arrival, I hurried to the parish library and took out as many adventure books as the priest would allow me. My favorite author was Salgari, who wrote about the pirates of Malaysia and the American Indians, that is, outlaws working on oceans or plains. I would then disappear in the *cesura* or apple orchard, or lie in the hayloft for hours at a time, reading and daydreaming. In my favorite daydream, I was Yolanda, the child of the black pirate, constantly sailing the ocean. My favorite place for action as a pirate was the Indian Ocean, or any ocean potentially rich for adventures as the Indian Ocean. From the library of his hometown, Turin, closed in by high mountains which he never left — Salgari gave me the perfect means to dream of the kind of ideal freedom from everything that oppressed me without my knowing it.

§ § §

VILLA FONTANA

"She died! Frau Spatzier is dead!" Francesca cried, running down the stairs of Villa Dolomitenblick. She threw herself, sobbing, into Mamma's arms. She had grown deeply attached to the old lady. It was also the first death Francesca had witnessed, since she was asleep when Papa died. Would Frau Spatzier have entered Paradise directly after leaving this earth, like Aunt Emma? Where was she now? Mamma assured her she was not in Hell. Perhaps in Purgatory, but nobody knew the ways of God. We should think the best and pray for her. So Francesca added Frau Spatzier to the long list of our family dead and we prayed for her every night in Latin, the most direct language, we believed, for communicating with God. We used the magic formula we had used for Papa. *Requiem aeternam dona ei Domine, Lux perpetua luceat ei, Requiescat in pace.* Wherever she was, she should rest in peace. Her death however, plunged us all into turmoil.

Mamma mourned Frau Spatzier for reasons of her own, which she explained to us later, after we had finally settled into a villa radically different from anything we had seen before in Merano. Not easy to accept at first, Villa Fontana was the best we could get under the circumstances, and we should be grateful for it, Mamma said bluntly one winter evening in our cozy new dining room. It was the first time in our lives Mamma had tried to explain to us how she viewed the world outside the walls of the family fortress. Mamma herself was a closed book for us. She showered us with attention but never allowed us into her personal world. She was always busy working. When she talked, it was about us. She herself was to be judged by her actions.

On that particular evening, however, she spoke at length with passion and directness as if she were in front of her students. We listened intently, carried away by her eloquence, caught suddenly in the magic web of a world we could hardly believe was our own.

Until then, war had been a literary experience for us, encountered in books at school. Mamma's shocking revelation made us aware of war as a reality. War could disrupt our own daily life, as it had once disrupted life in Athens, in Rome, and in Babylonia. That evening, Mamma made History real for us.

With the death of Frau Spatzier, she explained to us, our life in Merano had taken a turn for the worse. Frau Spatzier was a Tyrolean of the old school, a subject, as Mamma had been, of the Hapsburg Empire. She was a bit haughty, but honest, educated, reasonable, and, deep down, open-minded, which was unusual for any kind of Tyrolean, Mamma added as an afterthought.

Unfortunately for us, Mamma said, most of the Tyroleans around us now, especially the young, were irrational and ignorant. They had no sound knowledge of history. There was no doubt in her mind that these younger Tyroleans were fed fancy nationalistic ideas from "someone" — someone who for good or ill had gained absolute power in Germany. In time, she was sure the young Tyroleans would cause great trouble for the Italians. Everybody could see they were growing impatient with the way Mussolini was dealing with their problems.

Mamma did not blame the Tyroleans, who were once Austrians like her, not Germans. But she did not trust those among them who turned to Germany for inspiration and support. Mamma believed Germany was a country in great trouble. While Italy had changed alliances during the Great War to place itself on the side of the winners, Germany had lost. And losers in war always create trouble, especially if they are Germans.

The Great War, which she had survived in her troubled village and Papa in concentration camps, did not end because of a military victory, but because of German exhaustion. The peace treaty the victors concocted in Paris left the whole of Europe sick with a deadly illness, like the cancer that killed Aunt Emma. It was an illness for which no remedy had been found so far. Only fools like Mussolini, who spoke constantly of war, could believe one could cure the ills produced by war by fomenting another war. You do not cure tuberculosis with cancer.

Mamma had lived through the Great War on the Austrian side of the border with Italy and had witnessed suffering on both sides. The Italians suffered deeply, not only because they were unprepared for the fighting, into which they were thrust by politicians, but also because by their very nature they treasured life in peace. No "Mussolini" in the world could change Italian nature. No speeches. No songs. She had witnessed the Austrian Empire falling to pieces because no citizen of Austria believed in the war the Emperor had concocted with a bunch of bad political advisors.

Why did Mussolini talk so much about war and empire, when the whole world was sick and tired of both? Mamma did not have an answer to that question, but she refused to be tormented by it. She sought a simple remedy for the immediate survival of her own family. She saw us children living, like many people before us, in a kind of in-between period, with a painful past behind us and a dark future before us, against which there was no protection. Neither Mussolini in Italy nor Hitler in Germany could be trusted. Austria did not count any more. The Tyrol stood in a dangerous place between Italy and Germany.

So she made her own decisions, of which she made us part as she had done ever since Papa's death. We would weather the storm by taking advantage of what chance offered us. "People like us," she concluded in her usual matter-of-fact way, "will pay the price for what goes on between the Tyroleans and Mussolini, within a very disturbed Europe."

"I would like to live in Obermais," she continued. "But when Frau Spatzier died, I could not think of anyone who would sublet even the basement of his villa to an Italian-speaking family like ours with four children and a mother teaching in an Italian school, while Il Duce was mistreating the Tyroleans. I had to walk so far on a tightrope to get a roof over our heads and put up with many humiliations from the moment I made my decision to move among the Italians south of Grabmaierstrasse. In the end, it paid off, as you can see."

§ § §

Mamma did not easily accept the humiliations to which she had been subjected when we were forced to move from Obermais to Untermais. Fortunately, after the death of Frau Spatzier, one of Mamma's colleagues in school, Signora Lucia Locatelli, who had become a close friend, sweetened the pill for her by leading us firmly to our new destination, in a compromise with the Fascist government.

Signora Locatelli was a lively, direct and robust middle-aged lady, twice as wide as she was tall. The childless wife of an unemployed member of the Fascist Militia, an optimist and, mostly, an opportunist by nature, she was just the person Mamma needed at this difficult moment in her life, when her health was still shaky and our future bleak.

"Pina, Pina," Signora Lucia would repeat endearingly as she and Mamma sipped chicory coffee in our kitchen at villa Dolomitenblick shortly after Frau Spatzier's death. "Why don't you just accept reality? You can get a large apartment at half the price you are paying now, if you are willing to, how should I put it? If you are willing to join the club!"

As Mamma looked hesitant and unconvinced, Signora Lucia would become more insistent and specific, even rude: "You might as well resign yourself, my dear friend! Mussolini is here to stay and the Fascist organization Associazione Nazionale Combattenti (National Veterans Association) runs Villa Fontana."

"I can see that," Mamma commented sarcastically.

"Stop being so critical, or you'll get in trouble," Signora Lucia continued, "You'll end up in a hospital, as your doctor says. The Fascists will then take over your children."

That was it. Mamma agreed to negotiate the complex bureaucracy involved in subletting the ground-floor apartment of Villa Fontana, which was south of Grabmaierstrasse. Through the tedious dealings with the Association, the most useful and loyal friend we acquired was Comandante Prini, a short, sinewy and peppy Sicilian who had fathered thirteen children in as many years, all of whom were alive and well. He proudly explained to Mamma that he had had so many children to fulfill Il Duce's wish that the Italians should quickly triple or quadruple in number so as to remedy the injustices that had been imposed by selfish democracies. Thus, they could reconquer the world of the Romans. Prini had been compensated for his devotion with sumptuous living quarters for his family, the entire half of a dilapidated Villa.

"You have produced four children in four years!" Prini said, addressing Mamma like a brother in arms, having superficially glanced through the documents she had submitted to him.

"I am sure you would have continued to produce more if your noble husband had not died, a victim, as I can see, of those damned Austrians!"

Glancing at Papa's certificate, he commented, "He left you, as it is, with a bed full of children!"

Mamma, dumbfounded and plainly disgusted, declared that her children were born before Mussolini came to power, which wasn't true, but Prini silenced her with a smack on her back that almost made her lose her balance.

"Come on, Signora, one only needs to glance at you to realize that you are the best possible 'Donna Fascista' Mussolini could have wished for. I can see, my dear lady, that you were destined to produce soldiers for Il Duce's army, soldiers ready to fight against those haughty, decadent democracies."

He smiled at Mamma like an old friend.

"I am sure that if your husband were still around, he would have beaten even me in bringing little soldiers into the world. One a year over thirteen years."

I was afraid for a moment that Mamma would pick up her purse and march out of the room. Her face was as dark as the sky over our mountains before a summer storm. But she stayed, remaining silent, her eyes fixed on a life-sized color portrait of Mussolini in uniform that towered behind the tiny comandante. Although he had never seen a farm, Mussolini had the build of a farmer, short and stout, a torso wrapped in a tightly fitting, perfectly ironed black shirt, a fat stomach squeezed in by a wide, shiny leather belt, a square face with an exaggerated, protruding chin, a black fez hiding his bald cranium.

I was sure Mamma saw him, as I did at that moment, as a cardboard figure, unreal and unthreatening. That static puppet had nothing in common with the little dynamic Sicilian, who was wriggling and chattering incessantly in front of us, trying to pry into Mamma's most private business. When he shook hands with us at the end, his hand was as damp as his face, perspiring as if he had finished a difficult audition. A lonely stranger in an unfriendly land, Prini needed us just as much as we needed him.

"I never met anybody as empty-headed as that man!" Mamma commented dryly when we were finally alone on the street. "I don't know how Papa would have acted if he had been here. He hated heroics." She paused, then added as an afterthought, "He would have given in as I did. There isn't much else one can do."

We moved into Villa Fontana after the grape harvest when the vineyards and their Tyrolean owners were quiet. The Villa, which housed mostly Italian laborers, stood four floors high, surrounded by fenced-in vineyards. Linens were hung out to dry and the small yard between the building and the fenced-in vineyards, was filled with junk. Two worlds stood silently side by side, the Italians of the villa and the Tyroleans of the vineyards, suspicious of each other. They had nothing in common except their humanity, of which they were unaware most of the time.

On the ground floor of that villa there were two apartments combined into one waiting for us, six rooms in all, with kitchen, bathroom, two entrances, and a long terrace along the whole south side of the building. There was even a room for our young housekeeper, a new addition to the family from Mamma's village. Mamma led the work as we cleaned up the place and repainted it. With our sparse furniture, our new residence looked like a royal dance hall in a slum.

We prepared a narrow strip of land between the terrace and the vineyards as a garden for the spring. By the following grape season, Mamma was on good terms with the farmers who surrounded us. She would teach their children in exchange for as many grapes as we needed. As for the Italians on the upper floors of the villa, they were, like all Italians, the warmest possible human beings. But they also felt insecure and defenseless against the Tyroleans who surrounded them.

Signora Lucia, our inseparable friend, often sat on a bench on the terrace, admiring the work we had done. "You have the making of pioneers!" she remarked at one point, "You should be sent to Abyssinia!" We didn't know what she was talking about. Where was this Abyssinia? What did Africa have to do with us?

She and her husband introduced us to the Italians of Maia Bassa, mostly workers at the new chemical factory at Sinigo. They were fun to be with, relaxed, friendly, and lonely. They called the Tyroleans derisively "*crucchi*" (i.e. "krauts") and taught us scatological lyrics that made fun of the former Austrian emperor.

Mamma ordered us to stop the nonsense when she heard us, meaning that Signora Lucia had touched the wrong chord in her inner world.

We children identified Signora Lucia with the Sabato Fascista (Fascist Saturday). She exhibited the same hilarious vulgarity. We loved her because she loved us and we had fun with her, but deep down we knew she did not share Mamma's intimate world. Nobody shared Mamma's intimate world after Papa's death though her isolation surfaced only on specific occasions.

§ § §

One evening in the Spring, we overheard Signora Lucia trying to convince Mamma to send the four of us to Fascist camp in the Dolomites for the summer. Registering Mamma's interest, she insinuated that Comandante Prini could help us get admitted to the *colonia estiva* ("summer camp") of Planchos, in the heart of the Dolomites.

Mamma objected that she wasn't sure her children would be properly taken care of, but Signora Lucia was horrified. "You mean, you don't trust the Fascists who administer the camp? You don't trust our Duce?"

"Of course, I do," Mamma replied, bewildered, "but what about me? Spending a whole month without my children?"

Lucia laughed. "For God's sake, with the children off your hands, you'll be able to rest. You'll go back to your village. You'll sit on this terrace and stare at the sky."

Mamma looked at her friend like a wild animal caught in a trap.

"On this terrace alone? Back to my village? My world is with the children as long as they need me."

When Prini found work for Mamma at the camp, as a volunteer in charge of linens, she agreed to the plan. For a whole month, we lived in the beautiful Dolomites, among peaks of all shapes, pink at sunrise and sunset, as if they were covered with roses. But at a Fascist camp, there was no time for taking in the sights or simply sitting for a moment to rest. Life at Planchos involved twelve hours a day of uninterrupted activity, all done in unison, to the beat of patriotic music. All dressed alike, hundreds of girls and boys marched, exercised, and listened to speeches on the greatness of our country and of our Duce. And as we marched, we sang Fascist hymns.

We girls were happy. Not Neri and Mamma. Neri was often punished for trying to carve a few moments for himself out of a busy day. Mamma spent her days in a long, cold hall, overseeing the washing, drying, and folding of the hundreds of sheets and towels the camp used. Happy to watch us during the day at a distance, ready to jump into action if necessary, she waited anxiously for the evening bugle, announcing that we were all in bed. Then, walking through the long halls, she would come to give us a goodnight kiss, an apple or an orange hidden under her white apron. If we were sick, she saw to it we were moved to the Infirmary.

The echo of the last "Eja eja alala" in Mussolini's honor had hardly died out among the rosy peaks of the Dolomites when Mamma rounded us up, changed us into our homemade summer jumpers, and quietly led us home. "Enough with this empty rhetoric," she said. "Planchos will be our one and only Fascist experience," she proudly declared. But Il Duce thought differently.

On a sparkling clear day in June 1934, Mamma, Francesca, and I were walking home from the market, laden with vegetables and fruit for the week, when Il Duce's stentorian voice reached us from loudspeakers overhead.

"War is for man what motherhood is for woman. Proudhon used to say that war is of divine origin. Heraclitus, the somber man of Ephesus, finds war at the origin of all things. In the "Encyclopedia" I have established my theory with utmost precision from a philosophical angle. Not only do I not believe in everlasting peace, but I would also hold it as depressive and destructive of the basic virtues of man, which only in the bloody effort of war can shine in the full light of the sun."

As usual, Il Duce spoke very slowly, with long pauses to allow the words to sink into the soul of his audience. He was a superb performer and an accomplished speaker. We girls were usually fascinated by his speeches. But not this time.

As a commentary on his speech, someone had written a slogan in large black letters on the wall of a building in front of us: WAR IN 1935. We dropped our bags. Mamma's face went white. We could hardly make it home. Nobody could calm her, not even Neri. All of a sudden, after having lived disdainfully aloof from the politics of Rome, Mamma wanted us to help her discover against whom Il Duce was planning a war. She remembered Sarajevo, she kept on repeating, the shock of Sarajevo and the four years that killed her village.

The next morning, she bought a radio, a huge piece that occupied a whole corner of our dining room. She asked Neri to buy a newspaper every day. As we turned on the radio every morning and scanned through the paper, she shuddered at the idea that during the night the Duce might have led us into a war.

We tried to reassure her. To the best of our knowledge, there was no enemy of Italy in sight. The Germans, who were as poor as the Austrians, had acquired a new leader, the Führer, who was a Fascist like our Duce. Neri ruled out England. We girls excluded Yugoslavia, a recently created nation, comprised of several ethnic groups. On Fascist Saturdays, we had heard Il Duce repeatedly say in his speeches that Yugoslavia would fall apart on its own without any war, like a house of cards.

France, the most decadent democracy in the world except for America, was a possibility. We girls were taught some songs about threatening France with hand grenades and knives if it did not return Savoy, Nice, and Corsica to Italy. But Neri ridiculed the song as an empty threat.

"Word, words," he said. "Il Duce is a windbag."

We shut him up. Our villa had ears. The recent talk of war had made everyone in town look at one another suspiciously. The Fascists were all for a war at any cost, no matter against whom.

Il Duce denouncing Il Negus as our natural enemy surprised us all. Il Negus (or "Emperor") governed Abyssinia, a vast African country. Of course we had seen his name in the papers and heard it over the radio, but we didn't pay much attention to it, simply because Abyssinia, his country, was in Africa.

How wrong we were, Signora Lucia observed sarcastically. If we had paid attention to Mussolini's recent rhetorical strategy, we would have noticed the direct consequence of his policy of procreation. Our young nation, a land overflowing with productive mothers, had to expand beyond the Mediterranean, which was our natural habitat, since we descended from an ancient Mediterranean people, the Pelasgians.

What we would claim, according to Mussolini, was due us from selfish nations, such as England, that had colonized and exploited most of the available space on the globe outside of Europe. We needed *"un posto al sole"* ("a place in the sun") in recognition of our innate vitality and creativity and the prestige due to us as descendants of the Romans!

In regard to Abyssinia, what was at stake for us, Il Duce said, was nothing less than an empire that was conveniently located between two of our colonies: Eritrea and Somalia. England wasn't going to hand us that empire on a silver platter, he told us repeatedly in his fascinating speeches, though he didn't explain what England had to do with it. He stressed instead the fact that our empire had to be wrenched away inch by inch by our soldiers and "Blackshirts," as the Fascist militia was called. The savage Africans, for some inexplicable reason, fought against us, while at the same time longing to be liberated and civilized by us.

The whole situation, Neri insisted, was very confusing, except for Mussolini's determination to wage a war. In general, young Italians felt that Il Duce had the glorious future of our country at heart. Once upon a time, we had fought against the Abyssinians and lost. This was a unique occasion for us to wipe out forever a not very glorious page in our colonial history.

What really worried us, however, was England's support of Il Negus. For months during the fall and winter of 1935, we felt as if we were living on the rim of a precipice. Not only the League of Nations in Geneva, buffoons, in Il Duce's words, but England also was taking a firm stand against Il Duce's resolve to take hold of his empire.

At home, we lived on two fronts. The World Atlas in hand, we followed step by step the march of our soldiers from Eritrea into Ethiopia, fighting the battles of Makallè, Amba Aradam, and Adua. Our Fascist leaders insisted we should follow the example of our Duce. He had sacrificed his own son, Bruno, who was shot down in the Ethiopian skies after he had killed hordes of savage Ethiopians.

Thank God, Mamma remarked, we had nobody to sacrifice in our family. Neri was too young for the army.

On the other front, we followed the movements of the English fleet in the Mediterranean by listening to a short-wave radio broadcast. At that time, an English politician, the young Anthony Eden, decided to visit Il Duce and offer him Abyssinia in an inglorious compromise, without war, but Il Duce threw him out of the office after an argument ensued between the two. This we read in our newspapers.

"I never saw a better-dressed fool," Mussolini said of Eden, while Eden called Il Duce a vulgar clown and swore revenge. The revenge included sanctions by the League of Nations, which was dominated by England. Those sanctions became the flag under which we all united, even those who disliked Il Duce. What hurt us was the threat of an oil embargo and the closing of the Suez Canal, which would have cut off our soldiers in Africa from all food and ammunitions. How could we betray our own men? "Support our troops" was the clarion call of the day. We lived at the same time in fear and suspense when Il Duce moved into action as England was holding its elections.

"Oil embargo means war!" he thundered from his balcony at Palazzo Venezia in Rome; bent over the radio, we all shuddered. The British fleet had gathered in the Mediterranean. The smoke of its vessels could be seen from Naples. The writing was on the wall.

Il Duce, and all of us with him, were walking a tightrope. He was in constant contact by telegram with General de Bono, the old faithful Fascist who was in charge of our troops in East Africa. Their conversation was harsh and intense. De Bono was asking Il Duce for food, since there was none to be had in Abyssinia. Mussolini was ordering him to resist at all cost without food. The British, he feared, were about to close the Suez Canal. We listened secretly on the shortwave radio that gave us the background of the official news.

"Resist on what?" The general respectfully asked.

"Don't ask me on what!" Il Duce thundered back. "Resist, I say. Resist and win! That's an order."

"Should we declare war?" the general inquired, after he was ordered to cross the border between Eritrea and Abyssinia.

Il Duce replied furiously, "War? Declare war? Are you insane? All we need is a declaration of war! England is ambushing us in the Mediterranean."

De Bono should have realized that Abyssinia had to be conquered silently and his Army had to march as fast and as quietly as possible from the border of Eritrea to the Abyssinian capital, Addis Ababa. The world, England especially, was watching us. Thus Il Duce soon replaced De Bono with General Badoglio, the hero of the Great War, who had led the Italian army from the defeat of Caporetto to the victory of Vittorio Veneto.

In the meantime, with the threat of the embargo from Geneva and the British fleet moving close to our shores, demonstrations were organized all over Italy with patriotic, pseudo-religious fervor. On November 18, 1935, the day sanctions were inflicted on us, mothers gathered at the Capitol in Rome to throw their golden wedding rings into a big cauldron as a donation to the country in need. The rite was repeated in every town. Mamma joined the teachers of the Cesare Battisti in the patriotic act. From then on, she wore an iron ring with the date of the sacrifice. She was anything but enthusiastic about the war and giving up her ring, but she disliked Eden as a presumptuous British aristocrat trying to humiliate our stocky farmer, as she called Il Duce. She saw it as a case of the rich oppressing the poor.

When Il Duce asked us to give up our copper for ammunitions, however, she hid whatever copper we owned in the cellar. Over the shortwave radio, she had heard that our army, in order to counteract the dum-dum bullets provided by England to the Ethiopians, had used mustard gas on both fronts, in Somaliland in the south and Tigrai in the north, killing thousands of Ethiopians.

"Enough is enough," she declared, disgusted.

On May 6, 1932, Maresciallo Badoglio entered Addis Ababa, the capitol of Abyssinia. We had created our empire. The throne of the Emperor Haile Selassie was shipped to Rome for the king of Italy to sit on as emperor of Abyssinia. Peace was made with England after an undeclared war. Mamma sighed with relief.

Yet, Il Duce's bellicose spirit was not satisfied. On February 8, 1937, his militia entered Malaga, Spain, in support of a war waged by a Fascist ally, General Franco. Mamma shut off the radio in disgust, and for a long time no one in the family listened to the news.

§ § §

In Merano, tension between the government and the Tyrolean Resistance increased after Adolf Hitler, the new German leader, moved into bordering countries, planning to free all German-speaking people. Unlike Il Duce's speeches, the Führer's speeches were unbearably long and painful to listen to. He would talk for hours in the same high-pitched, shrieking voice. We shut the radio off. Yet, some members of the Tyrolean Resistance listened to him religiously because they secretly hoped for his support. They listened and acted accordingly.

At Villa Fontana, we had the uneasy feeling of not belonging to either of the parties, the Italian Fascists or the Tyroleans. In fact, we tried our best to keep aloof from both, and paid the price for it.

One night, deep in the icy winter of 1935, we were all sitting around the radio, listening to the news, when we heard a crack like wood splitting, from the shutters of the glass door that opened onto the terrace. As we raised our heads in surprise, we thought we saw a masked face appear and disappear between the boards of a broken shutter. We looked at one another in silence. All we could hear was the wind howling over the snow-covered vineyards. We sensed that there was something wrong but didn't dare to guess what. Neri was the first to speak.

"All the shutters of this run-down shack are hopelessly weak," he tried to reassure us. "Forget about it. It must be the weight of the snow on the rotten wood."

We had just retired for the night, when Bona shrieked in terror, "Help! There he is again! The horrible man!"

We all ran into the room Mamma shared with Bona, which was next to the dining room. As we sat on Mamma's bed, we clearly saw a masked face, whose devilish eyes looked down at us from the cracks of the shutter. The mouth of the mask opened into a horrible grimace. Mamma was furious. She ran to the kitchen and reappeared in the blink of an eye, holding a broom, which she blindly banged against the shutters, as if the intruder were a bat. Our maid cried softly from the back of the room, "Stop it! Stop it!" The four of us children stood up in admiration of Mamma's fury, but that night we hardly closed our eyes out of anger and fear.

The next morning at dawn, Mamma was on the warpath. It wasn't the first time in her life, she said, the Devil had come her way. First she marched to the office of Comandante Prini. He took her to the Commissariato and then to the Questura, the central police office. The Questore was a friend of Prini. He therefore received Mamma with respect and listened with interest to her report. The story, he said, fit a pattern of recent reports. He referred her to a recently created office in charge of terrorist acts. There, Mamma witnessed a long discussion among experts on who the masked man could be and on the possible reasons for his intrusion in our private life. Mamma was not extensively interrogated, because Comandante Prini made a solemn statement on her exemplary life as the Fascist mother of four children. He drew a picture of her as the ideal Donna Fascista. The Questore cut him short with a brusque "This is not pertinent to the investigation." Mamma sighed with relief.

Was she aware our having any enemies among the Tyrolean rebels? He asked her. Mamma, who was hardly aware of the existence of a resistance movement, was most emphatic in her "no." The conclusion anyway was that the act was political. The Italians were ruled out, so the culprit had to be some Tyrolean. They said they would look into the matter.

After hours of precious time wasted, which meant money lost from Mamma's private tutoring, she decided to go to the local police station on her own. There, supported by the conclusions reached in the previous office, she asked for a hand-gun and obtained it without any difficulty. She also asked to be taught how to use it. The head of the local police courteously complied. Back home, she placed the gun well in view on her night table and repeated to us the instructions on how to use it, so that we could remind her if she forgot. Anybody walking on our terrace during the day could see it.

Under Francesca's supervision, every night at dusk we went through the long and tedious operation of covering every single window or glass door of the apartment with blankets and sheets. According to Francesca, this would discourage the intruder's curiosity. After dinner and prayers, we almost automatically went by Mamma's night table to make sure the gun was there. That gun was slowly filling a void in our lives. It took the place of a police department we didn't trust. It also confirmed Mamma as the ruler of the family. The gun was an awesome thing and was never mentioned by us. It was up to Mamma to use it properly.

For a couple of weeks, the intruder did not return. We would have forgotten about him had it not been for the gun. Finally, one moonless night, the face made a fleeting appearance between the wooden shutters of Mamma's room.

"There he is!" Bona cried and we all ran silently into the room, our eyes not on him but on Mamma.

Mamma jumped out of bed in her long white flannel nightgown, grabbed the gun, and left the room. We followed her quietly. She left the apartment, climbed the stairs, and rang the bell of the apartment over ours. The two elderly sisters who lived there were not at all surprised to see her. She swiftly slid by them into the room over hers and opened the window. Her long hair loose, her slim white shape silhouetted against the starry sky, she stood immobile for a moment holding the gun firmly, with both arms raised over her head.

"I have a gun pointed at you," she said in her melodious voice. "I'm giving you a chance to leave before I shoot."

We were so tense, we didn't budge or utter a sound. There was an interminably long pause. Then Mamma lowered her head as if to protect herself and the gun went off loudly against the sky.

The intruder never showed up again. The day after the shooting, Mamma returned the gun, as she had promised. We never discovered whether the intruder was a Tyrolean rebel or an Italian Fascist, and the whole episode was soon forgotten.

§ § §

VILLA MOSKAU

"We must get ready to move!" Mamma announced bluntly one evening at dinner. We were speechless. Why move now, when we had finally found a form of peace at Villa Fontana, while the whole world around us was in trouble? At age fourteen, I was preparing for admission to the liceo. My sisters and brother had successfully followed me to the ginnasio, one after the other.

We studied with one eye constantly on the world around us. Recent events had radically changed our perception of life. School was no longer a haven, and the town around us was tense and restless. While Mussolini waged war in Africa with a wary eye on the English fleet in the Mediterranean, on the other side of our mountains, Hitler was starting his hypernationalistic program. Austria seemed to be a meager protection between us and Hitler while the Tyrolean resistance gained strength from Germany's.

Why move now, and where? We were upset by Mamma's sudden announcement, but she was in no mood to explain. She acted as if we had to solve the mystery on our own. Finally, on a chilly Sunday morning in March, as we walked home from church, she stopped at the crossing of Grabmaierstrasse with via Schaffer, a road that led north into the heart of Obermais.

"There are two villas in one park," she said in one breath as if to avoid interruptions. "They are more beautiful than you can imagine and different from any other villa in town."

She paused, then declared with a sigh of relief, "Finally free of Tyroleans and Italians, we'll be living with the Russians!"

"The Russians?" Neri burst out. "What are the Russians doing in Merano?"

Mamma looked at him condescendingly. She explained that the Russians had arrived in Merano long before the Italians. Relatives of Mademoiselle Messing, our new landlady, had long before obtained special permission from the Austrian Emperor to build two villas in Obermais to house sick Russians seeking special therapies. The Emperor and his wife would visit them when they came to Merano.

Though Catholic, the Emperor allowed the Russians to practice their religion, Russian Orthodoxy. Villa Borodino, the twin to Villa Moskau where we would live, housed the Orthodox chapel where their Pope officiated on special occasions such as Easter and Epiphany.

"What languages do you speak with them?" Bona inquired.

"German and Italian," Mamma said, explaining that they also spoke French and, of course, Russian.

Then, leading us single file on a narrow sidewalk up Via Schaffer, she made us stop in front of an elegantly chiseled wrought iron gate. Half-hidden behind it in a park of tall verdant trees of all sorts, paths meandering among them, two round marble fountains gurgling in their midst, stood the twin villas against the background of majestic white mountains. On one side was Villa Borodino, a dome over its Orthodox chapel. On the other was Villa Moskau, a construction of stone and artistically carved wood. Its main features were its wide wooden balconies, two for each of the main floors, each as spacious and well protected as a room. All balconies and shutters were closed on the second of the three floors of Villa Moskau, the one, Mamma announced with pride, we would soon occupy.

While we pictured our golden future on those balconies, Mamma, like a tour guide, lectured us on what she had recently learned about Russian history. She dove with gusto into Russia's resistance to Napoleon's invasion, speaking knowledgeably of the battle of Borodino, of the ensuing burning of Moscow, and of Count Tolstoy. He was somehow related to Mademoiselle Messing and her inseparable nephew, the composer Monsieur Messing. Both of them had once lived at the court of the Czar, which Czar Mamma didn't say, although certainly not the unfortunate one of the 1917 Revolution.

Listening to Mamma was like reading *War and Peace.* She had adopted nineteenth-century Russian history with the same enthusiasm as she had tackled the Italian wars of independence during our years in Villa Dolomitenblick, at the time of my admission exam to the Carducci. To my delight, it was Tolstoy's triumph over Cappelletti!

We entered Villa Moskau triumphantly on a radiant day in May. Mademoiselle Messing was waiting for us at the bottom of the majestic stairs with their red carpeting. They led from the first to the second floor of Villa Moskau. She was a tiny old lady, so thin and frail, one wondered how she could walk and talk. Her wrinkled, parchment-like face looked like the face of an Egyptian mummy reproduced in our ancient history textbook.

There seemed to be a secret entente between Mamma and the old Russian lady. They communicated by affectionate smiles, instead of words, while Mademoiselle Messing held Mamma's rough peasant hand with her long, thin, fragile fingers, as if to draw from Mamma the strength she needed to stand and act among us ordinary human beings. There was nothing normal about Mademoiselle Messing, beginning with that Mademoiselle, a title unknown in Merano.

We girls curtseyed to her, and Neri bowed his head while shaking her hand. When my turn came, Mademoiselle Messing whispered something that sounded like music to my ears. It was French. Mamma translated:

"Mademoiselle expects you to read to her in French during the summer, as soon as you are free from your school obligations." Then she whispered to me, "Don't worry. You have two full months to learn French. I'll see to it that you get some help." We all understood that my reading to Mademoiselle was part of our living arrangement.

Our apartment was situated at the top of two sets of stairs. A huge glass door opened onto it. The terrace outside the apartment was covered with wisteria in full bloom. Inside were four ample rooms as well as a kitchen and a huge bathroom, all comfortably gathered around a wide hall. The floors, even the kitchen floor, were made of shining parquet, the ceilings high, the wood panels delicately carved. In a corner of each room stood a huge porcelain stove, a different color for each room. The villa had been designed with love and care for people who needed comfort, perhaps on the model of some country house dear to Mademoiselle Messing in the outskirts of Moscow.

The dining room and the room Mamma assigned to Francesca and me opened onto the park. Their wooden balconies were almost as wide as the room itself and were sheltered from the northern wind by a glass panel. For herself and Bona, Mamma took the large central room, which had a veranda like window. Neri got the room overlooking the mountains. His room seemed immense, given its sparse furniture: a small bed and a chair. A whole corner of the kitchen was occupied by a big old-fashioned woodstove with a copper bucket for hot water and a pot to make tea, which Mamma called by its Russian name, samovar.

A Steinway piano occupied a third of the dining room. When we entered the room, a gentleman stood erect and stiff near the piano. He was of indefinite age, as lean as a rake, with a square olive-colored face and a prominent mouth. Black-dyed long hair hung straight down his neck. He introduced himself as Monsieur Messing and with him, as with Mademoiselle, his aunt, we all behaved impeccably.

Speaking German, he announced that, as soon as we had settled, he would start piano lessons for Francesca and me. He would provide the books. We later discovered that was part of the agreement Mamma had struck with him. In return for our piano lessons, she would teach him Italian language and culture, which was at that time the special subject for her private tutoring.

That very first night, after we had moved in our few pieces of furniture and eaten our dinner at our old dining room table, we gathered on the balcony. Mamma was lying in the leather armchair where Papa had died, her eyes closed. The fragrance of magnolias and wisteria filled the air, mixed with the penetrating aroma of incense from Villa Borodino. The park was bustling with a secret life of its own, of which only the song of birds and the humming, buzzing, and droning of insects reached us. We looked at one another and, without a word, we moved over to Mamma and held her tightly in our arms. She was speechless.

§ § §

For us, Villa Moskau meant having a home on another planet, insulated from the troubles of the world around us. With this privilege came certain duties. Almost every day, Mamma taught Italian language and culture in an Obermais villa where a Swiss lady, Fraülein Auer, ran a finishing school for wealthy young ladies from all over Europe. Instruction was mostly in languages, art, and music.

Fraülein Auer took over my training in French. She made me proceed rapidly from one level to the next so that by the end of June I had become reasonably proficient.

By July, Mamma delivered me to Mademoiselle Messing's inner rooms at Villa Borodino and, after an exchange of affectionate smiles, she abandoned me to my destiny. The oppressing July heat reached us past even the heavy blue velvet curtains that sealed off Mademoiselle Messing's boudoir from the rest of the world. She lay on a dark blue velvet sofa under a dark blue velvet canopy, adorned with a long golden fringe. On a low ebony table between us, stood a samovar surrounded by fragile light blue porcelain cups.

"Well, my dear young lady," she said in French. "Are you ready to help me spend the long hours of my afternoon? You know, I am almost blind."

Her soft, delicate voice reached me as if from another world, so different from the imperious voice of Fraülein Auer. Like everything about her, Mademoiselle Messing's French could not be measured on a normal scale. No matter what she said, it was pure poetry.

Leaning against her blue sofa, wrapped in a long black silk robe that fitted her slim, frail body, she raised her right arm to show me where I could find her favorite books on the shelves of her library.

She owned the French originals of all the Romantic poets, she said, but her favorites were Rimbaud and Baudelaire, whose poetry she recited to me by heart.

Up on her shelves a place of honor was reserved for the works of Tolstoy in Russian and French. Near them were Dostoyevsky, Lermontov, and Chekhov. On their right were Victor Hugo and Dumas Père. A little farther down I could see *Madame Bovary,* close to *Anna Karenina.*

I didn't dare confess that all of the authors she mentioned, except for Tolstoy, were unknown to me, but she seemed to be aware of that, because she whispered, "At the liceo classico, you honor only the ancient world. I hope to live long enough to open to you the world we live in."

Perhaps in consideration of my fledgling French, she put in my hands Daudet's *Lettres de mon Moulin (Letters from my Mill)* and lay back peacefully, while I read aloud to her as softly and gently as I could, in harmony with her world. My voice echoed in the silence of that mysterious corner of Villa Borodino, until I noticed from her regular breathing that she was asleep.

I quietly closed the book and climbed the ladder to reach the books on the shelves high up. I glanced at some of them, reading a paragraph here and there, cursing my insufficient French. Still, French was the passport that would allow me to travel through nineteenth-century Europe, experiencing a freedom I had dreamed of for years without realizing it. In Mademoiselle Messing's boudoir, I understood why the cultivated Russians loved French so much. It freed them from the prison of their own culture.

Suddenly, a book fell from my hands to the carpeted floor with a thump. Mademoiselle opened her eyes and, seeing me up on the ladder, broke again into a laughter again so pure that it filled my heart with joy.

Twice a week, Monsieur Messing showed up in our dining room for our piano lesson, impeccably dressed in his pressed black suit, his long black hair hanging down his neck. We started from the beginning, not only because Francesca had never approached a piano before but because I had learned the wrong technique from Schwester Annunziata, he said.

Putting in my hands an old copy of Hannon's *Klavier Virtuoso,* he abandoned me to my scales. Francesca, on the other hand, excelled from the very first lesson, grasping not only the spirit of the music, as Monsieur put it, but the coordination of mind and fingers which was indispensable for success.

At first, Mamma reproached me for not applying myself enough, as she was working hard to get Monsieur Messing to say a few words in Italian, in compensation for his piano lessons. He was a hopeless case, she told me, as if that could make me feel better. After that, I felt morally obliged to apply myself to the piano for hours until I could do all the scales in major and minor keeping my fingers in the desired position. But no matter how much I tried, Monsieur Messing played his best duets with Francesca, smiling at her all the while, whereas he confined me to scales.

I admired Francesca as she smiled back at him not only with her lips but with her sparkling blue eyes, shaking her mane of dark brown hair to mark the beats. She looked truly professional.

§ § §

In spite of my deficiencies, piano continued to enrich our lives during our years at Villa Moskau, a generous gift of our Russian friends. While we lived there, Mamma's private classes in Italian languages and culture for her German friends kept her wandering from villa to villa after her regular classes, from 4:00 to 8:00 p.m., except on Sunday. These lessons almost doubled her salary. Mamma's German students, inadvertently, introduced us children to a new aspect of the contemporary world.

The Führer was gaining status in Germany and his army moved into neighboring countries to liberate every German-speaking person, a policy that strongly encouraged the Tyrolean resistance movement. Another effect of Hitler's presence was a steady flow of German refugees who had, until then, lived peacefully at home, but were now crossing the Alps to find refuge in those beautiful villas that had once offered a pleasant home to the Austrian nobility.

Mamma's German students soon became her and our very best friends. They took a lively interest in us, in our studies, and in our lives. Middle-aged gentlemen and ladies, highly cultivated, soft-spoken and refined in spirit and manners, they were, like us, prisoners of the mountains, exposed only to tourists who visited Merano when the grapes were ripe. Yet they didn't mind their isolation

We befriended their children, who did not speak Italian nor attend school and hardly ever left their villas. Like their parents, they looked distant and melancholic. Without any reproach to Germany, which they had abandoned, these refined Germans went out of their way to proclaim their boundless love for Italian culture and language. As children of the teacher they loved, we were often invited to tea and strawberry parties in the spring and were showered with gifts at Christmas.

Our subject of conversation with our German friends was German poetry and contemporary art and culture. Together, we recited Goethe and Heine. They also introduced us to the mysterious, forbidden world of Marx and Freud. Mamma warned us never to ask any personal questions and never to reveal to anybody anything they told us, especially not details of Dr. Freud' theories or Mr. Marx's books.

Although Mamma seemed to know something of their world which we didn't know, she too was mainly in the dark about the reason they had left Germany.

"Let us enjoy their company as long as we can, she told us sadly after a birthday party. I am afraid they are not here to stay."

The mysterious shadow of Hitler hovered threateningly over us all.

The news of his invincible army marching into Austria and entering Vienna in March 1938 to the wild applause of thousands of Austrians took us and must have taken Il Duce by surprise because he sent half of his army up North to our area. Overnight, Merano was overflowing with handsome *bersaglieri*, members of the old army corps that dated back to the Crimean War. They rode on bicycles, turkey feathers in their hats, while sturdy *Alpini* showed off only one chicken feather on a different kind of hat. We girls were delighted by the show, which, however, ended abruptly. In 1939 I had hardly begun my studies at the University of Rome when Hitler and Mussolini signed the Pact of Steel, which was supposed to cement a sturdy alliance between the two leaders, avoiding, as far as we could judge, the threat of a Tyrol open to an eventual "liberation" for some, but for most of us an invasion. We in the family found relief in the thought that as long as the two "devotees of war," as Mamma called them, remained on friendly terms Hitler would not dare cross the border.

The Anschluss, however, as the Fiihrer's occupation of Austria was called, had immediate consequences for our generous German guests in Merano because back in Rome Il Duce proclaimed ___ — some said was forced to proclaim — that we belonged to the same noble race as the Germans, that is we were "Aryans." "Words", Neri commented. Yet this time, "words" had dire consequences that affected us directly. Not only our German friends, but many of our fellow citizens and close friends sold their villas and disappeared. Mamma took us to the Italian Church of the Holy Ghost under whose Gothic arches a solemn ceremony was held for three days at the time (a *triduo*). The music of the medieval hymns was so overwhelming most of the worshippers were silently weeping. That was the first time in my life I personally felt my family belonged to a community beyond the enclave of the two Russian villas. I remember distinctly Mamma's words one night as we came home from Church and listened to the Russians singing "dark clouds above us announce the hurricane." I don't think she herself knew what she meant. We didn't.

At the Liceo classico, Professor Morpurgo, a scholar of the history of ideas and economics, always dressed elegantly in a checkered sport suit of English cut with a minuscule Fascist badge on his lapel. He marched every day from the door of our classroom straight to his desk, as if we, his ten students, didn't exist. He questioned us once a trimester, calling us one by one to his desk. A memorable experience, because he hardly allowed us to speak; he answered his own questions. The rest of the time, he lectured in a monotone. While he talked, he never looked at us, keeping his head bent and rubbing his forehead with slow strokes, as if to elicit more ideas from his brain.

He lectured each time for two hours without stopping, keeping the ten of us of the upper classes, eight boys and two girls, in a sort of trance. During the three years of the liceo, in which he was supposed to cover the history of ideas in the western world from the Presocratics to Fascism, he spent a year and a half on Plato and Aristotle, then leaped a millennium to reach Giordano Bruno, Campanella and Vico, and gave special attention to Locke, Berkeley and Hume. Finally, he lingered endlessly on Kant and Hegel, then made room for Nietzsche and Schopenhauer. He completely skipped, without apology, the last section of the third volume of our textbook, entitled "Fascist doctrine."

In economics, he spoke at length on "liberalism" and on the "weaknesses of the democratic system." His tone was so ambiguous that we couldn't discern if he was dealing with the subject ironically or seriously. He advised us with a smile that we would not likely be questioned on that subject on the final exam. He defined the subject as well known to all.

I adored Morpurgo. When I saw him at a distance on my way to class, I would cross the street because I knew I would blush at the encounter. In class, I sat adoringly in the first row, never missing a word of what he said. He always gave me the highest grade, although, since I was never allowed to express an idea, I was not aware of what I had learned. As the years passed, I grew to believe that he and I had a secret understanding, by which Plato and Vico and Kant would speak to me, without forcing me to articulate my thoughts on their ideas to anybody, least of all to a professor like Morpurgo, who understood them so much better than I did. On one occasion, however, I had tangible proof that Professor Morpurgo had deeply influenced my own way of thinking.

It happened at the very conclusion of my classical studies, when I had already said goodbye to my beloved philosophy professor. The final examination opened with a six-hour essay, whose philosophical-historical topic was decided each year in Rome for the whole of Italy. In 1937, we were asked to choose a recent period in Italian history, to which a statement of the Greek historian Thucydides could be applied. In reference to the Athenians, he wrote

"We are as a people courageous and prudent, yet we manage to avoid being daring and are incapable of decisiveness."

Without hesitation, I applied the phrase to the Italian nineteenth century wars of independence, instead of to the current Fascist period. Morpurgo had restored my esteem for those wars, after the blow Mamma had inflicted on them when I was eight years old and she had tutored me for the admission exam to the ginnasio.

In the oral part of the final exam, the three examiners from Rome pointedly questioned me on the reason for my choice of that historical period for analysis. Why had I chosen, as the most striking moment in Italian history, the wars of independence, instead of the glorious Fascism of the present? I noticed with horror that my forthright response made them wink at one another. There was nothing in the events of the day, I said without hesitation, that could be compared with the Italian Wars of Independence for identifying the best in the character of the Italians. Most importantly, I added in a hurry, frightened by the stone-faced silence of the examiners, I strongly felt that we lacked the necessary historical perspective to judge the present. There was a moment of silence. Then the chief examiner courteously dismissed me without further questioning.

As I walked out of the room, a cold shiver ran down my spine and my heart pounded. I was sadly aware that at the close of my scholastic career I had again fallen into the trap of doing it "my way." I had blundered again, as I had at age eight on the admission exam. As a child, I could be excused for having acted instinctively and irrationally. At seventeen, given the present political conditions, my irrational act was inexcusable, because it could have serious consequences for my whole family.

I had not reached the stairs when one of my torturers called me back from the other end of the hall. He closed the door carefully behind us and said to me gently, "Do not worry. We all agree that you made the right choice."

I felt an urge to embrace and kiss somebody, but the somebody I would have liked to embrace wasn't there. I ran from the room down the stairs. Now that Professor Morpurgo had physically disappeared from my life forever, I suddenly realized how close we had been for the past three years.

As I walked away from the old Benedictine monastery, tears came to my eyes, not of nostalgia, but of gratitude mixed with a feeling of loss. That night in bed, I fumbled in vain to identify what Morpurgo had given me that had influenced my own way of thinking. One day during the difficult years that followed, it dawned upon me that it was his insistence on Plato's myth of the cave that had affected me so. Prisoners in a cave, their backs to the light, could only see the shadow of reality. That was the leitmotif of his teaching, and because of it, Professor Morpurgo had made me deeply aware of the subtle interplay of illusion and reality in the world in which I lived. He had made us witnesses to his own stubborn struggle to cope with a difficult reality. For three years we had had the privilege of witnessing his painful endeavor. Instinctively and unknowingly, I had been the closest observer of an intimate personal conflict. In 1938, Professor Morpurgo was forbidden to teach because he was a Jew. I had been a witness to his last three years of teaching. I learned later that after the war he was named Professor of Philosophy at the University of Genoa.

A month later, I went with Mamma to get the exam results. As usual, the grades hung from the ancient arched ceiling, written in beautiful black calligraphy on a white sheet. I had passed the state exam with the highest grades in Italian composition, philosophy, history and mathematics. Everybody hugged me, but for some strange reason, I couldn't share their excitement. I felt alone in a vast desert. I knew that those grades signaled the end of a form of security that had made me happy in spite of its illusions.

In his own peculiar way, Morpurgo had inspired his students to seek reality beyond the comfortable world of illusion. As our role model, he must have taken into account the fact that we, his students, had been born in the "cave" and had never seen the light of the sun as he had, before the rise of Fascism. Although he had chosen not to incite us to acts of rebellion, he had made us aware that there was something beyond our illusion. From now on, I would walk alone into that totally unfamiliar place. Morpurgo was my first secret love.

CHAPTER 3

The Dream of Rome

I owe both my success on the final exam in mathematics and my choice of a university to Mamma's uncommon ingenuity and acute common sense. This double gift came two years after we'd moved to Villa Moskau when Mamma decided that her children had left behind the age of summer vacations in the familiar rural environment of her native village. Having spent two summers working in town, they should now spend a whole summer in the absolute solitude of a high mountain. We needed a rest.

I had also warned Mamma, for whom success in our studies was of the utmost importance, that during the forthcoming summer, I would need time to prepare for my final exam. It would cover, besides fifteen Greek and Latin literary texts and an array of historical, philosophical, and artistic subjects, a basic knowledge of mathematics, physics and sciences. I explained to her my perplexity, which she shared, over the liceo's teaching method with regard to mathematics and the sciences. A good memory had served me well, but I was convinced that I was not prepared in these subjects, in spite of my apparent success in the classroom.

Not forgetting the incident eight years before when she had banged a cube on my head, Mamma now devised a more humane solution to my problems with mathematics. She worked out her plans rapidly, as was her habit.

A fifteen-year-old friend of Neri, Carlo Voragine, in love with rare stamps, had been recently expelled from the ginnasio for having stolen the most valuable stamp collection in town. We had become friends of Carlo's family during our stay among the Italians at Villa Fontana. His father was one of the highest military authorities in Merano, his mother a professor of mathematics on a leave of absence. In deference to the social status of his parents, Carlo, having been judged guilty, did not have to go to prison but was placed on probation. Since he was expelled from school, however, he had to prepare for the final exams on his own.

Immediately after the scandal, Colonel Voragine vanished in Africa. Mamma took it upon herself to persuade a depressed and lonely signora to remain in Merano to look after her son's private studies. In her practical generosity, Mamma found a way to help both me and the unfortunate lady by including mother and son in her fanciful plan for a vacation in a glacial wilderness. Signora Voragine would teach me math, while I would tutor her son in the humanities. This useful combination persuaded me to accept the summer adventure. Now all Mamma had to do was to find the proper kind of villa that a delicate lady of taste like Signora Voragine could accept. A villa in absolute, unreachable isolation.

Herr Brunner was one of Mamma's most faithful students and one of her best friends. He would have liked to marry her and adopt us, but since she was firmly opposed to remarriage, he tried to please her and us in everything we asked from him and much more. Mamma knew Herr Brunner owned a beautiful mountain villa. It was all but lost among the last forests of the dark and narrow valley of the mountain river Passirio, under the pass that indirectly connected Merano with Austria. Standing in perfect solitude in the shadow of a majestic glacier, the Villa Mamma dreamed of as the ideal residence for our summer in absolute solitude had no electricity but plenty of cold water and a cozy set of rooms on three floors. It was furnished like Goldilocks's. A vigorous torrent roared in front of it, drawing its foamy waters directly from the glacier.

Mamma arranged for us to spend the summer at Villa Brunner. When we arrived there, Signora Voragine embraced her with a deep sense of relief. This solitude, she said, was what she needed to cleanse herself of all the human ugliness of the past months.

That very night, she and I sat at the table in a kitchen lit by a fragrant open fire and a smelly oil lamp. Pencil in hand, she proved theorems and solved algebraic equations one after the other, silently, as if I didn't exist and she was acting exclusively for her own pleasure. This performance was repeated again and again every day in the house or in a green meadow near the brook, since she thought the noise of water was suitable to mathematical thinking. She never asked me any questions, never raised her head to look at me. She seemed to live in her own world, oblivious of me, while I remained near her in silent admiration. As with Professor Morpurgo, the miracle performed by Signora Voragine under the majestic glacier took place by force of her genuine love for her subject and my deep admiration for her abilities.

I don't know how it happened, but one day, pencil in hand, I began solving problems on my own. I had fallen in love with mathematics.

The complete isolation of Villa Brunner was not equally satisfying for every member of my family. Bona and I liked it better than the others. Neri longed for company. Francesca developed a bad cough. We all secretly longed for vegetables other than the wild herbs and the mushrooms of the meadows and more fruit than just the berries of the forest. Mamma was disappointed in us. She sadly confessed that we didn't have the making of real hermits or of real mountain lovers. In order to train us, she led us into the thickest forests at sunset. We remained desperately lost until the moon or some kind of star kindly showed her the way to our home.

As for food, we couldn't complain. We had plenty of fresh milk, butter, and cheese from the mountain dairy.

Unfortunately, the weather in August was cold and wet. But we stumbled along without complaining, in the hope that fortune would bring a touch of variety to our daily routine of long walks through the forests and endless hours of studying around the fire when it rained or snowed. Our prayers were answered twice, both times, in the wake of a frightful storm. The second time, the consequences changed forever the future of our family.

§ § §

Storms were an awesome phenomenon in this narrow valley. They came unexpectedly, often in the late afternoon of a warm day. A thick black cloud would suddenly gather between the glacier and the

Jaufen Pass. If we were in the forest, Mamma had taught us to run as fast as we could away from the trees and into the open meadows in order to avoid being hit by lightning or by a falling tree. If we were home, we closed all the windows and hoped for the best. Rain would soon whip the world around violently, enveloping forests and mountains with a thick curtain that would cancel them from sight. Here and there, a bolt of lightning made them visible for a fleeting instant, followed by the rumbling of thunder and often the crash of a tree. For a half hour or so, the forest would moan, victim of a merciless storm, and we would live in suspense within it and with it. When the rain stopped, we found ourselves immersed in a damp, palpable gray fog, which we knew would soon be scattered by the beams of the sun. Finally, up over our head, stretching majestically from the Jaufen Pass to the glacier, a rainbow's delicate colors announced the return of peace and normality.

We loved storms. By breaking our routine, they made us aware that no matter how carefully we planned our future, unexpected events could change it in ways we could never have dreamed. One afternoon in July, a violent storm caused an officer of the Alpine Corps, which was on summer maneuvers near the Jaufen Pass, to get lost in the forest. He turned up under our windows on his horse like a legendary prince in a fable. He was soaked to the skin, and he marveled at our villa, which offered shelter behind its sturdy walls and closed windows. We girls, who could hardly believe our eyes, had thrown open the windows and encouraged the handsome officer to come inside, which he did happily. We received him with open arms, understandably after a month of solitary confinement, and offered him everything we had available, berries and cream, plenty of homemade bread and butter, hot tea and chocolate. As expected, he departed with the last raindrops of the storm and left behind only the scent of a strong male perfume, which got us girls dreaming of a peninsula, leisurely and sensually stretched out, like a beautiful woman, on the shore of a blue sea.

The Alpine officer was like a swallow announcing the spring. One evening in August, at the end of another frightening storm, a sports car stopped in the misty sunset among the pine trees in front of our villa. Out of it, tumbled the three members of the Franchi family. We had known the Franchis since early childhood, as they had made brief visits to Mamma's farm in Tajo on their way to Cloz, a village north of Tajo. Cloz was the birthplace of Giuseppe Franchi, the father of the family, and of our newest aunt, Elvina, Uncle Silvio's industrious wife. Aunt Elvina was Signor Franchi's niece and godchild. He could therefore be counted as an acquired relative.

Giuseppe Franchi had emigrated as a young man from Cloz to Zara, a small Italian oasis on the Yugoslav Adriatic coast. There, married to a well-to-do local beauty, he lived comfortably teaching mathematics in a professional school, with his son Bruno, his wife, and his sister-in-law Rina.

We children remembered the Franchi visits as great events during our summers in the village of Tajo. Aunt Speranza would strangle a chicken, roast it on an open fire, and serve it with plenty of fried potatoes and fresh salad, the whole meal topped off by a huge apple strudel. The meal was served in a room used only on special occasions. As children we were confined to the kitchen and served the leftovers, a sure indication that the Franchi were very important people, worthy of the greatest respect.

The idol of the family was Bruno, a rather flabby adolescent who, we were told, excelled in everything he did – school, sports, and music. The third member of the family, whom we called Zia Rina, was a bony spinster with silver hair and matching silvery gray eyes. She was Bruno's aunt, who acted as a mother to him after his mother's premature death.

In Valtina, the Franchi visit was a most welcome surprise. Bruno, now a tall young man of twenty, moved briskly out of his sports car to embrace us, signaling that he intended to establish a new relationship, in which we were on equal footing with him. During the few days the two families spent together, we grew closer. As we picnicked on the wide wind-bitten meadows of the pass, climbed along the crevasses of the glacier, or searched for mushrooms and berries in the pine forest, we became aware that Bruno shared our desire to move beyond our families into a wider world. Of course, Bruno's world had been so far incommensurably wider than ours. As a child of affluence, he had always had everything he wanted. He lived near the sea. He had traveled by train, boat, and even plane. He owned a sports car, while we could not even afford a bicycle. Yet in our dreams, we children longed for a world beyond the one he had been raised in. Unlike Bruno, my siblings and I spoke three languages and lived in a bicultural, bilingual country coping with many problems. Poor from the start, we had been raised to fight hard for everything and to take nothing for granted. Therefore, we were more willing than Bruno to break with the past and to face the adventure of an unknown future.

After the Franchis had left, I came to envy Bruno for one and only one privilege: he was a student at the University of Rome. Upon hearing him speak of Rome, graphically describing the city itself and its new university, I made Rome my choice for the continuation of my studies. It was a silly thought, at first blush, impossible to realize, given my responsibilities to the family. Yet, I intuited that Rome was my gate to a kind of freedom — freedom from what, I did not know.

The real surprise to us three girls came when Mamma in-formed us, after the Franchis' departure, that the main reason for their visit was to choose a wife for Bruno. The Professor, his wife, and Aunt Rina had followed us girls through the years and finally made up their mind that we were the ideal pool from which Bruno could choose his companion for life. We giggled and declared without hesitation that Francesca should be the chosen one because of her recognized natural beauty and her invaluable human and domestic qualities. Bona was too young to aspire to the honor. I, according to my sisters, was too stubbornly independent and lost in my own world. When Bruno announced that he had chosen Francesca, I was delighted. Now, free to pursue my own dream of Rome, I could count on Bruno's help and support as my future brother-in-law. The dream of Rome now became my life challenge.

CHAPTER 4

Rome from Villa Moskau

My choice of the University of Rome and Mamma's approval of it were in no way motivated by any academic concern. In August 1937, Mamma and I did not know how an Italian university functioned. I would have liked to study medicine, but I knew I could not because it required attendance at all classes. Bruno assured us that in the divisions of the humanities and law at the University of Rome limited attendance was a common practice. I chose classical philology at the University of Rome.

At the time of our choice, neither Mamma nor I was aware of the deficiencies of the university system, particularly in Rome. Whereas the eight years of ginnasio and the following junior college – liceo classico and liceo scientifico, in which Greek was replaced by the sciences – were highly structured, with regular mandatory classes and frequent written and oral exams, the Italian university in its non-scientific divisions was dangerously unstructured. Based in theory on teaching through research, the Humanities Division of the Italian university was generally perceived by its ever-increasing mass of students as a marketplace. One could shop for a degree by registering for a prescribed number of courses that ended with oral exams. At the University of Rome, the one and only written exam in the Humanities ("Lettere") was in Latin composition. Oral examinations were scheduled for June and October. Lack of attendance, or limited attendance, which was due in part to insufficient physical space, was one of the major signs that the system did not work. Another was the difficult problem of the student-faculty relationship, which was left to each professor to work out. Usually, the more important the discipline, the more distant the professor. Latin Literature, the main subject, presented insurmountable difficulties for students on all fronts.

In the case of the University of Rome, the Fascist government had attempted to remedy the lack of physical space by building a walled-in University City (Città Universitaria) with separate buildings for each division, promenades with trees and flowers, a huge fountain around a statue of Minerva, the Goddess of Wisdom, a theater, and a Casa dello Studente (Student House) with eating facilities. The creation of a University City had indeed encouraged attendance on the part of students who lived in or near Rome. It remained, however, a not uncommon practice among students who came from afar and didn't have the means to live in Rome to limit course attendance to one month a year in order to collect the official class notes which they would then study at home in preparation for the exams. The Bidelli, or monitors, were sufficiently corruptible to provide students with the necessary signatures of regular attendance.

Mamma approved my choice of Rome because Bruno had assured her that I could obtain my university degree – *laurea in lettere* – in four years, while spending no more than two or three months a year in Rome, including the June and October exam sessions. I could therefore continue my regular work in Merano and contribute to the family's survival while setting aside money for my visits to Rome.

I personally had chosen Rome for more than one reason. Rome was the city of my dreams from childhood on. Also, being the farthest away from home among the possible choices, it would give me the opportunity to explore half of the peninsula I had longed to discover all my life.

§ § §

I can hardly recall my first Rome without the shiver of excitement I experienced during each of those very brief periods, one month twice a year, when I was allowed to enjoy the city on my own, during the spring and fall of 1938 and the spring of 1939 and 1940. For me, Rome was then, first and foremost, an escape. It offered me not so much a satisfactory continuation of my studies as a chance to disengage myself from the family responsibilities I had had to shoulder since Papa's death.

My idyllic view of Rome lasted two years. It ended abruptly the summer of 1940. After the Anschluss and the *Stahlpakt* (Pact of Steel) between Hitler and Mussolini, Hitler's invasion of the Sudetenland

and Poland in August 1939 led to a war between Germany and the Western democracies, while Mussolini, after the Abyssinian war, the war in Spain, the racial laws, and the invasion of Albania, was still holding on to a fragile neutrality.

Two very distinct images of Rome coexisted in my imagination when I chose it for my studies. The stronger of the two was the Rome of the great poets, whom I had learned to love during my eight years of classical studies, and the other was the complementary Rome of the great ruins.

In contrast to my understanding of classical Rome, with its objective rendering of human life in all aspects — spiritual and intellectual, physical and artistic — stood Il Duce's myth of Rome, inspired by an irrational, subjective patriotism and a passion for war. Like everyone around me, I had been bombarded incessantly by this irrational myth of Rome in Il Duce's speeches, the Fascist parades, and the Fascist youth organizations to which we had to belong, whether we wanted to or not.

Mussolini's myth of Rome was a personal and subjective political instrument for molding the amorphous mass of Italians (who until 1870 had been citizens of small states governed by foreign powers) into one powerful nation. The Fascist hymns were its most vivid vocal expression. We young people sang those hymns, hardly realizing that their words usually contradicted what we had learned of Rome in the classical school.

The money necessary for my brief Roman excursions was provided by the "school" my siblings and I had established at Villa Moskau. I was regarded by desperate parents in Merano as the ideal person to prepare their children for their exams, while my two sisters and brother, who were moving ahead successfully in the ginnasio, were accepted as support staff.

The school system determined the substance and method of teaching since the ginnasio liceo classico was the only road to university entrance. We four siblings knew how difficult that road was, how humiliating the defeats, how glorious the victories.

At Villa Moskau we offered assisted learning as an alternative to the way subjects were taught in school. Latin syntax, essay composition, Plato's ideas could all be approached in ways different from those pursued by the professors. Curiosity and interest were essential to success. But if a student resisted that approach, it was up to me to overcome that resistance somehow.

Most of our students came to understand the difference of approach in time to save themselves the humiliation and pain that came with obstinacy. Girls tended to open up like flowers in the spring breezes. Some of the boys were obstinate. Overall, ninety percent of our students passed the exams and became our best means of publicity.

At first, I taught Latin and Greek. When the requests for subjects increased to include the whole program of the ginnasio liceo, my brother and sisters joined me. We taught everything except modern languages, which were Mamma's specialty and which anyway we regarded as inferior to the classical languages.

Bona, the youngest, was usually assigned to support me and Francesca in special cases. Bona distinguished herself by her inflexibility – indeed her cruelty at times; she insisted that a boy learn what he had to learn. She became notorious for locking students in our bathroom, which was an ample room with a view of the mountains, until they had memorized seven classes of Greek irregular verbs.

Once, a boy known for his obstinacy left a message under her pillow. He drew a skeleton on a piece of paper and wrote, "Tonight you die." That boy, the son of Merano's police chief, was regarded by the ginnasio faculty as a total failure. However, with our help, he passed his final exam with an average mark of seven. He and his father became our friends for life.

This project was lucrative. Ordinarily, six months of tutoring would produce enough income to pay for a month in Rome, over and above, of course, the required contribution to Mamma's income for our daily life in Merano.

§   §   §

My first experience of Rome came in May 1938, after nine months of work at villa Moskau. The elegant arches of the Roman aqueducts, so light and ethereal that they evoked Ovid's magical lines describing the Palace of the Sun ("Regia solis erat sublimibus alta columnis," *Met.* II), rose suddenly before my mind's eye in the mist of an early spring dawn. I had been waiting for a first sign of Rome through a whole sleepless night on the train, sitting straight on my wooden bench between a soldier and an elderly gentleman. When my eyes caught the aqueducts' blurry lines softly emerging from a blue-rosy mist, I swore that Rome would be my city forever. Through all my life, the aqueducts have remained the symbol of Rome.

"Remember never to speak to any man on the train," Mamma had warned me as she gave me a last kiss before the train left Merano's little wisteria-covered station at 6:00 p.m. Her warning was preceded by a colorful description of how sly Italian men could be with young girls alone on a train, especially inexperienced Tyroleans traveling without make-up, their hair tightly braided around their heads. So far so good, I thought to myself. More than once, during the night, I pushed back the soldier, who in his sleep kept on falling on my right shoulder. The elderly man was toothless and harmless.

Mamma had organized all the basic details for my life in Rome so as to safeguard my virginity. When I stumbled out of the train with my little suitcase at the Stazione Termini, all neatly rebuilt in Fascist style, I found Bruno Franchi waiting for me. As Mamma had planned, he led me through the first city I had ever encountered in my life, offering a minimum of necessary explanation, such as "Wait for the green light to cross." There were very few lights. We went straight to the convent in Piazza di Spagna, where Aunt Rina had found lodging for me. He would be back after lunch, he told me as I went inside.

My bed was waiting for me, clean and neat, an orderly dormitory, and I went right to sleep. A bell woke me up for a lunch served in a cool refectory, a dish of *pasta al pomodoro*, a glass of wine, a salad, and a kumquat, a fruit unknown to me. The meal itself was preceded and followed by a long, stilted prayer to the Virgin. The imposing, severe arches of the main halls of the convent and the cold, distant attitude of the nuns, who seemed to regard me with suspicion, left me in an unpleasant state. This mood was magically dispelled, however, when I went out with Bruno for my first tour of the city.

He wanted to cover the whole of the ancient city in one afternoon, so I literally had to run after him. He explained the sites in a dry, matter-of-fact tone, racing ahead of me, not even turning his head. Yet, that first visit on a crystal-clear afternoon was the magical key that opened the city for me. Flowers of all sorts, mostly unfamiliar, occupied every open space, embracing the ruins and decorating the ancient buildings and the cloisters of the ancient basilicas. Birds sang, hidden everywhere in trees and bushes. Peace reigned supreme over the old and the new.

Whatever I explored on my own after that memorable afternoon in early May was like a gloss on a text inscribed in my memory with indelible ink. The Rome I encountered that afternoon was totally different from everything poets had written about it. For me, it was a precious stone tightly held in by the golden ring of the Aurelian Walls.

The next morning, Bruno took me to the university to confirm my registration for the exams I was going to take in June, for which he had kindly registered me ahead of time. The university had been recently built in typical Fascist style, similar to the station I had arrived at the previous morning, with reddish quadrangles surrounding a square fountain. From the moment I entered that university city, I was overwhelmed by a sense of being in transition. I knew that University City was a place where I would take exams in order to earn a degree, and then move on to something else. It was a way station.

My own Rome, immobile within the Aurelian Walls, gave off a distinct sense of permanence. The ancient Rome of the Forum and the Coliseum; the Christian Rome of Byzantine mosaics and Cimabue's frescoes; the splendid Rome of the Renaissance with its Palazzo della Cancelleria and Palazzo Venezia; and the eloquent Baroque Rome with its many churches – all lay there for me to enjoy to my heart's content. I owed my first Rome to Bruno.

Bruno vanished shortly after having given me instructions on how to get around on my own. He ended his duties by delivering me to an intimate friend of his Aunt Rina for a sumptuous meal. Signora Tacconi, who had moved to Rome from Zara with her adult sons, lived in Via Spallanzani, located in the residential section that surrounded University City. She became from that very first meal my point of reference for my dreamed-of future life in Rome.

A free, openminded lady of Slavic-Dalmatian descent, she immediately understood that I couldn't live in a convent. She helped me find a room with other students not far from her home. With the change of residence, my life changed radically. The villa where we lived, although rich in marble and imitation Renaissance furniture, was dirty and flea-ridden. However, the students with whom I shared the apartment, all Italian girls from the peninsula, enjoyed a freedom of movement I had never experienced before.

While my roommates were critical of the courses they were taking, I, who had to pay with my earnings in Merano for every day I spent in the Eternal City, soon became more critical than all of them. I found ways to enjoy Rome without attending courses; I figured out how best to prepare for the mandatory courses I chose not to attend because they were too boring. I simply bought the books of the professors, planning to read them later in Merano. Instead, I attended courses which were not part of program, such as "Roman Topography" and "Spirit as Pure Act", a course given at noon by the famous philosopher Giovanni Gentile, a man I instantly loved because of his warmth and his open-mindedness. He would lecture while walking around the classroom, addressing us individually.

In Rome, I was free for the first time to enjoy my life, with nobody forever reminding me of my obligations. I enthusiastically joined other students for bicycle rides through the Roman tombs of Via Appia and discovered pizza and Roman wine in the *osterie* of Trastevere. On one of those excursions, a tall Sicilian medical student with dreamy black eyes and long sleek black hair asked me to be his fiancée. I was so thrilled at the proposal that I delayed my refusal for a whole week. I felt highly honored.

In my daily letters to Mamma, I didn't mention the happy Roman diversions from my studies, but she must have guessed, because suddenly the trickle of money from Merano stopped altogether. If I wanted to complete my stay in Rome or even prolong it by one month, I had to find ways of earning money while there.

With the help of Signora Tacconi, I set up a system of private tutorials based on the model of our school in Merano. Rome, I discovered, had its own share of desperate liceo students in search of the kind of help I could provide. There were also Italian public officials who wanted to learn German, since Il Duce was getting closer to Hitler every day.

Mamma reacted ambivalently to my initiative. She correctly worried that the possibility of my working in Rome would become an alternative to working in Merano and hence would disturb the life of the family. By the end of June I had passed the exams in five courses with honors, having hardly attended two for a month. Back in Merano, excited by my unexpected success, I plunged into heavy tutoring at Villa Moskau for the whole summer, work which I continued through the fall and early winter of 1938, with only a brief visit to Rome in November to pass some exams and register for new courses.

By Christmas 1938, Rome had become for me something more than a welcome escape from Merano. Some of the courses I took called for much closer attention than I could give during my brief visits. It was, however, the life of the city that interested me most – a city basking in the peace that followed the wars in Abyssinia and Spain. Rome attracted many foreign tourists, intellectuals, and artists. My brief visits allowed me only the vague feeling of something mysterious going on between the majestic ruins of the Forum and the Renaissance mansions of the ancient noble families. There Count Galeazzo Ciano reigned, the minister who, besides being extremely charming, happened to be Mussolini's son-in-law.

An impenetrable mystery of its own, Vatican City stood on the other side of the Tiber, linked to it by a broad avenue, it was said, which Mussolini's initiative had created, destroying a whole section of medieval Rome.

I had caught only the vague fragrance of a *Roma Caput Mundi* (Rome Center of the World), but enough to make Merano and its villas seem pale and insignificant, including Villa Moskau and the Russian community that had generously housed us. Back at Villa Moskau, daydreaming of Rome, I tried to find new ways of earning an income that would allow me to prolong my next visit to Rome from January to June. Bona suggested that I earn my rent money by assisting our old school friend Rikland Wiese in Rome. For the past eight years, Rikland and her mother had lived in a villa in Obermais not far from our villas. The two had originally come to Merano from the Northern Sea, in search of sun and good weather, after the death of Dr. Wiese, a wealthy high official of the old Reich. Both had been tutored in the past by Mamma in Italian, then Rikland by me in Latin and Greek. Now Rikland, having successfully passed the final exam, was ready to move on to university. And she had chosen the University of Rome.

Rikland was a tall, robust girl, twice my size, interested in abstract subjects like contemporary philosophy. Her favorite philosophers were Nietzsche and Schopenhauer, her favorite book *Also Sprach Zarathustra*. She was an attractive girl but few could understand her when she spoke because of a birth defect that affected her throat and nose. Because of that, she spoke in a strange combination of sniffles and whistles. It took time and patience to work out what she was trying to say. By now, after so many years of living close to her, everybody around her in Merano had become accustomed to her way of speaking and accepted her for what she was – an intelligent and cultured young lady. But how would she fare among the Italians of Rome?

When I proposed to Frau Wiese that I act as her daughter's interpreter in Rome, if she paid the rent for a room we would share, she embraced me, weeping out of gratitude. She proposed not only financial help but also the strongest moral support. She offered to present my proposal to Mamma. In time, I convinced myself that my motive was truly one of Christian charity, not opportunism, and I promised Frau Wiese I would act not only as her daughter's interpreter but as her protector. I made that promise without giving the slightest thought to how I would carry it out. Mamma agreed. One starry January night, the two mothers saw us off to Rome at Merano's old train station. They both seemed relaxed, apparently trusting my ability to act as Rikland's guardian angel in the perilous environment of Rome.

My difficulties began on the long train ride, when Rikland insisted on speaking instead of sleeping. After the train crossed the Alps, she kept everybody awake and roaring with laughter, until I dragged her out of the compartment and forced her to spend most of the night standing near the window. She did not mind it because it was Italy that rolled by in front of her, the Italy of her dreams. She identified with Goethe's Mignon and kept on repeating "Kennst du das Land wo die Zitronen blühen?" ("Do you know the land where the lemons bloom?") She was becoming wild with excitement.

In Rome, however, where we settled in a room at Piazza Bologna not far from the university, Rikland turned out to be an ideal companion: good-humored, persistent, and resourceful. To my surprise, she possessed the skills of a detective.

To say that we were short of money is an understatement. I explained to my companion that until I could strike gold, hopefully with my tutoring, I had only enough money for one meal a day at the Casa dello Studente, a kind of International House supported by the government. For a while, Rikland offered to pay for a light dinner for both of us and did so until she discovered the Academies.

Supported by individual governments, the Academies in Rome offered residence to foreign artists, writers, and scholars. They also hosted exhibits, concerts, and lectures, which were open to a select number of Romans. Each event was followed by a buffet accompanied by wine and sometimes even champagne. Rikland found a way of placing us on the mailing list of as many academies as she could manage. Whenever we could understand the language of the inviting Academy, we enjoyed the event as well as the refreshments. When we didn't speak the language, as, for instance, at the Turkish and Romanian academies, we simply enjoyed the refreshments.

One night at the Greek Academy, Rikland overheard a slim and elegant Greek colonel tell a French colleague that he was planning to learn Italian and was looking for a tutor. I casually approached the tall black-haired colonel and we struck a bargain.

The next day, Colonel Ballodymos and I met at the Greek embassy for what, in his view, was a class in Italian. What he actually wanted was for me to read Italian newspapers aloud to him and translate them into French. When I tried to deviate slightly from the reading to introduce my student to a few rules of Italian grammar, he called me back to order, as if I were one of his soldiers who stood guard at the door. This went on for quite a while. At the end of each class, he paid me twenty-five lire, an enormous sum.

Rikland was delighted, even when I told her I was puzzled by the colonel's persistent interest in Albania. Nothing appealed to him as much as Albania. What did she think caused such interest? Was Ballodymos to be trusted? She laughed and gave a long sniffle. Why should I care? Greeks are Greeks. They are to be feared, as the poet said, even when they bring gifts. Sooner or later, he might turn his attention to Romania.

One day, the Greek colonel took me out for a ride in the shiny new embassy car. When we were far out of the city, he stopped, opened a box of chocolate, and offered it to me with a smile. I had just picked my favorite chocolate, when he put his arm around me and, forgetting about Albania, tried to kiss me. I put the chocolate back in its box and asked him to turn back to the city, which he did without showing any embarrassment. That day, had I not reminded him, he would have forgotten about the twenty-five lire he owed me.

The next day, despite Rikland's urging, I did not return to the embassy. I would have forgotten the handsome Greek colonel, had I not discovered soon thereafter the reason for his strong interest in Albania. From then on, I thought of him sympathetically.

§ § §

Shortly before I severed my connection with the colonel, I received a note on the official bulletin board of the Casa dello Studente, which I used as my advertising medium. A lady named Stefania Benita Marcantoni asked for my help in preparing her son Antonio for his final exam. They lived in Trastevere, across the Tiber, which meant they were true Romans. Her husband worked at the Ministry of

Foreign Affairs. After reading the note, Rikland and I treated ourselves to a double serving of *pasta al pomodoro* and an extra glass of wine. Then I rushed to cross the Tiber.

Signora Marcantoni's apartment, on the top floor of an old building, had a stunning view of the Tiber, yellow with mud, meandering around the Tiberine Island. Everything in her home, beginning with a huge poster at the entrance, spoke of Benito Mussolini, which explained why one of her names was Benita.

"Call me Nina!" Signora Marcantoni said, addressing me directly in the Fascist familiar style, using "voi" ("you") which had replaced "lei" ("thou"). A short, athletic woman with short thick black hair and huge shining eyes, Nina was dressed in the Fascist uniform, black skirt and white blouse. Her endearing manners and ready laughter made me immediately accept her invitation to join her for wine and cheese in her sunny kitchen, which exuded the fragrance of basil and garlic.

One evening in mid-March she angrily informed me that the Germans had occupied Bohemia without even informing Il Duce. It was, she declared, an act of disloyalty toward Mussolini, who had been deeply loyal to the Axis. On the other hand, she surmised that Hitler knew that Il Duce had problems at home. Italians, she intoned one night in disgust, were fickle by nature, which angered Mussolini. He had done his best to reeducate his miserable people in every possible way, even trying to change the climate of the blessed peninsula, convinced as he was that it had something to do with Italian softness of character. What Mussolini resented was that Hitler tried to humiliate him instead of helping him out. How could one otherwise explain the fact that he was occupying the whole of Europe, leaving no "'Lebensraum" ("living space") for us Italians?

It was in the context of the rivalry between Mussolini and Hitler about who would occupy what countries in Europe that Nina mentioned Albania. The only way to teach the Germans a lesson, she declared suddenly, was for Il Duce to occupy Albania.

"Why Albania?" I asked.

"Why not Albania?" she replied. Albania was up for grabs. Another country would be Greece, were it not protected by England.

From the latest reports, she declared, King Zog of Albania, unfortunately for him, was inclined to refuse our protectorate. This meant that we would have to create terror and confusion in Tirana before our landing, while assuring Yugoslavia and Greece of our proper intention

I ran home, dying to report to Rikland what I had heard about Albania. She had locked herself in the bathroom, vomiting. When she opened the door, she fell into my arms desperately sobbing.

"I know," she said sniffling, "I should have told you about all this before, but I was so happy I could hardly believe it to be true."

It took me some time to work out the facts in her rambling confession. Almost immediately after our arrival, she had met a handsome middle-aged Italian, Amilcare, a high official at the Ministry of Press and Propaganda. I remembered the man quite well from a party at the Romanian Academy. He courted her and came to see her, she confessed, right in our room while I was out. He took her to the best hotels in town, while I thought she was in class. He loved her. Yes, he loved her passionately, infinitely more than his wife. He promised he would take care of her and her baby. He was happy that she was pregnant because, as a Sicilian, a Fascist, and a Catholic, he loved babies. All he could promise Rikland was to keep her as his beloved mistress for the rest of their lives. No, he wouldn't have any other mistresses, he swore.

My reaction to her touching confession was rage. I threw the bag with her dinner on the table and screamed at her. How could she do this to me, betray our friendship? The trust I had in her? The promise I had made to her mother?

Surprised by my outburst, she embraced me and tried to respond to my questions straightforwardly. We talked at length, quietly, lying close to each other on the bed. I told her that I couldn't believe this drama had taken place under my very eyes. I thought of her as a true intellectual. Who would have suspected that while she kept *Also Sprach Zarathustra* on her night table, she was going to bed with a miserable, cheap Sicilian, who already had a wife and children, a

Fascist official of a ministry that even Nina despised because it didn't serve any purpose. How was I going to explain all this to honest Frau Wiese up in Merano?

Rikland stopped my sermon and, drying her tears, accused me of thinking only of myself. This was her business, not mine. She was older than me, and we didn't see eye to eye on the matter. Of course she had thought of her mother. There was no question that in Merano she would be ostracized by everybody, starting with her mother. Amilcare, with his proud Carthaginian name, was the love of her life. He had spoken to her of his beautiful village in Sicily. It sat perched on a rock, among orange trees and olive trees. Almost in view of Africa! With the last of her money, she would take a train down south to Sicily, the island of the sun, and die by plunging into Amilcare's blue sea.

Rikland's decision, sniffled out so quietly that I could hardly make out what she was saying, had the effect of a cold shower. Coming back to my senses, I realized how cruel I was being to her. I put Nina's dinner on a plate and served it to her. She was starving. Then I undressed her and put her to bed like a baby. When I heard her snoring, I settled our Roman business in writing, packed all our belongings, and walked quickly to the station where I bought two tickets for Merano. I woke Rikland and led her to the station as gently as I could.

Rikland seemed to board the train in a trance. She sniffled quietly for hours, sitting straight on her wooden bench, her eyes closed, while the train took us back home. When she discovered we were going north, she tried to declare that she wanted to go south. I explained to her as gently as I could that north was safer, at least for now. In time perhaps, God willing, we might go south.

During that interminable ride home, one image followed me obsessively through hills, plains, and mountains. It was that of King Zog, the king of Albania, kneeling near his wife, Geraldine, and their newborn baby in the wide hall of a medieval castle. Outside its walls, all around the city of Tirana, one could hear the crowds under Italian control, shouting against him.

Frau Wiese received the news of her daughter's misfortune with surprising calm, and so did Mamma. They both seemed almost happy to see us at home. God, they said, embracing each other, would take care of us. Rikland went quietly back to her studying and I to my regular teaching.

On April 8, I heard on the radio that King Zog had fled to Greece after Italian troops had occupied Tirana without resistance. I rushed to buy the newspapers. There was no reaction reported from either Yugoslavia or Greece. While working hard at night to prepare for my June exam in Latin literature, I was tempted to write to Colonel Ballodymos, but I didn't. My world now was not the world of Rome. At least not today's Rome.

On April 15, my whole family mourned quietly for Albania as we heard on the radio the Albanian representative Verlaci offering the crown of Albania to our king during a ceremony at the Quirinale. The king received it with his usual studied indifference. He did not seem to care about being king of Albania any more than about being emperor of Ethiopia. That was Mussolini's business.

My family listened spellbound to my explanation of his regal indifference. The few rebels who stood up for Albanian independence were quietly eliminated. Italian engineers were busy fixing roads that connected Albania to Greece, which, I explained to the family, could be Mussolini's next target. While we listened to the news in our spacious living room, with the sun setting over the snowy pink peaks, I thought without nostalgia of a Rome where my friend Nina was surely applauding Benito Mussolini in the crowd at Piazza Venezia.

When I returned to Rome in June for my exams, Francesca went with me to begin her university studies. Back in the city, I phoned the Greek embassy. Colonel Ballodymos was gone. Antonio Marcantoni had passed his exam with the highest marks in the class, as he had planned. Francesca and I were both invited to the celebration. If I ever decided to live in Rome, Nina proposed I tutor her younger son, Arnaldo, a good-for-nothing, she said, laughing, who was interested only in soccer. At the Casa dello Studente I found more requests for tutoring. I did not answer any of them, but I kept the names on file. Francesca and I soon went back home.

§ § §

The summer of 1939 in Merano was a long nightmare. We carried out our assisted learning program from morning till night on our balconies at Villa Moskau; I spent part of the nights on the same balconies, perusing Vincenzo Ussani's commentaries on Horace, Ovid, and Florus. Since the fright caused by the Anschluss was still fresh in our memory, we followed Hitler's movements behind the Brenner Pass with apprehension. Would the Alps protect us from a German invasion? The Tyrolean question, still unresolved, was like a thorn in Mussolini's flesh.

On September 1, the day Hitler's army entered Poland, Francesca was so shocked, she could not swallow. We calmed her with a hot bath. Remembering Nina's painful account of Mussolini's fluctuating feelings about Hitler, I tried to enlighten the family on Il Duce's worries and resentments. Until the very last moment, he probably hoped war could be avoided, and finally decided to remain neutral. But Mamma wouldn't believe that Il Duce had given up on the war.

At home now, we talked openly about Mussolini's nature and behavior as we never had before. My stay in Rome had taught me a new way of interpreting the world in which we lived. What I brought back from Rome, along with Professor Ussani's books on Horace and Virgil, was the image of Mussolini as a man who was undergoing his own personal human crises. He was a man like all of us, I told the family. Unfortunately, Mamma concluded sadly, we were paying for his mistakes and weakness.

In Merano, we lived in fear of Hitler's unpredictability. What if he decided to disregard his friendship with Mussolini? We were slightly relieved when, in his speech in Danzig, on September 19, Hitler spoke of Il Duce twice as a friend. Yet, the question of the Altoadige remained the subject of painful discussions between the two leaders. It was an obstacle and threat to their "friendship." Il Duce wanted an assurance from der Führer that the old border at the Brenner Pass, prize of the Italian victory in World War I, would be respected. Hitler, who had other worries, didn't hurry to make concessions to Mussolini, whom he didn't trust. Yet he promised the essentials.

On the other hand, the militants among the Tyroleans were determined to preserve their language and culture at any cost. They were Germans, not Italians. They didn't trust Il Duce to guarantee their rights. The solution to the conflict finally being considered by Hitler and Mussolini involved moving the Tyroleans who agreed to move to the other side of the Brenner Pass.

What leaked from the lengthy secrets between the two leaders was very upsetting both to those who decided to leave and those who never thought of leaving. If the farmers who had lived in the Tyrol for millennia were to leave, what would happen to the land? Who would take over the splendid vineyards and orchards, the pride and glory of the land? It was evident that Mussolini didn't care, provided he could get rid of the Tyrolean Hitler, who cared for the Tyroleans even less than Mussolini did, was interested in prolonging the dealings ad infinitum, so as to keep Mussolini in line in case he needed his help. Everybody agreed during our discussions at home that the Altoadige was strategically more relevant to Italy than Albania.

While the world around us was at war, I had very good news from my friends in Rome. Many of my former students expected me to resume my tutoring.

In June 1940, I was supposed to take the final exam in my major subject, Latin language and literature. Professor Vincenzo Ussani, who had taught the course in this subject, was a member of the prestigious Accademia d'Italia. An old Latin scholar and poet, he enjoyed the reputation of being aloof and distant from what went on among the students. Normally, out of the thousands of candidates forced to take the exam, only ten percent passed it. Puzzled by this phenomenon, I had brought all of his books with me to Merano, in the hope that the solution lay in understanding his method of interpreting the Roman poets. I didn't trust my few notes from the course. Mamma agreed with me that, in the best of all possible worlds, after reading his books, I should try to attend his course, which I had so far neglected.

Uncertain about the future of our own family, we felt very sorry for those among our friends who had decided to leave for Germany, but we were also worried about what would happen to those of us who stayed behind. Without envisioning the removal of our family from Merano, Mamma finally agreed that I should try to support myself in Rome for most of the forthcoming year 1940. Time would tell what the family should do.

Yet every time I was about to leave for Rome, something happened to make us postpone my departure: for instance, the attempt on Hitler's life in Munich on November 9, 1939, or the recurrent rumor that Belgium and Holland would be Hitler's next victims. There was also talk that the Germans, frustrated by the many difficulties hampering an agreement with Mussolini on the Tyrol, had decided on a plebiscite for the whole region. Il Duce accepted the idea of a plebiscite, but soon he suspected that this was nothing but an excuse on the part of the Germans to occupy the area. The plebiscite pacified the Tyroleans, promising as it did a settlement that would allow them to remain in their own land. They were given at least three years to leave for Germany. That, some said, meant an indefinite postponement.

Mussolini took precautionary measures, hoping to avoid any incident that might give the Germans an opening. Overnight, Merano was overrun by police and carabinieri. Il Duce's fears were justified when, toward the end of December 1939, a document was discovered in Prague which confirmed Hitler's decision to occupy Altoadige, Trento, and Trieste, and eventually even Lombardy. On Christmas Eve, the cathedral of Merano, packed with Tyroleans singing *Stille Nacht*, was closely watched by the police and the carabinieri. How could I leave the family under such precarious political conditions?

I was finally ready to leave in January 1940. At the train, both Mamma and I could hardly restrain our tears. We embraced wordlessly. I felt like a soldier leaving his homeland in danger.

CHAPTER 5

Love and War

I met Lyliana at the Casa dello Studente shortly after I arrived in Rome. The Casa dello Studente attracted mostly students with no connections in Rome. It was a comfortable, warm meeting place for students of all nationalities. I had even met an American medical student there. Fat and jovial, he addressed everybody by their first name and told us one day, maybe to impress us, that it took nineteen lire to make one dollar. For years, the dollar stood in my imagination as the king in the realm of money. English sterling was the queen.

Lyliana was a Bulgarian who had a degree in medicine from the University of Sofia. When I met her, she had been in Rome for a year, working in her specialization in obstetrics. Short and slim, she stood out in the crowd because of her boyish looks and her red hair. She smoked incessantly, mostly Nazionali, the most common, cheap, and vulgar kind of cigarette. She was witty and forthright. Not everyone liked her, but I did. And she liked me.

When I was introduced to Lyliana, Rome had lost its attraction for me. I was depressed. The city itself was cold, gray, and dreary. Since arriving there, I had spent most of my days in the library or at the Casa dello Studente because the cheap room I rented had no heat. But what I really missed was the warmth of my family. Twice a day, I wrote long letters home. They told in detail of my life in Rome and asked what was happening there. My classes had not yet started, nor had my tutoring, except for Arnaldo, Nina's son, who fortunately was as cheerful and ignorant about everything that interested his mother as a normal young boy could be.

In my loneliness, I was often tempted to use the few lire I had for a ticket home. I had almost persuaded myself that I could prepare better for the key exam in my specialty, Latin literature, in the seclusion of Villa Moskau, shielded by the mountains all around, than in Rome, a city with no borders, open to all winds.

What kept me going for a while were the daily letters from home, which included reports about the threat of uprooting the Tyroleans, who, at a distance, were "my people" more than ever before. The assisted learning program at Villa Moskau was blooming. Rikland's baby was beautiful, the picture of his grandmother. The archbishop of Bressanone/Brixen had officially declared that he would go to Germany with his flock when the time came. What was the Pope's reaction in Rome? It was a slap in the face to the Vatican in its relations with Mussolini. Neri asked me, "What did Il Duce plan to do with us?" I appealed to Nina who told me that at the Ministry they wanted the Tyroleans out of the way as soon as possible.

§   §   §

I had decided to move back to Merano to be together with my family and deal with whatever came when Lyliana asked me to move in with her. The friend with whom she had been sharing her room had returned to Bulgaria. She also offered to house Francesca at exam time, at no extra charge. I would have the room almost to myself, she said enticingly, now that she was an intern at the hospital. I accepted, and my life changed overnight.

Ten years older than me, Lyliana had experience in the art of living alone in a foreign land and in coping with severe financial difficulties. The room was spacious, sunny, and warm. It even had a telephone, a rarity in Merano. What I did object to was Lyliana's heavy smoking. When home for a few hours, she would lie on her bed, a cigarette in one hand and the telephone in the other, chattering in Bulgarian, enveloped like an odalisque in a cloud of thick smoke. When I complained, she smiled, said I was a baby, and ironically suggested I take up smoking, which I did, though unwillingly. I felt that there was too much at stake at this point in my life for me to risk losing the security of my newfound home.

Lyliana had become my role model. I admired the way she moved or lay in bed or brushed her teeth, even how she read aloud (in Bulgarian) from a thick book — the Bible or Karl Marx? — which she kept on her night table, and how she brushed her abundant red hair and packed her bag to go to the hospital. Nobody could keep Lyliana from doing what she had a mind to do.

I didn't live with Lyliana long enough to discover if my perception of her corresponded to reality. What mattered was that the perception worked for me at the time. With Lyliana as my role model, I plunged into studying for my major exam. I organized my tutoring to earn maximum profit in minimum time and made up my mind not to think about the present political situation, even though it was one of the main reasons for my feelings of helplessness. The strategy worked in the long run, beyond all my expectations.

On a wonderful blue day in March, my favorite waiter met me at the Casa dello Studente with a hand-written note in French. Someone who signed himself "an admirer" asked to meet me. Shortly after, a gentleman showed up at my table. He was definitely a "foreigner," though I couldn't tell of what nationality.

He was tall, dark-haired, olive-skinned, a gentleman, dressed in a checkered woolen jacket of foreign cut, gray pants, and a silk shirt. In lieu of a tie, he displayed an elegantly folded, light beige silk scarf, matching his shirt and his skin. He placed his umbrella on the back of his chair, which made me think he could be an Englishman, had it not been for the color of his hair and skin. In Italy, it was assumed that all Englishmen were blond and pale.

He sat down near me and ordered, in broken Italian, steak, potatoes, and salad, and a bottle of wine. "For two," he added, without consulting me. I could not detect any special accent. Since I was hungry, my protests were mild. By the end of the meal, I had agreed to tutor this mysterious man in Italian, for one hour a day at the Caffè Greco. He had heard of me, he said, through friends who admired me. Which friends, he didn't say. When I told Lyliana that night about the encounter, she warned me with a smile to watch out.

The next day, at 5:00 p.m. at the Caffè Greco, he introduced himself as Vassili. He had chosen the most romantic place in Rome to reveal his identity: a famous hangout of poets and artists since 1800, at the base of the Spanish Steps. Those steps, surrounded by azaleas in full bloom, connected the Church of Trinità dei Monti on the Pincio Hill with the Piazza di Spagna below. Another Greek, I thought to myself, who loves theatrics. Vassili was from Athens and had been educated in England from childhood. He had decided to stop in Rome on his way home from Oxford, where he had earned a degree in political philosophy, because he loved Italy and, of course, adored our musical language.

"What does a Greek see in Italy that is so extraordinary, since Italy is a Mediterranean peninsula not so different from Greece?" I asked forthrightly.

He smiled and answered without hesitation. "I came to see Mussolini. I would like to understand how he works."

I was startled. Did he know a certain Colonel Ballodymos? I asked. He laughed. The former Greek Military Attaché in Rome? Of course he knew of him, he said, but didn't know him personally. Vassili was the only son of a well-to-do Athenian mother, the widow of a Spartan. She was living now with a Greek orthodox priest, whom Vassili despised. I surmised that my new Greek friend had stopped in Rome on the pretext of learning Italian in order to delay his encounter with his mother's lover in Athens.

So far, we had spoken in French. When I broached the subject of Italian, Vassili laid down his rules: no grammar, no syllabus, no reading list. He wanted to hear me speak, tell him stories.

I laughed. "What kind of stories?"

"Stories about yourself, your family, your mountains.

How did he know that I came from the Alps? Was he in contact with some member of the Resistance in the Tyrol? Even if he was a spy, the young man was definitely different from anybody else I had ever met. He was witty and imaginative, which could have proved, I thought that night, that he was indeed a spy.

Anyway, even if he was a spy, I liked him and was happy when he proposed an honorarium that was twice as much as what Nina paid me for tutoring Arnaldo.

§ § §

At home, Lyliana warned me again, but in a vague way. Money couldn't pay for a woman's independence, she said. I ignored her warnings. When Vassili and I met the next evening at the Caffè Greco, we were both at ease and happy to see each other. The conversation centered on ancient Greek literature, first Thucydides and then Plato. I spoke in Italian as much as possible, switching to French when necessary. Vassili answered in French. He also recited in ancient Greek some words from Morpurgo's favorite passage in the Republic, about the prisoners in the cave.

When I spoke of Morpurgo, he warmed up and laughed.

"Don't make any mistake," he said. "A precipice separates modern from ancient Greece: Rome, Christ, and the Turks. What the two have in common is a love for freedom," he added, quoting Byron, a poet I didn't know. Unlike Albania, Greece would not be swallowed up by any power-hungry tyrant. He trusted that my love for ancient Greece or Rome would not excuse me from critically judging the present. I thought of Nina and kept silent. He changed the subject.

From that night on, I did not report our conversations to Lyliana. We had always refrained from talking about politics. I realized that I felt closer to Vassili than to anyone else in Rome. He spoke to me freely about his mother. I spoke of my family and of my nostalgia for life in Merano.

Vassili, I concluded after a week of meetings, was a lonely human being who badly needed a friend. And so was I. I was furious with myself for having suspected him of being a spy.

We began discussing art, first ancient art in the Forum, then Byzantine art in the churches adjacent to the Forum. On a late afternoon in April, after spending a couple of hours admiring the stunning mosaics of Santa Maria in Cosmedin, we climbed up to the wooded Palatine. We sat quietly enjoying the silence of an eternal sunset as we leaned against the trunk of a century-old olive tree. Beyond the Domus Liviae, the reconstructed house of the wife of Emperor Augustus, lay a silent Forum, its maimed columns rising among rosebushes and gigantic acanthus leaves. Vassili, his arm around my shoulders, leaned down and kissed me — a brief and unexpected kiss, which sent shivers down my spine.

"*Documenti!*" thundered an imperious voice beyond us. A stout policeman in black uniform informed us that making love in public places was forbidden by law. He then pulled Vassili up by the arm.

We both knew that explanation was useless, yet we tried to argue that we weren't making love. He had merely kissed me. "*Un bacio!*" Vassili said in his charming Italian.

"A kiss?" The policeman sneered. "Everybody knows what follows a kiss."

He had caught us just in time. Besides, in Italy, kissing in public was an offense against civic decorum. Kissing in front of Livia's House was an offense against an empress well known for her chastity and fidelity to her husband, the Emperor Augustus; kissing on the Palatine was a sign of disrespect for the cradle of ancient Rome, the birthplace of Romulus and Remus.

He paused for a moment, apparently thinking that we might be foreigners. Then he thundered again, "Documenti!"

He disregarded my university ID and concentrated all of his attention on Vassili's Greek passport.

"*Un Greco!*" he exclaimed finally with admiration.

But then he discovered that Vassili had entered Italy not from Greece but from England, which had recently blockaded us. Vassili, knowing the risk he was taking, promptly displayed the regular entry visa to Italy.

After Vassili agreed to pay a fine — in cash as the policeman proposed, thus avoiding any compromising written statement — the policeman shook hands with him, while looking at me scornfully out of the corner of his eye.

When he finally disappeared in the golden dust of sunset amid the ruins of the Forum, I burst into tears. Vassili took me in his arms and consoled me like a mother whispering to her child. Then he insisted on inviting me to dinner in a little restaurant he knew well in the Jewish Ghetto. "Aryans still patronize it," he joked. "In spite of the racial laws."

At Piperno, after more than one glass of wine and more than one serving of Jewish-style artichokes, Vassili said, "My heart cries out when I think of the Italy you live in and what is ahead for you."

"Why for me?" I asked. "Do you plan to stay?"

"No," he answered sadly. "I will leave, in spite of all the affection I feel for you. Soon my country will need me. There is nothing I can do for it here."

Then he took me in his arms and kissed me; the few people at the tables around us looked on with approval.

That kiss and those that followed, which Vassili always dispensed parsimoniously and under special circumstances, were important parts of a deep friendship that grew between us like a wildflower on rocks beaten by harsh winds. During the four months that followed, Vassili and I shared a silent understanding of the impact of the events taking place around us, while we suffered their direct consequences in our own lives.

I had lived through the Abyssinian and Spanish wars as Mussolini's subject. Vassili, who had lived those years in a radically different environment in England, helped me to envisage the tragic implications of a war that was at first nothing but a word shouted to a cheering crowd by a little man on a balcony. Even Lyliana, who first warned me firmly against any form of emotional involvement with my Greek friend, agreed in the end that our relationship was inevitable. Yet my aim was to study for the Latin literature exam I had to take in June.

In the two months Vassili and I were together in Rome, from April to early June of 1940, we lived two separate lives, while always remaining aware of each other's presence within those walls. Although his Italian had improved considerably, he insisted he needed my help now more than ever. That meant I could count on a steady income from my two daily hours with him. We were now focusing on a thorough reading of newspapers and magazines – national and international –, which we obtained mainly through the academies.

Vassili loathed the Italian press, with what seemed to me an exaggerated fervor, for being Mussolini's willing tool as he shaped the soul of the Italians. He premised his arguments by sarcastically stating that every country had the press it deserved. It was mainly through the press, he argued, that one distinguished a democracy from a dictatorship, the rule of the people from the arbitrary rule of an individual. Italy's press, the worst he had seen so far, was a parody of what a press should be.

I listened spellbound, not bothering to correct his Italian. He was opening a door for me into a world that was not completely unfamiliar. No matter what my reaction, he stood firm with regard to the invaluable advantages of living in a democracy.

We usually met in the evening and dined together. I spent the rest of the day studying or going from house to mansion in my capacity as a tutor.

Among my new students, I now counted several members of the Black Roman nobility, those ancient families who had sided with the Pope against the Italian king in 1870, when the king had taken over the Pope's city in the name of a new Italy. Often, after tutoring, I enjoyed relaxed conversations with my students' parents. Prince and Princess Lancellotti shared Vassili's very critical view of the Fascist regime, though not for the same reasons. Thus, Vassili became part of the complex background of my own very special Rome, adding to it, with a clarity and directness new to me, a democratic dimension in English/Greek style that deepened the attraction I felt for him. I entered the magical world of England, a step at a time, when he spoke to me at length of England as the country of freedom, where every citizen had the right to express his opinion, and consequently could live in ways I could not imagine. As for our legitimate desire to make our own place in the sun, he smiled ironically, and then with an apocalyptic tone unusual for him predicted that we would suffer the wrath of God. We would pay for what we had done to Abyssinia and Albania.

In our best moments, I told him he was my Greek Morpurgo. A modern Greek, he corrected me, who had the courage to defend himself against totalitarian regimes. A Greek who would fight Italy, if necessary.

§   §   §

Nina counterbalanced Vassili's theories with her concrete approach to Italy's political situation. She expressed her feelings with a passion that made every political act seem real, as if she had been there. Her favorite topic was Il Duce's relationship to the bold, bossy, and untrustworthy Führer. Mussolini, she said, was wavering painfully between his desire to wage war alongside Hitler, thus sharing the booty of the victory over France, and his sad awareness that the Italian army was in no condition to sustain even a brief war.

At her best, Nina shared with Mussolini scorn for the weaknesses of Italians, a mass of servile, inept, fickle individuals, each interested only in his own gain. All that was needed was a whip to make them function honorably. A good old-fashioned war would serve that purpose.

One day, unexpectedly, a quiet and rational Nina, straight out of Machiavelli's Prince, presented me with Il Duce's dream of a united Europe, a Europe in which a selfish, conservative, capitalist, internationally minded bourgeoisie would be replaced by selfless, passionate Fascist youth, fully devoted to the interest of the state.

Nina kept me spellbound mainly on one issue, which directly concerned my homeland: her personal reaction to the uninterrupted recent exchange of messages between Mussolini and Hitler. A sly Hitler, according to her, was about to invade the Tyrol while manipulating Mussolini's naive Latin soul with his continuous messages. In the end, Latin pragmatism would prevail because Il Duce would declare war on the Western democracies. Nina saw Hitler as the best possible means for Mussolini to reach the desired end. I was horrified and could not hold back from telling Vassili. He laughed and told me to ignore her.

I rarely mentioned Vassili to Nina. She was unaware of his existence. The two lived intensely in two opposite worlds. I needed both — each for a different reason. Nina was the source of important information, even if often of irritation. She was surprised at my reaction to the meeting of Hitler and Mussolini at the Brenner Pass. Il Duce had been mostly silent, she reported, as he listened to Hitler outline his plans for Europe after it fell. Horrified, I denied Europe would fall.

Nina looked at me in disbelief and then attacked me violently for the first time as if I were an enemy. What would be so terrible about the rejuvenation of Europe? She was fed up with the old decrepit democratic Europe. If we entered the war on Hitler's side, we would finally throw England out of the Mediterranean and rule our own sea from Turkey to Spain. Nina was angry at England for blockading us and confiscating the vessels that provided us with German coal. We should sink all English ships wherever they were and punish the nations that harbored them.

I shuddered at the thought of Greece, a jagged peninsula that hung defenseless in the heart of the Mediterranean, festooned with little islands harboring those British ships that attacked our ships, and of Vassili being forced to defend his homeland against Italy.

Not Chamberlain in England nor Reynauld in France nor, least of all, Roosevelt in America, Vassili told me, understood Mussolini's psychology. One had to live in Italy in order to realize that Mussolini's only aim was to rise through war, nothing but war, and conquer his Lebensraum through a glorious victory. Years ago, in faraway Merano, Mamma had discovered this on her own. Now though horrified, I felt powerless to rebel against the situation and I was angry at my inability to react.

During the spring of 1940, the whole of Europe was focusing on Mussolini, trying to get a hint of his intentions. I knew the names of each of the European representatives in Rome — Sir Percy Loraine of England, François Poncet of France, Teleki of Hungary, Phillips of America, and Sumner Wells, the spokesman for Roosevelt. England held the carrot and the stick. France claimed its old sisterhood with Italy. America longed to act as an intermediary. Yugoslavia hoped the Italian Army would not cross its borders. Hungary feared a German takeover and begged Mussolini for help. Finally, Greece tried its best to avoid the fate of Albania.

Although Rome was strangely quiet, Vassili and I increasingly felt the presence of Hitler, whose secret intentions could hardly be gleaned from his emissaries – an icy von Ribentropp, a Goering greedy for honors, a matter-of-fact Mackensen, and the Prince von Hesse, who, when in Rome, according to Nina, lived with the king, his father-in law.

From the old Prince Massimo Lancellotti, whose daughters were my students and friends, I acquired an understanding of how the king and the Pope viewed Hitler's activities. The Pope, the old Prince proudly related, boldly sent a message of sympathy to Denmark and Norway, nations that Hitler had recently invaded. Mussolini laughed when he was told of the Pope's message.

I was not surprised by Nina's interpretation of these stories, turning them to the glorification of her beloved Duce. Vassili told me that Mussolini and Hitler had made precise plans for a new Europe after their final victory. They would restructure the continent by displacing entire populations, so as to make each country coincide with the language its people spoke. I wrote then to Mamma that she should prepare to move the family. Where, I couldn't say. Perhaps to Rome, the place I knew best after Merano.

That spring, I was obsessed by the Latin literature exam. While the political crisis kept me in a state of anxiety, it emphasized the importance of a personal success which, I told Lyliana one night, would give me faith in myself. It was more than a point of pride. I repeated this to Vassili the next day. My exam had to be a victory.

Both Lyliana and Vassili asked me what I meant by victory. A personal meeting with Vincenzo Ussani, I told them, which only that exam could bring about. They were both puzzled. They knew that Professor Ussani was a member of the prestigious Accademia d'Italia and one of the leading classicists of his time. Did I seek the privilege of an exceptional connection? They also knew that this old luminary was considered an ogre by the thousands of stu-dents who had to pass his exam as a prerequisite for graduation. He flunked them by the hundreds, pitilessly, session after session. Each of them was surprised when I explained that for the past two years I had been looking forward to that exam as an opportunity to spend an hour with a very special individual who, through his books, had offered me a positive perspective on Rome.

My special relationship with Ussani, I explained, had developed out of my negative reaction to one of his lectures during my first brief stay in Rome, in May 1938. The auditorium where he spoke was packed with hundreds of silent students, everyone feverishly writing down what he or she caught from the monotonous, almost inaudible voice of that little old man sitting at the podium, his head bent over his notes. The little old man spoke about a certain Florus, a minor historian of the late Roman Empire whom I'd never heard of. Since I was madly in love with ancient Rome, I left the course. My time in Rome was a precious commodity. Instead, I attended Professor Lugli's course on Roman topography, mainly because of his frequent visits to the ruins of the Forum and the Palatine, where he would show us his recent discoveries. Lugli was irreplaceable.

Attending Ussani's lectures was a luxury I couldn't afford. If that famous scholar had something to tell me, I thought, he could do so through his books, which I bought with the little money I had left before my return to Merano.

The miracle took place during my long, silent nights at Villa Moskau, when, after a noisy day of work, Horace's poetry, as seen through Ussani's commentary, evoked in me an ancient Rome that no course in Roman topography ever could. Ussani, dealing with Horace, one poet to another, helped my old dream of Rome to survive, despite the blows it had received in recent times.

It was paradoxical to speak of a dream of Rome through the miracle of Horace's poetry while the heroic French army was being overrun by the Wehrmacht and Il Duce was about to join that Wehrmacht. Yet both Lyliana and Vassili listened intently, and each, separately, decided to help me keep my dream alive.

It was evident to us all that in order for me to have a successful encounter with Ussani, I had to stop my private tutoring immediately and dedicate all the time remaining, a little more than a month, to my studies. With touching generosity, Lyliana did not accept my rent for the month of May. A few days later, Vassili gave me his entire May tuition, leaving me free from all tutoring. I sent my students to a friend.

Around the beginning of April, Nina reported a typical statement by Mussolini on war. He said it was humiliating to remain with our hands folded while others were making history. It mattered little who won. To make a people great, it was necessary to send that people to battle, even if you had to kick them in the pants.

Everyone expected war, but when? Throughout April and May, Vassili and I endured the drama of Mussolini's hesitation in choosing a date for Italy's declaration of war. Vassili's continued stay in Italy depended on that decision. When, toward the end of April, Mussolini hinted at the end of August as a possible date, we sighed with relief. Then at the beginning of May, Goering's appeal to Il Duce for a speedy entrance in the conflict if he wanted to share the spoils made us panic. We wished Mussolini could follow the example of Franco, which had confirmed Spain's neutrality. Finally, we lost all hope when I discovered through Nina that on the morning of May 10, von Mackensen himself had visited Il Duce to tell him that Hitler's attack on the Western Front was about to begin.

I decided to close my eyes and ears to what was being decided and focus on my studies. But it was futile, since radios and newspapers blasted the news on the sequence of events that led us to enter the war on Hitler's side.

Brussels fell. Antwerp was destroyed. The Germans marched into France, and General Giraud and his staff were taken prisoner. In a nationalistic mood, the Albanians claimed Kosovo. Finally, on May 29, the Italian High Command was created at Palazzo Venezia, Even Badoglio was now part of the game, provided the war was short, very short, because Italy had no resources. On May 30, Hitler was informed of the date chosen by Mussolini: June 5. A last warning by Roosevelt was disregarded. Even the king was now resigned to war.

Hitler, however, asked for a change of date so as to give himself a chance to completely destroy the French air force before Italy entered the war. What about June 8 or June 11, he suggested. Mussolini, visibly annoyed, proposed June 11, the king's birthday, while trying in vain to obtain from the king the title of supreme commander. The heroic French resistance was faltering, when, on the evening of June 10, Mussolini finally spoke to the people from his balcony at Piazza Venezia. Vassili and I were in the crowd.

§ § §

The suspense created by the dramatic sequence of events preceding Mussolini's final announcement was just one of the disturbing causes of my self-imposed seclusion.

In mid-May, Francesca had joined me in Rome. From the very moment I picked her up at the station, I sensed a greater tension between us than the usual one caused by the difference in our characters and, more recently, by Bruno's presence in the family. Although not officially engaged, Francesca, at nineteen, a stunning blue-eyed beauty, didn't consider herself as free as Bona and I were. Far from resenting it, she almost boasted about it; she was beating Bona and me to the altar.

As soon as she got off the train with her little suitcase full of books, stiff from lack of sleep and elegant in her blue suit, Francesca told me that her stay in Rome would be strictly limited to taking the four exams in her specialty, German literature. She was badly needed at home, she said, indirectly reproaching me.

Although she liked our lodgings, she acted distant and re-served with Lyliana, our host. She took for granted that I should give up my bed for her and sleep on the floor. When I told her about Vassili, she didn't express any overt disapproval, but it was clear that she rejected him. I was surprised, but I surmised it was for political reasons. A Greek who acted like an Englishman, what an odd choice on my part, she said, at such a delicate political time. Did I know that Bruno was about to enter the army and would probably be sent to the Balkans?

§ § §

On the evening of June 10, 1940, Francesca refused to join Vassili and me in Piazza Venezia. She was tired from her last exam, she said. And anyway, whatever Mussolini said or did was beyond our control.

Swallowed up by the crowd that cried "Duce, Duce," although with considerably less enthusiasm than usual, Vassili and I were soon separated by a group of sturdy Fascists who had wedged themselves in between us, their armpits smelling of decayed cheese. Vassili succeeded in grabbing the collar of my jacket and pulling me near him, right at the moment when Il Duce was bellowing the first words of his speech.

Interrupted at regular intervals by the usual organized applause and shouts of enthusiasm, Mussolini told us exactly what we had been expecting. He was declaring war. It was up to us to carry it through with valor, dignity, force, courage, and all those virtues we Italians had inherited from our ancestors. At least this is what we thought he said. Most people around us were completely unimpressed, even annoyed. Some hadn't even heard who our enemy was. The veterans of World War I didn't show much enthusiasm for another world war. A reassuring note, however, as we fought to make our way out of Piazza Venezia was that the war would be short, very short, so short that we would hardly notice.

Vassili walked silently at my side, holding my hand reassuringly. We were both slightly disoriented by our first experience of a blackout. Then sirens rang loudly and we heard airplanes overhead. The crowd rapidly dispersed in the direction of what everybody said was a shelter, not far from the railway station. While we sat on a bench with many others in the shelter, a lone French plane let a few bombs fall near the railway station. I had brought along my Horace. My exam was scheduled for the next day.

Back home that night, I found Francesca waiting for me in her blue suit, her little well-packed suitcase at her feet.

"Mamma called," she said in a panic. "She wants us both back immediately. I went by the station. They say a few trains for civilians will be still available during the night. From tomorrow on, most trains will be reserved for the military going to the French border. I am worried about Bruno. He is in Zara." Then, turning to me, she implored, "Please come with me."

"Nonsense." I replied. "We'll leave tomorrow night."

"Is it for Vassili's sake that you want to stay?" she inquired in a hostile voice.

"No," I replied. "Tomorrow I have the most important exam of my life. Nobody can force me to leave tonight. Not even Mamma!"

Francesca picked up her suitcase and moved slowly, almost reluctantly, toward the door. As soon as the door closed behind her, I grabbed my cigarettes and flung myself fervently into the last text I intended to review. I was angry at the whole world, but especially at Mussolini.

§ § §

At 9:00 a.m. on June 11, I showed up at the grand entrance hall of the Facoltà di Lettere. My oral exam was scheduled for noon. Students roamed everywhere. They were depressed, angry, or worried, not however because of the declaration of war. The war, they laughed, was Mussolini's business, not theirs. Given his nature, it was inevitable.

Leaning against the wall, some girls were sobbing. Along with many others, they had flunked the exam that very morning. During the first half hour, the professor had disposed of twenty students. They all agreed he was insane. He machine-gunned his students, someone said, in line with the new war fever. I calculated, based on the number of students disposed of so far, when my turn would come. Many others had decided to withdraw, so my turn would surely come by 10:00 a.m.

I placed my two bags, filled with Ussani's books, near the door of the exam room.

"What's wrong with you?" a boy near me asked. "Why did you bring a library along? All he wants to hear from us are his notes on Florus. I have learned all of my Florus by heart."

"I don't give a damn about your Florus!" I retorted angrily.

He laughed. "She wants to teach the professor!"

"I know the girl," mumbled one fellow I barely knew. "A peasant from the Tyrol. just look at the way she braids her hair."

I knew they were attacking me because they were nervous, at least as nervous as I was. By then, I could hardly hear their voices. My eyes were on the door. My turn came even before I expected. I made a fast mental prayer to Papa and the band of angels with him in Heaven who were supposed to protect and support me.

When I came out of the exam room after more than an hour, I was attacked by the mob. What had happened to me? Did the satyr touch my knees? What did his assistants do while he entertained me? I was too excited to answer. Besides, how could I explain how Vincenzo Ussani had solved for me all the problems I had encountered in closely examining his books. Now I could read Horace, Virgil, Ovid, and Catullus as I had never read them before. How could I explain what a gentleman this professor was and how generous he had been when, looking at me with his clear blue eyes, he asked me all sorts of questions about my life in Merano and finally offered me the assistantship in a special project he led at the Accademia d'Italia?

Burning with holy fire, I ran as fast as I could to the Caffè Greco where Vassili was waiting for me. He held me in his arms in front of everybody and kissed me and kept on telling me he had never doubted my meeting with Vincenzo Ussani would be a triumph. I stopped him short.

"Now I must go home," I cried. "Home to Merano!"

"I know," he said sadly, letting go of me. "How I wish I could go with you."

On the night of June 11th, in the blackout at Stazione Termini, Vassili and I made our way among hundreds of soldiers looking for a train, any train, since all trains were going north. Somebody pushed me onto a military convoy and I lost track of Vassili.

"Vassili, come with me!" I cried as the train moved slowly away from the throng on the platform. The cheers and the songs of the soldiers drowned out my cries.

"Don't worry, young lady, you'll be safe among us," someone whispered in my ear, holding me tightly in his arms. "We are all going to the front together," he cried.

I protested that I had to go north to the German border.

"Why go to Germany when you can come to France with us? The war is against France, not Germany!"

Fortunately, a conductor arrived in time to save me from the drunken soldiers. He took me aside and told me that the train would be reconfigured in Bologna. He would place me in a car that would be part of a train headed for the Brenner Pass. He first hid me in a refrigerator, among carcasses of beef. Then, when everything was quiet, he led me to a sleeping car reserved for high-ranking officers.

"Lock yourself in," he warned me. "Someone will wake you up tomorrow morning in Bolzano."

I fell asleep before I could finish my magic prayer.

§ § §

"Say goodbye to Rome forever!" was Mamma's declaration of war when I got off the train in Merano. She didn't even embrace me. I guessed that Francesca, home before me, had told her of Vassili's presence in my life

At home, the war meant silence on my part. I resumed assisted learning program without saying a word to any member of the family. I knew that Mamma would have liked to speak, to explain, to accuse, to judge, to condemn, but I had made up my mind not to give her a chance. And as I worked day after day, from morning till night, on our sunny balconies, the ghost of Vassili pursued me.

Bona, then a sprightly fifteen-year-old, intuited what was bothering me and followed me into the park one night after classes.

"I want you to know," she said, "that I know."

"What do you know?"

"I know about the Greek. I mean Vassili."

"So?"

"And so I want to help you. I understand you."

We fell into each other's arms, crying. That night, I finally slept. The next day, we got to work together.

I called Nina from the post office for news about Greece. On July 3, Mussolini, she said, had accused Greece of offering shelter to English ships and planes. From that moment on, in spite of Greece's declaration of neutrality, he planned to occupy the Ionian islands. I had told Vassili to write "fermo in posta" ("hold at the post office") on any letters he sent me. One day, Bona victoriously delivered a long-awaited letter to me.

Life had become dangerous for a Greek in Rome, he wrote. He hoped I wouldn't mind if he joined me in Merano. If so, could reserve a room for him in a hotel? My very presence would reassure him. I begged him in a letter to come as soon as possible. Bona had found a nice room in a villa whose park adjoined ours. I was happy to be able to help him in Merano, as he had always helped me in Rome. Besides, how could I hide the fact that I missed him more than I'd expected.

When Vassili paid the family a courtesy call and asked me, in front of Mamma, if I could continue to tutor him as I had in Rome, Mamma shot him her nastiest look, as if he had asked me to be his mistress. After that meeting, he never again came to Villa Moskau.

Neither Vassili nor I could understand Mamma's hostility. At first, he thought her motive was political. But Bona assured him it was not, and I completely agreed with her. Mamma was anything but a coward. She was an expert in dealing with political pressure and had learned by experience the opposition's tricks. She stood strong as ever against Mussolini and his mania for war. Mamma would never refuse asylum to a political refugee, no matter the risk. It must be something, Bona argued, between Mamma and me, something she couldn't understand.

It was up to me to approach Mamma, she said. I needed to break my silence and explain my situation to her. I reacted violently. I had nothing to explain, I said. I hadn't done anything to deserve the treatment she was subjecting me to. Nor did I care to hear any explanation on her part. Bona dropped the subject.

With the arrival of Vassili's first letter, Bona played a major role in my relationship with him. She seemed at times as close to Vassili as I was. Since Mamma followed my every step in the hope, I thought, of catching me red-handed, Bona acted as a go-between for Vassili and me, delivering notes and arranging secret meetings. She would arrange for us to take walks across the vineyards from Vassili's villa, up to the foot of a nearby mountain.

As we sat in the cool shade of a gigantic chestnut-tree, a completely different Vassili rose from the cocoon of the fiery, aggressive young man who had taught me the secret joys of freedom from political oppression. This new Vassili dreamed aloud of his native Greece, while lying near me in a secluded corner of peaceful Merano, away from the Roman police. He spoke of the joys and sorrows in the faraway land of his childhood, a land I learned to love through the stories he told me during those idyllic encounters.

As a lonely child locked in the prison of an immense house during the interminable afternoons of a Mediterranean summer, he would listen for hours to the caressing music of the crickets hidden in the dry grass among the olive trees, until finally his mother would show up, silent, severe, and distant, her tall, slim figure draped in a long black dress. Without a word, she would open the heavy oak door of the white fortress to let him fly into the freedom of the fields. Enveloped in a wave of wild sage and rosemary, he would run barefoot across the olive orchards down to the sea.

While Vassili evoked the scene, he said he wished I had been with him to enjoy the silence of the land drowned by the roaring of the waves. As he expressed his last wish, however, holding me tenderly in his arms, the old Vassili reemerged, a man who could not dream without keeping in constant touch with reality.

I noticed with dismay that his eyes were on his watch. I was to meet Bona so that we could return home. I knew he did not want me to be late. I asked him then if he liked Bona as much as he liked me.

"I don't like you," he answered. "I love you more than I have ever loved anybody in my whole life. But what can I do for you, what can we do together, under the present conditions? Your people are about to invade my country, and I will have to fight against them. The time is coming when we will be forced to fight on opposite sides. How lucky we are to love each other today in the sun, before the storm darkens the world we live in."

He kissed me once more. Then we got up together and ran hand in hand down the mountain.

During those meetings, Vassili helped me to understand the reasons for my conflict with Mamma, which was the first and perhaps the only serious conflict we'd had in our lives. While I was living in my dream world, Mamma was facing the harsh reality every day, knowing that sooner or later I would have to face it too. Understanding Mamma's motivations didn't mean I had to accept her actions. I hated her with all of my might, even when I detected at our silent breakfasts that she had cried all night. Her hostility to Vassili was tied to her hostility toward Rome, I thought.

Vassili and I had forgotten about Il Duce for a while. Il Duce, however, hadn't forgotten about Greece. It was evident from news reports that he was getting angrier and angrier about Greece. There had been serious incidents at the Albanian frontier. Fortunately for us, however, Mussolini's attention at the moment was on Hitler, who was about to attack England. Why get involved in the Mediterranean when the center of the conflict was in the north? The Tyrol was deemed such a dangerous area that foreign tourists were asked to leave. Bona knew the local authorities who could delay Vassili's departure, so we survived day by day, taking meager solace in our surreptitious meetings. Then one day, Mamma confronted me.

"He must go," she said simply. "For his own safety. I'll be forced to tell him, if you don't."

Vassili left as quietly as he had come. On a hot evening in August, I picked him up at his villa and we walked together to the station. I didn't care about Mamma's reaction or anybody else's. As I watched his little train puffing away among the vineyards, I felt a sense of dread. An avalanche of loneliness was about to bury me in the quiet, peaceful oasis of Merano.

Back home, I entered the dining room while the family was quietly eating dinner. Sitting at my place among them, I attacked Mamma, with a violence I didn't think I was capable of. Relentlessly,

I accused her of destroying my happiness and plunging me into misery. She was mistaken, I screamed, if she thought that now, having eliminated Vassili from my life, she could hold me prisoner in Merano. I loved Vassili, but my life had to go on without him, and that certainly would not be in Merano. I needed some fresh air. She was suffocating me.

Mamma did not answer. How could she? My siblings were appalled. Had I gone crazy, or did my diatribe signal the end of an era in the life of the family? What finally stopped me was their awesome, awful silence. It was as if the world I had lived in till now had disappeared from sight, broken into a thousand pieces. Alone, surrounded by its ruins, I myself thought for a moment that I had gone crazy and would be taken to a hospital. Finally, Mamma got up and left, and the others followed.

For the next two days, I locked myself in my room, refusing the food that Bona brought. On the third morning, there was a knock at my door. I got up in a daze, not realizing where I was. There stood Francesca in her nightgown, holding a mug of warm milk.

"Drink," she ordered. "And then come help us. We can't waste any more time. I held the fort in your absence, as long as I could. Now I need your help. This is our chance to move the family to Rome."

She explained to me quietly that Mamma, who had been determined not to leave her mountains for any reason, had unexpectedly changed her mind. Francesca, under pressure from Bona and Neri, had deftly made her aware of the very favorable implications for the family if I were to accept the generous offer of my Roman professor. Mamma should hear the good news directly from me, Francesca said.

As I entered the living room, Mamma raised her head from her book, her eyes lifeless, her gray hair falling uncombed on her forehead. She had grown so old during the past months, I hardly recognized her. My first instinct was to throw myself into her arms, but she didn't give me a chance to.

"I know. I know," she whispered, as if to cut off useless misunderstanding. "You must leave Merano, and the others will leave, one by one, after you. I know, you have no choice. But for me, there is also no choice." She tried hard to hold back her tears. Then she blurted out in one breath: "You children are my world. I have no choice. No matter what happens to me, I must go with you, as long as I can help you. I can still contribute my salary."

In all my recent planning, I had never considered moving back to Rome without Mamma. Mamma's salary, no matter how small, would be the prerequisite for a life together in Rome. We needed Mamma with us in Rome, not only for her salary. We needed her for her moral support and her unconditional love.

Like lightning during a mountain storm, these thoughts dispelled the darkness in my mind. There was no need to forgive Mamma for having hurt me. Along with Francesca, she had just forced me to face reality. After our first emotional encounter, I sat down near Mamma and together we quietly planned how to leave Villa Moskau and go to Rome. While Mamma and Neri sold our meager belongings and the three of us girls closed our prosperous school, I dug out my Thucydides. In preparing for the forthcoming exam in Greek literature, I chose that singer of Greek freedom as the first author to study.

§ § §

After a brief unsigned postcard from Venice and a note from the consul general of Greece in Trieste saying that Vassili had left Italy for Athens, Vassili disappeared from my life. On September 14, the Axis attacked Egypt. One could read between the lines that the attack on Greece would follow shortly. What induced Il Duce to delay was his need for a success. Once the murderer struck his blow, nobody would come to help his victim.

It took a month and a half to isolate Greece completely. When it became clear that Yugoslavia, Turkey, and Romania would not come to the aid of Greece, the Italian minister of Foreign Affairs, Count Galeazzo Ciano, a professional pilot, led what he described in his diary as a "spectacular bombardment of Salonika." Greek aircraft put up a memorable defense against the Italians. By then, our family had reached Rome. Nina was more than willing to give me details about the formidable Greek resistance that followed and the cool or even disapproving reaction of the Führer to the Italian bravado. Every detail of her story made me cold inside.

During September 1940, thanks to the well-coordinated effort of every single member of the family, we prepared to leave for Rome. It was an immense relief to concentrate exclusively on family business. We joked and laughed together as we had done during our past moves, as if Rome didn't amount to more than one more villa among the many in our past.

On a late Sunday afternoon, a golden October day, all five of us were busy packing a huge trunk in Neri's bedroom. Beyond our windows lay fruit orchards and vineyards, the grapes turning blue and red, the apples, red and yellow. Our beloved Villa Moskau stood with dignity in the heart of Obermajs, discolored by age. The Russian community chattered in the park of Villa Borodino, as usual, after its Sunday meetings, incense in the air.

As we stuffed the trunk with items we considered essential for our new life in Rome, a bundle of papers surfaced from a dusty old box we were emptying.

"Should this be taken along?" Bona asked, handing Mamma an old newspaper in English.

"It is printed in Cincinnati", Mamma said, her eyes sparkling, "a marvelous city in a big state called Ohio, a beautiful state, a great city. Your father worked there in a bank and lived there with his wife in a white villa near a river."

"Whose wife?" Bona stammered in disbelief. "You mean Papa had another wife besides you?"

Papa married to someone other than Mamma was hard news for us to digest, and in America of all places, the most corrupt of all democracies. Mamma looked at us, as if surprised at our suspicions. She vanished into her room, then reappeared shortly after with two pictures — one of a two-story white house built on stone foundation, the other of Papa in a garden, wearing a Panama hat and holding a cigar. Finally, she dug out of her secret drawer a gold bracelet with a big F engraved on it.

"Flora was her name," she said. "She died of tuberculosis. I'll give this bracelet to one of you someday. Perhaps to the one who visits Cincinnati." She smiled to herself.

The room Francesca and I shared at Villa Moskau opened onto a wide balcony. The last night of our stay, after we heard Mamma and Bona quietly sleeping in the adjacent room, we tiptoed to the balcony. We sat there without speaking for a long time, drinking in the silent blue night. A thin slice of moon and a star hung between two tall trees.

"It was a hard decision for Mamma to make." I said, breaking the silence.

"Harder than we think," Francesca whispered. "She is very upset by the war. She lived through one war. That's when she met Papa. With his death, she lost everything. Merano is all she has left."

A cricket chirped nearby. The whole world lay in silence. We embraced.

"The two of us know Rome well," Francesca whispered as we were about to fall asleep. "Mamma knows she can trust us."

There was a long silence.

"What about America?" he asked. "I mean Papa's America. Why didn't Papa go back to America with Mamma after they married? What's the big secret?"

"Forget about America. It is a huge continent beyond an ocean, a big land that has nothing to do with Europe! Papa's America does not concern us in the least," I said.

We laughed together for the first time since Vassili's departure.

While the train moved slowly away from our little station, Mamma sat proudly among us on the wooden bench in the first compartment of the first car. She sat straight and motionless, holding her head high, her rough peasant's hands folded in her lap. Her green eyes wide open, she stared at the familiar mountains, their tops heavy with snow, then at the dark green vineyards, about to be widowed of their fruit, a part of herself she was giving up forever. The Adige River rolled by the train, a violent mountain torrent rumbling along rocks. One by one, we got up and kissed her on her forehead, as if she were a different woman from the one we had known so far, a kind of idol from the past whom we were taking along with us to Rome as a good omen for our future life in an unknown world.

Mamma, however, was anything but an idol. To prove that she was very much alive, she took my hand in hers and held it tightly. As she did so, a scene from the distant past rose vividly in front of me. I was five years old. Mamma and I were sitting near each other on a train that was slowly moving through orchards in bloom. She was taking me with her to the first school to which she was assigned in Italy, not far from Villa Soell in Gries, where Mamma, Papa, Aunt Emma and the four of us children had lived happily. I had never seen a school before and was curious and happy. The train meandered lazily among cherry trees while Mamma whispered something to me that made me shiver and cry. What had she told me? She'd had tears in her eyes. No matter how I tried, I could not remember.

CHAPTER 6

Vatican Adventures

It rained for weeks on end after we arrived in Rome. No place in the world is more lugubrious than Rome in the rainy season. The very soul of the Eternal City seems to dissolve into a thick mist as its ancient ruins and buildings, ancient and modern, get soaking wet. The Forum, not far from where we lived, was a swamp; the inside of the majestic Colosseum, a lake; and the churches, dark cold caves, except, of course, at High Mass. Our newly rented mini-apartment was a damp escape from the deluge.

After our uneventful journey from Merano to Rome with everyone snoring through the night, in spite of the rumbling airplanes over the train, we found temporary shelter in a modest boarding house in the center of the city. From there, we moved out to explore the Eternal City as immigrants from the north who had to find a decent home on a high school teacher's salary.

Automobiles were rare, and we traveled via streetcar. Nobody ever understood how Bona managed to fall from one such tram in motion. That was the occasion for Mamma's first clash with Fascist Rome. She dragged her daughter out of the emergency room, *Pronto Soccorso*, literally "Prompt Rescue," declaring contemptuously that the name was a joke. The nurses smiled compassionately.

Mamma's reaction to our selection of residences was even more vehement. She rejected outright the small apartment I had found on the eighth floor of a modest new building still under construction, just outside the 2000-year-old Aurelian Walls. She disliked the idea of the elevator, and the height made her dizzy. As for the stunning view of the walls, she stated that if they had been made of cardboard like those of the apartment building in question, they wouldn't be there for us to enjoy today.

The day we entered the tiny apartment which she finally rented, on the fourth floor of a small but elegant new building close to the Walls, we got the news that the freight train with our furniture had been bombed and many of our belongings had been destroyed. "We'll make do with what's left," Mamma stated stoically. Nina gave us a few mattresses, a table, a few chairs, and kitchen utensils to get started.

Professor Ussani kept his promise to help us. Through his connections at the Ministry of Education, he had gotten a transfer for Mamma from the high school in Merano to a huge one in Civitavecchia, which was Rome's military port. Mamma gratefully commuted by train to her new school two hours each way, six days a week, ignoring the Allied bombings. Her salary was indeed the indispensable base for our family's survival.

Day after day, Francesca and I plowed through a sequence of Latin words that would sooner or later find their way into an enormous *Vocabulary of Medieval Latin*. We perched on uncomfortable medieval benches in the cold humid halls of the decaying, but still magnificent, Renaissance building on the Tiber that housed the most prestigious Italian cultural institution, the Accademia d'Italia. Our work was neither challenging nor remunerative, but our pride was at stake. We were contributing to an imperishable enterprise.

Neri and Bona suffered, without complaint, the most traumatic experience of all of us, being rudely transplanted from the idyllic, small, family-style Liceo Carducci in Merano to a sprawling institution called Liceo Visconti in the center of Rome. In huge classes, they were expected to follow the state-established path to the final exam. They had suddenly become anonymous entities, left in the hands of numerous professors, all famous, some actually very good. In spite of the inevitable difficulties, they both completed their studies and were admitted to university, in 1941 and 1942 respectively.

Mamma was the first to profit from the war outside Rome. She was liberated from commuting by a successful Allied bombardment of the military port. Her school was reduced to rubble, fortunately hit at night, when it was empty. Thanks to Ussani, our protector, she was transferred from Civitavecchia to the Board of Education in the center of Rome. Thus, her salary continued to be the base of our survival. And circumstances soon required that we indeed build upon that base.

Rome had been declared an open City, its ancient section theoretically exempt from bombardment. However, what kept us fully aware of the war was the slow but steady disappearance, one after another, of food items from stores and their sudden resurfacing on the black market at three or four times the regular price. Given our budget, we gave up coffee, tea, sugar, butter, and meat, among other unnecessary items. Ration cards for pasta and bread, the main staples of the Italian diet, were not yet available.

Poldina, our maid, who helped us survive four years of war in Rome, gave the first alarm — the imminent disappearance of pasta. Poldina was a short wiry girl in her late teens who had joined us shortly after our arrival in Rome expecting nothing more than room and board plus Mamma's protection of her virginity. An orphan from somewhere in the Roman countryside, Poldina became our first link to Rome and its people. When she told us that another food item was no longer available, we believed her.

Mamma soon realized that we needed at least one more salary to deal with the black market. She decided how to get that salary during one of her long silences and announced her decision a dinner. We were sitting on Nina's chairs around our old table, one of the few surviving pieces of furniture from Merano. As she spoke, we could hear the rain whipping the blinds. Poldina, standing behind her, sadly confirmed Mamma's dramatic announcement: we were about to consume one of our last meals of pasta.

"Cousin Agostino" – Mamma pronounced his name with the respect due to a man who managed to eat three meals a day in spite of the war – "has told me that he has been granted a contract to build sewers for the government in Libya." She paused to gauge the effect of her words. Then she turned to me directly. "He intends to employ both you and Francesca as his personal secretaries. This is a wonderful opportunity."

I replied instinctively. "Francesca and me in an office, building sewers in Libya? You must be kidding! Neither of us is prepared for that type of job. Our typing is poor, non-existent! And what about our job at the Accademia? What about my dissertation?"

"Precisely," Mamma replied, ignoring both my job and dissertation. "Cousin Agostino has arranged for a crash course in typing and stenography for you both." She gave us the address we had to report to at 8:00 a.m. the next morning. The school was located in the vicinity of the Pantheon.

Before falling asleep Francesca joined me on the mattress I shared with Bona. We both liked Cousin Agostino, but she wanted me to come up with a strategy to avoid becoming his secretaries, which for us was the equivalent of slavery. "Don't you care about Ussani and your dissertation," she pleaded.

Sleepy and overwhelmed by the rain, I reassured her with a vague statement: "Don worry! Mussolini will never have us build sewers in Libya!"

"Never?" she asked.

"Never!" I replied. We both fell asleep, though I had no idea how I might carry out this promise. I was just happy that my independent sister looked up to me.

On our way to school the next morning, we took refuge from the endless rain in the majestic portico of the Pantheon, so we could gather our thoughts and coordinate our defense. Hand in hand, we joined the familiar flocks of young priests in black robes who waded across the piazza in small light steps, like black crows. In one of the dark, narrow side alleys, we discovered the dreaded typing school, the *Scuola di Dattilografia*.

In a humid hall filled with small tables, young ladies sat behind what looked like sewing machines. Francesca and I had no experience whatsoever with typewriters and had decided on passive resistance. I had to encourage Francesca, who showed some interest in typing despite the solemn vows we had just taken under the dome of the Pantheon.

Those machines, we agreed, represented the road to slavery.

A woman in a gray suit who was dressed like a nun checked to be certain that our names were listed on her thickly annotated school pad. Yes, Signor Sironi had paid for our weeklong training. We should sit down behind a machine and follow her instructions.

I disliked everything about the place except the woman in charge. With bones protruding from under her frayed suit, a blank face like Mr. Messing's, our Russian piano teacher in Merano, and fingernails spotted by the ribbons, that ageless woman in her silent efficiency bore touching witness to the helplessness of her world. I wished I could drag her out of that dreary school and run with her through an old Rome basking in the sun. But old Rome was drowning in the rain, while Francesca and I sat for two days, hour after hour, in front of a typewriter typing notes to each other in German with two fingers. That was our only escape.

On the third day, Francesca went to the school alone. I had to see Ussani, I told her, to apologize for abandoning his work at the Accademia and to submit yet another potential topic for my doctoral dissertation. I couldn't hope for his help in liberating us from the present impasse. Agostino would have been the obvious person to appeal to, since he was a most open-minded and practical person, but at the moment we were blocked by the gift he had offered us. Help, as Francesca put it, had to come to us from Heaven.

For some reason, I had awakened that morning thanking our paternal grandparents. In spite of the humiliations Papa's family had inflicted on Mamma, she admired his parents, Sior Augusto and Siora Maria, with a sense of nostalgia as legendary heroes within an empire that had vanished along with them into thin air. Francesca resented our grandparents' presence in our lives. Nonno Augusto was a ruthlessly ambitious politician in her view, a man who had forced his son, our own dear Papa, to sail for America. Nobody knew exactly why. If help came from above, had to come directly from Papa.

Ussani accepted my apologies for our withdrawing from the work he had given us. The *Vocabulary* of *Medieval Latin,* he said with an ironic smile, was just one of the casualties of the war. In me, there would be many more. As for my doctoral dissertation, he rejected the new topic had proposed on a major Roman author and surprised me with a proposal of his own.

"The time has come for you to go beyond those ancient authors to whom you seem to cling with typical obstinacy," he remarked thoughtfully. After a brief pause, much to my surprise, he completed his thoughts with an excitement that must have been like that of Dante's Ulysses when he looked beyond Gibraltar across the vast expanse of an unsailed ocean.

"You must look courageously beyond the lives and times of the Ancients and look to their resurrection. You must explore the new world which the Humanists built in their wake."

The Humanists? I had hardly ever heard of them! I was bewildered. Ussani supplied the historical background to justify his enthusiasm.

"Renaissance Humanism is a fascinating phenomenon that began in the early fifteenth century in a decaying Rome, after the Pope's return from captivity in Avignon."

Unfortunately, that was a period in Italian history I had almost ignored in my schooling.

"The field is virtually unexplored," he went on, with unusual enthusiasm. "I think you have the imagination and the persistence to contribute to its exploration. As for the necessary preparation to carry out the project, you'll get it as you go along."

As he spoke, I could see he wanted me to react to his offer with the excitement and awe of Christopher Columbus, when Isabella told him that he could set sail on an unexplored ocean. But I was not Columbus, only the most inexperienced of Columbus's sailors, one who had never sailed before. I stood dumbfounded in front of Ussani and the marvelous new land he was opening up for me. I could not share his enthusiasm. All I could do was listen politely to his plans for the first steps of my journey to this strange new land.

"At the dawn of the fifteenth century," Ussani began quietly, talking almost to himself, "Lorenzo Valla, whom we regard today as the one who made philology textual study, wrote a dialogue taking place among the secretaries of Pope Martin V, the pope who had brought the papacy back from Avignon to Rome and who, among other things, had founded the papal library.

"Valla's dialogue, entitled *De voluptate ac de vero bono,* celebrates the human senses, all five of them, as the greatest gift God gave man to enhance his creativity. He celebrates human sense against reason,

Epictetus against Aristotle, *voluptas* as the warm creative spirit of Christianity against the cold abstractions of pagan philosophy (e.g., Stoicism), the humanity of farmers and workers against the absurd abstractions of the intellectual elite.

"I think," he added with a smile, "that, after half a century of almost total scholarly neglect, the dialogue deserves attention by a young woman like you, who seems to have the right disposition at this moment in her life. He was approximately your age when he wrote it. The last edition of the dialogue, as far as I know, dates from the middle of the sixteenth century; it was part of Valla's *Opera omnia*. You can read the dialogue in that edition at the National Library. Then go to the Manuscripts Section of the Vatican Library, identify as many manuscripts as you can, and collate them."

Not wasting any precious time, my ninety-year-old mentor sent me off on this challenging expedition with his blessing and a note of introduction to Alcide De Gasperi, secretary of the Vatican Library.

"Alcide De Gasperi?" Mamma reacted to my story at the dinner table with unanticipated personal interest. "The name sounds familiar. Of course, De Gasperi was the main force of the Popular Party, I mean the Catholic Party, which was created in Trento in opposition to the Socialists. I was there at the time."

We looked at her in awe.

"That was a long time ago, at the turn of the century, she said pensively, "when I was a student living with a Monsignor at the Archbishop's mansion in Trento. Sior Augusto, your grandfather, who was one of our representatives at the Parliament in Vienna, knew De Gasperi very well. Sior Augusto was an enlightened man of the law who, in 1901, co-founded the Liberal Party, which preceded De Gasperi's Popular Party and did not see eye to eye with it. Yet the two, De Gasperi and your grandfather, respected each other. I am happy," she concluded with satisfaction, "that Alcide De Gasperi is out of reach of the Fascists, protected by the Pope himself in Vatican City."

When Mamma evoked a moment of her "golden past," as we called it, she acquired a special aura, which lifted her out of our everyday reality into the world of history. Sometimes, we would have liked her to tell us more about that past, but, after each of her sudden revelations, she would fall silent, as if her past was a treasure she could dispense only in bits and only at the right time and place. Maybe she sensed a lack of serious interest on our part or a kind of jealousy for the life she had lived without us.

The information Mamma provided that evening about Alcide De Gasperi fell on deaf ears. My own mind was elsewhere. Ussani had invested me with the specific mission of unearthing Lorenzo Valla's *On Pleasure* and Alcide De Gasperi played the role of gatekeeper to the Vatican Library, which housed that treasure. The powerful gusts of my excitement, as an explorer of new lands, swept into the background the glorious political past of Signor De Gasperi along with Agostino's Libyan sewers and the typewriters behind the Pantheon.

When the Swiss Guards at Porta Sant'Anna, upon seeing Ussani's note to De Gasperi, smiled at me on my first visit to the Vatican, I had the feeling that they had, in their colorful Renaissance uniforms, opened the first gate to my secret mission. Like the guards, the Secretary of the Library seemed to be there expressly to offer his services to an explorer like me. De Gasperi paid no more attention to my name than I did to his, and, after a fleeting glance at Ussani's note, he gave me a special permit to use the Manuscript Hall (*Sala dei Manoscritti*) beyond the regular hours, 8:00 a.m. to 2:00 p.m., five days a week. Then he reread Ussani's note and, lifting his glasses, he looked directly at me.

"My compliments," he said with a smile, "and best wishes for your research. You are lucky to work at such a young age with a scholar as unique as Vincenzo Ussani. Through the years, he has been one of our most faithful visitors. He is a man of vision, a poet who lives the life of the authors he studies. Too bad the young people of today seem to be afraid of him. You don't seem to be."

It was at that moment, encouraged by his directness, that I looked at the gentleman sitting in front of me with genuine curiosity and interest, finally oblivious of myself and of my mission. In front of me, on the other side of the bare desk, in a room furnished with remarkable simplicity, sat a man of uncertain age, tall, thin, pale or rather gray-skinned, so engaging in his manner that he made me feel I had known him for years.

De Gasperi's genuine cordiality, his frankness, his ability to enter my world with real interest in my needs even before I stated them, his total lack of the pompous rhetoric that permeated official life in Rome, from Mussolini at Palazzo Venezia down to the ushers at the ministries or the university, generated an intimacy between us that cancelled the difference in age and social status. Having crossed that bridge unconsciously, De Gasperi looked closely at my name on Ussani's note, got up from his chair, and addressed me with the warmth with which one greets a dear old friend after long separation.

"Maristella de Panizza, you must be related to Augusto de Panizza, perhaps the daughter of Gino, the son he lost to America? Once upon a time, I worked side by side with the Honorable Augusto. We did not see eye to eye on some political issues, but we shared a love for the people. I had a great deal of respect for the gentleman."

I had hardly confirmed I was his old friend's grandchild when he asked me in what way he could help me and my family. Opening my heart to him, I spoke at length about our lives in the Alps and in Rome. He listened with interest. When I came to Cousin Agostino's generous offer and Francesca's and my own negative reaction, he laughed heartily, went back to his desk, picked up a small address book and turned to me as if I were his equal.

"I hope you don't mind," he said, "if I send you to a friend of mine who could employ you with a decent salary. With your background in languages and your working experience in Merano and Rome, he will consider you a great asset to the institute he directs."

A little later, I left his office with a letter addressed to Commendatore Palma, a senior official of the Film Division of the Ministry of Press and Propaganda. Before we left, we exchanged addresses with the promise that our two families would soon meet, which they in fact did often during the war years. When I reached the Aurelian Walls on my way home, the rain had temporarily stopped. Glowing pink and orange streaks through mountains of clouds threw a warm light on the ruins of the Baths of Caracalla.

That night at dinner we subscribed enthusiastically to Francesca's favorite theory that what we were witnessing was a miracle performed by one of our many dead in Paradise. We disagreed on the choice between our beloved Papa and his harsh father who had disinherited him and hence forced him to sail to America.

The next day Francesca and I went separate ways. She was continuing her course at the typing school, but Mamma had accepted my alternative plans. I went towards the elegant nineteenth-century Rome, near Via Veneto, to Via Santa Susanna, which was the seat of the Film Division of the Ministry of Press and Propaganda. I had taken along my books in case the commendatore was not immediately available to receive me.

All day long I sat patiently in the reception room, without anyone paying the slightest attention to me. I skipped lunch, in case he might show up. Finally late in the afternoon I shut my book, having made up my mind I would identify the person to whom De Gasperi's letter was addressed. To my surprise, it was he who identified me, expressing curiosity about the young woman sitting all day long in front of his office. He led me into his office, apologizing profusely for what he called a misunderstanding on the part of his ushers.

He moved to his desk and after a brief telephonic exchange he declared, " We shall employ you as personal secretary to our "*Capo-Divisione*" (Office Head).

I could hardly find the strength to follow my benefactor down the wide stairs of the *palazzina*. I shuddered at my foolishness in refusing to take advantage, as Francesca had, of the opportunity offered by Agostino. Before I realized what was happening to me, I was sitting in a leather chair in front of the desk of a young, handsome, chain-smoking, elegant Roman executive who was inspecting me from head to toe from behind rimmed glasses. His name was Dr. Fortini.

For a whole week, I worked hard as Dr. Fortini's secretary and would perhaps have suffered longer if Dr. Fortini had not called me into his office on Saturday morning, and, without allowing me a word in my self-defense, pronounced my death sentence.

"You are fired!"

In order to soften the blow, he added with an ironic smile, "You might be an excellent scholar, highly appreciated at the Vatican Library, but as a secretary to a high executive you must learn how to type a presentable letter. I wish you good luck!"

I left the office without having said a word.

Fired! I had been fired! How could I tell the family, which was counting on my high salary? My first impulse was to go back to Francesca at the typing school, but that would have meant piling humiliation on humiliation, surely more than I could take without breaking down. In despair, I entered the nearby Church of Santa Susanna. Soothed by the solemn silence of its early Renaissance simplicity, I prayed with all the intensity I could muster. Then I ran straight to the Vatican, entered the Pope's City without even showing my pass, ran up the familiar stairs two steps at a time and plunged breathless into my friend De Gasperi's office.

His gentle smile and his innate serenity helped me to regain the faith in myself I had lost. "Why aren't you at work?" he inquired, and I blurted out the cause of my misery. I had betrayed his trust in me, I confessed.

"Is that all? Let us not be melodramatic. There must be a misunderstanding. With your knowledge of languages and your background they should employ you. You can be useful to them if not now, then in the near future. I apologize for the inconvenience, but you must go back."

With a bright smile lighting up his bony face, De Gasperi wrote a one-line note, which he showed me before sealing the envelope "Sorry to insist, but in my opinion Miss de Panizza should be employed even if she types with only one finger."

This time, the commendatore received me as promptly as De Gasperi had. He laughed when he read the note and immediately led me down from the Olympus of the *Capo-Divisione to* the basement, the realm of the filmmakers and the photographers. As we entered a long dark hall of shelves filled with newspapers, an old gentleman slowly moved toward us, limping from darkness into dim light, like a vision at twilight. He was in his sixties, of medium height, bald, leaning on a cane with a gold knob, dressed from head to foot with the punctilious elegance of old. He introduced himself to me with dignity:

"Marchese d'Adda Salvaterra."

"My dear Marchese," the commendatore introduced me, smiling in a slightly condescending way. "I have brought you a great helper for your most praiseworthy work."

"But, commendatore," the Marchese replied with humble pride. "I do not need any help down here. As you well know, nothing is happening nowadays, nothing, nothing worthy of being signaled by me to our cameramen for the production of our Film Journal. We lead a most boring life down here."

I became worried, but the commendatore, after a moment of embarrassing silence, regained the initiative.

"Do not worry, my dear Marchese," he declared, and I sighed with relief. "I assure you that soon, very soon, you'll be most grateful to me for having thought of you and provided you with a helper of such extraordinary qualifications as this young lady. I assure you that, unfortunately, in the near future we will have the most horrendous stories to report, one after the other, stories of great interest to our public. Just be patient, my dear Marchese, and trust the future. Rome, as you know, was not built in a day. I am sure the two of you will get along splendidly."

As soon as the commendatore disappeared and the two of us were left alone in that moldy, dark hall, the marchese raised his cane high over his head, an indication, I discovered later, of despair:

"Signorina, why do this to me?" He turned to me with a whining voice that soon turned angry and imperious. "Why do you want to ruin me? Here I am in this basement, in charge of signaling to the filmmakers and photographers events worthy of being used for our weekly journal, while, as I told the boss, there is nothing for us to report! I mean, we are well aware of shocking events that are changing the face of the world, but we have to act as if they are not happening."

Information on what was happening around us, hardly mentioned in the official press, flowed then from the marchese's mouth, item after item, like hot lava from a volcano. I listened, spellbound. Not since my dinners with Nina had I been given a chance to see our political situation so clearly.

"The Axis armies flee, defeated by the British in North Africa, and Graziani gets in a terrible fight with Mussolini. Five Italian divisions are pulverized in two days. The Germans, of course, laugh at us. We attack Greece on a historical date for Fascism, October 28, and the Greeks, much to our surprise, ridicule us by putting up a heroic resistance, killing off our badly equipped soldiers by the hundreds. Albania, the base for our Greek campaign, is, of course, in permanent revolt. The great question is Russia, but Hitler won't tell Mussolini what he plans to do about Russia. All we know is that Mussolini has asked the Germans for help against Greece, since we started that battle through our own stupidity, which even Mussolini has to admit. Why shouldn't the Germans laugh at us? Soon they'll annex the Altoadige, which is German-speaking anyway."

I tried to stop him at that point, but he went on with his soliloquy as if I wasn't there.

"And while all this goes on, down here in this basement we are forced to ignore it, to distort reality, so as to make the news fit into a celestial scheme."

Finally, aware of my presence, he changed his tune: "You must believe me when I tell you, my dear young lady, that down here we live in the dark about what is happening 'upstairs.' And suddenly you show up in this kingdom of darkness, where there is hardly enough work for me, to help me. You appear out of nowhere to deprive a sick old man of his work, so that eventually he will be kicked out and replaced."

Sitting near him, on one of the many piles of discarded newspapers, I took the marchese's hand in mine and tried to reassure him of my complete respect for his work and of my pure intentions. His plea had moved me deeply. I told how I had landed in his basement. Although he didn't understand much about my scholarly mission, he respected my desire to complete my degree as soon as possible by working with a set of manuscripts at the Vatican Library. When I finally convinced him of my absolute need to earn a salary for my family's survival as the only reason for my presence in his basement, he limped with energy to his desk which was hidden behind piles of discarded newspapers. He reappeared shortly with a thermos of hot tea and a box of chocolate.

"Hunger, my dear lady." He smiled with the satisfaction of one who has found the solution to a serious problem. "Hunger will soon be the common enemy throughout Europe. What brings us together, courtesy of Alcide De Gasperi, is our shared will to fight hunger."

While sipping the warm foreign liquid and munching on some chocolates, the marchese and I designed a way for him to continue his work exactly as before and for me to accomplish my mission.

The next morning, I was comfortably installed in front of a huge old typewriter in a corner of the long hall hidden behind piles of newspapers. There, during regular office hours, from 8:00 a.m. to 2:00 p.m., I typed, on Institute letterhead, the notes I put together every afternoon from 3:00 p.m. to 6:00 p.m. in the Manuscript Hall of the Vatican Library. As a relief from the typing, I sipped tea with the charming marchese, who spent his days at his desk scanning newspapers, enveloped in the mist of an aromatic cigar. For another diversion from my typing, I would also walk down the hall to chat with the filmmakers, who were usually resting from the work done the night before. One of them was Roberto Rossellini. I also befriended their secretaries. Soon one of them, a short Roman girl, all fun and efficiency, proposed to type the first chapters of my future doctoral dissertation if, in exchange, I could help her prepare for her exam in Latin literature. I happily agreed.

For a whole year, from late November 1940 to December 1941, when I defended my doctoral dissertation, the basement of Santa Susanna was for me the complement to my afternoon's work at the Vatican Library. The mornings I spent in that basement with its warm, witty, chatty, creative Roman inhabitants allowed me to take full advantage of my long afternoons in the wide, silent halls of the Vatican Library, where a lively, quarrelsome fifteenth-century Rome enveloped me in its mist.

The year I spent in the basement of Santa Susanna gave me the relief of a steady income as well as providing me with moral support that was crucial to my research. The marchese, the filmmakers, and the staff of Santa Susanna took as personal an interest in my work as I did in theirs, when circumstances finally led me to it.

During the spring and summer of 1941, through luck, intuition, and obstinacy, I finally got my hands on some early fifteenth-century manuscripts that allowed me to work out the solution to the key problem attendant on Valla's theory of pleasure — specifically, did he indeed disown the daring work of his youth as a mature scholar in need of a job from the reigning Pope? The evidence I found in those manuscripts was a clear "No."

I went to see Professor Ussani on a bright morning in mid-July with the product of my research neatly packed in two school bags. The city was as serene as if neither Mussolini nor Hitler existed, and as if there was no war. After I rang downstairs and the old custodian greeted me in his distinctive Roman accent, the heavy door closed behind me. I followed the old man up the worn steps, to the Rome of the ancient Popes and their friends the Humanists. It was Lorenzo Valla himself I was about to introduce to my venerable mentor!

That was what I did with all the eloquence that my recent discoveries inspired. Valla was a member of the court of Pope Martin V and the Pope's old scholarly friends who were intent on reviving all aspects of rediscovered Roman antiquity. At my age, twenty-one, Valla was ready to shock a still traditional academic world with a revolutionary idea, which he revealed through what soon became for me a drama in three acts, in the form of a dialogue between the goddess *Voluptas* (Pleasure) and the goddess *Honestas* (Virtue).

In Valla's dialogue, *Voluptas* lived life in its mercurial essence, true only to itself, not owing anything to anyone — in fact, spurning all kinds of authority and any form of artificial order to be identified with *Honestas*. The drama of *Voluptas* and *Honestas* came to life through real characters, those very scholars young Valla admired at a distance, who sat in a cloister near the Tiber when the Pope didn't need them, happily drinking and eating at the end of every session — that is, every act of the drama.

Voluptas speaks through a scholar who loved pleasure in real life and thus is called Epicurean. Making fun of his serious, even grim, opponent, properly called Stoic, who complains of man's tragic condition, the Epicurean celebrates each of the human senses in action, ending with a paean to *Voluptas* as man's — and also woman's — relationship to a benevolent Nature.

Having clearly defined his own ground, the Epicurean reserves Act II for the gleeful and even at times sadistic deconstruction of the world of *Honestas* as empty virtue for virtue's sake. He demolishes one by one the great Roman heroes who gave up their lives for their country. His attack climaxes in dethroning Aristotle himself, universally regarded as the *Auctoritas* — more precisely, in destroying his ideal of contemplation and tranquility of mind as the highest form of happiness to be found in life.

In the final act, a character, properly called "Christian," who is actually young Valla himself as a biblical David, brings the drama to a happy conclusion by overcoming the fear of physical death. Through Christ's redemption of humanity by His own death and resurrection, physical death is happily accepted as an entry to eternal happiness, the physical body being redeemed in its resurrection. The dialogue concludes with a celebration of Christianity that redeems the senses.

Had Shakespeare been aware of the possibility of such a happy solution to a most difficult existential problem, I suggested to Ussani, Othello's love for Desdemona could have triumphed over the treachery of honest Iago! He laughingly agreed. Ussani quelled with an ironic smile my youthful enthusiasm which had transformed the dialogue into a drama.

"Your enthusiasm promises well for your future work," he said. "But remember, you have a whole life ahead of you to develop an interpretation of your current research. There is much reading to do at the Vatican Library and elsewhere. Your enthusiasm proves that the field in which you are working has much potential.

"For the time being, however, you have to limit your conclusions to the results of your research, as a first step to a future critical edition. I hope you can publish these results in an article, but only after a successful defense of your thesis. As for the drama you envisage, I am proud to see it as the result of much future growth in your field. You have to widen your horizon."

Smiling, he concluded in a different voice: "I'm proud of your work so far and look forward to presenting your work to my successor in the Chair of Latin Literature, Professor Funajoli. He will set the date for your defense. I wish you good luck at the defense and look forward to what you will contribute to our *Vocabulary* at the Accademia.

§   §   §

Throughout a very difficult life that took him in search of patrons and protectors who could support him, Valla almost doubled his original labors in his last years, changing scene and characters, but he never abandoned his first daring idea. That was indeed what Ussani longed to hear, though he insisted that for the time being I should limit my attention to the philological aspect. I had to be patient. A critical edition of the work would be a solid basis for the conclusions I had drawn with such enthusiasm. My task now was to establish the text as the author had written in its different versions. The dialogue might be seen as a drama. But, for the time being, it was to be simply a text.

I could see, as I spoke for more than an hour, that Ussani was happy and proud of a Humanist who did not blindly admire classical antiquity but worked with it critically. That was what he had been trying to teach me through all the years we spent together. Nonetheless, he discouraged me from moving too quickly past philology, the close study of the text.

On that day, in the midst of Mussolini's war, my teacher was also happy that I had finally grasped the *voluptas* of his own teaching. What mattered for him was that I had grasped the clear vision of that young man among mature scholars and the courage he showed in being true to it. Ussani saw that the originality of the work was in young Valla's challenge to his elders' blind devotion to antiquity; in his using the revered past in order to build a better future. At the conclusion of the drama, the Aristotelian virtues of fortitude, prudence, and serenity of mind — gained by abstracting from the problems of everyday reality — are replaced in Valla's dialogue by the Christian virtues of faith, hope, and charity, not as theological virtues but as existential premises for every act of our own life.

How had I accomplished so much work at the Vatican Library in barely more than a year? Ussani inquired before I left. I happily told him of the support I had received from the Library, De Gasperi, and the filmmakers and photographers of the *Luce.* It was a part of the drama of my own life he did not expect.

§ § §

Hitler's invasion of Russia, which began in June 1941, brought a sudden, unanticipated change in my own life in the basement of Santa Susanna. Mussolini's long-standing jealousy of this independent Hitler, who simply ignored him, led indirectly to my contribution to the *Istituto Nazionale Luce* from June to December of 1941.

From January on, the defeats in North Africa, as well as the failure to conclude the war in Greece, had aroused in Mussolini a well-founded suspicion that the Germans had no respect for the Italian military. In June and July, we saw clearly how Germany lusted after the Tyrol: Hitler simply annexed the region. In North Africa, Dabra Tabor fell to the British, while Rommel complained about Italy's military inefficiency. The Allies bombed Naples and the Neapolitans did not react with the stoicism and the discipline of the Germans. Mussolini ordered that the alarm should sound in Rome every time it did in Naples, in order to prepare the Romans for what might happen. Italian laborers in Germany were treated like dogs. Worse, for any insubordination, they were actually exposed to rabid dogs in their camps. The Germans were particularly cruel in Greece, where starvation was even worse than in Italy.

For Mussolini, it was bad enough that Hitler had decided the Germans would go it alone on the Eastern Front. What upset him even more was the fact that the invasion of Russia seemed a great success. The Wehrmacht pushed on toward Moscow and Leningrad and the Russians precipitously withdrew. All this, at first at least, without Italian participation. Down in our basement, we laughed at the reports that Mussolini had ordered twenty non-existent Italian divisions to the Russian front, to the dismay of all of his generals and with no reaction from Hitler.

The *Istituto Nazionale Luce* was suddenly flooded with reel after reel of German films from the Russian front, a paean to the clear German victories achieved without Italian participation. The films were, of course, in German, with no subtitles.

The *Luce* didn't know what to do with them. How much of it should be shown to an Italian public already depressed by defeats in North Africa, the loss of ships, the casualties in Greece, the constantly shrinking rations? The Germans in the films seemed to be well fed, as did the crowds cheering them at home during one of Hitler's interminable speeches explaining why the intervention in Russia was necessary.

The problem for Mussolini and consequently for the Film Division of his ministry was how to make use of the German films in the best way for Italians. Under pressure from above, the executives of the *Luce* remembered suddenly that sometime in December they had employed a young woman who said she spoke German. One evening, during dinner, the doorbell rang at our home. A car was waiting to take me back to via Santa Susanna immediately. Our basement, as I saw it that evening, was a surprise. There was intense excitement and activity, and from that moment on, I became a member of the filmmakers group, sitting for hours on end helping them go through the most recent films from the Russian front.

I translated for the filmmakers as we went through the same scenes over and over, until they made sense. I tried my best to answer their questions, which wasn't always easy. I was asked to identify cities and rivers on maps of Russia spread all over the floor. The most difficult part of our task was to diminish the public effect of the German victories on a resentful Italian public. To this end, we had to cut short the interminable lines of hungry Russian prisoners and the impressive marches of the Wehrmacht. Other nuances escaped me though not the filmmakers, who made use of them, evoking laughter. The whole operation, although interminable, was not tedious. It allowed me to learn something of an art that was new to me.

Fortunately for Mussolini, Hitler began feeling the pinch of the first losses in Russia. Yet, the crowds of Germans applauding the Führer were, much to our surprise, as well fed now as they had ever been, while our own soldiers showed signs of starvation, as we all did. In November 1941, the ration of pasta was reduced by half. Our military losses continued to worry Il Duce, proving, he claimed, basic Italian cowardice and weakness.

On my personal front, things could not have been better. In November 1941, I defended my doctoral dissertation, *summa cum laude*.

CHAPTER 7

A School on the Tiber

"Don't tell me you were unaware that you must wear a Fascist uniform during the defense of your dissertation. Today in particular, November 18, the anniversary of the *Sanzioni* [Sanctions], the uniform is a must. In what world do you live?"

I would have liked to answer, but I had abundantly tipped that most efficient usher of the Facoltà di Lettere in order to be reminded of all technical details regarding my defense. I was moved to tears when he provided his own bicycle so that I could go quickly, in a downpour, to a friend's house nearby, and quickly change into her uniform, a black suit and a fez that kept falling over my eyes.

The three members of the committee were waiting for me in the great hall, dressed in their fancy medieval costumes, when I arrived, panting in a uniform much too large for me. Professor Funajoli introduced me. Cardinal Mercati's presence among the examiners made me turn quickly to my usual prayer to my beloved departed. A punctilious philologist, he could probably have destroyed my thesis if he had wanted, but he merely kept me under fire for most of the two hours allotted to my defense. Rightly so. Fortunately, Lorenzo Valla was on the *Index* for other reasons than "pleasure." He had exposed as false the document which, the Papacy claimed, legitimatized its temporal power. My dissertation summarized the substance of my research in a little more than a hundred pages. It lacked the necessary details to make the defense proof against assault. But I had met the deadline, thanks to Francesca and Neri alternating at the typewriter the night before delivery, collecting the essentials, among the many sheets spread on the dining room floor.

During the defense, I did my best to give from memory what didn't appear in my text. I was also aware that the research was incomplete. The results so far, however, were accepted. The topic —

Lorenzo Valla, the most daring of the Humanists — was declared "congenial," clearly in homage to Professor Ussani, who was establishing a new field of research. As for me, I knew by now that it would take the rest of my life to develop my findings.

The celebration of my successful defense in the basement of Santa Susanna was also my farewell party. A few days later, Ussani informed me that I had been appointed adjunct professor of Latin and Greek at one of the best schools in Rome, the Liceo Virgilio. I was twenty-one years old.

Before leaving the *Luce I* arranged for my brother Neri, who had just completed the Liceo, to be hired to replace me. The food situation was such that we had no choice but to turn to the black market. With the steady devaluation of the lira, even two salaries might not suffice.

§ § §

As I walked to my first meeting with the president of the Liceo Virgilio, I envisioned myself as a Caesar marching on Rome after crossing the Rubicon. I felt that Rome was due to me, as it had been to Caesar. But the head of the school thought otherwise.

Did I realize, he began in a monotone as we sat in his office overlooking the Tiber, the risks I faced teaching Latin and Greek in Section E of his liceo? His liceo was not a run-of-the-mill Roman school like the Visconti or the Giulio Cesare. The Virgilio was a refugium peccatorum, a "refuge for sinners." It collected the scum of Trastevere, the area that the Tiber kept properly separated from the rest of civilized Rome. Was I aware of what had happened to the young lady who, against his advice, had tried to teach in the section to which I was assigned? She was grabbed by the hair, dragged out of the classroom, and thrown down the stairs. Why did the Board of Education keep sending him frail girls instead of strong young men, when they knew the problems?

I stopped him short. I appreciated his concern for my safety, but I had no choice. At the invitation of Professor Ussani, I had given up a secure job. My choice was now between his liceo and starvation. He remained unmoved.

"It's up to you," he said finally, "completely up to you. I have warned you."

On my way over to my first class, I met an older colleague. "Good luck," he whispered with an ironic smile. I did not respond.

"Be courteous to your colleagues," the president had advised. "They are your only friends in this school."

As his plump figure faded from my memory, there was a moment of silence in the classroom. Then a vague murmur rose through the mob of forty or so boys, like thunder rumbling in the distance, and a few words reached my desk.

"She's just a tiny nothing, even smaller than the other," I made out. "She'll be easy to take care of."

"She braids her hair like a peasant, but her legs are not bad," someone sneered. There was laughter in the back, but there was silence in the front of the room, while a boy in the first row slowly opened his pants and dug out his penis. I had never seen a penis before, and it shocked me. That penis was intended as a weapon to beat me down. I looked at the boy who owned it, staring straight at him. He was a handsome young man of eighteen, well-dressed and defiant. He stared at me curiously, probably surprised his penis had not done the trick. He was taken aback when I asked his name. The class laughed.

"Marioni!" They yelled. "How do you like him?"

I froze inside. I was holding tightly to the roll book and to a copy of Euripides' *Alcestis,* which the class was to translate in preparation for the forthcoming final state exams. I opened the roll book. Yes, Marioni Cesare was among the names. I called him to my desk as my teachers used to do when they examined us in Merano. We feared that moment. But Marioni was not afraid. He strutted defiantly toward the desk, holding up his pants. The class roared. He knew he was the protagonist of the show. Now I had to take action. I handed him the *Alcestis* and asked him to read aloud the first line in Greek. Surprisingly, he got it right, still holding up his pants. Then I asked him who Alcestis was. "A king," he said, and everybody laughed.

Somebody from the back yelled, "She is a queen and she died for her husband."

"Her husband was a queen like Caesar," Marioni laughed.

But there was no echo to his laughter. A point for me, I thought.

Although I was at a loss as to how to move on, I was encouraged by that silence. They were silent, I thought, because I had rewritten their script. If they figured out that I was improvising, I would be lost. So I had to keep the boy captive as long as possible. No, the time had come to let him go free. But how did I do that? I must give him a chance, maybe to button up his pants.

"Why do you say Alcestis's husband is a queen?" I asked Marioni while he tried with his free hand to button his pants.

"I don't know," he mumbled.

"Then dig out the verb from that first line," I instructed him calmly. "That will be much easier."

He fumbled beside me. I must send him back to his seat, I thought.

"Sorry, Marioni, the class has lost a month of work. I need grades. There is not a single grade in this roll book. Today, you fail."

No reaction. I opened the book and called the first name listed alphabetically. The boy whose name I called refused to come up to the desk.

"You fail," I proclaimed.

The third boy showed up. He answered most of my questions, and the class whistled. I sighed with relief. We stood, the boy and I, side by side in front of the blackboard and wrote down the main tenses of a Greek regular verb. The fourth boy failed, however, as did the next two. Finally, I relaxed and spoke gently and quietly with the student who was with me as if we were alone, although I was loud enough for the rest of the class to hear. I explained to him that at the end of the year we would face a difficult exam together. Every moment from now on was precious. There was whistling in the back, but the front was quiet. Victory? Not really. The bell freed us all from the torture.

Outside the classroom I met face-to-face with the older colleague who had wished me luck.

"Were you spying on me?" I asked.

"No," he laughed. "I was sure you would make it."

The Marioni incident did have some consequences. A few days later, the principal informed me, with a satisfied smile, that I was being transferred to the "Liceo Visconti."

"A much quieter liceo," he commented.

I refused to leave. I had learned that Marioni's father, a Fascist leader of some importance, had asked for my transfer. Ussani supported my decision to stay. From December 1941 until Easter 1944, I taught Latin and Greek in Section E of the Liceo Virgilio, which was housed in a modern Fascist-style building stretched along the Tiber River. These were my best years in Rome.

I had just been confirmed at the Virgilio in early December 1941, when Japan joined the Axis with its sneak attack on the American fleet at Pearl Harbor. Delighted, Mussolini declared himself the first fan of Japan in Europe. In school and mainly at home, we were shocked beyond words. Francesca and I were crossing Piazza Venezia on December 11, when Il Duce croaked the news of "War on America" from his balcony. There was no crowd to applaud him. Enough was enough, even for a people as apathetic about the war as the Romans seemed to be.

Francesca and I rushed home through the deserted Forum. In the safety of our apartment, we closed the atlas we had consulted, disheartened by the incongruity of the Italian situation. Having proved incapable of subduing Albania, of overcoming the Greek resistance, or of driving the British from Libya, Mussolini had now engaged us, in the midst of a cold winter without food or coal, in a war against a country across the ocean, one whose people were well supplied and well fed. Now, again, we could do nothing but accept still another act of sheer lunacy.

The image of Vassili had been with me constantly during the past year, evoked by the painful events in Greece, causing me to feel a deep sense of loss. Now I suddenly felt, for the first time since his departure, that by not sharing Vassili's destiny at the onset of the war, I had lost not only him but the best part of myself. He had warned me about what would happen if Mussolini was not stopped.

Although at the time I had reproached him for suggesting the impossible, I wished now that I had sided with him, despite Mamma's orders, especially when he needed my help. On that cold evening of December 11, 1941, oppressed by the hopelessness of our situation and angry at myself, I looked at Mamma as if she had been the cause of my cowardice and of my consequent regret and shame. Sitting alone in a corner of our cold and damp dining room, dejected but unbent, her mother's rosary in her hands, Mamma was quietly crying. She glanced at Francesca and me with desolate eyes.

"Now," she said, "there is no more hope. I cannot fight any longer. You must continue the fight alone.

For days, she remained locked in the prison of her silence, which not even Neri's jokes could penetrate. She delegated to Francesca the job of running the household.

Before the Americans entered the war, though we spent many nights in the shelter, Rome was the most fortunate city in Europe; the war was felt mainly in the scarcity of food. For those who, like my family, could not cope with black market laws, hunger was a sharp stimulus to search for food.

Employed at the Virgilio, I did not have to look far. Some food came to me miraculously, shortly after I began my teaching, as a surprising gift of love. The innate generosity of my Roman students conquered my whole family. It suddenly allowed us to face our daily tasks with the energy generated by a full stomach. It gave us also the warm feeling of being accepted as Romans among Romans.

The students' generosity was less a miracle than the natural outgrowth of a trust which both the students and I wanted from the start. The students of the liceo in Rome faced the same problems as those faced by the students of the liceo in Merano. They shared the same curriculum and academic structure. But in terms of the process of learning, Merano stood at the antipodes to Rome. In Merano, the eight of us students had gathered the wood for our stove, while diligently preparing, in respectful awe of our professors, for a difficult final examination. When I entered my first class in Rome, I had the impression that I was expected to tame a herd of wild horses for the forthcoming show, the state exam.

That perception suggested my defensive strategy during my first tragicomic duel with my students.

I was surprised when, on the second day, a herd of students moved slowly in my direction with the bold request, "Okay! Let's see if you really can help us!"

Once I accepted their challenge, we had a real channel of communication, unimaginable before. For three years those students and I lived through the war in Rome as comrades in arms. Together, we plunged into Virgil and Euripides, Cicero's *Pro Milone* and Plato's *Republic* as our way to survive in the midst of war.

The war deepened our friendship. Marioni became one of my most devoted students. The night he fled north with his father, in the early spring of 1943, he left with me a collection of his poems, inspired by our translations of the Greek lyric poets. Marioni and his father were committed Fascists. The news of their cruel execution by a group of committed Communist freedom fighters near Turin caused widespread grief as well as fear for our community, our city, even our country. We feared especially that the much-anticipated liberation would plunge us into civil war.

In December 1941, our main war had been against hunger, or so I thought until I discovered that not all of my students were as hungry as I was. Some of them showed no signs of malnutrition. Their families, it turned out, owned farms outside the Roman Walls. Others had relatives who knew how to manage the black market. So they could afford to help me with food.

As the war worsened, friendship kept us together. We shared the anguish of a German raid on the school and the exhilaration of escaping Allied bombs outside the city walls during a field trip to the ruins of Cicero's villa in Tusculum: we wanted to have some fun together.

§ § §

Christmas 1941 offered the students a perfect occasion for their generosity. Rome was sleeping quietly under a light blanket of snow on December 24 when my family and I, leaving the Church of Santa Maria della Navicella on the Celio Hill, found in front of Bernini's fountain a huge basket of food and wine with a witty note from two students whose parents had a farm outside the Walls. The next day, we took our food to celebrate Christmas with De Gasperi's family in their modest, cold apartment.

I had been tutoring some of my students from the Virgilio, and I was soon joined by Francesca, who had taken over my Roman students when I began working at the *Luce*. Bona, who had passed her final exam, and Neri, when he was free from his work at the *Luce*, helped me as well. Mamma, first skeptical at the sudden turn of events, soon regained her old spirit and with it her native tendency for order and organization. She saw to it that our little school ran smoothly. The students' parents joined them and soon the best of Trastevere found its way to Porta Metronia, with our maid Poldina controlling the traffic.

As the food situation worsened, we improved our tutoring system. Even so, while this regularized our income, it lacked the gallant spirit of the original exchange. A colleague in the sciences told me one day that a group of professors had created a network of connections for private tutoring through some of the licei of Rome. The rule was: you send me your students and I send you mine. Success depended on the cooperation of individual faculty members of the licei.

My personal connections were modest at first, but because the range of subjects we offered as a family was exceptional — all those required for the final exam — every corner of our apartment, including the bathroom, became a classroom. Each of us, incluing Bona, worked so hard that most of our Roman pupils passed the exam. Soon our school was a real business because it obeyed the quicksilver laws of the war economy. One colleague, Professor Reginelli, helped us to establish guidelines for payment in food. A student named Russo, for instance, whose father had a flourishing farm near Rome, paid a ham for the essentials of Plato, Aristotle, and Immanuel Kant, not always with successful results. At times, our task was impossible. Asked to define Cicero's philosophy during the final exam, Russo declared him an "epileptic" rather than an "eclectic," mortifying Bona, who had been his Latin tutor.

In the summer of 1942, one of our Virgilio students offered us the ground floor of a fisherman's house in Sperlonga, a picturesque village in the South, overlooking the sea and surrounded by rich, unharvested vineyards and orchards. We had long dreamt of a month at the seashore. Mamma rejected the idea: the seashore was dangerous she said, though she couldn't exactly say why. Neri did his best to convince her that we had to take the risk. Forget about the sea, he suggested. Just think of Rome. The price we paid for being declared an "Open City" was to become an island cut off from the world. For us the world was the fertile land around Rome, an earthly paradise available to everybody. Wheat fields, olive groves, and fruit orchards not yet destroyed by the war awaited us, their branches heavily laden with fruit.

"Forget about the sea, Mamma," he concluded. "Just think of the fruit, the oil, the wheat."

Mamma listened intently. She probably would have given in, but our life changed suddenly. One hot day in June, I staggered home from a state exam and fell on my bed, unconscious. A physician friend sat by me for a long time, looking at me helplessly. He had a thermometer but no medicine. His diagnosis was typhoid fever. What I needed was clean water. Since typhoid was contagious, I had to be isolated from the rest of the family.

Mamma locked herself up with me in her room. She was immune, she proudly declared, since she had had typhoid during the last war. Some Austrian officers gave her cognac as a cure. The doctor laughed. It had taken her months to come back to life, due to liver complications. Furthermore, she reminded us, long before she was born, the youngest of Papa's brothers, Stefano, had died of typhoid fever in Rome. Rome at that time was a dangerous city.

Aware that these examples of past illnesses were discouraging, she added reassuringly that we shouldn't worry. Times had changed. Rome was safe now and she was the right person to help me get well fast.

I moaned and slept for a couple of weeks. It took a long time before I could sit up in bed — long enough for us to give up on Sperlonga. The students provided me with everything I needed: spring water, soap, chicken broth, and precious rice.

As soon as I could be moved, a new friend, the Marchesa Marignoli, drove me to Spoleto to convalesce with her at Villa Redenta. I wished Neri could have seen Villa Redenta. It was Paradise on earth. Why couldn't I live there forever? I wondered. While Bona tutored the Marchesa's daughter Flaminia, named after the ancient Roman road that ran by the villa, I rested under the olive trees in the park, delighting in the intense blue of the Umbrian sky, the smell of sage and rosemary, the music of the crickets. I would have lived there forever in blessed oblivion had Neri not reminded me in one of his funny letters from Rome that there was a war raging around us.

Bruno, Francesca's fiancé, a lieutenant in the Italian Army, was doing his best to survive the fighting in Albania and Greece. There was war in Southern Italy, war in Russia, war in the North — a war that echoed even in the Eternal City. How could I justify talking to the birds in the land of St. Francis? Mamma, he wrote, had gone with Francesca to Zara, in Dalmatia, to pay the requisite visit to Bruno's family, her future in-laws. Much to the Marchesa's regret and my own, I cut my vacation short and took the train back to Rome. I knew Neri was alone there. Mamma and Francesca were in Zara and Bona was with me in Spoleto.

CHAPTER 8

War at Potra Metrona

But Neri was not alone. Within the nascent community at Porta Metronia, men and women lived somewhat separate lives. In the shelter, during and after the sirens, Neri had joined a group of men — Umberto, Marcello, Fulvio, and an elderly man, a cavaliere, who was always ready to offer an opinion on everything. The men sat together, smoked, and talked politics, much as men did in any Italian village square. As women, though we were not excluded from their company, we felt obliged to attend to our work — domestic chores essential to survival. Watching our men and listening in on their discussions, we participated in their meetings only when we had free time.

Marcello, a former officer who had lost faith in the "National Cause," took pride in forming a political party, whose purpose varied according to developments in the war. After the German occupation of Rome, his party printed false identity cards bearing the seal of the Todt organization. Fulvio, an employee of the Ministry of the Interior, was the main source of information on national disasters, which increased in number and gravity as the war progressed. Umberto, by far my favorite, was a brilliant young man. He read every book in sight and attended every available lecture. As a Jew on his mother's side, he could not register in any university but he could attend courses. He lectured us more eloquently than any university professor on what mattered now — politics and economics, philosophy and history, ethics, and even religion. He spoke clearly and simply. Politically, he defined himself as either a Liberal Socialist or a Christian Socialist. Neither meant anything to us.

Umberto spoke equally well on the essentials of democracy, on the of laws of the free market, on the American Revolution and all that precious tea dumped in the ocean, and on *Das Kapital*, a book whose importance I had discovered in Merano as a young girl. Richly informative, he could arouse in his audience a feeling of euphoria. He said he did this to overcome the "numbness" that had seized us during our eighteen years of Fascist slavery.

Although fully enjoying the community of men in Rome, Neri remained as closely connected with his family of women as he had been in Merano. Thus, he was the first to perceive that the deep bond Francesca, Bona, and I shared, a bond which had helped us all cope with life in Rome, had recently been strained, causing Francesca to feel lonely. Bona and I had grown closer, while Francesca, after our adventures at the typing school, had distanced herself. She took over Mamma's responsibilities and behaved like Mamma, even adopting her eloquent silences. She lived in her own world.

What do you think is happening to Francesca? Bona asked one evening as we sat with Neri near the Walls after a day of hard work. Neri was happy to delve into the subject. Francesca, he thought, had been proud and happy when Bruno chose her as his future wife but now, uprooted from Merano and in a new situation in Rome, she resented our freedom.

In our efforts to survive in Rome, Bona and I had sought Francesca's cooperation, never worrying about her inner turmoil. In love with Bruno, she was the real victim of the war. Occasional news from the Albanian-Greek front came to her mostly via Bruno's family in Zara. In Rome, cut off from Bruno, she also felt cut off from our family, because nobody except Mamma seemed aware of her inner turmoil. She knew that we hated the war. She felt deprived of the intimacy we four children had enjoyed living in Merano after Papa's death, wandering from villa to villa, innocently certain that if we stuck together, we could overcome anything. In Rome, there were only occasional moments of family fun, mainly the Sunday lunches we shared with Cousin Agostino's family in their large sunny apartment in Via Bolzano. While we ate enough pasta, meat, and pastry to last us the rest of the week, we listened to readings from Dante's *Paradiso* by a Swiss Jesuit, Father Zullig, Agostino's spiritual guide and editor of the *Società Cattolica*. That was an interesting combination that gave us the chance to laugh at ourselves.

Following one of those meetings, Neri told Bona and me he had overheard Francesca and Bruno, during a leave from the front, discussing their official engagement. The marriage was to take place in Rome, one year later, in July 1943. The war wasn't going to stop Francesca from starting a family! On the other hand, Francesca and Bruno did not see eye to eye on Mussolini and the war.

On a cold, clear day (Neri told us), Francesca had sat with a uniformed Bruno on a marble bench in via dell'Impero, the broad avenue that ran through the Roman Forum. Above the bench were maps which Mussolini, after the Abyssinian war, had affixed to the imposing ruins of the Basilica of the Emperor Maxentius. The message conveyed by those maps — thanks to Il Duce, Rome had reconquered the old Roman Empire — struck Bruno and Francesca in starkly opposite ways as they watched a parade of flying *bersaglieri* and an army of young Fascists, chanting the most Fascist of all hymns, *Giovinezza*.

For Francesca, this was a carefree and joyful commentary on the meaning of those maps. Bruno, however, just back from the front, hungry and depressed, closed his eyes and waved the show away in disgust. To him those maps were merely an expression of Mussolini's megalomania.

"Send them to the front," he whispered to Francesca, "and they will give up their silly songs. There is no singing at the front."

A few days later, Neri, who had gone with Francesca and Bruno to Stazione Termini, heard Bruno whispering to Francesca, "I'll see you soon!"

"When?" an anguished Francesca asked. "Ask Mussolini!" were Bruno's last words as he disappeared in the acrid smoke billowing from an endless line of trains crammed with soldiers.

In July 1942, Mamma and Francesca left for Zara, an old Venetian colony and now a little Italian enclave on the Yugoslav coast, for Francesca's engagement party. Zara's picturesque streets were untouched and its little squares left to its fishermen, whose sing-song Venetian dialect expressed the city's only language.

Both Mamma and Francesca, however, felt the town's worries about its uncertain future. At any time, Il Duce could give up this little jewel protected by Germans in a bargain Hitler had imposed on the Yugoslav king. The city could also be wrenched from both Italians and Germans by the Croatian partisans, backed by England.

Bruno's family, the Franchis, lived in an imposing apartment building near the sea and had all the fish and vegetables they could wish for, the most welcome gift they could offer their two hungry Roman guests. Yet their lives were hanging by a thread. As long as the Germans remained strong, they had nothing to fear. They were prosperous, honest supporters of the Fascist regime and leading citizens. But the brutality with which the Germans treated the people around Zara was a guarantee of savage revenge by the Croatian partisans if and when the partisans took over. Old Professor Franchi, Bruno's father, would have to disappear quickly if he didn't want to be one of the first victims of that revenge. His only son, Bruno, an officer at the Albanian front, could hardly come to his aid. In case of trouble, he would have a hard time saving himself, because the freedom fighters hated Italian soldiers almost as much as they hated the Germans.

Francesca and Bruno's engagement was celebrated with a somber but rich dinner. Porcelain dishes, crystal glasses, polished silverware, and a lace tablecloth that had been in the Croatian family of Bruno's mother for generations, adorned the table. The white curtains waved gently in the evening breeze, the soft music of the sea gave the celebration a peaceful, even timeless feeling. It was as if the war did not exist.

The night before Bruno left, however, Francesca, in tears, told us that all hell had broken loose when Bruno defended what he saw as political reality against the staunch Fascist beliefs of his beloved father. And at breakfast, in his uniform, Bruno was cold and distant. We all knew, she said, that when he left Zara's peaceful island, death was waiting for him. The front was everywhere. There was nothing anyone of us could do to help him.

Francesca's visit to Zara was a harsh trial which left her perplexed about Bruno's future and the immediate future of his family.

Bruno stood with us one hundred percent against the war, Francesca assured us, but at what cost!

No day of the long fall of 1942 and winter and spring of 1943 was like the preceding. Yet, good or bad, they all rolled through our lives like the beads of Mamma's rosary when she held it in moments of crisis. News from Bruno was scarce, his letters laconic — just a few words, which only Francesca could interpret.

Rome was a city under siege. Food was scarcer every day. By Christmas 1942, because of the intensified Allied bombardments, only the most daring among our students could provide food from beyond the Walls. We all had to go out and look for food, while Poldina, after each bombardment, would stand in line for water at the spring near the Baths of Caracalla.

Usually the curfew sent us home as early as 7:00 p.m. When the sirens blasted, I, who had been designated *capo-fabbricato* (head of the building) would shepherd people into the cellar, where we spent our nights together. No bomb ever fell on or near our building until the fateful bombardment of Rome of July 19, 1943.

We eagerly anticipated the evening radio broadcasts. Lights out, blinds closed, doors locked, we gathered in our living room, which in fall and winter was cold and damp from lack of fuel, to hear the real news of the day from Radio Moscow and Radio London. As we hovered over the miraculous machine, the heavy silence was often broken by odd noises. After a while, if the transmission wasn't jammed, as often happened with Radio London, we could hear a voice telling us what was happening outside Rome. As we listened, we often felt cheated by not being where the action was. In spirit, we were certainly with the "others" — the people throughout Europe, from England, Norway, Leningrad, Stalingrad to Gibraltar, and those beyond the Atlantic, that huge unknown America that, according to Radio London as early as January 1942, was organizing arms and men to come to our aid.

Though there were frequent false reports of a German surrender, the year 1942 started badly for the Allies. Around April, the Germans began recruiting men from all over occupied Europe for their war machine. Their orders sent us women scurrying for places to hide those of our men who were not already in the army or in war work. Neri was for the time being safe at the *Istituto Nazionale Luce,* Bruno quite imperiled at the front.

From early fall on, our secret radios told us about the siege of Stalingrad and about Rommel holding off the British in Libya. By November 1942, however, the Russians had the upper hand in Stalingrad, managing to besiege General von Paulus, while the Allies were victoriously pushing back Germans and Italians at El Alamein in Libya.

The miracle happened, we thought, when, on Bona's birthday, November 8, 1942, the Americans landed in Morocco — 300 battleships and almost 200,000 men! Night after night, we breathlessly followed the Americans marching through half of North Africa to Tunisia in less than eighty hours! General Rommel was now losing one battle after another, with such serious losses of German and Italian soldiers that he begged Hitler to allow him to withdraw altogether from Africa. El Alamein was the final German/Italian defeat in Africa.

I was pained by the siege of Stalingrad. Among the German soldiers who died there was Hans Haller, one of my closest childhood friends in Merano. His family had given up their vineyards near villa Dolomitenblick and moved to Germany with their four boys after the South Tyrol pact between Hitler and Mussolini. All four boys were killed in Stalingrad. Their mother later sent me the epitaph she had placed on their graves.

By the summer of 1943, as the Allies marched through southern Italy, their deadly bombardments intensified. They landed in Sicily in July 1943. Rumor had it that the Americans who occupied Palermo, Messina, and Catania shot some Italian prisoners. We were as sorry for the prisoners as we were for the Americans, who were slowly taking shape as the heroes of liberation.

§ § §

It became clear that the Allies were giving priority to the Mediterranean over Northern Europe. That meant we would be the first to be liberated. The word partisan, i.e., freedom fighter, known to us only through the news broadcasts, applied mainly to members of the Russian and Yugoslav Resistance, led by someone named Tito. We were unaware of the existence of partisans anywhere else, certainly not around us in Rome.

By spring 1943, food in Rome was so scarce that Bona and I decided to join other women outside the Walls and hitchhike north on German trucks to get flour and other staples. The German soldiers on whose truck we landed with some other women one day warned us to jump out in the event of Allied bombing or partisan ambushes.

"Who are the partisans?" we asked.

"The partisans," one of the Germans said, "were created by God for the punishment of the Germans!"

His friend laughed, but we were puzzled. How could we be killed by Italians? we asked. The two Germans laughed again, sarcastically,

"It's obvious you've been living in a cocoon."

To be on a German truck was a sufficient reason to be *kaput,* he declared. We got back to Rome safely with two sacks of flour and a ham. No ambushes, only one machine-gunning incident, which we managed to escape.

Mamma could not understand how we could, in May 1943, accept our students' repeated offers of a month at the seashore. When the Sperlonga offer was seriously presented again one evening at dinner, Mamma left the room in protest. But the four of us approved the idea for one basic reason: food. Having risked our lives on a German truck for food, Bona and I were unwilling to try that again. We were now surviving on squash and water, plus half of an inedible loaf of bread a day. Others took risks. Why not we?

Francesca was the strongest supporter of the idea. She and Bruno had agreed to keep July 20 as the date for their wedding in Rome. A stay in Sperlonga was just what she needed. A call from Bruno's parents confirmed the date, even though, under the circumstances, they couldn't assure their presence. In view of this formidable news, a vacation on a beautiful beach seemed to all of us a godsend. Although trains were still running between Rome and Segni, the station closest to Sperlonga, we accepted a student's generous offer of a ride. Though overcrowded with soldiers, the roads were still passable.

Except for Mamma, our family had had no experience of the sea. We screamed with joy when we saw the expanse of blue water. Sperlonga seemed a painting, a flock of old houses perched together like birds in a tree. Our house was empty, dark and dirty. Mamma took one look at it and was ready to go back to Rome. But we cleaned it up and made it livable.

At nightfall, we heard the familiar rumbling of the gigantic American planes and felt the benefits of having abandoned Rome. With the rest of the villagers, we ran as fast as we could to the open fields. Spending the night amid vineyards or orchards of figs and apricots, we ate fruit still warm from the sun and drank the good wine we had brought with us. Then we lay on the soft ground and slept amid the fragrance of juicy figs. In the fields with the villagers we felt safe and free. And we made friendships, many of which would last for years. Neri met and fell in love with Elsa, one of the many daughters of a rich farmer in nearby Fondi. They planned to marry, but Elsa was killed with her family the following winter during the siege of Cassino.

In the mornings, we did not return to the village right away. We were invited to breakfast in the main farmhouse, and ate and drank our fill. Then we lazily explored the beach. We waded into water so pure, warm, and azure that we allowed ourselves to be caressed by it until Mamma called us back to the shore.

We ate freshly caught fish and then spent the hot part of the day sleeping on mattresses stretched out on the floor of the windowless cool cave that was our kitchen and living room. We slept until sunset, then, after a swim, wandered out with the villagers toward the orchards where we would spend the night. From our little paradise, we watched the bombardment, hoping, like everyone else, that we would find our house standing upon our return — and we did. Houses were damaged, but no one was killed.

In this extraordinary environment, Bona and I were briefly attracted to the same Sicilian medical student, a tall dark-haired Apollo chaperoned by a large mother. Among the vines and peach trees, we celebrated our being alive and well fed. Francesca, I suppose, dreamed of Bruno in the orchards at night. By the time we left the seashore for Francesca's wedding in Rome, we had collected such a variety of food that her wedding dinner was to be a sumptuous banquet.

§ § §

On July 19, 1943 we stood happily at the railway station in Fondi, all of us, especially Poldina, carrying sacks of all kinds of food. Neri helped us to find seats close to one another. We were enjoying the Roman countryside, Francesca lost in sweetest thought, when Bona, the quickest to perceive danger, grabbed Mamma by the arm and screamed: "The Americans are above us!"

The blue sky rained down bombs. Neri pushed the door open and we all jumped out, helping some elderly people. We ran for shelter under an overpass just as bombs hit the train. Billowing white smoke rose from the cars. Screams, then silence. People prayed. Mamma suddenly noticed that Poldina was missing.

"Where is Poldina?" she screamed. Neri left the safety of the overpass to check the area around us. Suddenly, Poldina appeared, triumphantly striding away from the car where she had been sitting all along, utterly unscathed. She was carrying a live chicken and some packages.

"Do you mean you were ready to give up the food for the wedding?" she laughed. "What world do you live in?"

Mamma, furious, dragged her back to safety, but Bona and I admired her courage.

A man who was with us during the bombardment became our guide for the slow walk to Rome. We saw corpses along the road, a wounded horse, its still warm intestines splattered over the pavement, and flies swarming about them. A child moaned, his mother kneeling near him. A house split in two, white curtains swaying in the breeze. An old man, bleeding, pushed along on a cart by a bleeding woman. "Move, move, get out of the way!" They were carrying bodies from a nearby station "Move, for God's sake. Where do you think you are?" a man screamed in Francesca's face. She looked at him dumbfounded and sat down, no longer able to face the endless road. Mamma yanked her up.

"Come on," she yelled. "You are not wounded. You must walk!" Her feet were bleeding. Neri carried her for a while on his back. The man who was with us when we jumped from the train helped Neri. Soon she was leaning on both of them, walking.

"Our house is still standing!" Bona yelled joyfully. "All we've lost are the windows."

Francesca was with us again, brought back to life by Bona's cheerful voice. Bruno was there, sitting on the steps at the entrance.

The first bombardment was meant to shake Rome from its torpor," he whispered as he took her in his arms. "You were lucky to be out of the city. I can't believe you made it alive."

Poldina took over the house as if nothing had happened. She mixed oil and eggs, and then broke up a chair to make a fire on the balcony. "What is a chair? We can sit on the floor," she laughed. At the gates of the church, there was a long line of couples waiting to get married. When Bruno and Francesca's turn came, the priest addressed them as Enrico and Maria. They protested. He pushed them aside.

"Get your name straight!" he yelled, and proceeded to bless the next couple, but Neri pushed the couple aside.

"For God's sake! Marry my sister first!" he shouted at the priest. "Marry her! They are here alive, miraculously. Marry them! Their name is Franchi!"

After dinner that night, we accompanied the newlyweds to Stazione Termini, overrun with soldiers. Many trains and the station itself had been badly hit, but a few trains still moved in the dark.

Francesca was lost. She held on to Mamma like a child. Then suddenly she vanished in the dark smoke that always swallowed our lives at the station.

Since he had a two-week leave of absence, Bruno took Francesca to Cloz, his father's village in the Central Alps, a hidden corner of the world not yet touched by the war. The old house near the brook at the edge of the forest happily received the newly-weds. Il Professore and Aunt Rina had escaped Tito's partisans by hiding for a month in Zara's graveyard, which was conveniently situated close to the seashore. Their devoted Croatian maid, who had brought them food every day among the graves, arranged for a sailboat to ferry them to the other side of the Adriatic. Tossed about by the waves for several days and nights, the old man vowed to the Virgin that, if he survived, he would give up politics and dedicate his life to peace. We were relieved when the news reached us of their safe arrival and the unplanned reunion in Cloz.

§   §   §

On July 19th, 1943, Rome got its first heavy bombardment. The whole Quartiere Prenestino, including the Basilica of San Lorenzo with its Byzantine mosaics, was destroyed. Electricity, water, and telephone service were gone. Help was scarce or nonexistent. People clawed through the rubble to dig out their loved ones.

Unlike Berlin, Hamburg, London, Milan, and Turin, not to mention Stalingrad, Leningrad, or Moscow, Rome had been spared aerial attacks. We reacted with plain disbelief. Wasn't Rome an "Open City"? Umberto, the best informed among the young men in the building, sneered at us when we said this. A few days before July 19, he had heard on Radio London Churchill and Roosevelt begging us to choose between our lives and Mussolini.

"How can we get rid of Mussolini?" asked the ever-pragmatic Poldina.

That bombardment, as hard as it was to take, answered her. Bona, Neri, and I spent the day cleaning up the glass from our broken windows and standing in line for drinking water. Like others, we survived for a couple of days in total inertia, until we got news of Francesca's safe arrival in Cloz. Then Neri, nineteen, left for Terni, where he was to report to officers Training Camp.

Bona and I, alone with a silent Mamma, accepted a ride back to Sperlonga. We knew what dangers we were facing by leaving the city and moving south toward the sea. Although the Germans seemed convinced that the next Allied landing would be in Greece, and General Rommel was put in charge of the Greek theater of operations, we in Rome expected them to land close to us. Perhaps close to Sperlonga.

As a student of mine drove Bona, Mamma, and me southward, bouncing over a pock-marked road, Bona and I admitted to each other that all we longed for now was to break the magic circle that had kept us prisoners of Rome, open city. Now Bona became my most faithful companion as we tried to deal with life beyond survival. We did not know exactly what that meant. The next iron circle that kept us idle prisoners was broken for us by circumstances beyond our control. Bona and I were swimming together in the turquoise water of the Tyrrhenian Sea when Giovanni, the shared-boyfriend whom we had recently discarded, called to us from the shore: "He is gone!" he kept shouting. His joyous voice reached us over the lapping of the waves, "Mussolini is gone!"

We rushed out to get to a radio. The village fishermen and their families gathered on the beach, hardly daring to believe the extraordinary news: Mussolini had been asked to resign. The Great Fascist Council, the supreme organ of the regime, had asked the king to take over. A new government had been formed headed by General Badoglio.

The king had had Mussolini arrested and spirited him away in an ambulance to the island of Ponza, south of Rome, not far from Sperlonga. Bona and I were giddy with joy. "To be delivered to the Allies!" we cried. Mamma, who wasn't hoping to witness that delivery, asked us to pack and move back from Sperlonga to Rome. But we said we have other things on our minds besides our personal safety.

Although there was no official announcement that the new Italy would cease fighting, Bona and I took it for granted that an armistice would be signed. That was evidently the reason for the coup. Umberto had told us that the very day Rome was being bombarded Hitler was meeting with Mussolini somewhere in the north of Italy. Nobody knew what went on between them, but everybody guessed the Duce was being warned by the Führer not to agree to an armistice. What could Mussolini say but "Amen"? That's why he, back in Rome, had been dislodged by his own party!

The news that followed Mussolini's disappearance from our lives left us almost as dumbfounded as the bombs of July 19, which, in our minds, were directly connected with the fall of Fascism. Twenty years of Mussolini's leadership, climaxing in his alliance with Hitler, were wiped away by a combination of forces we could hardly identify and interpret. I was twenty-two when Fascism fell; Bona, the youngest of us, was eighteen. In my diary, I read a mixture of astonishment, embarrassment, fear, and mostly confusion. After July 25, when Mussolini lost his power, we were asked to face a world about which we knew nothing and for which we were unprepared. What would Badoglio and his government do next? Who would shoot at us first — the Allies or the Germans? Would the Allies let us join them, or simply shoot us for having fought against them? What would the Germans do to our own soldiers, who had been fighting alongside them? What would our soldiers do?

§   §   §

We had our first answer right in Sperlonga. As we stood with the fishermen on the beach, a couple of German soldiers joined us. "Fascism *kaput!*" they said, and laughed as if they were relieved. The next day, those same soldiers told us to clear the beach. The whole seashore was being mined against a feared Allied landing. Bona and I asked the soldiers to let us have a last swim. Surprisingly they joined us. They were Poles. Like us, they were looking forward to the end of the war.

We reached Rome just before the second bombardment, on August 13. Mamma, Bona, and I, caught in the center of town, joined a crowd of silent Romans in a shelter under the tomb of the Unknown Soldier in the Campidoglio. The bombing was heavy, though not as heavy as the first; there was less damage and a quicker recovery. Besides, the air was clear. Fascism was gone. We were quietly but unenthusiastically tasting something like democracy. There was talk of new political parties which would allow us, the people, to be represented in the government. We were also slowly regaining some joy in living. Yet, clouds still hovered. Francesca was back in Rome, sad and alone. Since the armistice had not ended Italy's part in the war, Bruno was still in Yugoslavia, forced by the Germans to "punish" the partisans.

We had also lost Neri to the army. Fortunately, he was stationed close to Rome. In case of danger, he could find refuge at home. The four of us women were left alone to survive as best we could. That meant rebuilding our little school with the help of my old students, finding food, following the news, and waiting patiently on the precipice, a precipice that was to open wide on September 8, 1943.

"Democracy is humanity at best, not because we believe that a republic is better than a monarchy and a king is better than nothing and nothing is better than a dictatorship, but because it is the natural condition of every man ever since the human mind became conscious not only of the world but of itself. Morally, democracy is invincible. Physically, that side will win which has the better guns. Of faith and pride, both sides have plenty. That our faith and our pride are of a totally different order cannot concern an enemy who believes in shedding blood and is proud of its own."

This definition, offered at the time by the Russian writer Vladimir Nabokov, who had taken refuge in America, could have been, in part at least, our own on and immediately after September 8, 1943.

Rising from his afternoon nap that day, Hitler learned from the BBC that Italy had surrendered to the Allies. Furious, he ordered the Wehrmacht to hold as much of the Italian peninsula as the Allies had not already taken. At the same time, the Allies launched — as Radio London put it — Operation Avalanche, a landing on Salerno beachhead, not far from our beloved Sperlonga. The armistice had the consequences we feared. The Italian soldiers who did not immediately surrender to their former ally, were massacred by the thousands in Greece. Even many who did surrender were shot or deported to concentration camps as traitors. The members of the Italian navy who had survived the Allied bombs before September 8 and the German submarines shortly after that escaped to the island of Malta.

In Rome, caught between the Allies and the Germans, we managed for about twenty-four hours on our own. It was during those twenty-four hours that we got a brief taste of democracy as self-government. Then the guns changed everything. That evening started as uneventfully as any since July 25. During a break between afternoon and evening classes, Bona and I were playing tennis with Adriano, a former student. Our public courts were among the most picturesque spots in Rome. They had been built under the ancient Aurelian Walls at Porta Metronia, right next door to our building. Mamma and Poldina were out on the grounds of Villa Celimontana nearby, picking edible herbs for our dinner. Adriano had brought along some bread and grapes for Francesca, who was pregnant. The heavy air promised a storm, when my first evening student, Luna, approached me with a peevish air. "Armistice," he whispered and disappeared. We ran home.

Mamma, Francesca, and Poldina were huddled over the radio. They motioned for silence. "Unconditional surrender" was the official message of Premier Badoglio to the Romans, endlessly repeated, while he drove away from Rome with the king and his family. Nobody knew where they were going, only that they would stay safely out of German reach, under Allied protection. Everybody seemed relieved. The war was over, at least for us. Our men would soon be home. The siege of Rome had ended.

Bona and I were worried. How could the king and Badoglio abandon Rome without warning or defense?

From the rooftop we enjoyed a clear view of the plains almost to the sea. As the rumble of the artillery grew louder, bright flashes of light lit up the sky. Neri told us that the Germans were besieging

Rome. He had jumped on a truck at the first news of the armistice; now, back home, he got rid of the uniform he hated.

Neri joined Umberto, Fulvio, il cavaliere, and the rest of the men in their political discussion, focusing on who was pushing their way into Rome. As we listened, we women began to worry. What if it was the Germans? The men reassured us: some chocolate and chewing gum had found their way into the Eternal City. Yet they all agreed with us that the Allies didn't stand a chance of taking Rome since we were totally unprepared to support them.

After a sleepless night, Bona and I went searching for food. At a corner of Via Nazionale, a group of *Blitzmadel* (young German female soldiers), protected by German police, waited for a truck. A few German soldiers moved around with their cameras, like tourists. The bars were full as usual. We entered one to get an ice cream.

The morning of September 9, a state of emergency was declared. We could hear the guns. Ministries closed; there was no sign of any government. It looked like each man for himself. Helpless, we'd have to face the Germans as they pushed into the city. Towards evening, a plane dropped a few bombs; no one seemed to care. Bona and I joined Poldina at the Baths of Caracalla to get more water for the eventual siege.

Early September 10, Bona and I set off again in search of food. We took streetcar #22 to the Central Markets at Porta San Paolo. In the vicinity of Porta San Sebastiano, a screaming crowd stopped us. We jumped off the streetcar and ran in different directions but soon found one another again, both lifted by helpful hands onto a truck full of vegetables rushing towards the center of the city. A truck full of vegetables! We filled our bags with red and yellow peppers before jumping off at the Colosseum. The Celio Hill separated us from Porta Metronia. By now the heavy artillery was so close that shells fell around us. Santa Maria della Navicella, at the top of the Celio Hill, was locked. We took our chances and ran down the hill, under fire, towards Porta Metronia.

On the roof terrace, we were joined by my student Franco Ferri, who brought along much needed food and gossip. The radio announced that we were now negotiating with the Germans. But with Badoglio gone, who were "we"? Who was in charge of the city? While we talked, we heard on the radio that negotiations had fallen through. Then there was silence. Only one newspaper, the *Popolo di Roma,* would write that we, the Romans, wished to know the truth.

Guns revealed that truth. At 3:00 p.m., the building shook as it was falling apart. We ran from the roof down into the shelter where men were silent, while women wept and prayed. Suddenly, someone screamed, "My God! They are here."

There was a noise at the entrance of the building. Two German soldiers came into the shelter, supporting a young blond comrade, his face disfigured, his body spattered with blood. They took the door off its hinges and gently laid the wounded soldier on it.

"Schwein!" they cursed us, eyes flashing, and disappeared.

That evening, when we left the shelter, we found the Germans camped around Porta Metronia on our tennis courts near the Walls. After a burst of gunfire, they moved to a building on Via Amba Aradam and set up a machine gun at the entrance. When a man came by, they shot him dead. His body just lay there.

Towards evening, fighting subsided between the two ancient gates, Porta San Sebastiano and Porta Latina. Another battle had taken place not far from there at Porta San Paolo. Part of an Italian division defended that gate heroically to the last man against an overwhelming German force. Some civilians died in the fighting.

After days of unbearable heat, rain fell softly through the night. A conquered Rome lay in silence.

The next morning, Francesca brought a carabiniere, a young, sturdy, taciturn man, home from church. He ate everything in sight, including Francesca's precious breakfast, then left wearing Neri's pajamas, after having abandoned on our bathroom floor the uniform which his army was so proud of. That carabiniere was the first of many uniformed men who were to come by, exchange their uniforms for any clothing available, and move on, entrusting us with an address of a relative somewhere in the Italian peninsula. From that day on, our apartment, like many others, became a shop where my students and I collected men's clothing of all kinds, including priestly garments, to replace the uniforms.

The desertion by the Italian soldiers and the help we gave them were not inspired by a love for the "democracy" we had lost with the departure of the king and Badoglio. On the contrary, some of us regarded the democratic "forty days" under Badoglio as the direct cause of our present misery. Resistance to the Germans in Rome, as far as our family was concerned, was an act of self-defense by the oppressed provoked by the behavior of the oppressors. When General Kesselring became the Supreme Authority in our city, it was the cruel enforcement of his orders that made resistance our highest priority, more important even than our basic physical needs.

On September 11, both the radio and posters all over the city told us that martial law had been imposed. The radio also brought the news of unconditional surrender. A message from Kesselring reached us between two love songs: Rome would be punished as the traitors' capital and it would be the immediate rear-front created by the Allied landing in nearby Salerno.

Resistance to the Germans did not prevent the Romans from acting as they always had, using ingenuity to survive. Shortly after the occupation, Neri and his friends and Bona and I joined some Romans in our building on a perilous expedition. We had heard that there was food in abandoned Red Cross trains at the San Paolo station where the fighting had taken place a few days before. We found the trains and, yes, there was food, more than we expected. As we were dragging a sack of sugar and a bag of rice up a slope, we were caught by two German soldiers. They forced us at gunpoint to abandon our loot. It looked like we had become victims of some article of the newly imposed military law, when, as we talked with them, we discovered that one came from the Südtyrol, the other from Slovakia. What started as an arrest with the risk of imprisonment and deportation ended in a pleasant encounter across mountains and wars.

"We are right to release you," laughed the Südtyroler, "because according to international law you are legal recipients of Red Cross goods!"

Unfortunately, a heavy exchange of gunfire at the Baths of Caracalla, forced us to abandon half our loot. We divided what was left among the neediest members of our building.

Shortly after this incident, the Germans began a manhunt that continued through the eight months during which they occupied Rome. Under Kesselring's orders, all Italian men between the ages of 15 and 60 had to report to a military command to be employed as workers near the front or sent north to feed the German war machine. From that day on, the Germans hunted Italian men while the Italian women sought better hiding places, food for their men, and eventually false identity cards to allow some of them to surface for brief periods for a breath of fresh air.

Fortunately, Rome had catacombs and churches of all sorts and sizes. Some were two or three levels deep. The final refuge was the Vatican which, thanks to a highly diplomatic Pope, did its best to help us survive.

The Germans, on the other hand, tried to surprise us in more than one way. On September 12, Mussolini, who had been moved from the island of Ponza to the top of a mountain in the Apennines, was freed by German paratroopers. Although the announcement was official, we refused to believe that he was alive until he spoke to us in his all-too-familiar voice on September 18. It was a very weak speech to which we listened out of curiosity.

By now, however, our main attention was elsewhere. Rome had changed. German roadblocks were set up everywhere to seize Italian men. There were relics of recent bombardments, buildings half-destroyed. An Italian armored vehicle stood in the middle of Via Gioberti, covered with dried blood. Commissars took the place of ministers. The newspapers, heavily censored, wrote only about futility, except for one speech by Churchill on September 22 which was reported in its entirety. Nobody understood why. We knew the Allies were fighting their way north from the southeast, the Americans heading up from Salerno.

The main difference between pre-armistice Rome and the one we lived in now was the presence of German soldiers. Tanned, their heads high, their faces impenetrable, the Germans seemed to ignore our presence as they began to systematically remove all transportable goods from the city. They looted public buildings, private houses, and even churches, where they used the priests as porters to carry off everything they wanted. We were witnessing a highly organized Sack of Rome, more efficient than that by the Huns in 410 or that by the Spanish and German soldiers of Charles V in 1527. The German invaders treated Rome the same as every other European city which they had occupied.

We, the women of Rome, dumbfounded and helpless but unharmed, were spectators of that tragedy. To make things worse, under the leadership of a resurrected Mussolini, Hitler imposed on us a new Fascist militia whose behavior was much rougher than the Germans' had been. They sneered at us and took advantage of the German presence and support to get revenge for having been ousted during the Badoglio interregnum. General Graziani, as the official Italian authority to represent the old Alliance, and Kesselring, who dispensed the death penalty freely, left us waiting helplessly for the next blow.

It took us some time to shake this sense of helplessness. When we did, however, we tried to make up for lost time. In our family, the focus was on Bona and myself. With no news of Bruno, Francesca became deeply depressed, refusing even the meager food we offered her.

While Umberto, Fulvio, Marcello, and the other young men of our building were in hiding, Neri was still recklessly moving around the city. Twice on September 24, he was hauled onto a German truck. Twice he escaped. When he arrived home the second time I forbade him to leave. He had received an official notice signed by a Fascist to report the next day to the *Servizio del lavoro* (labor office) which meant he'd be shipped off to Germany. For two days I walked all around Rome trying to find a hiding place for him.

Umberto and the boys, home briefly, sat with us around the dining room table discussing options. Neri could take to the countryside, joining those rebels called "partisans" who, it was said, had been seen in the mountains of Abbruzzo, east of Rome. But if they really existed, exactly where were they? Seeking them out would be dangerous. If he was captured by the Germans, he would certainly be executed. Another possible alternative would be hiding in a monastery or a church.

I investigated all of the religious institutions around. They were filled. The catacombs were reserved for important people like high-ranking prisoners of war or German deserters. Neri could be declared dead. But I hadn't been able to find a doctor who would sign his death certificate. I kept investigating the possibility of his working for victims of the war. I also harbored some hope of making him a member of the Order of Malta.

One night, an old friend from Merano, Comandante Prini, came to see us, now an important official in the new Fascist militia. While he was in the living room describing his Fascist hopes and asking for Neri to join him, we kept Neri locked in the bathroom and told Prini he was somewhere in northern Italy serving his country. We managed to entertain him through the evening without cutting our ties. We were still convinced that he was a good man at heart, although he could not explain to us why the Germans had stolen 40 tons of gold from the Banca d'Italia, attacked the mint, and taken truckload after truckload of tires.

The only relief I got was my teaching and some reading I did at night, often by candlelight, when everyone else was asleep. History seemed to flow from the past into the present as I read Croce's *History of Europe,* while the present took shape in strange ways – a booklet on Communism by Luciano Berra, applying Stalin's lay mystique to contemporary Catholicism, and Trotsky's *History of the Russian Revolution.*

Teaching was sheer pleasure, as was my wandering from home to home for my private tutoring.

Finally, in October, we had news of Bruno by way of friends. He was safe, near Fiume in Istria in the northeast, not far from Venice. He was, we felt, better off than we were, living as we were in a republic created by Mussolini with a Constituent Assembly that considered the Fascist party a state, while the Senate was dissolved and justice administered through special tribunals.

At night, when we were not confined to the shelter, as many as ten of us listened intently to Radio London, following the Eighth and the Fifth armies as they fought their way towards us from the southeast and the south. On the eastern front, the Russians were moving towards Leningrad. We were so deeply immersed in the war that we had forgotten what life in peacetime was like. I thought at times of my friend Hans Haller in Stalingrad, who was ready to die, he had written to me, if that would save us from Communism. I was ready to fight against Hitler, not because I was moved by conscience or a sense of duty, but because Hitler transgressed all human laws. I was ready to fight for survival. I was fed up with ideals. In my rare moments of "peace" I tried in vain to understand what had happened to us. I never looked to the future.

CHAPTER 9

The Germans – The Women's War

With the start of the liceo term on October 1, I slowly gained a new perspective. We discussed politics all the time, since a radical change had taken place in the academic community without our noticing it, a change not evident in my home community. Among my colleagues, there was as yet no indication of the collective rage and feelings of helplessness that overwhelmed us at home, provoked by the condition of Rome after the armistice. Still, the fall of Fascism on July 25 had given many of us at the liceo a gleam of hope that some kind of political change was possible.

Most of my colleagues openly declared themselves "anti-Fascist," a new word in our vocabulary, and looked to the Allies a liberators. Those who disagreed with the anti-Fascists did not exactly side with the Germans and the neo-Fascists. They stood aside, in silence. Many could not decide which direction to go. As for me, I stood against all slogans and empty rhetoric and simply distrusted all exaggerated forms of nationalism.

After October 1943, two Italies existed. From Rome to the Alps, Italy was a neo-Fascist republic with Mussolini as puppet premier and Kesselring as military ruler of Rome. The regions south of Rome lived under Allied auspices with Victor Emanuel III as king and General Badoglio as Premier. The area between Rome and Naples was a battlefield.

On October 3, King Victor Emanuel appealed to all Italians to resist the Germans. The night before he spoke, the Roman sky was lit by fireworks falling slowly towards us in multi-colored clusters, carried by the winds here and there like kites. Defying the curfew, we threw open our balcony and laughed like children enjoying a forbidden game. When we finally closed our windows, the sky over Ostia still on fire, we felt elated as never before. Those fires brightened our night. Slowly, we were perhaps learning what it meant to be free.

As those lights fell from the sky, suddenly the image of King Zog of Albania surfaced in my imagination. Where was King Zog now? Where was Vassili? Did they still believe in freedom?

Despite the abnormal conditions, Roman schools and the university operated as usual. I saw the carabinieri in regal uniform standing guard at the Tomb of the Unknown Soldier under a flag with the king's coat of arms ripped out. A week later, the Germans packed all the members of the corps into trucks and drove them north. How wise one carabiniere was — the day before, he had left his uniform in our bathroom and happily moved into the world dressed as a priest.

I continued to find refuge in my nightly reading and took to pondering the many questions of the day. I was puzzled by the difference between the Italians and the Russians in their reaction to the war. The Russians fought in self-defense. The Italians had been sent into battlefields by a war-besotted Mussolini. How could one expect us to organize a resistance like that of the Russians?

Usually my meditations were interrupted by sirens, Allied planes visiting us by night.

During the day, as the Allies fought to reach Rome, the family struggled with everyday problems. Perhaps what kept me going after September 1943 was the determination to preserve what I could of life around me — the members of my extended family and my students.

The Germans kept us in a state of fear. One day, a truck paused in front of me, a German soldier jumped off and grabbed two young boys who were walking nearby, hoisted them into the truck, and vanished. It reminded us of the way a vulture in the Alps would drop out of the sky to snatch a rabbit. It was so quick the boys couldn't let out a scream for help. Having seen this, I skipped my tutoring session and spent the afternoon answering questions from the parents of the boys, by then on their way to Germany.

That night, an order from Kesselring decreed deportation for anyone housing men called to service or caught listening to a foreign radio or reading a foreign paper. Another day, while watching the

Germans removing luggage from Stazione Termini, I saw some Fascist militiamen drag two young men out of a bar and load them into a German truck. Women circled the truck and tried to free the men. The Fascists shot in the air, pushed the women aside with the butts of their rifles, and rushed off.

"Cowards!" the women screamed, sitting helplessly on the sidewalk. I realized that Neri had to vanish immediately.

At home a soldier who had come to abandon his uniform in our bathroom informed us that some of the Italian army had withdrawn into the high mountains of the Central Alps. At night these former soldiers descended into the valleys to get food and help from the villagers. Some deserters had found shelter in the hills near Rome but they were difficult to reach because of the fighting in the Alban hills around the city and further south around Monte Cassino.

Some Germans seemed reluctant to act against us as harshly as they had been ordered to. After they deprived us of most means of transportation, including bicycles, I sat in one of the few surviving streetcars near a German officer who looked so miserable I was tempted to speak to him in German. Seeing the hatred all around him I thought better of it. A few days before, I was told, a German officer threw down his weapons in the St. Peter's Basilica screaming at the top of his lungs, "God, you are my witness that enough is enough. I can't stand it any longer!" Swiss guards spirited him into the Vatican.

Stories about the resistance in Naples worried us. We were told that some Italian sailors had barricaded themselves in the Admiralty (Palazzo dell' Ammiragliato). The Germans who were billeted in a mansion opposite it took a hundred civilians as hostages. For every German killed they killed a hostage.

Realizing in despair that I would not be able to protect Neri on my own, I decided to contact the National Liberation Front and offer them my collaboration in exchange for help. Before I could do anything, however, we learned the Germans had ordered the neo-Fascist government to pack up the Ministries (now Commissariats) and prepare to move north.

They would take along as many Italian men as they could.

Faced with this new emergency, Umberto found a way to be admitted to the University Clinic for Infectious Diseases. The day he left our building a joint German/Fascist patrol rushed into our neighborhood. Mamma and Signora Serafina, Umberto's mother, who had visited her son among children suffering from diphtheria, reported that he was sad and depressed. That very night we heard on Radio London that the British were 140 kilometers from Rome! Would the Germans declare a state of emergency before leaving? What would that mean for Neri and his friends? Would they kill them or take them along?

During the night of October 6, the SS — the most feared German unit — removed all of the men in the building next to ours. The most recent communication from the SS ordered Neri to present himself to a barracks. Early in the morning on October 7, I took Neri to the hospital on the Tiberine Island. Situated in a very picturesque location, the hospital was cheerful and almost cozy.

His leg in a cast, Neri lay on a bed in a room with three other men, all pretending to be accident victims. From his bed, he enjoyed a beautiful view of the Tiber while spending his days reading and talking. Either Bona or I would bring him meals, which he would share with his friends.

Neri was much better off than Umberto, to whom I also brought food. To reach the university clinic I crossed the section of the city that had been heavily bombarded in July and August. Houses were blown up, smashed, or cut in half. Piazza del Verano in front of the Roman Cemetery was itself a cemetery. When I entered the city of the sick, I felt even worse.

The people I encountered were shadows of those the bombs had missed. Slowly dying in pain and hunger, an army of phantoms lived in dirty crowded quarters, just waiting for death. The second day I visited Umberto, I knew what to expect and felt less depressed, although I was twice stopped by interminable funerals with four or five coffins each and crowds of moaning women.

Umberto, tall and lanky, was at his best when speaking in public, shy and withdrawn in private. Nervously walking among the cots of children suffering from diphtheria, he told me about his many frustrations as a victim of racial laws, his love for journalism and politics, his worries about the future of Italy, and his distrust of the political organizations that were growing around us. I listened without interrupting and promised to do my best to help him. He entrusted me with the manuscript of an article he had completed at the hospital. I promised him I would care for his mother as I cared for mine.

He laughed, "Do you realize my mother is Jewish?" Yes, I knew his mother was Jewish. So far, the Italians had refused to deliver the Jews to the Germans. Now that we were in German hands, however, we had to prepare for the worst.

Day after day, Bona and I wandered from hospital to hospital with food and messages. The food problem was worsening. Our private tutoring in Latin, Greek, History and Philosophy had been reduced to a trickle. By now, my only students were members of noble or affluent Roman families like the Lancellotti, the Serlupi, or the Marignoli. It was impossible to feed our men and ourselves on our two salaries. We took everything we owned to pawnshops, while Poldina established secret connections with blackmarketers. My Virgilio students, those who were still around, had become members of the family. One was courting Bona. They did whatever they could to get food.

Umberto had already found his way out of the hospital via his Vatican connections when I learned from Neri's doctor that the Germans were visiting other hospitals. Neri had to leave his hospital as soon as possible. With the help of my closest friend, Natalia Lancellotti, he found shelter in the labyrinthine underground of our parish church, the Church of the Nativity, in Via Gallia.

"Remember this is a temporary and unsafe shelter," the parish priest warned me every time I showed up with a bag of food for the refugees there. But finding Neri a permanent hiding place was my highest priority. Hope for a rapid liberation had faded because the Allies were stuck for months at Monte Cassino, halfway beween Naples and Rome. Nobody knew why. Some surmised that the Americans disagreed with the British, others insisted that the German army was much stronger than they had expected. We became resigned to living in a state of siege as prisoners of General Kesselring.

In Rome, every day of that cold winter of 1944 was more difficult than the preceding. What kept us going was our belief in the importance of Rome. How could the Allies turn their backs on Rome when they were just a few miles away? Meanwhile, we survived day by day, vaguely aware that there was an underground political organization. But those who had only insignificant contact with it, like myself, did not deem the group supportive of our efforts to survive. So we were not pleased when they committed subversive acts that put our own lives in peril.

§ § §

One day in late winter, I was tutoring a young Marchese Serlupi in his family's mansion in the center of the old city, when the German police blocked the entrance to our narrow street. In a nearby alleyway called via Rasella a bomb thrown from a building had killed thirty German soldiers about to enter a restaurant. Since no one claimed responsibility for the act, the Germans executed over three hundred Italians shortly thereafter. We were horrified and wept bitterly, even though we did not know any of them. The deed confirmed what we knew. Everyone was in danger.

One night Poldina awoke me in despair. The Germans were kidnapping Signora Serafina. Even before I entered her apartment, I heard the screams of *"Raus, raus!"* (Get out!) Three soldiers stood near the bed on which Signora Serafina was kneeling. They wanted her out in five minutes. Mamma, Francesca, and Bona stood near her, holding her hand and arguing with the Germans. Women around her joined hands in prayer, Mamma kept arguing, trying to learn the reasons for the soldiers' act of brutal violence, delaying it, hoping that something would change their minds. Francesca and Bona were busy packing the essentials for Signora Serafina to take with her.

I ran upstairs and called an emergency number at the Vatican. Umberto needed to be informed immediately, I said. Back in the apartment, I approached the soldiers. For a moment they seemed to listen.

We can confirm, assured them in my most courteous German, that the lady is not Jewish. There is a mistake.

One of them dug out a sheet with names on it and peevishly pointed to her name. It had a big yellow star next to it. *"Jude!"* he screamed in my face in a violent rage.

We all stood there for a moment frozen in horror.

"Jude!" he repeated, more quietly this time. Helpless, we trembled with rage. We knelt near Signora Serafina and dressed her as if she were already dead. Before dragging her away, the Germans cleared the room of all the women and children moaning in the background.

"Raus!" they roared and the crowd vanished down the stairs. By speaking calmly to the Germans, Mamma and I were allowed to accompany our friend down into a waiting truck. Once Signora Serafina was inside, the truck was sealed. Then we fell into each other's arms weeping. Without waiting for the end of the curfew I ran to Piazza di Spagna where I thought I would find Umberto. He wasn't there but I was assured he had been informed of his mother's fate and our Vatican friends were already in action.

The next day Signora Serafina returned to our apartment. She had "become" an Aryan and had the identification to prove it. That night, sleeping near Mamma, she wet her bed.

The horror of what had happened left us feeling utterly helpless. We desperately wanted to break through the walls of the city and scream our pain to the world.

§ § §

Two months had passed without news from Bruno. Francesca was by then five months pregnant. One night in November, a man in his thirties who looked gloomier than any deserter came to our door and asked to speak with her. He had been on an overloaded military ship with Bruno, he said, that sank not far from the Italian coast. He was one of the few who had survived.

Francesca listened without showing any emotion. I gave the soldier two blankets so he could sleep on the floor of our entrance hall, then joined Francesca in her bed. She was moaning silently. I tried to comfort her and convince her that Bruno was surely alive. The man couldn't know for sure. When a boat sinks, one worries about saving oneself, not about counting survivors. I kept talking to her until she fell asleep.

A week went by. Mamma tried to give Francesca hope with stories of men who, during the Great War, had been given up for dead and then reappeared years later, very much alive. But we knew that her brother Damiano had never made it back from the Russian front.

Not a day went by without news of someone caught by the Germans, tortured, deported, or shot. We had worked out a scheme by which, at the first sign of a raid, Neri would escape by way of the roof into the next building. As for Bruno, there was nothing we could do but pray. Perhaps he was better off, we told Francesca, wherever he was than caged up in Rome. The last we had heard, he was in Fiume. Maybe he was safely with the Yugoslav partisans. Francesca was horrified. "No!" she screamed, "Not that!"

Late one night in the depth of the winter, while we were all asleep, Poldina came into the room I shared with Francesca.

"Someone is downstairs," she whispered, "trying to get in."

Francesca heard this and thought immediately that it was Bruno. She ran downstairs and threw open the door. A gaunt Bruno, famished and shivering with cold, fell into her arms. The story he told was not like any of Mamma's stories of the survivors of World War I. Stories of survivors, he laughed, are all different and all the same. What matters is the ending. Bruno who was taciturn by nature had suddenly become talkative.

"One more mouth to feed," Poldina complained the next day when Bruno showed up for lunch, but the family was happy to be together again. The meal of two small barely edible baguettes, boiled herbs mixed with squash, and a few chestnuts was as usual divided in two. The biggest portion went to Francesca who was seven months pregnant, the rest was divided equally among the six of us, five members of the family plus Marcello, a friend Neri had brought along when, after the episode of via Rasella, they had been evicted from the Church of the Nativity. Nobody dared complain. With secret connections in the Resistance, Marcello turned out to be very useful to us.

However, our main problem was not the lack of food but the Gestapo checking every building. By this time, no Italian adult male could justify being in Rome unless he had papers to show that he was a worker for a German organization like the Todt. After a long family discussion, I was assigned to get papers for Neri and Bruno. I had no idea where to begin and was terrified of the Gestapo. Yet I was proud of having been chosen and of Bona offering to help. Mamma and Francesca were both more worried than excited, but Neri, Marcello, and Bruno urged me on, sure that I would succeed.

With some advice from Marcello, I set out to find an under-ground organization that could produce the needed documents. Since I had lost contact with the National Liberation Front, I approached the Communist organization Umberto had introduced me to while he was in the hospital. But I had no luck with them either. I remember my meeting with them in October. I entered the room discreetly and found a meeting in full swing, the first political meeting I had ever attended. The leader was a tall, thin man with small, deep-set eyes, under an aquiline nose, and bony hands. He reported that they had agreed to get rid of the monarchy. What stuck in my mind, however, was not the issue in question, since the neo-Fascists had already acted by creating their Republic of Italy, but the recurrence in the speech of the word "power," as in "power of the right," "power of the left," "power of the center." While the word made me worry, another recurring phrase, "De Gasperi in power," was reassuring.

De Gasperi was still, I assumed, the Secretary of the Vatican Library and a friend of the family. To hear members of the underground refer to that modest, witty gentleman as the future arbiter of power in Italy suggested to me that power could be used not only against us, as Mussolini used it or Kesselring. Power could also work for us.

I also recalled my humiliation at that meeting, when two young men my age took active part in the discussion, while I remained silent, uneasy, feeling out of place. When someone, finally, addressed me as the typist for Dr. Bruni, all I could say was that I was nobody's typist and would never be.

"I teach Latin and Greek," I stated proudly and even the most somber of those Communists burst out laughing. What did that have to do with them, they wanted to know. Holding back tears of anger, I explained I was a representative sent by Umberto, of the Christian Socialists, about whom, I added humbly, I knew absolutely nothing. I was angry with myself but mostly with Umberto for having launched me unprepared into a political meeting.

In a later conversation with Dr. Bruni, the leader of the group, I got a better understanding of the nature and purpose of the many political parties that had blossomed during the forty days of Badoglio's tenure. Where was I during that important period in the history of Italy, Dr. Bruni inquired. "In Sperlonga," I replied. He looked at me pensively, "And what were you doing in Sperlonga?"

"I was with my family," I answered candidly, surprised by the question. "We swam and ate."

Although disappointed that I hadn't broken through Rome's Walls on a useful mission, he accepted my political naiveté as a matter of fact. His somber face broke into a brief smile, and he finally dismissed me with an oracular statement, "Rome will be ruined by its stubborn political ignorance.

Remembering the humiliation of that first meeting with the Communists, I didn't approach them again. I lacked the political credentials to ask for a favor. Marcello, aware of my difficulties, turned to his own party, whatever it was. They had what we needed, the stamps of the Todt organization to be used on passes for Neri and Bruno. In return, Marcello said, Bona and I were expected to contribute to their cause by encouraging German soldiers to desert.

Bona was given nails to spread on the main streets of Rome where German trucks often crossed the city. I was entrusted with a more delicate task, to approach the Germans when they were busy fixing their flat tires and urge them to desert. Most of the Italian army had deserted. Helping Italian soldiers desert had become one of our main activities. Why not help Germans as well? Marcello assured us that, if they left the front with supplies and arms, they would be taken care of by the underground organization that provided the fake identity cards.

Bona and I would have liked clearer details on how to deal with the German deserters, but Marcello, having gotten his passport to freedom, had left for parts unknown. With Neri and Bruno safe, Bona and I felt free again. Once in a while, mindful of the promise we had made to Marcello and his mysterious organization, Bona spread nails on Via dei Trionfi and Via dell'Impero, the broadest thoroughfare from the south. When these succeeded, I would strike up a conversation with a German soldier fixing his truck.

I would first study the soldiers from a distance. Deciding whom to approach was tricky, given the great difference between Italian and German soldiers. The armistice had created the ideal conditions for an Italian soldier to desert. But the Germans generally did not trust Italians. Those who came through Rome were not allowed to speak with Italians. The consequences of desertion were also very serious. German deserters who were caught were shot after summary trial. Their Italian accomplices were also shot.

Bona and I made our first attempt in a nonchalant way, like two schoolgirls on holiday. We approached four soldiers with a truck near the Colosseum. They were fat, jovial, and laughing while they fixed a flat, the result, we hoped, of Bona's nails. We approached them, trying to match their mood, as if there was no war. We talked of everything under the sun except desertion. They told us all about their homes. Two of them came from the vicinity of Munich. One, named Hans, was the owner of a Bier-Keller and he looked it. He seemed to prefer Bona to me.

Against all the rules, we exchanged addresses. One of them even had a visiting card, a rarity in those days. What a mistake, Bona and I agreed later. We hadn't discussed desertion yet, Bona reminded me, and we sighed with relief. Two weeks later, Hans called from the outskirts of Rome. He had half a lamb for us. We thanked him and sent Poldina out to get the unexpected and very welcome gift, which we shared with the neediest people in our building. No desertion was in sight, but at that point we didn't care.

Unfortunately, other encounters with German soldiers followed. Some took place near our building, in the immediate vicinity of Porta Metronia. Although we kept our address a secret, we were not careful enough to deny that we lived in the neighborhood. We went through the "operation" a couple of times without giving our names or address and hoping no soldier would show up.

One day in mid-March, however, we were faced with what we should have expected. It hit us like lightning out of a clear sky.

As usual, it was Poldina who sounded the alarm, shortly after midnight. "The Germans! The Germans!" she shouted. As I jumped out of bed and, dragging a sleepy Bona, staggered into the entrance hall, what startled me was Poldina's voice. Sometimes she cried wolf but that night the danger clearly was real. Her round black pupils reflected stark fear. Her lips trembled. Her alarm was more frightening than an American bombardment.

Our men were at home with their false identity cards; the Germans had come to arrest them. Why hadn't I tried to hide them away from home, at least in a cellar! Home was a trap. Maybe Marcello had been caught and tortured and had talked. Or maybe the Gestapo had caught the man who made the false Todt identity cards and so had come to arrest us all.

The small entry hall was crowded. Mamma and Francesca, wearing only nightgowns, stood surrounded by five soldiers. All were peevishly listening to Mamma who was interrogating them as if she had come to arrest them. The one among the soldiers who spoke German acted as interpreter for the others who, I learned later, were Czechs. After a while, Francesca took Mamma's place. Her German was better and her questions more focused. All five soldiers were mere boys, barely 18 years old. They had come directly from the front bringing with them a truck loaded with weapons, rice, cigarettes — everything they had been told the partisans exacted to support them as deserters until the war ended and, God willing, they could return home.

Francesca addressed her questions to the one who spoke German though with a thick accent, Sergeant Kheminski, a Pole.

"Which partisans contacted you? Who precisely told you to desert and under what conditions? Who gave you our address?"

"The teacher!" he promptly replied.

"Which teacher? Francesca pressed on.

Sergeant Kheminsky pointed at me. Both Mamma and Francesca turned to me, dumbfounded. There was a moment of silence and then an intense attack in Italian, Mamma and Francesca both loudly upbraiding me. They spoke almost in unison with a vehemence justified by the difficult situation in which those five soldiers had placed the whole family. I tried to remind them that I, and Bona with me, had acted in good faith and with the full consent of the family.

"What consent?" Francesca shouted.

I responded with controlled rage. Did they think I got the identity cards for Bruno and Neri because of my good looks? I had to give something in return. That something was helping the soldiers to desert, and bringing weapons and food to the partisans. We had spared Francesca and Mamma the risks. Bruno and Neri were fully aware of the dangers involved.

Bruno and Neri had escaped to the terrace, ready to jump from there into the next building if Poldina gave them a signal. But Poldina did not budge from the hall. Being more in control of these unexpected developments, she had brought out five chairs for the Germans to sit on while they waited for us women to decide their fate.

Poldina was the first to realize we had to focus on those five soldiers. Since we could not send them back to the front and could not keep them with us, we had to find a hiding place for them. We reminded ourselves that those "Germans" were really victims of the Germans; they were citizens of countries overrun by the Germans. They were legitimate deserters, like our own men, and it was our moral duty to help them.

I tried, in vain, to phone Marcello, the key to the mysterious organization. Next in line was Umberto. Poldina summoned him from his mother's apartment. He told us that Marcello's organization could not take responsibility for the deserters.

I was stunned and asked what I could do with five deserters. I could sell the food they had brought on the black market and use the money to support them. But just doing that would be a tremendous task. And what about the weapons and the truck? Umberto suggested that once I had found them a hiding place, the organization would take care of the rest.

What followed was a frantic series of proposals, all rejected. While the family argued with Umberto, Mamma took me into her room. She was dismayed, she told me, that I didn't even know the name of the organization that engaged me in such a risky enterprise. Didn't I realize that the lives of those five soldiers depended on us? If they were caught and shot, it would be on our conscience. Was I ready, when I accepted the task, to sacrifice those five in order to save Bruno and Neri? She always suspected that Marcello could not be trusted. Umberto was different, but he didn't seem to carry much weight in Marcello's organization.

She spoke softly, without anger, more to herself than me. Upset by her unexpected rebuke, I told her the whole story. Sometime in early March, Bona and I had found their truck parked near the Walls. I suggested desertion to them and all five agreed enthusiastically. Evidently, they felt cut off from both the army in which they were forced to serve and the country whose language and people they didn't know. I told Mamma that I knew it was hard for her to understand. I, myself, only now understood the reason they had accepted my proposal to desert.

"Of course, I understand," Mamma interrupted with feeling. "I understand, because I witnessed the tragedy of their fathers in my own village in the first war. They were all there, Poles and Czechs and Hungarians and Croats and Serbs, camped in our village, ready to be shoveled onto a battlefield. I lived with them during their fearful hours before they were sent to their deaths. Your father taught the villagers, who were all against the war, not to hate them, because they were more miserable than we were. He called them the real victims of the war."

Bona called us back to the entrance hall. We had to decide before dawn.

"Call Maria Romana De Gasperi," Mamma suggested. Maria Romana and her family are fighting for survival just as we are. Besides, the Vatican seems to help everyone in danger no matter of what race or army.

I called and spoke to Maria Romana, the eldest of De Gasperi's four daughters. I explained briefly, but forcefully, our duty to help "the rest of Europe enslaved by the Germans." Here, this very night, in our own apartment, there was an opportunity, but we needed help.

Everybody listened spellbound as I spoke and then waited anxiously for the reaction. Maria Romana said she needed to think about it. She would call back.

When the telephone rang, the five deserters held their breath. Maria Romana had called the nuns and had arranged for them to be hidden in the Catacombs of Santa Priscilla. We sighed with relief — but only for a moment. What about the truck? Would the nuns take over the truck with the weapons and the rest? Maria Romana laughed. Evidently not. Umberto volunteered to take care of all that.

To reach the catacombs of Santa Priscilla we had to cross the whole city. I had a curfew permit so I was assigned to sit between the two soldiers up front and guide the truck to its destination. Umberto would ride with the other soldiers in the back of the truck. The ride was uneventful. When I spotted a German, I would crouch under the wheel.

The nuns were courteous and matter-of-fact. Evidently, they were used to this. They would provide shelter and civilian clothes for the soldiers, but they expected us to help them with food. I assured them there was enough food on the truck to feed their guests for the rest of the war. They smiled incredulously. The war would go on forever, they said. One of the nuns added that our soldiers would be in good company. There were German deserters as well as Allied prisoners and eminent Jews. She seemed to take pride in the mixture.

Lucifer was setting in all its splendor in a pearly sky, when I returned to the truck. But the truck had vanished. Relieved that Umberto, whom I fully trusted, had taken care of it, I slowly began my long walk back home, happily free of responsibility.

Nobody in the family had gone back to bed. In silence, we shared boiled water with a bit of chicory before I left for school. Life went on, day after day as usual. We were anxiously awaiting Easter. The believers among us hoped to gain some strength from Christ's death and resurrection. I was among those who believed in the power of our beloved dead. So I prayed for them as I walked home from the liceo.

We had almost forgotten about the five German deserters, when they all showed up one day dressed as civilians, asking for food, but we had none for them. Bona and I gave them our five-day ration of bread and begged our students for help. But the American bombardments had created a barrier that only a few dared to cross. Rome was a city under siege. The deserters, however, were hungry. They didn't speak Italian, they reminded us. How could they ask for food? Would we please keep our promise?

Bona and I gave them food for the day, but they were still hungry. I explained to the sergeant that they should not depend on us to feed them; they should contact Umberto and Marcello. They told us that someone had taken care of them for a while, after the nuns had sent them away because of lack of food. They had been given Todt identity cards and an apartment. For the rest, they were told they were on their own.

At Easter, we looked for the five deserters to share with them whatever we had, but we couldn't find them. As time passed, I feared the Gestapo had caught them. Umberto had vanished with the truck. I never saw him again. I was terrified when someone in our building reported that on Easter Monday the Gestapo had arrested an elementary school teacher in the building across from ours. They released her the next day. She wasn't the "right teacher," someone joked.

"There is still justice even in the world of the Germans!" was Poldina's comment.

Although we didn't talk about it, we all worried that the deserters had been captured. Bona and I lived in fear and hunger, more fear than hunger. Being in a permanent state of fear made me feel less hungry.

April days were long, the evenings peaceful. Rome was as beautiful as when I had seen it for the first time with Bruno in May 1939. On a serene April evening, after dinner, Bona and I took a walk through the park of Villa Celimontana adjacent to our home. The air smelled of wisteria, the birds fluttered among Roman pines and myrtles, but all we could think of or talk about was food, no matter of what kind, just food, something to fill our empty stomachs. We talked also about freedom, freedom from fear and hunger, freedom from family obligations, freedom from everything that seemed to have taken over our lives, and finally freedom from despair. We yearned for a reason to hope. Rome had become a prison.

The next day, we walked to work as usual, through the ruins of the Baths of Caracalla and along the Tiber. It would have been an ideal walk under ordinary circumstances. Every morning, Bona tutored children of the branch of the Lancellotti whose mansion was between Piazza Navona and the river. We would part at the Virgilio.

My first class moved painfully slowly. The students were hungry and sleepy, and so was I. My second class, the third and last year of the liceo, required concentration. We were reviewing Euripides's *Alcestis* for the state exam. Half the boys were absent fearing a German raid. When the custodian, an old Roman from Trastevere who loved me dearly, entered the classroom without knocking, I knew instinctively the Germans were in the building.

His pale wrinkled face betrayed the news.

"Where are they? Who are they looking for?" I whispered.

"In the president's office" he answered. "Four of them. They are looking for you."

He handed me a note scribbled in a hurry by the president, "You must leave the building through the courtyard and then move immediately to the house in Piazza Navona."

I had hardly glanced through it when the old man snatched the note from me, chewed it slowly and swallowed it. My students and I stood for a moment dumbfounded. I climbed through the window into a courtyard with three of my students, who knew the labyrinth of old Rome much better than I did. We avoided via Giulia, fearing that German soldiers would be there, and went through back alleys of ancient Papal Rome. We reached Piazza Navona, quietly basking in the April sun.

Natalia Massimo Lancellotti was waiting for me at the main gate of her home. She was my closest friend, my age, intense and quick in mind and movement. She had a beautiful face with bright blue eyes and shiny black hair. We embraced and quickly decided on a plan of action. It was Natalia who, alerted by Bona, her cousins' tutor, had contacted the headmaster of the Virgilio. In a quick note, Natalia had asked the headmaster to help me escape from his liceo and meet her at her home on Piazza Navona. Bona, she assured me, would join us shortly. The Gestapo, we surmised, must have gotten to the Virgilio at almost the same time as Natalia's messenger.

Bona arrived, and we dispatched the students to check my home at Porta Metronia and report back to us about the situation there. Natalia's mother, the elderly Belgian Princess de Merode, and her husband, the stately patriarch, were waiting for us in her bedroom. The shutters closed, Natalia, Bona, the prince, and I surrounded the princess in a twilight atmosphere evoking the past, to decide how to manage this problem.

The princess was lying uncomfortably on a sofa. Bona, pale but composed, repeated what she had told Natalia earlier. She had called home, as she usually did during the morning to make sure nothing unusual had happened, and was surprised to hear a German voice. The voice informed her that her mother had been badly hurt in a serious accident and wanted to see her two daughters as soon as possible. Bona had silently put down the receiver.

We waited in silence. Then the Prince began to speak, looking off into the distance. He said there should be no doubt in anyone's mind that the deserters had been caught and probably tortured and had told what they knew. So, the Gestapo had identified me and probably also Bona as accomplices. Nobody could predict how the Gestapo would treat Italians who helped German soldiers to desert. But presumably the accused would be allowed to offer a defense.

The situation was clear. The Germans, the prince declared, held the high cards. They had taken over our home during our absence expecting to find our two men, themselves deserters, with an old lady and a young woman about to give birth. Bona and I were now to become their hostages. In practical terms, we had two options. We could disappear, that is, hide in the attic of the Lancellotti mansion, joining Italian deserters until the Allies arrived. Or we could march right into the mouth of the wolf.

He looked directly at me. If we chose to hide, the Germans would probably arrest Bruno and Neri, who had the same fake Todt identity cards as the deserters. Our men would presumably be punished for their own crime. The German who had taken over our home was well aware of the likely consequences of that arrest for poor Francesca and Mamma.

If I gave myself up, it would be up to me to try to explain the human reasons for our action and so lessen the gravity of our transgression. Of course I would have to avoid, even under torture, naming any accomplice. Mentioning a name would betray the trust people had placed on me.

He had complete confidence in me, he said; in fact, he couldn't think of anyone who could manage this better. It would be facilitated by what Machiavelli called the concrete reality of facts. Both he and his daughter Natalia were certain that I had no idea of the name and whereabouts of the organization which had manufactured the fake cards and presumably sponsored the deserters. If I had known anything, I would surely have turned to the organization for help when the deserters showed up. But my ignorance would save me, because the source of the fake identity cards was the only possible item of interest to the Germans. A few more deserters hardly mattered, given the present military situation. The Allies were advancing rapidly. People said that General Clark had decided to get to Rome as soon as possible.

He knew from German sources within the Vatican that the Germans had no alternative but to give up Rome and open a new front. Of course, he added as an afterthought, we were all in the hands of God ____ and of Churchill who might pressure the Americans to land in Normandy instead of Italy. Then we would all be lost. The prince's vision of where Bona and I stood had the beneficial effect of shielding me from the shock of recent events. As I listened to him and reason began to take precedence over emotion, I developed a plan which would let me survive within my community of family and friends.

My defense, the prince continued, if I was allowed a defense, should focus on the basic humanitarian reason for our action. It was not an act of rebellion against the German army, but rather of compassion for soldiers who were exhausted, and it was inspired by our own longing, after four years of war, for peace and normalcy.

As for Neri and Bruno, they were victims of the armistice, as were thousands of other Italians. They had the merit of having opted for neutrality instead of joining the partisans.

Rehearsing my defense generated the faith I needed in myself. While the Prince was speaking, I felt what a firefighter must feel at the moment of entering a fire. To face the fire I would need faith and hope that I could make it out alive. With fine intuition the prince added an ironic touch: although nobody could guarantee Bona and me a safe exit, we had no reason to believe the Germans would sentence us to death or torture us. In the worst case, he surmised, they might send us to a concentration camp — but concentration camps were in Germany, which could not be reached from Rome at the moment. And he believed Rome would soon be liberated. Nonetheless, he assured us that his own family and other old families in Rome would support us before the German authorities.

Having decided to give myself up, I begged Bona to hide in the Lancellotti's attic, but she declared that she would share my fate. Natalia would accompany us home to offer the Germans assurance of our exemplary behavior as citizens of Rome.

Meanwhile, my students returned. Downstairs, they met Poldina, who had escaped from the bathroom through the roof. She told them what had happened. As usual (the students commented) what she did not see she made up. The Gestapo entered the apartment and one man went straight to the telephone. Two other soldiers pointed their guns at Bruno and Neri and ordered them to the back of the dining room, near the balcony. A fourth soldier examined their papers. He questioned Neri in a low voice so as not to disturb the one by the telephone. (Poldina could understand some German.)

Mamma was standing erect, answering the German officer's questions in a gentle but calm voice. After a coarse opening, he seemed to have fallen under Mamma's spell. She didn't know where her two daughters were, she said. What did they do? They taught all over the city. In what subject? Mainly Latin and Greek, but also other subjects. The officer smiled.

Near Mamma, Francesca, crying, was praying aloud, *"Requiem aeternam dona ei domine."*

"What are you talking about?" the German asked Francesca. "She is saying the Latin prayer for the dead," Mamma quietly responded.

He laughed rudely. "Your sisters are not dead yet, although they might be soon." (Poldina stressed this comment.)

"She is praying for her father not for her sisters," Mamma corrected him. "He died long ago when they were babies. But he is here right now with us today."

Just then the telephone rang and Francesca started to cry. Mamma looked at her with concern and then turned to the German.

"She should have a chair!" she said in a firm voice.

"Certainly," he answered with a grin. His eyes shone with victory, as he answered the telephone.

"Your mother," he said, "is unconscious." He pronounced each word slowly. "You must come home immediately if you want to see her alive."

About ten minutes passed in silence. One of the soldiers had brought up two chairs, one for Francesca, one for Mamma. Suddenly, the telephone rang again.

"No," the German told the caller, "Your mother is unconscious. She wants to see you. Aren't you her eldest daughter?"

He smiled as he replaced the phone and mumbled something in German which Poldina did not understand. At precisely that moment, Francesca fell to the floor. Mamma poured a glass of water, sat with Francesca on the floor, and helped her drink it slowly, while rocking her gently and whispering in a strange language.

At that point, Poldina quietly fled through the bathroom window and the terrace into the next building. She wanted to reach the Lancellotti, she said, but first she had to see what had happened to the family.

§ § §

When we arrived at our home, I was relieved that Natalia spoke to the German officer without fear.

"There must be an error," she said in fluent, elegant German. "These two young ladies, close friends of mine and of my family, are law-abiding citizens." She then introduced herself as Army nurse Princess Natalia Massimo-Lancellotti. She was undoubtedly hoping to impress the German officer with her titles. He shook hands with her like a comrade.

Then, looking her in the eye, he said, "My dear princess, it is not up to you to decide the guilt or innocence of your lady friends. I am here on duty. While we talk, our soldiers are fighting and dying a few miles from here, as you well know. I am here to protect their interests and," he added with sarcasm, "Germany's interest in a country that has chosen to fight this war with us to the finish. I am here to investigate the matter further. So far, however, I have clear evidence that your two honorable friends have violated military law. They have encouraged some of our soldiers to desert and leave the battlefield with valuable military material. Judge for yourself!"

At that, without waiting for her reaction, he pushed her aside and took hold of Bona and me. He ordered a soldier to handcuff us. Francesca freed herself from Mamma's arms and jumped towards the German in an attempt to stop him. He shoved her violently aside and forced us out of the apartment.

§ § §

The thought of Francesca and her baby weighed heavily on both Bona and me as we left the apartment. The pain we had caused her and Mamma was worse than any fear or humiliation. We could read that pain in their eyes. The hardest thing was to be cut off from the family.

Afterwards, neither of us could recall a single detail of what happened between our house at Porta Metronia and the prison in Via Tasso. We had become numb the moment we were taken away. What woke me up in the darkness in which we were plunged was a woman's voice.

"I am Neva," she said. "What's your name?"

Since I didn't answer right away, she went on.

"I keep busy counting the days. I have been rotting in this cell for five months and two days. I have never been interrogated. I have never learned why they arrested me. What about you?"

The warmth of this human being brought me back to earth. With both arms around Bona, I asked Neva to guide me to a place where we could sit down. Neva was delighted to help. Her eyes were accustomed to the darkness. Lying on a blanket on the floor, Bona and I finally burst out crying as we told Neva our story. We cried about the family we had left behind.

Neva guessed that by showing up at home we had saved Neri and Bruno, who by now were probably free. They should be thankful for what we had done for them. That thought had never occurred to us, and we felt grateful to Neva. We stopped crying. Then she told us all about where we were — an apartment building that had been converted into a prison. Once a day, a soldier would give us a loaf of German bread and water; hours later, another would bring some soup.

There was no way to know the time of day, or what day it was, except by asking the soldiers, and they spoke only German, a language none of the women spoke except Neva, who knew a few words. Twice a day we were allowed to go to the bathroom escorted by a soldier. Most of the women in the cell were rarely called for interrogation. Nobody could explain why she had been arrested.

"We must be careful," Neva warned, adding bitterly, "Lucky are those who are called. It means that the Germans are interested in them, in which case they disappear, sent to either a concentration camp or another prison, nobody knows exactly where. Some are actually freed. Yet, to be freed you have to go through an interrogation and I have never had one," she concluded.

Neva was an actress from Trieste. "I am a Slovene," she stated proudly, sure that this was better than being an Italian. I waited for some light to see what she looked like. I imagined her blond and beautiful, and so she was. Among our fellow prisoners, she mentioned a descendant of Giuseppe Garibaldi who had liver trouble and at times moaned for hours; a prostitute who entertained those wanting to hear her lurid tales; a nun who led the rosary every night for those who wanted to pray; a mother worried about her children at home; and a gypsy in a colorful costume who predicted the future every day for anyone willing to listen. The gypsy, she said, was the least disagreeable.

"Forget about the rest. You'll be better off in the end," she concluded and I wondered if the long months of forced cohabitation were the cause of her bitterness. When I got to know the rest of the members of my new family I didn't find them as bad as she had made them out. That first evening, I hardly listened to her, because Bona was burning with fever. I got up from the floor and violently shook the door of the cell.

A woman laughed loudly, "This new guest thinks she's in a hotel."

I waited patiently leaning against the door. When I finally heard the stomp of heavy boots I whispered a call for help as sweetly as I could in German. Almost immediately the door was opened slightly and behind a huge shadow I saw a beam of light. I told the soldier in German of Bona's fever. Not long afterwards, he brought a cup of coffee and a couple of aspirins. His name was Heinrich. After that, we felt lucky when Heinrich was on duty. I got help for Signora Garibaldi and permission to go to the bathroom for urgent cases. I became the interpreter for my friends in misery.

Heinrich had been a fur merchant in Berlin. The English bombs destroyed his house and store and killed some members of his family. His wife and children were now somewhere in East Germany. After a few days, Heinrich showed me pictures of a handsome boy in school uniform and a plump little girl under a tree in flower. I told him about Merano's orchards and for a while we experienced some peace and normality. We were both fed up with the war.

On the night after our arrest, I had my first interrogation. What I recall is an intense light shining harshly in my eyes and the officer's metallic voice. The two together upset me. With much effort, I finally recalled the reasons I had planned to offer in my defense. As the interrogation went on, I stuck to my story of basic hatred for war and said that love for those who had been forced to fight had led to my transgression.

I had carefully memorized what the interrogator had said to Natalia before he had me handcuffed. I recognized my transgression of a military law. I stuck to my humanitarian reason as my basic motive and I thought I succeeded in conveying my feelings sincerely and passionately by keeping my eyes shut against the blinding light and by ignoring the metallic voice that cut into my very being.

Surprisingly, after a series of questions and answers, the German officer allowed me to speak without interruption. I spoke passionately what I truly believed. When I finally opened my eyes, I realized that the officer had shut off the blinding light and was listening quietly, like an ordinary human being. The interpreter was gone. There was a phone call and my interrogator left the room.

Back in the cell, Bona fell into my arms crying. Neva warned me not to reveal anything of what had gone on. Not everybody could be trusted! When I summarized the meeting, she commented, "So far not bad." There was room for some positive developments. I was encouraged.

At the second interrogation, the officer focused on ferreting out the source of the Todt seals used on the cards, just as the prince had predicted. On the basis of my earlier testimony, he tried to make me feel guilty by accusing me of irresponsibility, saying that acting without any support from a responsible organization was tantamount to leading those poor young boys to a firing squad.

I did not react, so he elaborated the details of their imminent death, insisting that they would have never thought of deserting had I not encouraged them. Then, taking advantage of the fact that I was upset, he brusquely moved to a completely different subject. He couldn't believe that a sensitive and cultured woman like me would let herself blunder into such an enterprise without knowing precisely where to turn when the soldiers showed up. My reaction was instantaneous and vigorous.

All my anxiety vanished; I recalled verbatim the passionate defense the Prince had suggested. I envisioned the five of us in the dark room at Piazza Navona. The Prince's inspiring words had radically changed me. From that moment on, I saw clearly that my duty was not only to my family but also to society.

I did not know how the Todt seal had been copied, nor had I ever been interested in it. What inspired me to help the five Polish and Czech soldiers desert with the truckload of food and weapons was my hatred of war, every kind of war. I spoke of how I had interpreted the armistice as the inevitable reaction of people tired of war; those deserters did not even speak German. I spoke of Neri and Bruno, who had chosen neutrality. Of my obstinate search for ways to hide them so they wouldn't be deported to Germany. But mainly I insisted on my instinctive hatred for war, war in all its aspects, a hatred I may have inherited from my father. In fact, my interrogator now lowered the lights so that I could open my eyes.

He listened and did not ask me for any names. Had he asked, I would surely have avoided mentioning anyone who had helped me — Marcello, Umberto, the Prince, Maria Romana De Gasperi, or the nuns of Santa Priscilla. I don't know how I would have reacted if he had tortured me or tricked me into revealing names by threatening to harm members of my family. But he never did.

As the Prince had predicted, he must have realized that his army was retreating and was abandoning Rome. In any case, what made me useless to my captors was my political naiveté. He focused on the source of the Todt seal; nothing else seemed to matter. He also volunteered the information that the deserters had in fact mentioned it, but I didn't believe him.

"Yes," he said contemptuously, "in that case those four poor boys would not be shot and you and your sister would not be sent to a concentration camp."

With that he sent me back to my cell. Clearly what lay ahead of us was a concentration camp in Germany, about which, fortunately, I had no knowledge whatever.

Back in the cell, Neva, hearing my report and thinking of other cases she had heard of during her months in prison, concluded that he was hinting at the SS's decision about our crime. What would save us would be the Allies capturing Rome. We rejoiced together every night as we heard the bombs exploding over our building. We would either die or be liberated. But I was tormented by worries about the likely fate of the deserters.

Bona had never been interrogated. Like many other women, she was allowed to leave her cell during the morning to shake out her blankets. During the following weeks, I was not called either. Neva commented sourly, "They've lost interest in your case. Now only a miracle can help you."

Neva taught me some useful exercises. She also taught me some English in exchange for my teaching her some German.

"English will soon be the universal language," she whispered. "Lucky are those who can greet the Allies in their own tongue."

She was obsessed with the presence of spies among us. "The Communists," she kept repeating, "could ruin Italy and the whole of Europe."

To avoid thinking about the deserters, Bona and I asked the gypsy to predict our future. We also listened to the prostitute's lurid tales. At night we recited the rosary with the nun and we consoled Signora Garibaldi when she had painful attacks. Our best hours, however, were thinking and talking about our family. We talked of Papa's mysterious past and of the equally mysterious romantic relationship of Papa and Mamma when they lived wholly separate lives, of their longing for each other through the Great War, of the years Papa spent in a concentration camp. In our prison, Mamma's war suddenly became very real to us, though it was a different kind of reality from our own.

We dreamt of our two grandmothers about whom Mamma had often spoken, one an Austrian peasant, religious and conservative, the other an Italian Baroness, agnostic and liberal. I had met Papa's mother only in her coffin, a wrinkled mummy's face with a rose in her hair; Mamma's mother instead I knew as an old, gigantic, senile woman with just one long wiggly tooth. According to Mamma, both had lived the intense life of love and heroic sacrifice; while one was very poor and the other wealthy, they nonetheless shared both joys and pains. Both had miraculously survived their war, but each had suffered from war. I don't know why we thought of them in prison. I guess we longed to get our minds off the deserters and our responsibility for their fate. We never mentioned them.

§ § §

One day the German officer summoned me to his office. He handed me a sheaf of papers in Italian and asked me to summarize aloud their contents for him in German. The papers dealt with deserters from the front as reported by Mussolini's neo-Fascists. Another time, he handcuffed me and took me out in his car. I was terrified at the thought of what might happen to me. He took me to the official Italian prison, *Regina Coeli* — the name means Queen of Heaven — on the Tiber, not far from the Virgilio. I was also terrified by the prospect of being separated from Bona. I begged him to leave me where I was. He laughed. "You'll stay where you are," he assured me, "at least for the time being."

At *Regina Coeli*, he made me interpret for an Italian prisoner who appeared to be as badly off as I was. He was pale and thin, and I hardly recognized him as a student I had known at the university. I was numb. Perhaps he was better off than I was. On the way back, I got up enough nerve to ask the Hauptsturmführer, as he was called, about Francesca and her baby. Smiling, he assured me that they were well, guests of that princess who seemed to be so attached to me.

"How do you manage to befriend high-class people in Rome being a foreigner, a German from the South-Tyrol?" he asked in a bemused way. "We have been besieged by princes and princesses asking that we free you." He laughed when I answered that my passport was my tutoring, mainly in Latin and Greek. He wished he knew some Latin, he said, speaking for the first time like a human being. I was moved and thought, for a moment, that there might be some hope for us.

Neva and Bona relaxed when they saw me back in the cell. A first, they thought I had been sent off to a concentration camp. There were also other reasons for hope. The bombardments were more and more frequent. No new prisoners had joined us in our cell. The officer's activities suggested that the Germans were emptying the prison, Neva surmised, and she was right. One day, Bona and I and four other women in the cell, Neva included, were allowed to leave the cell to work, cleaning and translating. A week later, we were allowed to sleep at home and report to the prison every morning at 6 a.m. For several evenings in succession, the German officer himself accompanied Bona and me home.

The family was terrified by his appearance at our home. What did he want from us? I summoned up my courage and asked him.

"Nothing," he said, "I want nothing else but your company. I have been alone for years. I want to come back to Rome after the war." These were to be his last days in Rome, he added. He closed our case shortly before he was transferred, as part of the army SS, to Stalingrad. We were surprised at his attitude, to say the least.

We were all surprised by everything he said. We listened as if in a dream. Before he left, he smiled and turned to Mamma, speaking as if he were alone with her. "You shouldn't worry," he said. "Your foolish daughters are safe."

He had closed our case, he said, despite some difficulty with his superior, and recommended that we be transferred to a concentration camp in Germany only when the roads leading north were viable.

Neva was right. I learned much later that he had classified us as of no interest in the present emergency. The Germans were preparing to leave Rome. The German army had to use those roads to set up a new front against the Allies beyond Florence. As for him, he was needed at the Russian front.

In his talks with Mamma, he came very close to admitting that the war was ending. He didn't seem very upset about it. Once he came to our home bringing his guitar. Sitting on one of our dining room chairs, with Neri and Bruno in front of him, this very German officer who had arrested us, saving the very men he could have arrested in that very room, after drinking the wine he had brought along, struck up a nostalgic song whose refrain was "Annemarie." As he sang, he became a different person, someone like Heinrich, the Bavarian soldier who had given us the lamb for Easter, or even like the deserters.

Before leaving Rome a few days later, he took Bona and me aside and warned us to keep our eyes and ears open. At the first sign of the Allies approaching, we could safely stay home. Until then we had to report every morning at via Tasso. The Gestapo was capable of sudden punishments which the Italians deserved anyway, he added with perverse satisfaction, for having betrayed their ally. After his departure, he added, we should be careful. We would lose our only protector at Via Tasso. It was up to us not to play the wrong hand again. We certainly didn't. Every morning we went from home to the prison until we saw the first American vehicle at Porta Metronia.

His last words at our home were for Mamma, who reminded him of his own mother. "You are a wonderful lady," he said. "I hope your daughters will be like you some day."

§ § §

All through the night of June 4, 1944, we could hear the tanks rumbling along, and the bombardments eased off. An endless line of German soldiers filled the main streets of Rome. They shuffled along through Porta Metronia moving North, their faces blackened, chains of machine gun cartridges slung over their shoulders. The retreating army ignored us.

Francesca's little girl, Antonella, who had been born during a bombardment while we were captives, watched the show from our terrace. Bruno, Neri, Bona, Mamma, and I decided to walk to the center of the city to enjoy the first day of freedom with the rest of the Romans.

German soldiers crowded the *Corso*. We entered the Church of San Carlo. Its baroque immensity echoed with the exhilarating sound of a powerful organ. A hymn of victory, we thought at first. On a side altar they were celebrating what looked like a wedding. There was a bride in white — but no bridegroom. We learned later that a young woman was taking her vows. Kneeling at the altar, she had just raised her veil. A priest in ceremonial robe was holding her long black hair in one hand. In the other he had a pair of scissors. As the organ played the *Te Deum laudamus,* the woman's long black hair fell to the ground.

CHAPTER 10

The Liberators

On June 4, 1944, Rome's ruins and its buildings, its parks and its streets smiled under an avalanche of flowers. As the Germans slowly moved out, we could hear the armored cars approaching from the south. Living south of the city, we would be among the first to see the Americans. At dawn, crowds of Romans gathered on Via Gallia, the main thoroughfare, to welcome our liberators with profound thanks. We were also curious. We had no idea what they would look like or how they would dress. None of us had ever heard the sound of their language, which was English. We knew that not only the Americans and the British, but also the South Africans, the Indians, the New Zealanders and the Australians had sent contingents to Rome. Each one, we were told, spoke a different kind of English. All eyes were on the Americans!

At Porta Metronia, we were lucky. Real flesh-and-blood Americans were the first to arrive — four or five soldiers in odd open cars called "Jeeps."" They were handsomely dressed, if a bit dusty. They were as heavily armed as the Germans had been. What struck us was their superb boots that reached almost to their knees. I could not believe that any nation could produce shoes with such leather. For two years, I had been wearing sandals which Maria Romana De Gasperi had taught me to make out of leather bags, two thin straps of leather over a piece of cork.

The Americans smiled, talked loudly, and threw us candy, mostly the sticky kind. Chewing gum would become their trademark. They lifted up women to ride with them, embracing them and singing. I was in a daze, as if Rome had been suddenly projected into a new world. Our future with the liberators seemed to be still a dream, not a reality.

When I walked to Piazza Venezia the next morning I saw Indian soldiers dressed in the liveliest colors undoing their turbans amid the ruins of the Forum and combing their long black hair in the Roman sun. An unreal show, a fable, an adventure out of the *Orlando Furioso*! Not only was Rome now free from the Nazis, but its gates were open to the whole world in its magnificent variety.

Like everybody around me, I was excited and numb. We were overwhelmed by another miracle which our liberators brought to pass. The very day they came, they distributed bread at no cost. It was a kind of bread we had never seen before, snow-white and velvety soft. As big a surprise as the leather boots. Manna in the desert.

The ecstasy lasted just a few days, about as long as the distribution of the bread, because by the third night drunkards were reeling through the streets. It became unsafe for a woman to be out at night.

Those Romans who had not experienced the Gestapo romanticized the near-childlike behavior of the German soldiers. They would religiously visit the Forum and the Colosseum, guidebooks in hand, like regular tourists. Some paid good money to rent the few carriages that remained and went shopping for souvenirs from the peddlers who now, of course, were selling this merchandise to the liberators for their dollars.

Why didn't the liberators show respect for the Holy City? Most of us women gladly forgave their weaknesses when we thought of how anxiously we had longed for them and how hard they had fought to liberate us. A peaceful Rome, venerable for its antiquities and the seat of the Pope, was the ideal place for them to relax, even if that meant breaking some rules.

When law and order were reestablished, the old problem of survival returned, as pressing as it had been before. There was widespread unemployment except for jobs connected to the Allies, devaluation of the lira, and a flourishing black market with food at sky high prices.

A few days after liberation, I was put in charge of finding work for the whole family, except Poldina, whose job was to keep the household going. Schools were closed and Mamma, Bruno, and I were unemployed. I was worse off than Mamma and Bruno since I had a yearly contract with little hope of renewal. Private tutoring was unavailable. Although my old Virgilio students kept in contact with us, they too were now struggling for their own survival. My professor and protector, Vincenzo Ussani, was banned because he had dedicated his *Vocabulary of Medieval Latin* to Mussolini.

With all of our previous sources of income gone, Cousin Agostino came to our assistance again just as he had at the beginning of the war years in Rome, with regular five-course Sunday dinners, followed by readings and commentary on Dante's *Paradise* by a Swiss friend of his, the Jesuit Father Zullig.

Agostino's central office was in Milan, in northern Italy, and he needed to be there to conduct his business. A few days before departing with many others for the North, before Rome was cut off from northern Italy, he came to us in our tiny apartment at Porta Metronia. He was the only person I knew in Rome who trusted God more than man and so had an objective perspective on his personal interests. Still, what he offered us was unusually generous. Sitting in our dining room, a heavyset man with a sizeable paunch, he asked us to take over his large apartment at Via Bolzano. All we had to do was live there and enjoy the place as if it was our own. He had prepaid the rent for a whole year, which would give us time to start rebuilding our lives.

So we moved to Agostino's apartment, crossing the whole city on foot five times with Antonella's baby carriage and a cart overloaded with our belongings, especially books. Agostino's apartment was fully furnished: three bedrooms, a huge living room, a roomy kitchen, two bathrooms, and a balcony running along the whole apartment. The family had left it with linens and even food as they hurriedly departed.

While the move was easy, we still had to find money for food. The Allied Military Government (AMG), across from the Palazzo Venezia in Piazza Venezia, was looking for apartments to sublet and paid a good price for them. As our first source of income, we could rent out our old apartment.

None of us could speak or understand English. Since I had learned a little from Neva in prison, I was put in charge. Realizing how important my presentation would be, I gave myself three days to learn the essentials of this new language on which we depended. What mattered, Neri declared, was speaking not writing. I should give up my professorial prejudices and learn English by listening to the soldiers on the street.

"Why don't you just go to the AMC?"

I reacted angrily and decided to do it my way. I picked up the military newspaper, *Stars and Stripes*. After three days of intense study, I felt almost ready to present my case with dignity.

"Good morning, sir! I have an apartment for rent," I would say, and after that I would face the unknown.

It was early morning when I joined the already long line in Piazza Venezia. I was given a number over 300. Calculating that my turn would come around 2:00 o'clock, I sat on the ground like the others, leaning against the wall of the mansion, my eyes closed to discourage conversation. Waiting had become a way of life. Empty and exhausted, I soon fell asleep.

"Wake up!" the man near me pushed me gently, cigarette in hand. "They are calling your number!"

As I walked up the stairs of the AMC headquarters, I rapidly repeated to whomever I met the English sentence I had learned by heart: "Good morning, sir. I have an apartment for rent!"

That sentence carried me safely from one office to the next, from that of South Africa, to New Zealand, to North America.

"Come with me," each soldier I met said kindly, and I followed him, happy to have added a new phrase to my limited vocabulary. "Come with me," I repeated to myself, excited to capture the key to English. When after a last "Come with me," a New Zealander emitted a long series of interconnected words, a whole sentence that was like Arabic to me, I had reached, without knowing it, a safe harbor. He left me with a gallant military salute without expecting any reaction on my part.

"Come here, Cinabro!" somebody yelled to somebody else in the back of the office. The officer who spoke was a tall, slender young man in a khaki uniform.

"A signorina here has an apartment for rent.

It was an unexpected pleasure for me to hear that the American pronounced my sentence as if it were his. His mellow, deep voice gave weight to each word and a rhythm to the whole that I had missed in my own version. I was so delighted I could not restrain myself from repeating after him as loud as I could: "I have an apartment for rent."

"I hear her, Corso, I hear her. It's Bové who needs an apartment."

Though I did not understand their words, I caught three names, all of which happened to be Italian; Cinabro, Corso, and Bové. Corso was the young man near me, Cinabro was in the back of the office and an invisible Bové turned out to be the key to my success. I was as tense as a spider about to pull a fly into its web.

Cinabro soon joined Corso and, laughing together, they ferreted out Bové from a dark corner of their office. Cinabro was a dark-haired, skinny, short man whose bright eyes spoke more eloquently than any words. Bové was the most colorful of the three, two huge brown eyes with long eyelashes brushing thick glasses every time he blinked. He was short and slim with hairy, bony, nervous hands and a thin triangular face lightly shaded by an almost imperceptible dark beard. His tall boots accentuated his bow legs. What struck me was how the three young Americans enjoyed a kind of camaraderie; it must have come from spending hard months together. Corso and Cinabro loved making fun of Bové, who seemed to enjoy it.

Nobody would have guessed that the three had come from a battlefield. They spoke to each other as rhythmically as they walked, lightly swinging on their shiny leather boots, their speech a slow tango with charming rhythms and a brusque stop here and there as if to pick up strength for the next swing. If that was English, it didn't resemble any language I had ever heard. I stood dumbfounded, as they spoke to each other, curious about what would happen next.

"E c'osì, mia cara signorina, lei ha un appartamento da affittare." ("And so, my dear young lady, you have an apartment for rent.")

That was Cinabro addressing me in fluent Italian with no trace of an accent.

"And according to my friends, I am to be the fortunate resident of the apartment," Bové continued where Cinabro had left off, in equally fluent Italian.

"Naturally with my approval," said the tall, elegant Corso; his Italian didn't flow quite so easily. "I am the captain in charge of this office. Nothing is allowed out of this office without the proper seal. We all know that nothing is official in Italy without a seal."

Corso's Italian had a strong Southern flavor and a strange undertow of something I couldn't define. It was obviously the Italian of a foreigner, but which kind of foreigner I couldn't say. Always speaking tongue-in-cheek, Corso was the funniest of the three. They all burst out laughing in unison as if to applaud their improvised play.

Before I could react, the last actor in the show introduced himself as Captain James Corso and ceremoniously presented the other two as his subordinates, Lieutenants Joseph Cinabro and Claude Bové — Jim, Joe, and Claude for short. Then he added, "We are all Italian-Americans and we want to practice your beautiful language."

Upon hearing this, I burst out laughing. They looked at me in astonishment, thinking perhaps there was something wrong with what they had said. I reassured them that I enjoyed their performance. I was not laughing at them but at myself. Their request for help in Italian struck me as the most unexpected solution to the latest problem, how to survive without knowing English.

I said that I could show them Rome as a student of archeology and also help them practice their Italian, which in my opinion, was already very good, if they would introduce me to English. They agreed enthusiastically, especially after learning that I taught Latin and Greek and had a degree from the University of Rome. Each of them held a degree from a different American university.

Sitting around a desk with the three musketeers, as they called themselves, I drank and ate unfamiliar things — Coca-Cola and potato chips, I learned later. My American friends had as much trouble imagining my Alpine life as I had imagining Kalamazoo,

Cinabro's home, or Philadelphia, Corso's home. They were taken aback by my total ignorance of Schenectady, Bové's hometown. How could I not know about General Electric? Cinabro joked.

"How could you not know about Rome and Florence?" I replied.

He did know, he said. He had taught history at a college in Michigan. As for Bové, Corso joked, he was the most erudite of the three, having earned a degree at Harvard.

"What is Harvard?" I asked, and they laughed.

"The greatest university in the world!" they sang in unison.

"Whose world?" I asked.

Evidently, Cinabro concluded, we didn't have much in common. Then Corso, suddenly serious, mentioned the deaths of so many Americans on Italian soil. I felt deeply embarrassed. Yes, we owed our freedom to those who had died, and I saw no way we could ever repay them for the lives they had given up for us. How could we call them friends without knowing anything about them?

"Now, now," Cinabro broke in, visibly bothered by my silence. "Don't be upset. Otherwise, our signorina here might reproach us for having been too slow in coming to her assistance."

Out of a drawer came a bottle of Campari to celebrate our friendship and future collaboration. Corso insisted I should be introduced to an American drink they called "Roman Coke" and replaced the Campari with a bottle of rum. Having had already a taste of his rum and coke, he proposed to teach me a new song called "Amapola." Bové, however, who didn't drink, reminded his friends that it was late and I probably hadn't eaten all day, which was true. My family must be worried about me.

Without bothering to remove bottles and glasses from their desks, they gave me a ride home in their jeep. Before we jumped off their strange vehicle to face my family at Agostino's apartment, Corso wisely reminded the others in English that I had originally come to their office to offer an apartment for rent.

"And so, Bové, the moment has come," he continued in Italian, "for you to declare to our signorina, before she introduces us to her family, the sum you are willing to pay for renting her apartment. Cinabro and I will chip in so that we can use it together."

Bové mumbled something to himself. The other two winked at each other as he proposed a sum which seemed exorbitant to me, ignorant of the exchange rate of dollars. Bové was calculating the rent in lire.

"Bargain! Bargain!" the two officers encouraged me. "He is a scrooge!"

They bargained on my behalf, doubling the sum he had proposed.

"Okay." I heard myself saying with nonchalance. That was the first time I used the word.

"Okay!" Cinabro and Corso echoed, laughing at Bové who had apparently agreed to double the sum because he didn't want to lose face. Mamma and the rest of the family couldn't believe their eyes that night when Lieutenant Bové left millions of lire on the dining room table for the first month's rent. It was light after darkness. We had solved for a while the problem of food.

§ § §

From that moment on, I was obsessed with learning English. I loved the language but couldn't quite grasp its special music. Every time I tried to enter the dance I felt out of step. It was disheartening. So I decided I would focus on reading and writing. Speaking and comprehension would come later. I needed to get a job as soon as possible, and a reading knowledge of English was second best, after fluency in speaking.

Fortunately, after their first, most welcome, visit, the Three Musketeers became friends of the family and the *Stars and Stripes* grounded our friendship. Almost every night, the three officers brought along their Colonel, John Fisher, a taciturn man who stood out because he was tall, thin and supple. He was, Cinabro told me with a conspiratorial air, of Anglo-Saxon origin, while the Three Musketeers were of Latin origin. According to Cinabro, that meant they were discriminated against as "inferior." The lowest on the scale were the Negroes, he said. The Italians came next, then the Irish. The English and Scots were at the very top. Cinabro was my bible for American politics and sociology. I listened to him, spellbound. I had never seen a Negro in my life but felt immediately troubled by their low position in society.

The four officers, I soon discovered, had been risking their lives together since the Americans first landed in Morocco. They were part of the Counter-Intelligence Corps (CIC), a group of linguistically gifted Americans who interrogated prisoners of war. Since he was monolingual like most Americans, Fisher had to depend heavily on his subordinates for the success of his unit.

For me, Fisher's monolingualism was most useful. Very much aware of my eagerness to understand him, this Anglo-Saxon pronounced English very slowly and clearly. He then wrote down what he had said in order to show me the relationship between written and spoken English. I wondered if, in civilian life, he had taught in a school for the deaf, because he was the only American who made me see what he said. He was also very encouraging. When one day I understood the whole of one of his favorite stories concerning his unit, he was very pleased.

I learned that his unit always landed immediately after the first wave of soldiers, so that they could work with the first prisoners. At their landing in Sicily, Fisher noticed that Bové, usually very disciplined, disposed of some of his weapons while holding on to his typewriter as he waited to be lowered into the landing craft.

"I will punish him for that," he said to himself angrily, when and if both of us survive this damned landing.

They both survived. But Bové was not court-martialed. Asked about his discarded weapons, he explained that it was necessary; he had seen an overloaded raft with soldiers and their equipment swallowed up by the sea.

"Since I was too overloaded to survive the landing, I had to choose between a machine-gun and a typewriter. I decided the typewriter would be most appropriate for my job. So I dumped the machine gun."

"That's how my best soldiers are," the Colonel said. "They are Americans, they have a mind of their own."

I owe to Colonel John Fisher my first and only English grammar book. We perused it together. Since English is an Indo-European language, its grammar was easy to learn, we were happy to discover. He was especially pleased when I told him that his name was the German noun Fischer without the *c*, derived from the Latin *piscator*. I was sure that if the war had not been Colonel Fisher's most pressing business, he would have cheerfully become one of my Latin students. In any case, the war allowed him to stay in Rome long enough for me to learn some English.

Fisher was not my only teacher. He was part of the team I had assembled after my first visit to the AMG at Piazza Venezia. Cinabro, who was a writer by vocation and a lover of literature, brought me books that were way over my head, like *Moby Dick* and the poetry of Edgar Lee Masters.

He patiently read excerpts of these books to me, but was usually too tempted to educate me on what the real America was like, so that we never spent much time on literary English. In his view, everything in American politics had gone wrong. The Constitution, itself a monument to democracy, was often ignored. Corruption was endemic. Europe had to be careful lest it be misled by the Americans.

Bové, on the other hand, was amusing. He brought along a mandolin and, supported by Corso who loved to sing, sat with us on the balcony under the stars, drinking tea, the only luxury we could afford; we had found it in abundance in Agostino's kitchen. According to Corso, Bové was a romantic who had spent his time at Harvard studying French, Latin, and American history, instead of the laws of Wall Street, which he was supposed to learn. Bové laughed. He knew that Corso admired him.

Although Bové, or Claude, as he asked me to call him, was the only single man of the four, he was the family man among them.

Not only did he pay his rent promptly for the two months he spent in our apartment, but, noticing our desperate scramble for food, he organized a kind of food drive, mainly, he said, to feed Francesca, who was breast-feeding Antonella. Every night our American friends brought a stack of sandwiches made with their soft white bread. They were filled with a brown substance they called *peanut butter* and a marmalade they called *jelly*. Claude also brought along some kind of round cakes called doughnuts and gave us American coffee, besides of course chocolate and candy in abundance. Mainly because of him, we soon associated liberation not only with the departure of the Germans but with some relief from the hunger that had plagued us for so long.

Aware that the responsibility of finding jobs for the family fell mainly on me — I had by now mastered a kind of pidgin English — Claude took it upon himself to help. He got me a job at the censorship office where I dealt with Italian correspondence. That, he said, would give me time to improve my English.

For my part, I did what I could to please him. Of the four who took part in my tours to the archaeological sites of Rome, he was the most faithful, the most interested, and the most critical. Cinabro and Corso were generally aloof, appearing mainly interested in the relationship that might develop between Claude and me.

"Bové is made for you," Corso hinted more than once, "and you are made for him."

"Beware," Cinabro warned me. "Our friend Corso has been trying to marry off Bové ever since we arrived on Italian soil. He likes him a lot, but thinks he needs to shake off the life he was leading in Schenectady where he was supporting his mother and four sisters with a miserable job at some kind of depot. As an escape he had a girlfriend. She was only an escape, just as Harvard was from the prison of his Italian-American family.

"Corso thinks you're the right woman for him at this point in his life. He is the fourth in a family of eight children, four boys and four girls. His family comes from the south of Italy near Naples. Mine comes from the mountains of Abbruzzo. That's not the same thing," he said more than once. "But it doesn't matter where our families came from, because we, I mean Corso, Bové, and I, were all born in America which has very little in common with southern Italy. You are so different from the girls we met in Southern Italy and so is your family. Perhaps we are in for a surprise as our army moves north and we will find many girls like you. In any case, Corso thinks you are just right for Bové. What worries me, though, is that everybody here in Italy is so naive about America, even you who have studied and read."

"You see," he continued. "Bové is an intelligent man and a real musician. He's an artist and a bookkeeper at the same time. But he takes America at face value. He doesn't look at it critically. He is a patriot who swears by the flag, not an intellectual who contests ideas. He is a conventional American who thinks one can break new ground just by plowing along, following rules and regulations. It horrifies him that I am a socialist at heart, and am aware of the tremendous social injustices that the capitalist system imposes on our people. He is not even a businessman like Corso who practices the art of using money to make more money. At times I think Corso is right. What saved Claude from the boredom of the most bourgeois American life was the war. Perhaps a woman like you can save him from falling back into his pre-war pattern. Anyway, the decision will rest with you, if he proposes. I don't want to influence you. But whatever you do, beware of Schenectady."

I was both puzzled and put off by Cinabro's views of America and of Claude, but I was not in love with Claude so I did not pay any special attention to these warnings. Besides, life was moving on so fast that there wasn't much time for reflection. When Cinabro received new orders to move to the front, which was now close to Florence, he joked about it. He was grateful to the army, he said, that provided him with the best possible tour of Italy, first Rome, then Florence! As for Claude, not long after Cinabro's departure, he was transferred to the island of Corsica to supervise a prisoner-of-war camp.

My whole family was saddened by their departure, but we knew that the liberation of Rome did not mean the end of the war. On the contrary, the very same day the Allies entered Rome, their northern contingents landed in Normandy where fighting was more ferocious than anywhere else. This meant that the Mediterranean campaign would not get replacements and had to count on the forces already in place. It also meant that Italy would remain cut in two by the dividing line established by the German resistance north of Rome.

Personally, I felt morally obliged to show our American friends that we were putting whatever we had learned from them to good use. While working at the censorship office, I kept on the lookout for a job in which I could use my fledgling English. Then I could pass on my own job to Bona, whose English lagged behind mine.

CHAPTER 11

Regina Coeli

Good luck returned, this time through another branch of the Allied army. Rome had long ago lost most of its public buses and trams. Because of my job at the Censorship Office, I had gotten a pass that allowed me to flag down any Allied vehicle and ask for transportation. The driver of the first military car I stopped was a major from New Zealand, a short, wiry man with bright blue eyes and a tiny blond beard, just enough to confer on him the dignity of his rank. He not only agreed to take me across the city to where I worked, but proposed to pick me up at day's end. After a couple of days, it seemed proper to me to invite Major Taylor to meet my family, an invitation he must have read as romantic interest.

The major was not surprised to be received cordially. On one visit he even performed some Maori dances, which were much easier to follow than his English. Shortly thereafter he asked Mamma, using me as an interpreter, if she would object to his marrying me. He had a lot of land and many sheep in New Zealand where I would be treated like a queen. I answered for Mamma that she could not agree because she needed my help in Rome; New Zealand was too far away. Not surprised by my refusal, he still offered to help me in whatever way he could. I told him then as clearly as I could that I needed a job where I could use the little English I knew. A few days later, he introduced me with an eloquent speech, of which I didn't understand a word, to the AMG division where he worked, the Palace of Justice. There I was assigned to a certain Captain Freeman, a policeman from California, who, with the help of his handsome, tall, gray-haired English mistress, governed the Regina Coeli ("Queen of Heaven"), the official Roman prison on the Tiber River.

Given my limited knowledge of English, I was asked to organize the files of the prison in the registrar's office. The change from political prisoner of the Gestapo to assistant to Captain Freeman in an ordinary Italian prison struck me as odd. Even so, organizing files and answering requests, I ended up being useful to many Italians who had been imprisoned for up to four years without trial. Even a murderer, the Italian prisoners insisted, has the right to trial and I agreed. The captain had assigned me to work in another office and be available in case of emergency. That was where my English was needed and that is where I finally failed miserably.

I could read and speak English to some extent, but had trouble understanding speech, especially on the telephone. Claude knew that emergencies were common during war and had insisted on daily oral exercises which included singing and dancing to "Twinkle, twinkle, little star," "Tell me the tales," "Onward Christian soldiers," and "Amapola." Singing in darkness was a congenial way of improving my oral English. Claude assured me I shouldn't have any difficulty if I kept up working on oral English. I did my very best, but evidently it was not enough.

When an emergency suddenly arose at the Regina Coeli, my American liberator was unfortunately in Corsica. It happened on a sunny morning in October, the sort of day on which Rome shines from the seven hills down to the Tiber. The Captain and his mistress had left in the early morning with Carretta, the director of the Regina Coeli, to attend the trial of Questore Caruso, the head of the Roman police during the German occupation. The trial was being held at the Hall of Justice, a huge rococo building on the Tiber not far from the prison. Questore Caruso had been in charge of the Roman police when, in the spring of 1944, the Germans had shot over three hundred political prisoners in retaliation for the killing of thirty of their soldiers in Via Rasella. The executions had terrorized us.

Since the captain was away, I had to take charge, and I was very uneasy about it. Only the presence of a trustworthy carabinieri, who had been with the Captain and Miss Ann since Sicily, reassured me. The shutters were closed. I was completing a translation when the carabiniere rushed into the office.

"Signorina!" he shouted, "look through the shutters. They are marching against us.

"Who?" I asked.

"The women who murdered Carretta." The carabiniere was beside himself. "Phone Allied Headquarters in Piazza Venezia." We need help.

Then he told me that, to protect the Regina Coeli against the attack, he had lowered the emergency gates. The prisoners were safe. There was nothing for us to fear from the inside. I needed to protect against any attack from the outside. So I must call headquarters to enlist their help.

"Tell me what happened," I insisted, to gain time. I didn't like the idea of being the safety valve for so many people. What if I couldn't explain in my poor English or, worse, couldn't understand what was being said on the other end? I needed to get ahold of myself. The carabiniere trusted me. What we didn't know was that, at the trial's end, after Caruso had been sentenced to death for consenting to the German massacre, some women in the audience had decided to take justice into their own hands.

To avenge the death of their sons and husbands, they broke through the police lines. The condemned Caruso was whisked off into the underground cells of the Hall of Justice, while Carretta, our prison director, was on his way out of the building in the company of Captain Freeman and Miss Ann. Had the women mistaken Carretta for Caruso? Both men were middle-aged, short and stocky, with square faces.

Like the Furies, the women had flung themselves on Carretta almost dragging the Captain and Miss Ann along with him. In an attempt to escape, Carretta had dived into the Tiber and tried to hang on to a small boat. A man on the boat cut off both his hands. Someone had fished Carretta out of the Tiber, probably already dead. They finished him off and were dragging his body triumphantly down Lungotevere, the road that ran along the river. Those Furies were taking their revenge on the Regina Coeli.

We heard banging on the main gate, which the carabiniere had ordered shut. Someone rushed up and said that a mob of ferocious women was crucifying Carretta on the outside of the gate. I ran to the telephone and called AMG headquarters. Since they seemed to already know vaguely what was happening, I tried to give them the essentials in my best English. I thought they understood, but I could not make out their answer.

"Are they coming to our help, yes or no?" the carabiniere asked. Behind him stood the nuns from the women's prison who had such faith in me.

"Of course they are," I lied. "They're on their way over."

Everyone embraced me. I was embarrassed, but pretended to be happy. I later discovered that the AMG headquarters had told me that they could not come to our help because it would be taken as interference.

No one ever discovered my failure to understand the message, however. As the carabiniere and I looked through the closed shutters, we saw the captain driving a tank across the Tiber, the first ever. He had the body of his friend Carretta removed from the gate, while (we were told) the dead man's wife and two daughters watched from the other side of the river. When everything had calmed down, he did something unusual. He invited me, the carabinieri, and the nun into his office for a hearty American lunch, a real treat for someone who had been living on two potatoes a day.

However, the nun and I had an unexpected reaction to the day's horror. To the astonishment of our hosts, we devoured the entire meal. The Captain did not touch his food, but drank copiously from a bottle of whiskey. He took advantage of the occasion to insinuate that I had recently broken the AMG law by buying a ten-kilogram sack of potatoes from the nuns in charge of the women's prison. The potatoes were part of the provision assigned by the AMG to the prison. This was a crime, he told me, which in a democracy would be punishable by months in prison.

I shuddered. While I was learning much about life in a democracy, there clearly was still much to learn. I suddenly saw myself in the same situation as many of the prisoners whom I had just recently helped, accused of a crime of which I was unaware! In one breath the Captain shouted at me, "In our democracy nobody is above the law, not even the president of the country."

To my surprise I understood everything he said, but it did not make any sense. What had I in common with his president? Was he, like me, on a diet of two potatoes a day?

Shortly after that disheartening experience, I resigned from my job at the Regina Coeli and gave up working with the Allies altogether. Miss Ann tried to dissuade me from resigning and Captain Freeman himself apologized for his accusation, which he had learned was unfounded. I thanked them but stood by my decision. I had to admit to myself, sadly, that I had failed. My English needed improvement. But there was more to it than that.

Freeman's reproach had set me thinking about the relationship between the law and the individual in a democracy. If a law was made by the people and for the people, a principle I accepted as one of the main tenets of democracy, how should I be judged? Although I had broken a law by buying those ten kilos of potatoes from the nuns, wouldn't my action be justified, at least in part, by the fact of my present state of hunger? In my work for the prisoners of the Regina Coeli, I had often dealt with similar cases. Now, being personally affected, I began to think that the law to which Freeman appealed might not work for my own people. I considered the troublesome question of the relationship between the strong and the weak in a democracy. How far could the strong Americans apply their democracy to us weak Italians? I concluded that I wasn't yet ready to work for the Allies. Indeed, along with my English, my understanding of their political system needed improvement.

CHAPTER 12

St. Peter's

My old students had begun showing up asking for tutoring, so I returned to my pre-liberation pattern of conducting classes at home, while continuing to exercise my English in daily letters to Claude in Corsica. Claude wrote to me about the boring life he led, after months on the battlefield watching prisoners of war work in the rocky mountains of a secluded, yet peaceful and picturesque island. He also recalled his life in Schenectady with his brothers and sisters. At the age of fifteen, his parents had separated and he was left in charge of his four younger sisters. He wrote about his father, who often treated his wife and children harshly, and of his sweet mother who suffered in silence. He wrote about the difficult life of an Italian-American scornfully called *WOP* in school by the WASPs, the White Anglo-Saxon Protestants, and of his wonderful years at Harvard — he was still paying off his debt. He was thankful, he wrote, that the war had helped him to pay off many debts and to meet me. Would I like, some day in the future, to escape from all the difficulties of a troubled Europe to a little white house in Schenectady? Perhaps a two-story wooden house with room for a big family? I tried to imagine a kind of dollhouse covered with snow most of the year, under the watchful eye of a huge General Electric plant not far from the thunder of Niagara Falls. Seen from troubled Rome, it had its attraction.

I wrote to Claude mostly about the present. I told him everything that went on at the *Regina Coeli,* especially the dreadful story of the emergency. I wrote that I trusted him and admired him for the straightforward, down-to-earth way he lived his Americanness. I also liked his ability to solve problems directly without much talking. Truth and justice for him, I thought, were never abstractions. In his world the law was made for man, not man for the law. If American democracy was what he practiced, I was all for it. But what hurt me at the moment was the humiliation I had suffered at the prison.

He wrote back that I should forget the episode at the *Regina Coeli*. He and his friends knew me much better than that odious policeman from California. He wrote that he admired me for my intellectual curiosity, the product of a thorough classical education, which would be much appreciated in America, if I ever wished to join him there some day. He might even decide to stay on in Europe, if he wasn't assured a fresh start at home.

He finally asked me in plain, simple English if I was willing to marry him. I answered,

"Yes, I am." And that was that.

§   §   §

At twenty-three, I agreed to marry Claude because I was attracted by the mystery surrounding him and by his candor and directness. "Take me as I am," he often said.

In my imagination, he had become a living image of America. In accepting his proposal, I also accepted the challenge of discovering not only a husband but also a world totally unknown to me. Perhaps only by making America my home would I find the answer to some of the questions that had troubled me during the German occupation of Rome and the days following Liberation. I couldn't even formulate many of those questions at the time, but they took shape slowly, one by one, during the two years Claude and I spent in Italy as husband and wife. They arose in reaction to the events we lived through together, while Europe was painfully recovering from the ravages of the War.

When I met Claude I was not in the best psychological condition for falling in love. I learned to love him as I lived with him, day in day out in postwar Italy. No doubt, as a self-centered young woman, I loved him for selfish reasons. He not only represented the security I had longed for much of my life, but he also genuinely enjoyed my company and he showed it. He loved me, he said, when I took part in discussions with him and his comrades. He showed me off at meetings and official parties of all kinds, in part as a miraculous

Pygmalion. He took pride not only in my achievements but in what he thought were my natural gifts, such as my ease in society, my ability to help people understand issues dear to me, and my ability to get out of trouble. He was proud of little things such as my dancing, and even my very modest swimming. He ordered the best possible bathing suit and dancing outfit for me from his sisters back home. What attracted him to me, I often thought, was his image of Europe — and of Italy in particular.

More than anything else, however, as we lived together, he increasingly trusted my ability to work beside him for the betterment of his post-war place in American society. Our marriage at the very end of a long war signified to him that he would never go back to where he had been before. I would assure the success of his ambitions upon his return to America.

Cinabro's warnings arose once in while, like a cloud obscuring the sun, mainly when we discussed starting a family. But even on that issue Claude quieted my worries. There would be no family before we had settled somewhere on the other shore. That somewhere was no specific place. We had an entire continent at our disposal. In his opinion, I would be a perfect American, a pioneer better fit for the West than for the East.

§   §   §

Our decision to marry delighted my family. They all loved Claude. During the exhilarating but difficult post-liberation period, he had helped us deal with our poverty in a practical way. Claude, the family declared, understood poverty not as a stigma but as a challenge. He had been poor in childhood. Yet he seemed to think of poverty in America as something different from what we were now experiencing in Rome. This made him truly one of us, Mamma concluded, and everyone agreed. Even Papa, she assured me, blessed our union.

Mamma's easy consent to our marriage was also due to the fact that, by late November 1944, the general condition of the family had improved, as Rome had returned to more or less normal conditions. Mamma and Bruno got back their posts as tenured high school and junior college teachers. Francesca, who had successfully passed her doctoral exam in German Literature with the well-known Professor Gabetti, was now temporarily employed as headmistress of a troubled school in Trastevere. Bona, who was about to complete her degree in Roman History, had grown very close to a young German/Polish officer who was on fellowship leave from the Gothic Line, i.e., the front in northern Italy which ran from Pisa to Rimini. They had met in an English Literature class at the University of Rome taught by Professor Mario Praz, known as *"l'Innominabile"* (the Unnamable One).

Of all the members of the family, only Neri was not settling in to post-liberation life. After a year in hiding, he had returned to his studies in engineering, but with little enthusiasm and even less success. Even Poldina had moved up to a new stage in her life. She was engaged to the local baker and we had pledged her dowry.

Surrounded by everybody's love, under Mamma's wise tutelage, little Antonella was growing rapidly right in front of us, a happy child out of danger.

As for me, whose world suddenly pointed beyond Gibraltar, the main question was if I should give up my plans for an academic career. With Claude's approval, I decided I would not. But that was easier said than done.

My career had been moving along two parallel lines. My main ambition was to pursue a university career under the direction of Professor Ussani. At the same time, however, to earn a living I had to get tenure as a Professor of Latin and Greek in a liceo, which required finishing among the top one thousand or so candidates in the state exams. In postwar Italy, the process of elimination of all persons connected with Fascism and with Mussolini in particular, had hit Ussani, who had been expelled from the Italian Academy for having dedicated to Mussolini the *Vocabulary of Medieval Latin*. At eighty and in frail health the blow had nearly killed him.

Ussani's demotion did not mean that my yearly contract at the liceo would not be renewed. I hadn't been called back to teach because the Virgilio was temporarily closed. But it did mean that I had to give up, at least for now, all hope of working at the university. Without a powerful mentor, a university career was inconceivable. I had to concentrate on getting tenure in Latin and Greek at the liceo, the best avenue for eventually moving on to the university.

The state exam consisted of a six-hour composition in Latin on a literary subject, followed by an oral exam that covered Latin and Greek literature. One could advance to the orals only after passing the written test, which most candidates failed. I had failed the written test once, mainly, I thought, because I had trained myself, for months before the test, to write Latin in a rich and florid Ciceronian style. Chastened by that experience, I decided to undergo a radical stylistic purification and learn to write in the plain style of the Gospels.

I had recently received the happy news that I had passed the written exam and could go on to the orals, if and when the Ministry of Education decided to offer them, which nobody expected to happen after the armistice under the neo-Fascist republic. I was ready to write off those orals as victims of the war, when we suddenly learned that, since the bureaucratic machine was once again operating, I should prepare for the orals. All of this happened shortly after Claude and I had decided to marry. During the first two years of our marriage, the usual Greek and Latin authors accompanied me on my tour of Italy as a war bride, as they had done throughout my whole life.

Colonel Fisher and Captain Corso, both still in Rome, were delighted at our decision to marry. Having both acted as links between us during Claude's months in Corsica, they now helped engineer his temporary transfer back to the AMG in Rome. The marriage, they decided with Claude's approval, should take place in the Vatican — where Claude had been assigned in 1944 to assist the Japanese ambassador — with all the pomp the circumstances allowed. Even before Claude's arrival, Corso assisted me in collecting the documents which the Church required. We needed a baptismal certificate, so Corso extracted Claude's with much difficulty from some church in Schenectady. However, when I presented it to my parish, Santa Agnese, famous for its catacombs on the site of the child martyr of the Roman persecutions, the old priest laughed outright.

"What do they take us for, these Americans — born yesterday?" he exclaimed, glancing at the document. "Who in the world would believe that this typewritten piece of paper is an official document and not a fake produced in one of their offices in Rome? Send it back and ask the American parish priest to place the proper seals on it." In despair, I brought the document back to Corso. A few minutes later he brought it back to me replete with a number of seals from his office: Top secret," "For your eyes only," "Confidential."

"Didn't I tell you," the priest commented triumphantly when he saw it, "that all we have to do with these Americans is to make them respect us?"

§ § §

Claude and I married on February 2, 1945, with the special blessing of the Pope, in the third chapel on the right as one enters St. Peter's. My family and best friends were around me, Natalia Lancellotti first of all. Colonel Fisher gave the bride away.

§ § §

From 1945 to 1947 I accompanied Claude as his wife all through Italy on his different assignments. We traveled by jeep and truck across the Apennines over roads that bombs had destroyed. We passed piles of ruins, once towns and villages. Yet, once we arrived at our destination, we always enjoyed decent living quarters and had more than enough food to eat, which made me feel miserably guilty.

The change in my life since marrying Claude was so radical that at times had to pinch myself to be sure I was the same person who, just a year before, did not have enough water or bread. In those days, I almost blessed the bombs falling around us because they might have shortened the nightmare we were living.

But it wasn't only food and sleep and water for a shower that made a radical difference in my life. By marrying an American officer I had entered a totally different world from the one in which

I had lived so far, both in my small town in the Alps and in Rome. I missed my school and my students. It saddened me to think that they were now a thing of the past. Following my husband through a ravaged peninsula in Operation Peace, I missed the chance to participate as an Italian in "Operation Democracy," which took place with the appearance of political parties I had hardly known so far. I was left out of the people's slow and painful struggle to rebuild their lives in a new context. I was no more part of them than I had been during the war.

Yet, throughout those three years with Claude and the Allied Army in Italy, while I was in an ideal position to observe, I was more than simply an observer of what went on around me. I became Claude's most welcome assistant in his effort to understand the political confusion and the consequent suffering of the people around us. In Caserta, Florence, Udine, and Zones A and B at the Yugoslav border, I witnessed the sad results of the war. I listened to the pleas of many persons less fortunate than me, people who felt abandoned and were often subject to the revenge or greed of their neighbors. I learned that no war ends in peace for the countries that have been invaded and destroyed. For Italy, establishing peace was a long and painful process. I witnessed its first stage.

Unlike Germany, which had started the war, and the countries which Germany invaded and forced into the war, the Italian government had deliberately chosen to enter the war on the side of Germany. And then it had changed alliances and government in the middle of the conflict and had eliminated a foolish dictator while an insane, frightening one was ready to take his place. The government abandoned Rome and its entire army to their fate and, with them, two-thirds of the country, when it signed an armistice with the Allies from a safe haven in the south. Italy also had the biggest, most powerful, and most disciplined Communist party in Europe, while northern Italy was witnessing the birth of a harsh new Fascist party to oppose it.

In my travels throughout Italy as Claude's wife, I saw what I could never have seen had I remained in Rome: the effects on individual citizens of Italy's tragic political choices. Their suffering continued long after peace was declared.

During the first months of our marriage, Claude and I stayed in Rome at the AMC. It was a real blessing because it allowed me to contribute to the support of my family with the crumbs that fell from the rich table of the liberators. This was what every Roman was trying to do. In cheerful contempt of Captain Freeman's lofty words on the sacred character of a law imposed on us by America, I happily disposed of the cartons of cigarettes due to Claude, who did not smoke. Magically, the black market turned cigarettes into food for my starving family.

At first, it was hard to believe, but I could rely on Claude to pay bills. Every night, like a model bookkeeper, he recorded what he spent, penny for penny, in a special notebook. That, I thought, was how Americans managed to live in affluence. When there was excess, Claude sent it to his savings account in Schenectady for our future needs. Such savings reassured me that the pleasure that had suddenly become part of my life would not be short-lived.

The great change in my life was meeting people from all over, talking freely of the present and the future, learning for the first time in my life what had happened before liberation and was happening now in places far away from Europe. I had not paid attention to the war against Japan that had followed Pearl Harbor. I never knew, for instance, that the battle of Saipan in the summer of 1943 had cost thousands of American and Japanese lives. For the first time, I felt with horror and dismay the tragedy of the atomic bomb and Hiroshima. Though the bomb was widely considered necessary in order to end the war, nonetheless so horrible was it that it changed life on the planet.

And then there was Fun, which became dancing through the night with Claude and his comrades in the elegant Hotel Majestic on Via Veneto, Rome's liveliest street. When we retired in the early morning to the apartment Claude had rented near Via Bolzano, the only conversation we had was about my shoes whose soles I had completely worn out in the hours of uninterrupted dancing. Fun was our shared reaction at the end of the war.

Fun was also my long-standing interest in the theater that led me to my first contribution to my American husband's business operations. Among all the contemporary playwrights, Eduardo de Filippo represented the quintessence of Italian theater in his fusion of improvisation and text. As author, actor, and director of his own plays, de Filippo seemed to me an Italian miracle. He cast his brother Peppino and his sister Titina as actors. Of all of Eduardo's plays the recent *Napoli Milionaria* stood out as the most immediate artistic version of the complex drama of war in Naples.

I took Claude to see the play again and again and discussed it with him at length before we introduced ourselves to de Filippo after a performance. I had slowly become convinced that Eduardo's Neapolitan tragicomedy of the war, if rendered in fluent English, could be successfully produced for a New York public, among whom, I was told, were many Italian-Americans of Neapolitan origin. I was also attracted by Eduardo's own special message in the play, the moral redemption of the city of Naples.

Eduardo was as delighted to meet Claude and me as we were to experience the genuine warmth that was one of his innate gifts. I stood aside, with Eduardo's American wife, in admiration of the growing intimacy between our husbands. Before leaving Rome Claude identified, through an American friend in Rome, a possible angel for the play in New York. He also signed a contract with de Filippo for a translation of the play. It was my first successful deal as public relations officer for my American husband.

The first obvious result was the choice of where we would live in North America: New York City, more specifically Manhattan, as close as possible to the theater district, near Times Square.

§ § §

We left Rome in May for the Allied headquarters in the old Royal Palace of Caserta. Claude was assigned to write its history. I lived in a room in town so infested with bedbugs that had I not become a friend of those soldiers who were in charge of sanitation and disinfection, one of the most important services in the Allied army, I would have asked for a tent and camped in the main square.

We reached Florence just weeks after liberation. The bombed-out bridges over the Arno River gave the city the look of a mortally wounded soldier. Claude taught French, Italian, and Spanish at a newly opened University Training Command. I had a chance to learn some Russian with Claude's comrades and, unexpectedly, consult Latin manuscripts in libraries still closed to the public. My spoken and written English had improved so that I could use it regularly in conversation, in letters, and in my diary. In Florence at the Hotel Majestic, Claude's comrades introduced me to my first readings in contemporary American literature, in particular Steinbeck and Faulkner. I also acquired a more sophisticated understanding of contemporary American politics. Soldiers at the University openly criticized decisions of their government, without being punished for it. In Florence in 1945, a new world opened up.

Claude was allowed to live with me in a room we rented in the home of an impoverished Italian general, on trial for the most common crime at the time, collaboration. I shared the indignation of the general and his wife for what they were enduring. Claude, however, tried to explain that those who had suffered persecution and torture before liberation were now seeking justice. Mixed with their desire for justice was the thirst for revenge.

It was painful for Claude, as an American, to discover the consequences of an armistice which had temporarily cut the peninsula in two. In the north, a real civil war raged until April 1945 and continued sporadically after that.

Claude and his friends became important instruments in the long and painful effort of healing and reconciliation. By the time we left Florence, the city had buried its dead and briefly glorified heroes, then moved on to rebuilding its bridge.

The contrary was true further north. On April 25, 1945, a band of Communist partisans captured Mussolini and his entourage in the mountains near Lake Como and promptly executed him and his mistress to avoid delivering him to General Alexander, the commander-in-chief of the Mediterranean campaign. This type of execution was the common procedure for the Communist partisans, who were very powerful through northern Italy.

Though many disagreed, I instinctively felt that Mussolini's death was in line with his life: he was executed not by an anonymous soldier but by the Italian people, whom he had betrayed. I moved north alongside the Allied army with the conviction that the moral force of democracy does not come from ideologies but from the people themselves as they grow aware of the rights they have as people and the duties that go with those rights.

CHAPTER 13

Venezia Giulia

The Treaty of Versailles in 1919 assigned to Italy, as one of the victors, the South Tyrol (Trentino-Alto Adige) and the Italian-speaking region to the northeast bordering Yugoslavia, Venezia Giulia. At the end of World War II, the three main cities of Venezia Giulia were Trieste, Fiume, and Udine, the capital of nearby Friuli. Shortly before Claude was assigned to the AMG of the area in December 1945, Venezia Giulia and Friuli had been divided by the "Morgan Line," named after the British officer who arranged this for General Harold Alexander, Supreme Allied Commander of the whole Mediterranean Operation.

Though the general originally wanted to keep lines open between the U.S. Army and Austria, he and President Truman both thought that this area, with its large population of Italians, should remain in Allied hands while awaiting political settlement with Tito at the Peace Table. The Morgan Line was the result of Tito's claiming the region for Yugoslavia. When Claude arrived at AMG headquarters in Udine, the Morgan Line was the demarcation between the democratic and communist ideologies. Zone A, the cities of Udine, Trieste, and Gorizia, were under the AMC, and Zone B, the Istrian Peninsula, was under Tito's control.

Zone A was administered democratically but an improvised Communist administration replaced the Italian one in Zone B and the Yugoslavs displaced the Italians. Italians who resisted were summarily tried and executed for Fascist crimes or simplyy anti-Communist attitudes. Those who could escape fled for their lives. Starting in late 1945, just when Claude was transferred from Rome to Udine, the refugee exodus peaked in 1947. Claude served first in Tarvisio on the border between the zones. Shortly thereafter, he was named governatore, i.e., civil affairs officer, of the whole area between the rivers Isonzo and Tagliamento in the Friuli region. His seat was Latisana and San Vito al Tagliamento.

§ § §

In January 1946 we arrived at Udine from Rome by military plane and by truck. Udine was bitterly, cruelly cold. It was, they said, the coldest winter in history.

"Sorry. No civilians allowed upstairs."

Claude had tried to get me into the AMG building at Udine, an impressive ancient construct, but the sergeant on guard was adamant. There would be no exception to the rules.

I was freezing. All I wanted was a blanket and a cup of hot soup. I dreamt of a fire. We had traveled for hours in an open truck through the snow. I had refused an offer to sit by the driver.

"Are you cold?" The South African sergeant asked unnecessarily as Claude vanished up the staircase. Claude found me three hours later sleeping peacefully on a bench, wrapped in an olive military blanket, an empty cup of tea next to me.

"Be careful," the sergeant had said. "People around here are not to be trusted. They'll try to snatch away this blanket."

That olive blanket became my lucky charm in Venezia Giulia.

Claude's particular concern when we arrived at a new post was how to discharge his duties with me around. Here, he had to figure out where to park me and how to dress me. I was wearing a thin woolen dress and a light coat. We entered our new world through a bar in the center of town. The dingy room was filled with men enveloped in thick smoke. There were no women. They sang a song in "friulano," an incomprehensible dialect which I learned eventually: "O ze bel o ze bel chischiel de Udin," a hymn to the old castle overlooking the town.

Attracted by both the music and the vitality of the people, we squeezed in at the bar. I was ready to deal with the questions that my presence as an Italian woman with an American officer would arouse. We ordered cappuccino and Claude was given a *fisarmonica* (an accordion) on which he improvised. We conversed in Italian interspersed on their part with "Okay, Officer," and repeated requests for cigarettes. When I told the crowd that my husband did not smoke, there was an embarrassed silence. No cigarettes and a wife! I explained our presence in Udine. I was one of them and we needed a place to stay. The Allies had taken over the major hotels.

A few hours later, two of the men accompanied us to a small pensione, clean and decent, they assured us. "You might not like some of the women there, they are refugees," our new friends explained on the way over. "But you know, refugees have to survive." That was the first I had heard of refugees.

The pensione was fine. After a good night's sleep under heavy blankets, we started preparing for departure. Claude had been assigned to a post high up in the mountains at the border between Zones A and B. The name of the village, Tarvisio, was hardly visible on the Italian map, but it was printed in large letters on Claude's military map.

Before the war, you could reach this village only by way of two meandering mountain roads, both of which were now nearly impassable. After the armistice of September 8, 1943, the zone had become a battlefield between Italian and Slovenian partisans who had both fought against both the neo-fascists and the Germans.

Claude was enthusiastic about the assignment. His major concern, once again, was my clothes. Of course, there was the black market, but Claude was a staunch believer in the sanctity of the law. He rightly felt he had to set an example for others. I was left on my own to find myself clothes for the mountains.

In Udine, Claude worked from 7:00 a.m. to 7:00 p.m. I began my day with breakfast at the bar. In the morning, the bar was clean and pleasant. The doors were flung wide so that the icy air would drive out the night's smoke. A squad of women washed and scrubbed the floor. Those women solved my problem.

Siora Turon, the owner of the pensione, herself a refugee, introduced me to her domain, the kitchen, a large room with an immense corner fireplace. Cooking went on from early morning until late at night. It was wonderful. I had often dreamt of warmth and the sweet fragrance of food during the long war years in Rome, where we had only a gas stove. But there was much more than warmth and food in this extraordinary environment; the Siora was an advocate for knitting, which would become a major industry in the area.

When her women were through washing and scrubbing, they sat around the fireplace and, following her direction, took up their knitting with the same energy with which they had scrubbed the floors. Siora Turon sat at the table drawing and cutting models, and deciding on stitches and colors.

"Most of these women are like me, refugees," she explained. "We have lost everything, so we have nothing to lose. We are making ourselves a new life." Then she added, "You have seen war so far from a narrow perspective, a Rome separated from the rest of Italy. Rome would never understand what we have gone through."

She was a stocky woman in her fifties with a long, thin braid of blond hair pinned around her head, and piercing blue eyes, which, no matter how serious the situation, were always laughing. I listened spellbound. She faced Claude one evening over a drink at the bar. I needed, she told him, the kind of suit that would allow me to face the Alps like a soldier — a ski-suit. The next morning I was introduced to the refugees' workshop, a vast basement filled with tables and old sewing machines at which men worked busily. Two days later, I walked into the bar at the pensione to general applause.

"I wish you'd had that suit on when we married," Claude said, with a laugh.

Back in our cold room, while warming up in bed, Claude asked me the question I feared, "How much?"

"Only two cartons of cigarettes," I whispered, "and I got a pair of mountain boots in the bargain."

I did not wait for his reaction. I turned on my side and went to sleep. Two days later we left for Tarvisio.

Claude was assigned a command car and driver, Enrico, a tall, slender, taciturn young man with a stoic face marked by a deep, recent scar. He had thinning blond hair and was slightly cross-eyed. His left hand trembled; he tried to hide it.

That night I told Claude I did not like Enrico. I did not trust him. Claude replied that the road to Tarvisio presented serious difficulties, besides the problems of the season and the condition of the road. Since it had been the center of the fighting between partisans and Germans during the last year of the war, most of the villages in the valleys had been burnt down or made uninhabitable. As a consequence of recent political complications, some deserted mountain villages served as a shelter for the loose bands of Titini, or Tito-partisans, most of whom were hostile to the Allies.

However, after much checking, we realized that Enrico was the only person at AMC headquarters who knew his way over the mountains. He had fought there as a leader of the partisans. People who knew him thought him outstanding. My opinion did not count.

Enrico laid out his non-negotiable terms: he intended to leave at 6:00 a.m. in a closed command car with snow tires. The road, which ran along a precipice for long stretches, was a sheet of ice. He would be forced to drive very slowly in the light of day because no one would come to help him if there was trouble. If everything went well we would arrive in Tarvisio by dinnertime.

The morning of our departure was blistering cold. Claude and I were ready at the bar when Enrico entered stomping his heavy boots on the freshly mopped floor.

"I did not get what I asked for," he declared in his rumbling bass, "and I am not going to leave under the present conditions."

It took Claude hours of bargaining to get another vehicle. When he finally was presented with an open command car, Enrico remarked sarcastically, "I still wonder how you won the war!"

Then he disappeared. A few minutes later he returned with a huge sheepskin in his arms. He nodded to me to get out of the car and gently wrapped the rough smelly sheepskin over my Antarctica ski suit. When Claude thanked him, he replied, "You should have thought about it yourself, knowing full well that this woman spent the whole war in a greenhouse." Then he added as an after-thought, "I really do not understand why you want to drag her up there."

From my early months with Claude in the army I had learned not to react to such remarks. I swore to myself that I would not speak to Enrico during the whole trip.

Of the two meandering roads to Tarvisio, one passing through Gemona, the other through Caporetto, our guide chose the latter, without explanation. He was in a black mood because by the time we left Udine it was already 2:00pm, close to sunset in the narrow valleys. Shortly after the car started moving, I closed my eyes and fell asleep.

When Claude woke me, I was stiff with cold. We had to wade a torrent on foot, while Enrico tried to get the car through. Putting my frozen feet in icy water was the best thing I could do. The cold stimulated my circulation, and I mentally thanked Siora Turon's brother for the completely waterproof boots he had handmade for me, all for a half carton of Lucky Strikes. Claude's feet were soaked.

After crossing the torrent Enrico took a road that climbed a mountain and soon we were in the midst of a brilliant winter landscape. After an hour, however, he turned back to the valley. While slowly climbing through it, we went through several villages. As Enrico had warned us, the villages were completely deserted, their houses burnt or severely damaged by gunfire. On the main gate to a church someone had scrawled in large red letters *"Ritorneremo,"* ("We shall return"). All that survived of the villages was the cemeteries, whose crosses were still standing, displaying the names of the deceased and some gentle prayers. The car advanced so slowly that I could almost read those names.

A cold wind whipped flashes of light snow against our faces and I pulled my sheepskin over my head, disappearing under it. Enrico burst out laughing heartily, and as he laughed the deadly silence of the world around us dissipated like fog. I was relieved, as if I had been freed from a prison. Claude took out the thermos of hot coffee and the two men drank from it.

As the cold gray day slid imperceptibly into a dark velvety night, Enrico's voice soared from the foggy valley into the open sky. In waves of heartwarming bass, he sang a song which Claude and I could not understand. His voice smelled of the earth when, on the first warm day of spring, the ice melts and the first flower pierces the arid soil. It reminded me of sitting around the fire eating hot cornmeal while the men, just back from the fields, their boots muddy and their hands dirty, tell dirty jokes, and the women, who move around to serve them, absorb the fragrance of the male bodies and dream of the night they will spend close to them in their matrimonial bed. His voice sounded of children playing noisily in a village square in front of the church at sunset during summer Saturdays, while the bells ring to announce the day of the Lord. Enrico's song was a paean to his village.

Suddenly the fog lifted, the clouds broke, and a half-moon cradling a bright star shone over the snow-covered pines. The moon and the star came and went between the white branches as the car moved slowly along. Enrico's song embraced winter and summer, Christmas and Easter. It was a hymn to peace.

When we reached Caporetto, we got out and walked around the village, a living monument to the Italians' worst defeat by the Austrians in 1917. That defeat spurred the beaten army to the final victory at Vittorio Veneto in 1918.

"I know of a place where we can rest," Enrico announced. He led us to a house that was still intact among the ruins. A thin plume of smoke rose from the chimney towards the moon and the star.

An old man and a woman huddled near the fire in a large empty kitchen. The wall facing the road and the window were badly cracked. Gunfire had recently hit the building, but even so everything was neat and clean. The woman, dressed in black, a black handkerchief tied around her head, was busy turning a thick wooden ladle in a large pot of polenta over the open fire. She hardly noticed our presence. The man signaled us to sit down. Then, to our sur;rise, Enrico announced in a matter-of-fact tone we would all share the dinner. We sat in a circle around the fire, a huge wooden platter of hot cornmeal topped with cheese on our knees, a glass of local grappa by our side.

§   §   §

The next morning's sharp cold air reminded me of what had happened the night before. As we ate and drank around the fire, Claude thanked our hosts for their hospitality. The old man, attempting a smile, tried to explain that he was only doing his duty.

"We all owe our lives to him and his friends," he said, pointing to Enrico.

Enrico raised his glass full of grappa and swallowed it in one gulp. "To my American friends," he said, "who crossed the ocean without knowing what they would find on the other shore. They believed, perhaps, that they were keeping Hitler at a safe distance from their own land — a good enough reason. But is it a sufficient reason for thousands of young men to risk their lives fighting for a land they had never seen before or hardly ever heard of?"

"This," he said, turning to Claude, "is what I do not understand. But," he continued, "you do not understand us, either. You come to us from another planet and look at us with interest. You risk your lives to set us free. I admire you for the way you dress. Yes, you wear these uniforms and boots made of the best leather. And I admire your equipment. I admire you for the honest, frank way you look at us and our problems. For the way the Allies are handling the whole affair with Tito. But, I ask myself day after day the same question. What made people like you cross the ocean to come to a village like Caporetto? What is your personal interest in us, when it was the Japanese who destroyed your fleet?

"For us it was a different story. When I took to the bush I was a deserter from an army deserted by our leaders. I was pursued by another army that had invaded my land and taken over my home. I wasn't drafted as you were, I guess. I had said my farewell to arms the very night our colonel disappeared from our barracks in Ancona after the armistice on September 8, 1943.

"Among those who fled with me was my captain. I was a corporal. We stuck together, the captain and I, because we shared what counted most for us — the land where we were born, a language which few understand, the polenta and the grappa we are eating and drinking now, our mountains, the trees of our forests. My captain was caught, months later, by the Germans and hanged like a bandit from a tree. I ask myself why I survived."

Claude was looking keenly at Enrico, impassive, unperturbed. It must be his long experience as interrogator of war prisoners, I thought. Perhaps he was wishing he had his typewriter with him. Claude had hardly touched his grappa. The old woman had fallen asleep, wrapped in her black woolen shawl. The old man was avidly drinking in Enrico's words.

"The armistice left us to our destiny," Enrico continued, "We had to steal guns and beg for food. But as the months passed, there were more and more men and women like me. All of a sudden it wasn't just us Italians. We had German deserters and British prisoners who had escaped and Russians. Up here in Friuli our best comrades were the Slovenes, with whom we shared our mountains. Together we followed the progress of the war, on our radios and through the Allied prisoners. What made us partisans was your decision to focus on the landings in Normandy, at the expense of the Mediterranean. But I understand why you did it. After conquering Rome and Florence, you lost interest in the rest of Italy. We in the north had to fend for ourselves — we had to get rid of the Germans on our own.

"The front along the Gothic Line forced us partisans to fight on. Italy was on the other side of the line. It was a terrible winter, and we had to find ways to survive. In Friuli, we learned much from our neighbors, the Slovene Titini. They had Tito, and an ideal to fight for. We had no leader and no ideals. Our best-organized group was the Brigata Garibaldi. We wore red kerchiefs around our necks and we didn't tolerate acts of banditry. We were the Communist partisans and proud of it. Our region, deeply Catholic, produced another army, called Osoppo. The two armies fought side by side against the Germans. But things changed dramatically after the peace treaty."

Enrico stopped. I assumed he was tired. His left hand was trembling; he hid it in his pocket.

At this point Claude, who had been very attentive, spoke. He was interested in what Enrico was saying and wanted to know more, he said. Was the civil war, which raged in the Friuli before the Allies intervened, as bad as the German occupation?

"No!" Enrico yelled. "You have it all wrong. The first cause of the civil war was the German occupation and then the support the German army gave to the neo-Fascist regime. Northern Italy was forced to live the real war separated from the rest of the peninsula. Before the armistice, life here in Friuli went on normally, just as it did on the rest of the peninsula."

Enrico's sudden outburst had awakened the old woman. Claude offered her his thermos of coffee, a luxury only the Allies could afford.

"There were bandits among us freedom fighters. Even bandits, however, were useful to the cause, because they were never just bandits. A daily column in the local press, *L'opera dei fuori legge* ("The work of the outlaws"), contributed to confusing the two. We partisans were forced to hide. Our own families in the cities and villages were our natural protectors. The Germans took their revenge on them whenever they couldn't get at us. The neo-Fascists were far worse than the Germans. My own parents were farmers in Nimis, a village not far from here. My father and brother were killed by the neo-Fascists, my mother died shortly afterwards. We killed, too. Mostly in revenge. We held trials and executed the prisoners immediately after the verdicts. But the Fascists killed us without trial. I was almost executed myself. I survived by playing dead, but I was seriously wounded."

The old man interrupted him and the two spoke briefly in Friulano dialect.

"He's suggesting that I tell Carlo's story," Enrico continued with a faint smile, "I will do my best. There are so many stories, I don't know where to begin.

"Carlo was both a bandit and a supporter of our cause. His real name was Tarcisio Ceccutto. He was twenty-six when he was hanged by the Fascists. As leader of the partisans' Friuli battalion, he attacked the barracks of the Alpini in Tarcento, where he killed a German captain and aided the Garibaldi battalion in the successful attack on Vedronza. After the armistice, over two thousand British prisoners working at the factory of Tor Viscosa escaped through the surrounding fields. Carlo was instrumental in placing them with families. He even stole a police boat and ferried groups of prisoners to a British submarine waiting at Marano Lagunare, five kilometers off the coast.

"At the same time Carlo killed, at times indiscriminately, even people on his side. He killed a pregnant woman who had been falsely accused of being a spy and a respected doctor accused of having erroneously declared dead a young man hanged by the Fascists. Carlo shot the doctor at dinner in the presence of his family. When the Fascists finally caught him and several other members of his group, they kicked them through the streets of the village, then hanged them one by one from a tree. Twice, Carlo's rope broke. He was kicked and insulted and forced to climb back on his chair while the relatives of those he had killed shouted obscenities and insults. The bodies hung there for days before their families were allowed to retrieve them for burial. The Germans never took part in these shows, as far as I know."

His voice resonated in the cold, empty kitchen. The fire had almost died out. Claude got up and moved towards the woodbin. The old woman, like a tiny skeleton wrapped in black, made an effort to get there before Claude, but he helped her back to her chair. He gathered some straw and kindling and soon a roaring fire sent warm golden light onto the beams of the ceiling and on the white walls around us. A ray of cold moonlight came through the cracked window.

"Grazie, Officer," Zoan, the old man, said with a smile. "All we needed was a fire."

Breaking the heavy silence that followed, Claude began to speak almost inaudibly. In that silence, I was suddenly overwhelmed by a terrifying feeling that we were all dead and it was the fire, not Claude, speaking to us.

"Often during this war I thought I would have a lot to say about it, but now that the war is over, there is nothing to be said."

Only the crackling of the fire broke the awkward silence.

"For months, after our first landing in North Africa in 1942, I could not forget the faces of two friends with whom I had crossed the ocean. They were farmers from the midwest and had never seen the ocean before. They asked me what I thought we would find on the other shore. We had been told again and again we had to fight Hitler, who had taken over Europe, but that did not make much sense to them. Why didn't the Europeans fight Hitler themselves? Japan was different. This ship, they said in jest, is going the wrong way. Now those faces have vanished. Perhaps my friends are dead. I have seen so many die around me, especially when we landed at Anzio. My job was to interrogate civilians caught in the squeeze between the German army and the Allies.

"Of course I could say plenty about Rome, where I met my wife, and about Florence, with its destroyed bridges and its damaged historic buildings. I could talk about the many beautiful things I've seen in Italy. But I have nothing to say about the war I fought, absolutely nothing except I am glad it is over, it is finally over.

"The war I fought was very different from yours. You fought for your village. We were told we were fighting for the Four Freedoms. I doubt that my friends who died were willing to give up their lives for the Four Freedoms. The war was a dirty job. We never said so in our letters home, but we all felt it. We had to get through this dirty job, and we got through it in the best way we could. We were proud of our units. We loved our friends and were proud to fight beside them. Yet our main motivation was to get it done and go home. Just like you. Except that our home is back on the other shore. That is the great difference between us. We were lucky. Tonight I felt how lucky we are to live on the other shore. Yet, what you said made me proud to have fought on your side. It gave me a solid reason for fighting and makes me feel at home with you."

He paused to feed the fire.

"Yet there is not much difference between your war and ours, Claude continued, looking at the fire and playing with the embers. "War, no matter what war, just or unjust, yours or mine, is all about hatred. You kill in order not be killed, but in order to kill you must hate. I still wonder how the SS could kill those hostages in your village square. Did they hate you Italians so much? I don't think you can be ordered to kill. Killing is something you do on your own.

"Before we landed in Sicily, a general (they say) tried his best to arouse in his soldiers hatred for the Italians. Once we've killed them, he said, we can see if they were good or not. But we have to kill them first.

"I come from a small town in New York State called Schenectady," Claude went on. "I had never seen Italy before I landed in Sicily, but at home my mother and father spoke an Italian dialect. They couldn't even speak English properly. My father crossed the Atlantic twice, paying for these trips with gambling winnings. On his second trip he married my mother Giuseppina Miele. They had three children in Italy and five in Schenectady, I was the first of the Americans. The Irish boys in school called us *dago* and *wop*, but we were still Americans.

"When we landed in Italy, I discovered what it means to be an American of Italian descent. In Sicily, I couldn't hate the Italians, any more than I could hate my mother and father. Yet, during this war, I must have killed some Italians. And down in the south, I witnessed the execution of three Italians accused of spying.

"The war gets so confused in my mind at times that I wish I could forget it. Now that the war is finally over, I understand why some of our soldiers deserted. Perhaps they didn't want to kill. Perhaps they couldn't get themselves stirred up enough to kill. All they wanted was to go home. Many of the Germans also wanted just to go home, and they also deserted. Yet, Hitler succeeded, more than any of our generals, in making his soldiers feel proud. Perhaps he succeeded because the Germans hated the Communists from the start; they saw them as a threat to their homes."

Claude picked the biggest log from the woodbin and flung it into the fire. As it hit the embers, there was a shower of sparks.

"If we must hate, that was definitely an advantage they had over all of us!"" Enrico's laughter broke the gloom. Zoan brought out more grappa and served Claude first insisting he should swallow his glass along with him, which, to my surprise, he did. I also drank my share and fell asleep without realizing it.

§ § §

We began climbing the mountains at sunrise, under a metallic sky. Enrico followed the steep ascent of a road which was passable in spite of its bumps.

Now that the ice was broken between us, he admitted that the night before he had been afraid to face this part of the road, because he knew Tito's partisans had taken over some deserted villages. They would never dare stop a car during the day, he said, muttering "Cowards" almost inaudibly. But during the night, who knows, and then he feared we would be left alone because they would have taken him away with them.

At a certain point the road skirting the precipice was so icy that not even the special tires Enrico had requisitioned seemed able to keep us from sliding perilously. He suggested Claude and I walk on the inside of the road and he proceeded slowly ahead of us, waiting for us at every turn.

The sun shone triumphantly when, on the very crest of the mountains, we reached the village of Tarvisio. At a point where Italy, Austria, and Yugoslavia meet, Tarvisio, a huddle of houses clustered around a church with a tall steeple, stood silent before us under a thick blanket of snow. Peace on earth, goodwill to men — it could be the perfect Christmas scene. The village rose on a plateau surrounded by the snowy tops of the great mountains.

As we entered the AMC officers' quarters, we were met by the happy aroma of food and a chorus of cheery voices from the dining room. The officers' living quarters consisted of a two-story chalet about half a mile from the village. Constructed of stone and wood, situated at the edge of an impressive pine forest, and providing an imposing view of the mountains, the chalet was a dream home for lovers of the Alps in winter.

While Enrico and Claude were busy unloading the luggage, I entered the chalet. Three Allied officers were coming out of the dining room to meet us. When they saw me alone in the entrance hall, wrapped in a rough sheepskin, a heavy woolen cap covering most of my face, they stopped for a moment in some surprise. They told me later they didn't know what to make of the strange dirty bundle rolling into their house.

"Perhaps this is the woman," whispered one of them to the others through the loud laughter.

He was a tall stout officer with thinning blond hair and a deep voice. A South African captain, I later learned. I am sure he thought I didn't hear him, but since I did, I answered with a laugh that, yes, I was the woman, and I hoped they were not disappointed.

§ § §

Our three months at the chalet began with that rude but jovial first encounter, followed by proper introductions. Everybody knew Enrico. The AMG of Tarvisio consisted of three officers — a British major, a South African captain, and a first lieutenant from New Zealand. Claude was replacing the fourth, an American who had just left. The team governing the Tarvisio area seemed as taken with the idea that a woman was to be added to their household as with the arrival of a new American officer.

Without the PX and the American rations, the AMG diet would be sharply reduced. This was the very first matter brought to my attention. Consequently, I was to be driven to headquarters daily to gather as much food as I could, and I would supervise the kitchen so that the jolly spirit prevailing so far at AMG meals would continue and perhaps even improve.

Throughout our stay in Tarvisio, I fulfilled this expectation to the best of my ability. The chalet's kitchen had an excellent local cook, three assistants, two housecleaners, and as much extra help as I thought necessary. The whole village was at our disposal, since all its inhabitants were unemployed. The members of the staff would become my closest friends and collaborators during our stay. Nothing connected with the kitchen had ever been of particular interest to me. My task here, however, went beyond the kitchen itself. I was put in charge of the food as a way to make the presence of the Allied authorities acceptable.

My task, which looked at first like a full-time job, included finding the food as well as cooking it. As soon as I discovered the talents of the Friulani around me, however, I simply became a point of reference at the center of the process. My presence was indispensable at 9:00 a.m. at the rations headquarters in the village where I would have coffee with the sergeant in charge of supplies. This young man, from South Dakota, welcomed me each morning with a bright smile. I was present for lunch also and especially for dinner. Dinner was particularly lively because it was preceded by a cocktail hour. The alcohol was provided once a week by the non-American members of the AMC.

Maria Rosa, the cook, was a genius at inventing all sorts of recipes using the canned American rations, something no American cook could have envisioned. The housecleaners, who were able to move freely across all borders, provided — all black market prices — eggs and fresh poultry, venison and fish, even fresh vegetables, a rarity in Tarvisio. One of the drivers, a baker by profession, prepared fresh bread and cakes daily. The meal was always topped off by American coffee and British Scotch, which was new to me.

The dinners were so successful that I could hardly put an end to them, except when an inspection of some kind was scheduled for the next day. My guests, especially Captain Jones, the South African, usually came to the dinner table after a session at the bar. Conversation flowed like wine, smooth and tasty, moving freely from the casual gossip of the day to more serious political or literary matters. The war was a thing of the past, a bad storm they had weathered in good company, fraternizing among allies who had come together from the four corners of the earth, thanks to Hitler. The rest was to be forgotten. The political problem AMG was currently facing in Venezia Giulia received hardly a mention. We regarded Tarvisio as a way station before going home.

My guests spent the whole day at work in the village, with just a pause for lunch, Italian style. Nothing that happened in the office was ever mentioned in my presence. Even Claude, when I could spend an hour with him before going to bed, never said a word about what went on at work. The AMG chalet was, for me at least, a happy Nirvana. I began to think of Udine and Caporetto as a nightmare, even though Enrico was there to remind me that they were real. But in Tarvisio, even Enrico seemed carefree.

The peace of Tarvisio gave my life another dimension. Daily letters from my family in Rome spoke of the immense difficulties my sisters and brother had to deal with as they looked for work. They encouraged me to prepare for the forthcoming state orals which would secure for me a tenured position teaching Latin and Greek in a liceo. I dug out my Homer and Virgil, Horace and Herodotus from my duffle bag and placed them neatly on a pine desk in our living room, where I could peruse them while my guests were at work. My oral exam would take place in Rome in May. I had passed the written exam two years before, seventeenth among a thousand candidates.

The British major was enchanted by my books. He began declaiming Homer in Greek to Captain Jones who, ignorant of Greek but good in Latin, fell on Virgil. The New Zealander listened with envy to both and asked me how long it would take him to learn the basics of Latin. Claude knew Latin well and proposed to teach him. I asked them all the obvious question, "Why don't you work on Italian first?" That led to using the cocktail hour for Italian conversation.

Two months went by happily with only one semi-serious contretemps. Captain Jones drank more than the others. As a kind of remedy for this excess, he slept naked covered only by a sheet, the window of his bedroom wide open no matter how cold it was. The chambermaid suggested I keep an eye on him in the coldest nights to make sure he didn't freeze. At first, I was a bit worried, but as the nights went by and he showed up every morning for breakfast punctually at 7:30 a.m., pink-cheeked, I forgot about his strange habit. One night, however, shortly after midnight, the maid woke me up whispering, "He is dead."

I jumped out of bed and knocked on his door, which faced my bedroom. No answer. I knocked again. Again no answer. We finally decided to enter his room. From the open window a full moon shone on a huge pinkish naked male body lying motionless on the floor. I rushed to get Claude who called the two other officers. Jones's heart was beating, they said. With great effort, since he was quite large, they managed to get him onto the bed. They massaged him with alcohol and then covered him with heavy blankets. When he finally came to, he looked surprised to find us all in his room. The major had a hard time explaining to him what had happened and why we were there.

He laughed heartily, "You are all jolly good fellows, he said, "and I thank you all, but none of you can make me change my ways. Not after four years of this lousy war."

§ § §

My constant companion during our stay in Tarvisio was Wolf, a white German Shepherd. Wolf followed me on my long walks on skis or on foot into the thick forest that stretched from the back of the chalet up to the crest of the mountain. He warned me of dangers by jumping in front of me and thus preventing me from going ahead. He lay at my feet when I sat down in the sun and licked my book when he decided that I had read enough and we should move on to do something more interesting.

Wolf belonged to the chalet. The AMG had found him there when they took over. The dog's relationship with the staff was special. There was a secret entente among them and a secret language. Maria Rosa told me he would bark only in case of danger.

On a sunny day, Wolf and I were following a path deep into the forest along the tall pines heavy with wet snow. Suddenly, Wolf stopped and threw himself in front of me. Then he jumped up, barked furiously, and bounded into the forest. A few minutes later I saw the black shadow of a man disappear about fifty yards away, not fast enough for me not to notice that he was heavily armed. Wolf came back to me and showed me the way home.

As soon as I reached the chalet I called Claude at his office.

"I should have warned you this morning," he said, "Tito's partisans have infiltrated the area. We are taking care of them. They are not dangerous to us but they certainly are to the Italians." My reply seemed to surprise him, "But I am Italian."

Wolf had already communicated the incident to Maria Rosa and her helpers when I showed up in the kitchen. As I sat down to take off my boots they all crowded around me. During the night the Titini had kidnapped Beppe, a friend of Marco, one of our employees. There was alarm in the village. Certainly the officers were taking care of it; I shouldn't worry. They introduced me to the elements of the coming dinner: venison as the main course, a special Tarvisio-style creme caramel for dessert.

Spring arrived just before we left Tarvisio. The pines, free of snow, glistened. The snow was melting in spots exposed to the sun and patches of tender green grass were beginning to show here and there. One day, we saw the first flower of spring, the *bucaneve,* piercing through the snow. I could not believe my eyes. I embraced Wolf who could not understand my sudden joyous outburst.

The *bucaneve,* literally "snow piercer," was the main topic of conversation at dinner that night. My New Zealander friend, a true lover of nature, took a few hours off the next day to explore the forest with me. He restrained me from picking any flowers. Perhaps, he said, the *bucaneve* was an endangered species.

On March 15, we left for Claude's new assignment in Udine.

§ § §

Enrico drove us to Udine, this time in the small Fiat we had in Tarvisio, over a now passable road, slowly descending through the deserted foothills of the Alps to the Adriatic coast. The snow was melting and the fields smelled of earth, grass, and cow manure. The scent of new life was in the air.

In Udine, while Claude was at the AMG headquarters getting his orders, I visited with Siora Turon and my old friends. Claude picked me up at the pensione after dinner. He was received with wine and songs. I was now billeted with him at the AMG hotel, he announced, but I refused to leave the pensione.

The next morning, Claude gave me, as a belated Christmas gift, but mostly as official recognition of my work in Tarvisio, a splendid fur jacket of gray lamb, fitted at the waist, with a hood that made me look like a Little Gray Riding Hood. It had been made by Siora Turon; I had become their honored customer. From then on, I wore that fur jacket, giving it up only when the flowers were in bloom. I had never dreamed of owning anything so elegant.

I slept at the pensione out of loyalty to Siora Turon and her women, but my life radically changed. From my first day in Udine, I was officially received in AMG society. That included not only the officers and the mostly British military commanders still in place, but also the high society of Friuli. The region was anything but peaceful, I was told. Marshall Tito, with his territorial ambitions, created serious worries for both Truman and Churchill. The Allies were cooperating with Italians to counteract Tito and his partisans.

On my first day, I was invited to a dinner given by Colonel Bright, Claude's new British superior. A thin, wrinkled, witty lover of horses, he smoked cigars and sported a riding crop. I sat between Colonel Bright and the person I thought was the Italian guest of honor, Count Manuel de Asarta. I was told upon entering the dining hall of the AMG hotel that the Count was to be our host during Claude's stay as *governatore* of Latisana and the surrounding region.

During dinner, served Italian style with plenty of excellent local wines, Claude and I traded jokes with Major Kenyon, the mayor of Cervignano, Brigadier Howard, who commanded the 2nd AA Brigade, and Colonel Bowman, head of AMG for Venezia Giulia. Colonel Bowman invited us to our first horse race, at Ajello. Brigadier Howard and Colonel Bowman were quite impressive, both tall, slim, witty, sporting blond mustaches that contributed to their British air. At dinner, Colonel Bright seemed to be interested in Roman history and literature, while Count de Asarta dove straight into the topic dearest to him, our forthcoming arrival in his territory. I learned that this was the reason I had been invited to the dinner. He was waiting for us, he said, "with open arms." He pulled out a map of the region and opened it over his plate.

The count was short and stocky, with a reddish complexion from the days he spent in the fields. He spoke Italian to me without a regional accent; to Colonel Bright he spoke in British-accented English. He was witty and often sarcastic. I listened, impressed by his analysis of regional politics and his remarkable historical, political, and literary knowledge. I was to discover that he was as fluent in French and German as he was in English.

As we waited for dinner, he told us that his estate extended along the Tagliamento River. He pointed out that, while newcomers to Friuli might regard the Tagliamento as just another river, it had witnessed in 1797 one of the most significant battles Napoleon fought on Italian soil, the battle of Codroipo against the Austrians. The peace treaty signed in Passeriano, a short distance from Fraforeano, the count's estate, better known as the Treaty of Campoformio, marked the end of Italian independence. The last independent Italian state, the Republic of Venice, was sold by Napoleon to Austria. The count's library contained some of the original documents related to the event, as well as many secondary sources.

Having established the historical importance of Fraforeano and of his library, the count turned to me with an offer that didn't seem to me to be genuine. However, it became clear that he meant every word. He could not believe it, he said, when Colonel Bright told him that he could have Claude and me as his guests. He knew we were an exceptional couple — Claude an alumnus of Harvard who spoke Italian, French, and Spanish, and I, a student of classical philology, disciple of Giovanni Gentile, and assistant at the Accademia d'Italia to the philologist and poet Vincenzo Ussani. Besides, I was a lively lady who was sorely missed already at the AMG chalet in that godforsaken outpost of Tarvisio. He would place his rich library at our disposal.

He stopped speaking as the waiter asked him to fold his map so that he could be served. But before obliging, he showed me the map, so that he could entertain me with its contents for the rest of the dinner. I wanted to know whether the count knew that a partisan had recently murdered Giovanni Gentile in his villa in Florence. Did he know that the famous Professor Ussani had been deprived of his honors by the new Italian government because he had dedicated his *Vocabulary of Medieval Latin* to Mussolini?

Meanwhile, Claude was lost in conversation with the countess, a plump lady of uncertain age, admired for her worldliness, who spent as much time as she could in Rome.

§ § §

Latisana stood at the very heart of a troubled area, between the Isonzo River to the east, which more or less marked the border with Tito not far from the Morgan Line, and the Tagliamento River to the west, roughly the border of the AMG zone with Italy. The region was overrun by Italian refugees from Trieste and the whole area of Istria, including Fiume and Zara on the Dalmatian coast. Moreover, Tito's men raided the zone at regular intervals. Only the Allied presence could hold them back.

But Claude and I and the count and countess were to live together like a happy family. He put his villa at our disposal.

"He takes us for lightning rods," I whispered to Claude, as we left the dinner.

"What's wrong with that?" Claude replied. "Isn't the AMG a lightning rod for the Italians in this godforsaken part of the world? We have ceased to be a military unit. Our task is purely political. We are now warriors of peace."

I liked that expression, although I hated the word war. I realized by now that the reason I had helped the German deserters in Rome was simply to get them away from the front. What I had seen and heard about war in Venezia Giulia reinforced my convictions. Peace, however, turned out to be a more complex matter than we had envisioned that night at the AMG dinner in Udine.

The count's villa, in the heart of Fraforeano, about 15 kilometers from Latisana, was a country fortress within a large park which was already bright with the signs of spring when we arrived. It was flanked by workshops and stables for cows and horses. The majestic river Tagliamento flowed at its side.

We arrived at noon in the tiny Fiat Topolino. The count and his niece, a young woman my age, the mother of two children, married to an equestrian, were at the gate to receive us. While the count's butler attended to our luggage, we lunched in the family dining room. A white-gloved waiter silently served local dishes with local wines on a square table.

The display, to be repeated daily for months, was a tribute to beauty and harmony, which his eyes seemed to caress: the elegant porcelain, the silverware, the delicately embroidered napkins, the antique furniture, the oriental rugs, the half-drawn golden curtains, allowing only a partial view of the park, the prints and etching of Roman ruins in the Friuli, the pictures of landscapes darkened by age, and fresh flowers from the garden. Conversation flowed like a limpid stream in the shade of huge trees. It skirted unpleasant topics with the nonchalance of those who have been through enough battles to consider them a part of life.

At our first lunch, Claude took the lead with detailed questions about his new post, starting with refugees and raids. The count answered these. But he seemed to evade questions about economic conditions, unemployment, and his agricultural workers. It was up to Claude to find that out, I learned later.

After lunch, Claude left for his office in Latisana and I was shown our quarters, which comprised the whole southeast wing of the top floor — a living room, a bedroom with an antique canopied bed, and a spacious bathroom with an antique bathtub. Spring flowers from the garden abounded. The rooms offered a bright view of the park and the river.

The countess assigned two attendants to us, a charming woman and her teenage daughter. While helping me unpack, they told me that the rest of the family worked in the fields. Everybody at Fraforeano worked for the count.

The view was wonderful: huge trees covered with fluffy green, like chicks just out of the shell; the wide Tagliamento flowing so peacefully it almost seemed to stand still. I thought of Napoleon and of the battle of Codroipo, of men running for their lives in every direction, when I suddenly saw a strange sight. In the distance, three tall, slim trees seemed to be moving along the high riverbanks.

I called Anna and Lucia to explain. They laughed. Those were not trees, they were three women carrying firewood home on their shoulders, bundles weighing up to 175 pounds, a distance of five or six miles! Later in the spring, I met some of those women during a walk along the riverbank. Tall and sturdy, dressed in black, with black kerchiefs covering their hair, they moved along gracefully, balancing those great bundles. They kindly stopped so that I could take their picture, and then we chatted.

They asked me to show their picture in America.

§   §   §

In the early afternoon of our second day, Claude sent his interpreter to take me to Latisana. I found him in his office surrounded by local officials who were trying to brief him on the problems of the area. Though they talked slowly, with ample gestures, they were all talking at once, some in Friulan dialect, some in Venetian, some in broken English. Claude was listening attentively but seemed relieved to see me.

"Let's show the lady the town," they proposed, thus allowing Claude to end a meeting bristling with unsolvable problems. The frustrating aspect of his work was that, though he could see the issues clearly, he could not find meaningful solutions. The solutions had to come in their own good time, not from America but from the people themselves.

It was Wednesday, market day in Latisana. Tables and benches displayed silks of all kinds, in ironic contrast to the town's lack of basic necessities. Yet that was, as I learned later on, a hopeful sign of a return to normality. Latisana was the center of the silkworm industry, though most of the spinning was done in Lombardy.

The buildings that were still standing after the heavy Allied bombings were typical of the laguna's architecture, loosely related to venetian architecture. The Ufficio del Governatore displayed only two flags from its balcony, the Union Jack and the Stars and Stripes. For political reasons, no Italian flag was permitted, and the two exhibited impartiality towards the Slovenes of the region.

The Slovenes, however, were nowhere in sight. I learned that they were hiding in the bush. They came in stealthily from beyond the Morgan Line to kidnap or execute "enemies of the people," encouraged by Tito to prepare the region for possible takeover after the Allies left. But fortunately, General Alexander and his army, with backing from Churchill and Truman, gave no sign of leaving.

For a year at least, Latisana and the region between the two great rivers was the theater for a covert but stubborn struggle between the Allies and Tito, without developing into open conflict. The AMG kept control of an explosive situation. What the count had explained to us in Udine emerged tragically from our first encounter with the people in town.

§ § §

Both Claude and I were stunned by the poverty we saw that first day. Refugees from behind the Morgan Line were everywhere, mixing with the locals, who did their best to help them even though they themselves needed help. In the Cold War, Latisana was still suffering from the preceding war. Except for the center, the town was a pile of ruins, eighty percent of the houses destroyed by Allied bombardments or German raids. The people lived in tents along the river, with no hope of a roof over their heads anytime soon. It was painful for me to live at the count's mansion, an Italian among Italians but unable to help the refugees. I had been warned in Udine that as a war bride I was strictly forbidden to interfere with my husband's work.

For the next year, Claude worked in his new post within well defined parameters. He was a superb listener, offering a whole new experience to the residents of the Tagliamento area. Even if he could, at best, do little for them, his presence among them counted, and not only because he wore an American uniform. By his very behavior, he made them aware of the basis of a democratic way of life. If you want your views respected, you must respect the views of your neighbor. A piece of wall in Latisana, remnant of a bombardment, still bore the infamous Fascist motto *"Mussolini ha sempre ragione"* (Mussolini is always right). When Claude expressed his opinion, he made sure people knew that he did not think he was always right.

Claude was also an excellent organizer, virtually addicted to order. But much to my dismay, he was not decisive. A soldier gets to make very few decisions on his own, and even now, with the AMG exercising a political rather than a military role, all the important decisions came from Udine. Still, I thought that Claude did not take advantage of the opportunities he did have to make a decision. Of course, because he strictly followed orders, his work was valued in Udine, and Colonel Bright showed his support in more than one way. The whole area on the other shore of the Tagliamento, centered in San Vito al Tagliamento, was soon added o Claude's area of responsibility. Most practically, our little Topolino was replaced by a jeep.

All the residents of Latisana applauded the arrival of the jeep one bright morning, especially the Governatore's driver, Giocondo. Jeeps were an endangered species at the time in Venezia Giulia so we considered ourselves lucky to get one, even if its windshield had two bullet holes. Slovene bullets had made the holes, killing the Italian driver and severely wounding the American officer sitting next to him, on the road from Udine to Gorizia. Claude refused to replace the windshield. Further, to ward off bad luck, as he put it to the Latisanesi, he baptized the jeep *Maristella,* painting the name in large white letters just under the pierced windshield.

Our driver, an outgoing Friulano from the plains, who considered his role as our driver to be the highest honor, offered to teach me to drive. Given my innate inability to deal with any mechanical device, only the screams of an admiring crowd saved me from driving straight down the banks into the river. The crowd cheered my daring maneuver to get out of trouble and I passed the test with flying colors.

Twice a week, Giocondo drove us to San Vito where, while Claude was busy at work, I was the honored guest of the local nuns and their blossoming kindergarten. I had lots of fun with the children and provided them with large cans of powdered eggs from Claude's military rations. I also spoiled them with chewing gum, the treat they loved most. The gentle nuns in turn, learning that I had married without a dowry, embroidered tablecloths and napkins of the brightest orange and blue cotton cloth woven in the region, so durable that they lasted over fifty years. The nuns presented them to us during a moving Christmas ceremony.

The most challenging events were the weekly trips to Trieste for our military rations and the monthly excursions to Gorizia to pick up Claude's pay. Because of the damage suffered by our jeep on the outskirts of Gorizia and other accidents, we were always careful to protect ourselves. We rode in the backseat and let Giocondo drive a hundred miles an hour in dangerous areas.

Trieste, recently taken by General Freyberg but shared for a time with Tito's partisans before it was declared neutral territory, was a sad sight. With empty roads and silent people, it had a sense of impending doom, hardly befitting a city once known for its vitality. Gorizia's medieval castle now proudly displayed the Stars and Stripes and its wide streets were often the setting for military parades dominated by tanks. Those parades told the Slovenes that the Americans did not intend to relax their hold on the region.

The black market flourished in Gorizia, as it did everywhere there were American troops. Giocondo adored Gorzia.

§ § §

My life ran parallel to Claude's. Both of us appalled by what we saw, we reacted in different ways.

"I am a soldier," he would tell me. "I have to take Colonel Brights's briefings seriously. For him, the Morgan Line business is exclusively a military problem."

"Don't you see the human side of it?" I would suggest. He would smile.

It took Claude a while to realize the tragic human problem for which there was no practical solution. He had become an almost perfect executor of the military orders he received. As an Italian civilian, I immediately understood the Morgan Line problem as the most complex he had faced yet. I had never imagined that peace would mean what we were now seeing in Venezia Giulia. In twenty years of Fascism, we had always heard Communism described as the prime enemy of individual freedom. Throughout my adolescence, I had never questioned that. Now I rejected Communism as fiercely as I had during the dark years of Fascism because Stalin and his ally, Tito, acted just like Mussolini and Hitler.

The refugees in Venezia Giulia cried out for the right to live in peace. Even their painful silence spoke eloquently as they crowded in the main square in front of the church. Mothers hugged their children to them; the old leaned on the young. If one dared to talk, it was to tell the story of how Tito's men had abducted and executed young sons right before their fathers' eyes.

I often repeated to myself Roosevelt's words, pronounced in Chicago in 1938, which I had written in my diary and knew by heart: "The only sure bulwark of continuing liberty is a government strong enough to protect the interest of the people, and a people strong enough and well enough informed to maintain sovereign control over its government." How could the Italians, as weak as they were, led by an almost nonexistent government, possibly protect their liberty?

I worried that the Americans had an insuperable problem trying to understand the political and social situation in Italy as we understood it. I groped for a way to present the matter to Claude during one of our evening discussions. The fragrance of magnolias filled the air. Frogs croaked in the swamps along the Tagliamento River. The world around us was peaceful, as if it had never been touched by war. Yet we both knew that a new war was brewing, against yesterday's ally. The Italians around us would have to choose between liberty and a new form of dictatorship. I was horrified at the thought of a Communist Italy.

"Perhaps you should try to imagine," I suggested one evening, "what it would have been like to live the best years of your life as a prisoner in a windowless castle. Your life is dictated by the lord of the castle. You have no contact with the outside world. After a while, you can't imagine anything different from what you are accustomed to. You accept and never question. Then you are suddenly freed, and you find yourself unable to make choices.

"The motto of the castle where I spent my adolescence was *Mussolini is always right*. It was painted in big black letters on all the public buildings. I am now fighting to gain a sense of the liberty of which Roosevelt speaks. If I ever do cross the ocean, I'll do so aware that I did not conquer liberty on my own. It came to me at the cost of so many lives. Yet those lives will have been spent in vain if you don't help the people you freed make the right choice now in Venezia Giulia."

§ § §

While Claude did his work, I spent hours in the count's library doing research and looking into new fields, such as the history of Venezia Giulia. I took long walks on the banks of the Tagliamento exploring this wide, gently flowing river. This natural phenomenon was new to me, since the Adige in Merano is a mountain torrent and the Tiber an intrinsic part of ancient Rome like the Walls or the Coliseum. I would sit amid the canes and high grass on the river bank and take off my clothes for a swim. I also walked into the fields of wheat, corn, maize, and barley, where the count's people worked. I listened, sitting on the grass at the edge of a field, as the women in particular spoke of their concerns. Though they had enough to eat, they and their children had never owned and never would own anything, not even the beds on which they slept. How different this was from the farmers in Tyrol who owned their fields and owned their home

At night, Claude and I discussed the thorny issue of the workers' resentment. Both Tito's partisans and the Italian Communists were exploiting it. Claude had often warned the count about it. The AMG worried about subversive acts in the forthcoming national elections. The Communists were determined to have a say in the government. Would the Demo-Christians, the strongest center-right party, be able to counteract them? In Venezia Giulia, it was difficult to separate the issue of political justice from the strictly territorial ambitions of Tito.

I couldn't clarify Claude's views on this question. Isolated in Fraforeano, I hardly read the newspapers or listened to the radio. Italian politics came to me mostly from the count, who could not be objective about social problems because he had vested interests. Caught as I was in the awkward position of being an Italian among Italians but not one who could actively contribute to the creation of a new democracy, I began to feel the desire to cross the ocean and build a new life.

In late spring I went to Rome to take my oral exam. I also met at length with Eduardo de Filippo to discuss Claude's proposal to translate his play, which now more than ever both Claude and I felt would be our strongest connection with Italy when we went to America.

Otherwise, it was disheartening to be in Rome, a city groping for identity under a fledgling democratic government. I was glad to return to Latisana with my mother. Her presence stimulated both Claude and me to tour Claude's republic, as she called the region. We spent sad days in a Venice that was deserted and in the similarly deserted Roman ruins of Aquileia, where we met some congenial Slovenes who were as horrified by Tito's political maneuvers as we were.

Back at the count's estate, sitting next to me in the shade of the park's centenary trees, Mamma unexpectedly called up memories from a time long before my birth. Through her stories, she was trying to unravel for herself the relationship between her family and the family of the man who was to become my father. On the one side were poor ignorant farmers, on the other, wealthy intellectual aristocrats, who owned most of the valley. Yet each respected and helped the other. She could not explain how it happened. I often lost her as she pursued her memories.

Of all the rooms in the rural fortress of Fraforeano, Mamma most loved the count's library. What attracted her, she said, was the smell of old books mixed with the fragrance of roses in the park. Sitting on a leather chair, book in hand, she would be transported to the library of my paternal grandfather, Sior Augusto, in her native Alpine village. She recalled finding herself there in the company of my grandmother, Siora Maria, feverishly searching for information about Cincinnati, a mythical city on a mysterious continent, to which the family's adventurous son had escaped. Both she and Siora Maria had fallen in love with that unknown city on the Ohio River.

Suddenly, the bird would fly back from the distant blue and land in my lap. She told me I must visit Cincinnati as soon as I settled on the other shore. She was now envisaging my future in tomorrow's world, where America and Europe would stand side by side. Mamma was more worried about the future of Europe than of Venezia Giulia. There wasn't anything I could do here, she said categorically, not in Venezia Giulia, not in Italy, not in Europe. While Europe was waking up to the harsh reality of reconstruction, I should face life courageously in America. She was keenly aware, she said, that the separation would be painful for both of us. But there was nothing else that we could do.

As for Claude, for whom she had affection and respect, she advanced her opinion with some hesitation. The Americans would be a greater help to Europe in peace as civilians. It was time for him to help Europe from across the Atlantic. Once we settled in America, she added, Bona, who had recently married Eddie Kostka, would follow us and then Neri and she herself would come.

During her stay with us, Mamma showed herself to be a firmer believer in America than either Claude or me. She was, Claude commented one evening at dinner, the real American among us. "European-American," he corrected himself. "That is a new brand of American."

Claude and I both sorely missed Mamma after she returned to Rome. Claude warned me I would miss her even more in America. The night she left I cried myself to sleep. Still, the thought of her made us stick to the decision to move on to the next phase of life.

During the long summer nights, as we listened to the odd music of frogs and crickets flooding our bedroom, I wondered what New York would be like. I knew we would stay in New York, because de Filippo had approved the final translation of *Napoli Milionaria* and expected it to be successful. We could not let him down. I was both excited and frightened at the idea of leaving Europe. I didn't know what to expect. Fraforeano, only a few miles away from the troubles of Latisana, had given me the most comfortable life I had ever lived. High-class entertainment, as Claude put it in one of his letters home. The count, often joined by his son Vittorio and his niece, had an intense social life, with summer parties in the park. The whole of the Udine AMG were the count's honored guests. They reciprocated by inviting us to the Ajello horse races.

In a spurt of enthusiasm I decided to learn to ride. The horse the count provided, however, was anything but tame. More than once he simply threw me. Still, I persevered until I could take short rides in the countryside. I enjoyed every new experience; it had the feeling of exploring a new land.

As summer turned into fall and the park became a palette of rich colors, my talks with the count became more frequent. We were, I realized, two lonely souls searching for a political truth which we could not easily define. We suffered frustration for not actively taking part in the development of a new political order. The count had grown attached to both Claude and me. He enjoyed my company in his solitude and admired Claude's skills in the complex business of the refugees and reconstruction.

There was nothing Claude would not do for me. If love means trying to please the beloved in all possible ways, certainly Claude loved me more than anyone. And I loved him in return. He had given me both hope for the future and a new faith in myself.

So that we could see a bit of Europe before leaving it, Claude suggested a trip to Paris. I opted for Switzerland instead because I wanted to see a country that had not experienced war. It was my first trip out of Italy. On the way, we celebrated my first Thanksgiving, in Milan with some of Claude's colleagues. At that point, anything was an excuse for celebration. We then stayed overnight with the count's sister in a chalet near the border. She was an elegant lady who had been one of the women-in-waiting for the Queen Mother. Switzerland seemed unreal to me, a sort of fairyland inhabited by self-satisfied people I didn't think could manage in today's world. Would America be like that? I asked Claude.

"No way!" Claude laughed.

During the Fall I decided to take up my research in Renaissance Humanism, interrupted when I was arrested in April 1944. Claude provided a jeep for my weekly visit to the Marciana Library in Venice and made arrangements for me to stay overnight at the Palazzo Guggenheim, which had been requisitioned by the Allies. The hours I spent collating manuscripts in a damp and freezing library were followed by delightful walks on little empty streets along canals smelling of moss. The luxury of a warm bath, thanks to the Allies, crowned my Venetian days.

Venice has never been as attractive to me as it was those days: silent, empty, mysterious and also damp, dirty, smelly. A city slowly drowning in its own mysterious silence.

§ § §

Life in Fraforeano had its own dramatic moments, letting the count know that change was coming. One summer morning, I was in bed, mulling over how to organize my day between the library, walks along the river, and visits to the refugees of Latisana, when Anna, our chambermaid, burst into my room.

"They killed the poor boy," she sobbed. "They killed him only because he was engaged to Marisa."

She grabbed my hand and dragged me in my nightgown down the stairs into the courtyard. There was the poor boy, hanging from a tree, to the right of the gate. What struck me first was how the body seemed to long for the earth below. But the rope around his neck prevented his body from reaching the earth a couple of yards away. Somebody had done that, and it was the thought of that unknown somebody and of this action that frightened me so much that I began to sob. I joined the other women who had gathered in front of the tree, the boy's mother, his grandmother, his fiancée, Anna and her daughter. The count, Claude, and the farmers found us there, Claude said later, embracing like the holy women at the foot of the cross.

The count was livid. The farmers were horrified but also angry. They said they knew the killers and would get revenge. The place chosen for the crime, at the very entrance to the villa, showed its aim — a warning to all those who worked for the count.

Some said the killers were Italian Communists connected with the Titini. The Titini Communists among the farmers argued that this was untrue. But everybody knew that the killer was a Communist. Marisa, the boy's fiancée, was the count's personal secretary.

Claude took firm control. As the representative of the law he telephoned the local police and ordered two of them to take the body to the Latisana police station. Then he called Udine and initiated an investigation. He never made public the results of the investigation. Claude warned the count that his farmers were an easy prey to subversives in the area. He should take whatever steps were necessary. The count answered that he was aware of the danger, but at a loss as to what to do.

§ § §

Late summer can be stifling in Bassa Friulana. Claude and I spent nights in August wishing we could silence the relentless frogs and crickets. Under the white canopy that protected us from hordes of mosquitoes from the swamps, we yearned, in vain, for a breath of air. One dawn Claude kicked the canopy open and announced angrily that he was going to work. The sun was high in the sky when I arose. I had a leisurely breakfast. Anna and Lucia had closed all shutters to keep out the heat. A bouquet of peonies filled the room with its acrid aroma, reminding me as always of the night before my father died.

I had never enjoyed so much peace and beauty in my life as here in Fraforeano, I thought to myself, when suddenly a loud noise came through the shutters: the crunching of running feet on the gravel of the courtyard. Before I could wonder what it was, the count knocked at my door He was pale. His hand shook on the doorknob.

"Would you kindly come down with me," he said with his usual courtesy, "to face the crowd gathered in our courtyard?"

He said he was willing to meet with them, but they had come armed with axes and sickles and, he thought, even firearms. His very appearance might be the spark that set them off. He withdrew to his library. My first reaction was to call Claude's office, but, of course, the line had been cut. The count sank into an armchair, holding his head in his hands. Since Claude had taken the jeep, I sent Giocondo to Latisana by bicycle.

Waiting for Claude there was nothing else I could do but face the crowd, which I did with apprehension. They shouted questions. I tried to answer. They explained why they wanted to see the count. I listened. All this time, the count sat in his library. When I heard the familiar rumbling of Claude's jeep outside the gate I could feel the count looking down at us from behind the closed shutters. By the time the count met with Claude, he had regained his natural color but not his eloquence. He remained silent for the rest of the day.

Claude addressed the crowd American-style, telling jokes, as if they had come to visit. He then asked the farmers to choose representatives with whom he could discuss their grievances. Finally, holding my hand, he walked slowly out of the courtyard with them and their wives.

Negotiations went on for weeks in Claude's office in Latisana. Claude was in daily contact with Colonel Bright in Udine who came to Fraforeano to speak with the count. He never spoke with the farmers.

In the dispute between the parties, Claude acted as arbitrator. He believed his task was to help both parties, within the law. But which law? The British colonel in Udine reminded the American officer that there was still a war going on in Venezia Giulia and no law existed except for the military law imposed by the AMC. Beyond settling disputes between farmers and landowners, the duty of an AMG officer, Claude was reminded, was to keep the area free from Communist infiltration until a political settlement could be reached and peace established. The farmers would have to wait for that peace to resolve their grievances.

The count was so upset that it took him some time to regain his composure. That evening he silently embraced me at dinner. I had grown so fond of him that I could listen to his arguments with some understanding, but by now I knew that the problems were far beyond him. Born and raised on a vast estate that had been in his family for centuries, he was obviously inclined to hold onto it at all cost. He was no St. Francis and was not likely to have a dramatic change of opinion. What was so unjust, he would ask us, about defending one's own property?

We had come to Bassa Friulana as foreigners. We left for Rome, almost in tears, as members of a family.

In Rome, we learned that I had passed the state exam, ranking high among the thousands of candidates. This good news won me an assignment to the liceo at Frosinone, close to Rome. I could have bargained Italian style to keep the job, but the day I got the news, I resigned. Maybe I felt guilty about keeping a job away from another Italian. More likely, I simply wanted to burn my bridges so that I could devote myself completely to America. Now I began to say goodbye to all my friends. In Rome, the first one I visited was Professor Ussani. He did not know how American Universities worked, he said, but he had a friend at Columbia University.

"Where is it?" I asked and rejoiced to hear it was in New York. Sitting at his desk, he wrote a long note to his friend. "I have recommended you to him," he added as he folded the letter, "but you must remember to send me those American soups, so good for my delicate stomach."

The last person I visited was Natalia Massimo Lancellotti. We sat on her bed and reminisced about the happy days she had spent as our guest when Claude taught in Florence. We had enjoyed our weekends as guests of the orchestra conductor Igor Markevitch, with whom Natalia was madly in love. She explained to me sadly that her family had forbidden her to marry him because he was divorced.

That was the last time I saw Natalia. Her mother visited me in New York two years later and told me that Natalia was in the Congo, working as a nurse.

By now I was like a steed chomping at the bit. Nothing could keep me from crossing the ocean, not even my family. But it broke my heart to say goodbye to Mamma and the family, especially Francesca's little Antonella, at the Stazione Termini, as Claude and I left for Viareggio. I had forbidden everyone to come to Livorno to see me off. After a week spent with many other war brides in a hotel in Viareggio, I sailed for New York in early February, 1947, on a Liberty Ship, the *General Muir*. At the pier, I was greeted by two of my old Virgilio students with a copy of their verse translations of some Greek lyrics.

CHAPTER 14

Times Square

In the very early morning hours, the Liberty ship *General Muir* slipped unobtrusively into New York harbor. At that time, curled up as usual under my military blanket down in the ship's hold, I felt as if I were quietly skimming a smooth surface. I refused to open my eyes. I had been unconsciously longing for that feeling since the ship left Gibraltar to face an angry Atlantic. I had been longing for that smoothness for two interminable weeks while our *General* was assailed by mountains of roiling water, its keel tilting perilously as if out of control. What I suddenly experienced now was a soothing lightness as if I were skimming over a field of flowers up in my Alps, hardly touching their tops — a dream I'd often had after an illness.

This gentle gliding was a miracle: peace after the storm, with blue skies revealing new horizons. Though the miracle vanished, I was left with a sense of having been privileged to experience it.

The sound of the siren made the war brides around me jump off their berths and run to join their soldiers on deck. I clutched my duffel-bag making sure it contained the two precious items which justified, at least partly, our venture into the New World: Claude's translation of de Filippo's play *Millionaire Naples* and the letter by my venerable professor. To the two I had added a letter of my own, scribbled here and there in moments of respite from the strange life I had been leading.

Cara Mamma began a long letter I wrote her. From the moment we left Rome, she had filled my heart and mind as everything I was leaving behind: my whole life so far, from my father's sad death amid the flowers of the Dolomites and the fairy tale villas of Alpine Merano, almost unreal at this distance, to the German occupation of Rome and the civil war in Venezia Giulia. Nobody could guess, as I left Rome and then the military port of Livorno if, when, or how this turmoil would end. All I knew was that I was leaving my whole life behind me forever. Shutting that door left me deaf and blind. Fortunately so, because had I been fully conscious, my departure would have seemed to me a betrayal — as in fact it did later, a betrayal of the family I had promised Mamma that I would support when Papa died.

Mamma had supported my decision to marry Claude and go to America, but it was my decision and mine alone. I wanted to break through barriers and move freely beyond them. I was fed up with the Europe I was leaving behind. Claude as my husband stood for a freedom and security I had never dreamt of. I loved him as I loved the open skies he had brought with him.

The fearful crossing ended, I stood on the deck of the *General Muir*, facing not the unknown but Manhattan — my fixed point from now on. Thus I closed my letter.

Writing to Mamma I was really trying to face the pain of separation and understand it. What I wrote revolved around issues I discussed on the *General Muir* with Cinabro, Peter Viereck, and John Dos Passos, author of a novel on Naples to be called *The Gallery*. Claude listened in silence; he seemed more worried than I was about what to expect.

§   §   §

I had written the first version of *Cara Mamma* in the toilet of the military train that took us from Rome to Livorno. I withdrew to the toilet to cry freely, ignoring the knocks at the door. ("In America," Claude had warned, "never cry in public.")

Mamma was surely horrified to learn that her daughter had to be checked for venereal disease. I went through the exam at Viareggio along with the other war brides. I also wanted to amuse and puzzle her with what came next. We were treated like royalty at the hotel — excellent food, a military band playing at dinner, an elegant double room with balcony overlooking the sea, and pleasant though strange entertainment. After enduring the venereal disease exam, our lives were nothing but fun.

We war brides were put through a demanding program of Americanization, supervised by a plump captain and carried out by a squad of well-meaning nurses with much good will but little elementary Italian. The program must have been designed in the abstract. There was a cooking class to introduce us to American food, though roles were often reversed: the nurses were happy to be introduced to Italian cooking beyond pizza and spaghetti.

On the other hand, many wives were bothered by the warning that, in America, if your husband was a construction worker, he would leave in the morning to reappear only at dinnertime. Thus, to avoid divorce, wives had to prepare a lunch box with sandwiches made of baloney — the Italian equivalent of which means "bullshit." Of course, when children joined the family there were more lunch boxes to prepare, this time with peanut butter and jelly, like baloney, exclusively trans-Atlantic products. Most brides who knew nothing about their husbands in civilian roles were amused by the lunch boxes but puzzled and even troubled by the notion of divorce, which seemed to be part of American life.

"What about being abandoned by your husband in Nebraska" my roommate asked, "and you don't know any English?" I reassured her she could turn to the Italian consulate for help. She hardly knew how to spell her name in Italian, she confessed. We laughed but stopped short when we realized we were being harsh. "The Americans are so well meaning," my illiterate roommate said, "that it's a crime to make fun of them." Despite not knowing how to write, she had memorized the basics of American geography.

A very serious problem at the hotel in Viareggio was the separation of mothers from their babies for hygienic reasons. Only nursing mothers were allowed in the nursery where babies were kept, crying so loud they could be heard throughout the whole floor. Mothers often broke into the nursery. The problem was becoming so acute on the *General Muir* that the captain and head nurse thought they might be forced to crack down and impose military discipline. But sea sickness solved the problem. Most mothers could not move from their berths.

At the hotel, our captain exercised his paternal role at breakfast and dinner, entertaining us (through an interpreter) with the rudiments of American history. The interpreter forewarned us to laugh at his jokes, even when they didn't make much sense to us.

As I wrote my letter, I wondered how Mamma would take my stories with her unlimited admiration for Americans, whom of course she knew only through the impeccable Claude and his friends. So I urged her not to jump to conclusions but wait for future impressions. Thanks to my experiences both at the hotel in Viareggio and on the ship, I learned to take my companions as individuals and avoid generalizing.

When we finally left the hotel, after being regaled at breakfast with *O sole mio* and *Stars and Stripes*, I was given a sign to be displayed when we embarked, stating that I was an "N.P.W.B" (non-pregnant war bride). Pregnant and nursing war brides took precedence over everyone else. Undoubtedly a delicate thought on the part of our paternal captain, but I felt a sense of achievement at crossing as "myself" alone.

§ § §

The port of Livorno was crowded with military craft of all kinds, huge, gray, and dreary to someone like me who had never set foot on a ship and hardly ever seen a port. When we left the bus, we were surrounded by a crowd of relatives of the war brides. The ensuing confusion explained why our departure had been so carefully orchestrated. Here and there some military police had to forcibly separate clusters of tightly-embracing relatives. Sobbing continued unabated, in full view of those of us on deck, even after the departing bride had disappeared. Then I finally understood — I wrote to Mamma — why I said my good-bye to the family where I could cry alone undisturbed. As usual, Claude was right.

Our arrival in New York was different. The soldiers were the first to disembark. They walked slowly, overloaded with their gear. Next came the war brides, some clutching babies, others with a cardboard sign announcing that they were pregnant, others like me dragging their duffel bags. Last came the crew. The line moved slowly under an icy drizzle. We were about to part, each passenger going his or her way alone from here on, each, as a GI poet had said to me that last night at dinner, "to a different port in the great sea of being." He was surprised that I knew he was quoting Dante. But Dante didn't matter at this juncture, I declared. I wanted to read William Faulkner and Edgar Lee Masters.

Some of the GIs on the ship were exceptional people. Captain Cinabro, for instance, gave me some advice that, he said, could help me avoid obvious traps once I started my life in America. I stored his words in the back of my memory, just in case. What bound us forever was a Europe we shared and the *General Muir* that had brought us safely through two weeks of storms to the other shore. Now we had to give up both.

In Staten Island, the line was very long but orderly, unlike the line in Livorno. Here, the relatives and friends of the returning heroes were somewhere out of sight, at a distance from where the docked ship was disposing of its precious cargo. I barely made out the Statue of Liberty in the fog, busy as I was heeding the captain's orders, dragging my bag out of the bottom of the ship. As I quietly stood in line waiting to be debriefed, America met me with a sense of peace, order, and emptiness. For two weeks I had been either seasick or in the dream world of Dramamine. Now, as tired as the soldiers, I was mainly homesick. The military port of Livorno lay lost beyond an ocean.

§ § §

From now on Claude was to be my all. He loved me in his own American way with an admiration I did not deserve, for qualities that in my world were taken for granted. Yet that's just what I needed then. Through two years of marriage I had slowly grown to identify that American soldier with America, a country that would allow me to be reborn and to make a fresh start. During these two years of happy marriage I had learned to take Claude's presence near me as a guarantee of the new life that would allow me to help those I had left behind. Claude never spoke to me about democracy or freedom in the abstract because he knew by experience that, like millions of other European victims of ideologies, I had come to distrust them all. He knew that after the last year of war in Rome, which ended for me in a Gestapo prison, I was desperately longing for a personal freedom that would give meaning to liberation. Having lived together through the civil war in Venezia Giulia, we both knew that the unpredictable nature of the parties which freedom and democracy had generated in a liberated Italy might well plunge the country into civil war. War generates political and social confusion. Only America, I thought, could save Italy.

Claude had made me aware of the strange irony of my birth in the bank my father directed, not in Cincinnati, but in Bolzano, capital of the old Austrian Südtyrol which the Peace of Paris in 1919 had delivered to Italy. Claude had an unbounded admiration for Mamma, who, after the bankruptcy, raised us as her husband wanted, on her own, and our, hard work. My family, Claude remarked, had thus avoided the Depression which had forced his own father into bootlegging. Yet it had made me and my siblings prisoners of Mussolini's Italy, whereas my father in his short life had known the world. Claude was well aware and proud that he had walked into my life to break the chains that held me prisoner, like a slave in Plato's cave. He was proud of showing me not with words but with actions that he had freed me from a world of appearances.

For all these reasons I had grown to love Claude as one loves life after a long illness. If his way of understanding the Italians after twenty years of Fascism and four of war came from his earlier life in a democracy, I enthusiastically embraced that democracy. During our two years of marriage I had followed him from Rome to Caserta in the South, to Florence, and finally to a Venezia Giulia threatened by a former ally. I was proud of having Lieutenant Bové as my husband not because of his uniform but because of his practical handling of the first insoluble problems between Tito's soldiers and the Italians. During the past three years, from the liberation of Rome to our departure from Italy, Claude had offered hope of a better life not only to me but to all the victims of war who had met him. And finally, I was proud of his friendship with Eduardo de Filippo, to whom I had introduced him.

Claude Bové was a practical man. He taught me oral English through popular songs like "Tell me the tales" and children's rhymes like "Star light, star bright." A born musician, he was the first to teach me, patiently, how to sing in tune. The only songs I knew before were the Fascist hymns which I would yell out in unison with an army of girls and boys. As for my written English, when I began composing in a diary on the model of my first English Bible, *The Stars and Stripes*, he agreed to correct it in collaboration with his Colonel. He replaced my Shelley with Melville and made gentle fun of my love for Edgar Lee Masters.

What he did best, however, was inculcate some rules for life in America, which I would follow as if they were a doctor's Rx. About crying, he emphasized that I should avoid crying in public, but crying in private, he added, had the power to change me inside. So my family managed, together with me, to avoid tears at my departure. When finally, to everybody's relief, the whistle blew and the train began moving away slowly, they all raised one hand silently; I kept my own hand out the window as long as I could see them. Then Claude joined his friends, and I ran to the toilet to have a good cry. Claude was right. The woman who walked from the toilet to the compartment so he could show me off to officers and nurses as the model war bride was different from the one who had left Rome. When I learned I was not on the list for the *General Muir*, the first ship to depart for New York, I acted differently from the other war brides. They barricaded themselves in the dining room and had to be removed by the MPs.

I stopped the Captain in the hall as he strode past leading the brides to dinner. I showed him the precious document I had in my duffel bag — the translation of *Napoli Milionaria* for which Claude had found a sponsor in New York — and told him that I was expected in Manhattan with my husband as soon as possible. At the dinner-dance that evening, to everybody's surprise he asked me for a dance. Dance I could, better than anybody else. Three days later we were on the *General Muir*.

§ § §

The morning of our arrival at Staten Island we could not see Manhattan from the dock where we had disembarked. Housed within a fort made of little white huts, enveloped in a thick fog, we spent a few days undisturbed, with our dreams. The soldiers were being debriefed. As for me, suddenly bereft of all dreams, I held on to Claude as to my anchor. But then something happened that shook me. When Claude came back in civilian clothes and I saw him like myself, a powerless nobody, I was shocked. Like Cinabro and the others who had impressed me with their sharp perceptions of what to expect and, mostly, not to expect from their homeland — including Peter Viereck who on the ship seemed to tower over the rest for his intellectual acuity — Claude without uniform seemed naked. On that deserted dock, he also seemed shorter, thinner, even helpless. The skyscrapers of Manhattan looming behind them, cold in the blue like the wind that swept them, those Americans whom I had deified as liberators laughed and joked as if to forget all that. Shedding their uniforms, they seemed to lack something essential. I was suddenly frightened at the prospect of having to face life on my own. That evening I couldn't eat, that night I couldn't sleep. Claude noticed my feelings.

"You can settle the Columbia matter on your own. That's your business," he said at breakfast. "As for *Millionaire Naples,* I'll take care of that. The Theater District on Broadway is a great place. You'll enjoy it."

To please him I used an idiomatic expression he had taught me.

"Broadway gives me the creeps."

I reassured him that "our Eduardo" was indeed the greatest Italian living playwright — that he had bet on a good horse — but, like me, he was tense and frightened at setting foot in New York. I was making him tense, he said.

§   §   §

In the crowd of American civilians welcoming their heroes home was Peter Bove, Claude's brother, a blue-eyed middle-aged gentleman who seemed at ease in his beige sport-suit topped by a dark fedora. He was the first American civilian I met. After him I met his family, and then, before long, the Schenectady family. We were in for a series of encounters over three weeks that had nothing to do with Mr. Cowan, the man we hoped would produce Eduardo's play, or with New York's Theater District, or with Columbia University. I had imagined America in the abstract, a sort of land without real people, a place where we could "go to work" immediately in the heart of Manhattan and try ourselves out there. Like Christopher Columbus, I intended to get all the gold I could and get it fast.

We would get to Cowan and Butler eventually. The first America I was to meet was obviously through Claude's extended family. Their America, not mine. People, plenty of people, who insisted on seeing me and enjoying my presence among them and who would not advance our project one inch.

So, as I came ashore, my first act had to be an act of humility. It was not easy at first and not always pleasant. It took me a while to develop a taste for it. Most of the time I enjoyed it and in the end it paid off. They were all heartwarming human beings.

Long before we arrived, Claude's extended family had agreed that my American experience would start as guest of Peter Bove and his family in Montclair, New Jersey. I had known Peter by way of his intimate correspondence with Claude. Peter was the most successful member of the Bové clan. Some of the evidence of his success, I learned, was his living in Montclair rather than Schenectady. Claude had described to me the pattern of his brother's success, often ironically but still admiringly.

Peter, it appeared, had successfully crossed the bridge into the Anglo-Saxon world and so had anglicized his name by dispensing with the accent on the *e*, while Claude, at Allied Headquarters in Caserta, had employed the accent to show the link of the Bové clan to Napoleon's brother when he was king of Naples. That's why Claude insisted on the accent. But didn't Claude in Rome anglicize my name from Maristella de Panizza Inama to Mary Bové shortly after we married, in order to facilitate my life in America?

Peter changed his name, dropping the accent, after a long upward movement in a society that favored Anglo-Saxons over Italians. After high school, Peter abandoned his father's '*storo*' in the Italian-American section of Schenectady, took out a loan to attend Harvard, and got both a degree in business and an Anglo-Saxon wife. He never lived in Schenectady again. His wife Beryl was a sturdy, independently wealthy yet hard-working graduate of Wellesley College; her father was one of the founders of the "Five and Ten" stores. Peter had met her while singing in the choir of a Protestant church at Wellesley.

Now in February 1947 the father of two and an executive of the New Jersey Telephone Company, Peter welcomed Claude back, seeing him as a potential partner in an import-export business of which *Napoli Milionaria* was in some way to be a part. He continued to be Claude's role model, as he had been throughout his adult life. Claude had followed Peter to Harvard with a loan that the war had allowed him to repay and — thanks to the war and the conquest of Rome — he now boasted of a war bride who, though poor, was socially not inferior to Beryl. Among the Bové the ambitious Peter Bove was for many reasons the closest to Claude in his determination to start life anew. For me, Peter Bove was an example of the social mobility for which the Old World envied the New. He had succeeded in moving upwards *in loco* without having to go through four our bloody landings as had his brother Claude.

CHAPTER 15

Montclair

Montclair received us in icy silence under a veil of snow. Peter and Beryl's comfortable white house on a white lawn, one of many, lay not far from the mansion of Beryl's parents. Everything inside had an air of tranquility. Yet, in spite of my good intentions, the peace of a family whose daily life didn't arouse my interest soon declined into boredom. The house itself looked like a doll-house with cute furniture and white lace curtains. I marveled for a moment at the wide Frigidaire overflowing with bottles of milk and juice, nicely packed meat, butter, and jam, frozen vegetable and fruit, whereas my own home in Rome or in Merano had not even had an icebox. But we didn't miss one, since Mamma in Merano took us children daily to the market in between school hours, much to our delight. In Rome, we ate what we could get off the black market. I don't remember any leftovers.

What bothered me most in Montclair was the guillotine character of the windows. During my long hours alone or with Claude in Peter's house, the children were in school, Peter at work, and Beryl running errands or attending church or PTA meetings, I sat for hours near one of those windows wishing I could lift the lower half and let the outside air flow into the overheated house, air cold and pure, smelling of the pines that adorned the lawn. But the windows would not budge. Of course nothing kept me from opening the front door — which to my surprise was never locked —and running down the lawn to another lawn and then another and another. Montclair was a world without fences. It took me a while to realize that what oppressed me in a world naturally free was the Old World pressing on the New and almost spitefully trying to kill it. I tried in vain to counteract the feeling, but only one thing seemed to attract me: Times Square. Why didn't Claude take me to Times Square? When I asked, he told me to be patient; we would go to Times Square.

The best part of our time in Montclair was the evenings. We gathered around the fireplace and Claude was asked to entertain the Bove family and the guests invited to honor a returning hero and his foreign bride. Claude would give a breathtaking version of the landings in Morocco, Sicily, Salerno, and finally Anzio, landings which led him to Rome and to me. Though I knew the story by heart, I still marveled to hear again how, on the first landing, he got rid of his machine gun in favor of his typewriter. Then came the stories of the internecine wars in Venezia Giulia between Tito's soldiers and their Italian Communist allies, and a harrowing description of conditions in Italy, which only America could remedy. According to Claude, a third World War was on the horizon. A brief presentation of me as a war bride from a German-speaking region in Northern Italy, once Austrian, offered him the opportunity to develop an important issue: All wars not fought in self-defense constitute a crime against humanity. His best example was World War I, and he told my father's story.

At the dawn of the century, my father had settled successfully in a bank in Cincinnati, Ohio, close to Beryl's hometown. Here he found the personal freedom denied him by his family in Europe. In 1896 his father had disinherited him and sent him into exile, with a ticket Southampton-New York-Chicago, for having married a prostitute, that is a woman not of his social class. Lovesick mothers can accomplish miracles. In 1914, when his father died, his mother, the old Italian Baroness Ciani, conceived of a ploy to lure her son back from Cincinnati for a visit in Südtyrol: she had designed a superb book on life in Cincinnati before 1914 based on letters he had written her daily, beginning in 1900. A young school teacher in their village, the Baroness's closest companion after her husband died, wrote most of the work. The plan worked. By the time the masterpiece was completed, in May 1914, with maps of Cincinnati and charts of its history, her son was back in Südtyrol. As expected, he fell in love with the young teacher. He would have married her and taken her to Cincinnati, had it not been for the war. Among its many tragedies, it separated the lovers. The armistice of the "most useless and criminal war ever fought in the West," as he wrote to her, finally brought the two lovers back together, both exhausted but ready to start a family and educate it for a world without war. Of course I, born in a bank as the first product of that miraculous marriage, was destined from the beginning, in papa's eyes, to cross the ocean, which I finally did, but not before I had lived through years of Fascism and another world war.

Much to my surprise, *Napoli Milionaria* and Eduardo de Filippo, the most popular Italian playwright of the day, were never mentioned during those lively first weeks in America. In the peace of Montclair, Claude's mind seemed to be on wars and how to avoid them. The fact that he didn't refer to de Filippo's play for the purpose puzzled me.

The ten days I spent with Peter, Beryl, and their lovely children left me with mixed feelings: gratitude for their warm hospitality, but dismay that there was no movement on our project, a project which I thought central to our future in America. I kept longing for Times Square, which I thought was the theater district, while Claude and Peter discussed the import-export business they planned to start together. Claude made no move to contact the producer, Cowan. Lou Lawrence, his connection with Cowan, had told him to wait for Cowan to make the first move. We had to be patient, he said in response to my complaints.

§ § §

"You don't know anything about America yet," he comforted me one night as I lay awake and disappointed. "Peter," he explained patiently, "has cleverly assembled, for our evening meetings, the best of New York's business world. You must know that rich businessmen work on Times Square or Wall Street, in Manhattan, but sleep in lovely little towns like Montclair, where they send their children to school, while their wives are active in church activities — Protestant churches, of course."

That left me even more curious about Manhattan. Who actually slept on the island, people who couldn't afford Montclair? But my mind was on Manhattan only as a means to an end, how to get *Millionaire Naples* to Broadway. I asked Claude why he didn't mention de Filippo and his play during those evenings in Montclair. His answer left me speechless.

"Naples? That's the very last thing to mention. Naples must come as a surprise. A public relations office will take care of it, once Cowan has confirmed that he will put up the money to produce the play. Eduardo's Naples with its unsentimental, witty humanity will enlighten an American audience, once we have an audience. But I am not de Filippo nor the public relations person for this play. Peter's task is to introduce us to a congenial audience. You must have faith in me and patience. We have just set foot on American soil. Cowan doesn't even know we are here. What if Cowan doesn't keep his promise? Then we'll have to find someone else. Peter is opening doors for us. The old man sitting on the sofa near you last night is a well-known investment banker and a big shot in the Republican Party, which as you know is the party that Peter belongs to."

To reassure me further, Claude reminded me that he treasured his European experience in Italy more than anything else in his life. He wished we were back in Europe. To dispel all doubts, he proposed that next day we see Times Square with Peter and his family.

Next evening we went to Times Square, not to go to a theater, which I would have loved, but to become acquainted with the theater district. The visit was worse than a letdown. It was for me an emotional disaster. Called a "square," it was anything but a square in the Italian sense. It was framed by gigantic billboards with some of the figures moving and even puffing smoke in a phantasmagoria of lights. Within the square itself, a confusion of people who, like us, did not seem to know where they wanted to go, while cars swished by — I had never seen so many cars at once in my life — predominantly yellow vehicles, which I was told were taxis. I held on to Claude's arm like a child, a strange feeling that stayed with me for quite some time after my arrival in America. I was afraid that by losing him I would dissolve in that immense frightening crowd. Noticing that Claude was hanging on to Beryl and Beryl to Peter, I was crushed by a sudden anxiety and I lost all points of reference. What if everybody around us in this crowd felt just like me? What if life in America was indeed endless movement, a hanging on to each other because each one had lost himself? In Times Square, I felt lost as never before.

A vague curiosity about what actually took place in the theaters behind their multicolored lights was soon dissipated by a sense of disorientation. Finally, all curiosity gone, I withdrew into my own little world that I so despised before crossing the ocean and thanked God when Peter shepherded us into a noisy restaurant. I ate my steak and drank my beer in silence. I had no questions the entire evening. Ashamed of myself, I could hardly hold back my tears, and was relieved only when I finally withdrew with Claude into our quiet little room in Peter's villa, on a white bed, enveloped by a deep silence we could happily sink into.

After a good night's sleep, Claude admitted that, looking at me in Times Square, he was afraid I would completely abandon our project. His pragmatic approach to the problem reassured me. He mentioned a certain Elia Kazan and the plays he directed on Broadway. Some day we should go to see those plays. Claude obviously knew more about theater than Peter did, I thought, while Peter knew America better than Claude.

"The secret of success," Claude reassured me, "is to run right through those lights that frightened you. That's what we'll do!"

We both agreed it was time for us to move on from Montclair to Schenectady, Claude's hometown.

CHAPTER 16

Schenectady

Both Peter and Beryl had given me a detailed rundown on what to expect in Schenectady. Peter had spoken tenderly of his mother and had joked about his sisters, to whose education he and Claude contributed. Laura, the eldest, had earned a Master's degree in Spanish, Gertrude, the youngest, a degree in nursing. Martha and Jill had dropped out of college and both now worked as secretaries. Beryl, who loved Ma and the girls, had warned me about the father, a mysterious character at best, a gangster at worst, who for years had kept the family, all nine of them, in a state of fear and anxiety. I knew that Claude, as a young boy, was the only child who lived alone with the old man in his '*storo*' in the Italian-American ghetto. In his teens, Claude had joined his mother and four sisters in a residential section of town, mainly because they needed his help. From what I had read and heard while still in Italy, I admired the constant, almost stubborn, support the family members gave each other through the years, daring even to call Pop to order when he misbehaved. I learned in our correspondence of a harsh exchange of words between Pop and Claude about a house for Mom and the girls that Pop at first refused to buy. Peter and Laura had insisted that Claude should contribute part of the sum.

"It isn't up to me," Claude wrote in Italian to Pop from Italy, "to support a family which you put into the world. I have risked my life in this war and, therefore, intend to put the money I have earned in the bank for my future family, not for the one you built and must support."

I was puzzled by Claude's behavior regarding money. The liberal way in which Peter handled it made Claude stand out. He was afraid of money as much as I was but in a different way. He recorded every penny he spent, how he spent it, why, the monies he paid back, and who owed him money, no matter how little. I was raised to look on the little money available as exclusively for services, and so I had much to learn if I wanted to match Claude.

Back in Italy, Claude seemed to have a lot of trouble getting his sisters to understand that they had to urgently send what I needed. This wasn't charity, it was giving back the money they owed him. Laura and mainly Gilda replied to Claude's insistent requests that life in America had never been so hard as during the war because of shortages and strikes. The result: in need of plain walking shoes, I received after a month a package with two pairs of patent leather high-heeled shoes. While Claude fumed, I sold this luxury on the black market and had a friendly nurse buy me a pair of sturdy nurse's shoes at the PX. From then on, by selling Claude's ration of cigarettes, I managed my own and my family's basic needs. The problem of survival was solved for me but not for Claude.

The black market was a natural phenomenon, an attempt to stimulate a stagnant economy. In a besieged Rome we depended on the black market. Claude, however, regarded any contact with the black market as criminal. So he turned back to his sisters, nagging them about what they did send as well as what they did not. I had imagined life in Schenectady as out of touch with the reality of war for a civilian in Europe, imagining it as bourgeois and boring. Among Claude's sisters, however, there was a spunky one: Jill, her name an English version of Gilda, the victim in Verdi's *Rigoletto*.

Though by necessity a secretary at General Electric, Gilda made the best of what she had: a soprano voice and an irrepressible *joie de vivre*. Whenever she could, she showed up in public for beauty contests in spite of her unfortunate bow legs; she went to parties, was furious at the strikes as well as the war. Patriotism was not her forte, though she supported the troops.

One act in particular endeared her to me. Of all the people she could have turned to, she dared to ask war-hero brother Claude for a $180 loan to buy herself a fur scarf. Claude was furious, but I insisted and he did lend her the money. Jill was also the only member of the family willing to write Claude that he should stay abroad if he wanted to have a good time, because life in Schenectady was dreadfully boring. Any war was preferable to this boredom. She seriously considered joining the Army and regretted that she was too young when the war broke out.

§ § §

On the train from New York to Schenectady, Claude showed me a picture of Pop, a robust giant, with dark hair, a bushy mustache and a heavy chain across his chest. He had crossed the Atlantic alone at the beginning of the century and had later re-crossed it, paying for his ticket by gambling in the ship's hold. He returned to his native town, Cervinara, near Naples, only to kidnap and subsequently marry tiny, industrious, blond Giuseppina, who bore him nine children on two continents. The first infant was buried in Italy, where three other boys were born. Cristoforo, Luigi and Pietro became Chris, Louis, and Peter as soon as Pop crossed the Atlantic for the last time. Claude, the fourth boy, was the first to be born in America.

When I met the family, Chris, Martha, and Gilda worked at General Electric, Louis had disappeared, Laura taught Spanish, Gertrude had just gotten her RN degree and was about to marry a doctor. The girls' lives were to become more colorful with the arrival of their husbands. But that was yet to come. Meanwhile they lived decorously with their mother on Eagle Street, parallel to State Street, the main thoroughfare in Schenectady, an honorable address by American standards. Pop lived alone in his '*storo*' in the Italian section. Claude had warned me that the language his sisters spoke with their mother was a Neapolitan dialect infused with English.

"English, he said, and only English is the language you should speak with my family."

§ § §

I owe to Schenectady my first American discovery, the encounter with what was to become my most faithful American friend. I met it the first time in February 1947 by train, in May by ship, often those first American years by car. It has been flowing for the past forty years below my apartment. I still follow it today on foot, every day, in every season.

It was clear to me from my first encounter that the Hudson River is not a river. The Hudson is a god speaking a language you can understand only if you hear the words in your heart. As the ship glides along the Hudson's shores, thick in spring with fresh vegetation, you dream of an unknown land hiding, behind those shores, and of Indians and Europeans, their eyes wide open to its still intact marvels and dangers. As the train meandered in February 1947 along the majestic curves of the Hudson, taking Claude and me away from New York, I felt an inexplicable happiness, as if the whole world was mine. An effortless conquest, America's first gift to me. It was as if a tacit agreement had been reached between me, survivor of war-torn Europe, and an immense, untouched world.

I was to have that same indescribable feeling of peace and elation again, forty years later, as I sailed on a small boat, guest of my youngest daughter Donatella, in Africa, on the meandering Zambezi, before it leaps a mile into Victoria Falls. On the train to Schenectady, I tried to explain to Claude the surge within me of a joyful sense of freedom. A freedom, I said, based on a tacit understanding between an unknown, penniless war bride and an immense continent. Claude made gentle fun of me, as he usually did when he thought I was being too imaginative.

"Just wait," he said, "this is only the beginning."

"The beginning of what?" I asked. I thought my conquest was complete, from beginning to end.

While Claude softly elaborated on what, according to him, was the American miracle, I fell asleep, lulled by the gentle rocking of the train and the fascinating song of the Hudson. And as I slept serenely, I dreamt of being home again. When I woke up, a chain of low mountains drew an undulating line at the horizon, bathed in the deep orange of sunset. On one side of the train, a forest of trees, their trunks as white as snow, glided by us, sweet and silent like purgatorial souls led on by a thin sliver of pale moon in a pink sky.

"Those mountains have a funny name", Claude told me. "The Dutch who settled here called them Catskills."

"What about the trees? I've never seen such elegant trees."

"They're white birches. We have them all over New York state."

Hudson, Catskills, and white birches. Love at first sight.

§ § §

Schenectady gave Claude the reception that he had missed when the *General Muir* docked. Mom and Claude's four sisters and his brother Chris were at the station with their friends and Claude's friends, as well as correspondents from the local newspapers, depot employees, representatives of veterans organization, which included executives of General Electric in whose shadow the city lived.

Italian-American associations played a major role in the reception, which included singing and flowers and short speeches. Italy was glorified for its Roman past in a way that reminded me somewhat of my Fascist adolescence, as well as for its less glorious recent present, which most Italians were not proud of. Claude was the hero they needed to show their patriotic spirit, their rejoicing at the end of a war that cost so many American lives. Claude's return from overseas was also an occasion to reaffirm the part that Italian-Americans had played in the war and in American life in general. The affection and gratitude shown to Claude were both genuine and moving.

When, however I became the focus of general attention —with interviews, pictures, flowers, and speeches — I was unsure of my role. What did they see in me that had to be celebrated? What had I done to deserve a special reception? Of course, I wished I could tell them about the magnificent play on Naples and the war, but that play lay some place in New York on a producer's desk. Did they know I was just a nobody blinded by the lights of Times Square? I was even more embarrassed when I heard Claude, a short distance away, singing my praises: "You'll see that girl some day in Washington." How could he say that? I had hardly reached Schenectady and he was sending me to Washington, when all I wanted was to be in Manhattan.

In the happy confusion which embraced me, Captain Cinabro's voice echoed in my head:

"Beware! Beware. A young and pretty Italian war bride can easily become a victim of political causes. Causes provoke wars, as you well know. Do not become an instrument of some patriotic ideology, in the celebrations our home-towns will put on for us."

He laughed and I asked him to explain.

"They might welcome somebody like you, naively thirsty for all expressions of American life, and at the same time fresh from the war we fought against Fascism with the help of the Communists. It will be hard for you to believe that some Italian-Americans feel ambivalent about Fascism. After all, we Italian-Americans had our moment of glory under Mussolini. You cannot imagine what it means to be treated as inferiors. Mussolini forced America to respect Italy and Americans of Italian descent. That's how the Italian-Americans saw him. Now, I know you hate Mussolini, but after all, the war opened up the world, and you, because of Mussolini's war, have crossed the ocean with us and are about to land on the other shore, home with the liberators!"

Now, at Schenectady's reception for the return of the hero and his war bride, Cinabro's *Beware* surfaced unexpectedly. Could it be that the attention this singing crowd poured on me now had some hidden motive? The victory against Fascism was a *fait accompli*. What about Communism? What did they know in America about Communism? Claude had learned about it first hand in Venezia Giulia. Some friends of Peter in Montclair had told me there were too many Communist sympathizers in the theater and warned me to beware of the American Communists. But Claude said not to bother: Peter and his friends were Republicans and conservative. Claude was an open, straightforward person with nothing to hide behind his thick glasses. What I needed most in facing America was a clarity of perspective that only Claude could give.

Like shadows conjured by a flickering light I put aside Cinabro's remarks. They just confused me. I quietly settled into the idea that these Italian-Americans showering me with photos, interviews, and flowers had taken me for a symbol of Italy, their own country of origin, a country they dearly loved. Yet, I wondered seriously whether they had placed their love on the right country. Had they forgotten that their sons had not gone to the Italian peninsula as tourists, and that many of their comrades had died just as they landed in Sicily, Salerno, or Anzio? Had they forgotten about Mussolini and his alliance with Hitler? And hadn't we been responsible for having kept Mussolini in power for so long?

Claude's four sisters stood vigilant guard over me. Getrude, the youngest, and her fiancé, a young doctor named Jimmy Purcell, rescued me in the simplest, most natural way. When they noticed that I was ill at ease, they literally carried me out of the hall, tucked me into their car, and drove me to Eagle Street and then to a restaurant.

§ § §

I had never enjoyed in Italy an experience like the welcome the Bové's of Schenectady gave me. Excellent food, superb wine, and operatic music sung *en famille*: Jill as Gilda in *Rigoletto* in Mantova, then as Violetta in *La Traviata* in Paris, and finally as *Tosca* in Rome. Jill was short, thin, with black eyes in an expressive face, wearing a long purple skirt. The tenor, a young man, tall and slim, stood at her side.

After a moment of silence Alfredo's voice in Verdi's *Traviata* singing a hymn to love in a Paris salon made everybody in Schenectady's crowded restaurant giddy with the desire to waltz: "*Beviam dai lieti calici, spira dolcezza Amore...*"

Gilda as Violetta stepped in vigorously after Alfredo's strong and melodious voice transported the audience into a world of universal, passionate love.

"*Beviam, beviam!*" (Let's drink.) As the solo glided into a duet, couples pirouetted around the long table. Those who remained joined in the singing. The Chianti was succeeded by Vinsanto, sweet and strong, and then by Asti Spumante.

A baritone, short and rotund like a middle-aged innkeeper, brought tears to our eyes as he evoked the warm sun of Provence that his son had forsaken for Violetta under Paris' clouded skies, *La Traviata's* sinful love.

"*Di Provenza 'l mar' il sol, chi dal cuor ti cancellò....*"

How could love make Alfredo forget his noble — even modest — southern origins? A remorseful Alfredo stepped in, ready to console his aristocratic father, when the audience called out: "We want something Italian!"

Gilda with her fiancé complied and promptly moved south to Castel Sant'Angelo. The audience looked at me in respectful silence as the painter-lover, about to be executed, called up the image of his beloved Tosca remembering when, under a starry Roman sky, she had opened the gate of his country garden and, freeing herself of her garments, thrown herself into his arms:

"*E lucean le stelle e fremeva la terra... O dolci baci, o lan-guide carezze quand' ella lieta... il suo bel corpo disciogliea dai veli...*"

A powerful Tosca, standing high on her chair, her little hat like a butterfly hardly resting on her short curls, stepped in with a passionate aria. She had no intention of disrobing herself of her purple suit in front of us or of kissing in public.

From Rome we moved further south to Sicily, where Gilda crowned the performance as a willful, almost violent Santuzza in *Cavalleria rusticana*.

During dinner, people casually moved around. Early in the evening, a man had pushed his way in to sit next to me: an older man who towered over everybody, an imperial head centered on great broad shoulders. A black woolen suit tightly fitted his gladiator body as if it were part of the body itself. Under his jacket he wore a vest or *panciotto*. A gold chain drew an elegant curve across his prominent stomach.

This giant did not speak at first. At least, not with words. He spoke with his black, piercing eyes fixed on me while he devoured whatever came our way. His eyes made me uneasy, asking too many questions. During the performance, he seemed to live in a world of his own, enjoying the arias at a distance. Finally, when we descended from Paris to Provence — the old father lamenting his son lost to the love of Violetta — he turned and asked in a deep mellow voice:

"Do you like the aria?" His English was Italian accented.

From the tone of his voice and the expression of his dark eyes, I knew he piled into that question all the others he had asked me with just his eyes during dinner.

"I like the people around me," I replied. "They make me live that aria in a new and different way."

"You are not one of us," he stated. "You look at us with curious eyes, trying to understand why we live as we do. You come from a different world with which we have little common."

The giant's statement suddenly cut me off from everything around me.

The performances had by now reached Rome, the Pope's fortress, Castel Sant'Angelo. The giant turned to me suddenly.

"You should have seen Gilda at the beauty contest in Schenectady years ago when she was eighteen. Her brothers and sisters staged her entrance. The poor girl counted on her voice because she is hopelessly bowlegged. But the rules of the contest forced her to wear a bathing suit. You should have heard the whistles of the audience as soon as they saw her legs. But then Claude and Chris and Laura and Martha and Gertrude and all the friends they had recruited drowned out the whistles with their applause, until she was allowed to sing. Then everybody quieted down and she came out of there with a prize, a modest prize but still a prize.

"You look at us with curious eyes," he repeated. "I tell you now what you don't know about us. America has been cruel to us. But the time will come when we'll be given a chance to sing. My own children are fighting for a modest, very modest, place in the sun. Mussolini gave us a chance to dream, but it was a futile dream."

He stopped to fill his mouth with forkfuls of spaghetti alla marinara. Then he picked up where he had left off.

"Dreams in America are fed by an instinct of survival. Take me for instance. I first worked with lumber. A kind of honest life. But then came the Depression and too many children around me. I made do as a bootlegger. Those were the good old days. I survived by gambling and breaking the law. It was a hard life, but not a bad life. I always was free and am still free in my '*storo*' — as I could never be free where you come from."

Instinctively, I told that giant in some detail about Cinabro on the *General Muir* and about my worries that very night. He smiled. Then he took my hand in his. "I would never cross that ocean back to Italy," he said in his deep voice.

"Your Cinabro is one of us, but he was abroad for too long, talking with soldiers, reading too many books. He has lost touch with us, but he knows we have preserved a wisdom the Italians in Italy have lost, a wisdom that comes from long striving for survival. I left Italy like many others because I was frustrated by the hopelessness in Italy. What Italian we have preserved here is our joy in living. We kept it alive in America even during the Great Depression when everyone else had lost it. Then came the war against Italy — a war we hated but had to fight anyway. Italy caused that war and you as an Italian were part of that war. But how can we not love someone like you? You are what tore us apart all along as our children were fighting that war on the other side of the world. Yet, we cannot hate you any more than we can hate ourselves. You were once our enemy, but then you married my son."

That giant was John Bové. Next day I went to visit him in his '*storo.*'

§ § §

As we drove to Pop's store, Claude reminisced about his childhood. He remembered, when the family was still together, Pop as a gambler, impulsive and hot-tempered. When he didn't win he struck hard. One night in the family kitchen he struck the winner in the chest with a kitchen knife. The wounded man had to be snuck off by the other gamblers, while Pop sat in a corner of the kitchen, his face buried in his hands, and Josephine led Claude and the four girls upstairs. Peter, who still lived at home with his brother Louis, moved bravely towards his father. But his father hit him in the groin. That night, he left the house never to return.

Pop took along with him little Claude to help him in his store. Ma Josephine supported the girls, working as a seamstress in a factory. Claude got up early every morning; before going to school, he had to deliver the Italian newspaper *Il Progresso Italo-Americano* and pick up fresh vegetables at the market.

Claude didn't mind the work. He remembered mainly the happy hours he spent with the books he hid in the back of the store, among cases of pasta and cans of tomato sauce. After work, he would sit on a box near the stove and strum the mandolin. Pop made him work very hard, but also saw to it that he was treated properly by society. When an Irish boy in school called his son *Dago* and threw an inkwell at his face, Pop, without a word went straight to the school, picked up the boy, who was playing in the schoolyard, and gave him such a spanking that he surely never again called anybody names. Short, slim, bowlegged, Claude grew up in Pop's school as resistant as an iron rod and just as inflexible.

Claude ended his reminiscences with a smile: "Peter showed me the way to Harvard, but it was Pop who gave me the stamina to make it there once I was admitted. Life was not easy at Harvard for a penniless Italian-American."

§ § §

On the way to Pop's store, we stopped at the depot, a long one-story buiding so indistinguishable from its surroundings that it has totally vanished from my memory. Inside, men and women were sitting behind typewriters. They all got up when we entered, shook hands with Claude and told me with pride that he had been by far the fastest typist of all.

"Alcamisi had a hard time replacing you!" They laughed. "But we followed your heroic deeds in the army and we are all proud of you," said the man who appeared to be in charge.

Then they all took turns telling us how difficult life had been in Schenectady during the war and still was. Hard work and shortages of all kinds. Claude led me by the arm out of there without the usual talk about my achievements. He was visibly annoyed. Perhaps like me he was thinking of the Italy we had left behind.

"The Italians," he had once written to his father who was complaining about daily life in America, "are like a mass of people who don't know where to go. Nobody knows what will happen next. A country as damaged by the war as Italy has been is no longer a country. It is a territory where people try to survive. There is no joking here. They are waiting for help from America. I don't have enough paper to tell you the conditions of Italy today. The rest of Europe, I guess, is no better off."

§ § §

John Bové was waiting for us at his grocery store, proud to show off his kingdom. The place looked more like a store-room than a regular store; it was filled to capacity with all kinds of Italian foodstuffs -- pasta and oil and wine and varieties of spices stacked all over. As we sat on stools munching salami and parmigiano on Italian bread, Pop examined me attentively with his ox-like eyes and probably found me to his liking because he insisted on our staying as long as we could.

When we left, we carried with us the fragrance of spices mixed with the smell of caciotta and fresh ricotta, fresh tomato sauce and a special kind of oregano Pop grew in his courtyard.

"All products of the good old earth," he commented.

His dark brown eyes shadowed by long dark eyelashes — the eyes Claude had inherited — as mysterious as a deep lake, followed us with an odd tenderness as the car slowly backed out of the narrow alley. I never saw him again.

§ § §

After the visit to Pop, Claude led me through a quiet neighborhood of little white houses more or less alike into a large park. It was amazing. The park was a cemetery that seemed to me like the one in "Spoon River!" As we sat on a bench among barely distinguishable graves, the soft ground sprinkled with snow, Claude was cheerier than I had seen him be in days.

"This is where I want to be buried some day!" he said more to himself than to me. But then he turned directly to me with a strange statement.

"I know," he said, "you are dreaming of a different life for us than the life of my people here."

"We are not like *your* people here," I answered. "We are different from them, much more different than I expected. Your father knows it. He said so to me. The war changed us both. It made you different from them, just as the war drove me across the ocean, far from my own people. You and I can't live like your brother and sisters. We foresaw all this in Europe. Now we have to face reality."

Claude jumped in. "You don't seem to understand what surviving means here. Life is much harder than I expected — shortages, unemployment, lack of housing...."

"No, I don't," I admitted, "but you don't either, because we haven't faced life so far in America. All we have been doing is visiting and looking at how others live, and celebrating."

I knew that what I said would hurt him. Perhaps I said it on purpose.

"I have hardly paid my Harvard loan," he said coldly, "and you want me to launch myself into the void?"

"You have $10,000 in the bank. We agreed...."

"You have hardly held a dollar bill in your hand and you speak of my $10,000. I mean, you don't know the value of a dollar. You survived through the war somehow or other. You never planned your life carefully, money-wise that is."

I had never felt so angry in my life, not since Mamma had unceremoniously dismissed from our house Vassili, my one and only boyfriend. He had taken refuge among us when Mussolini was about to attack Greece. After he left, I never heard from him again. I was so angry with Mamma then for her attitude towards him that I went on a hunger strike for twenty-four hours and eventually made her promise to move the family to Rome.

I spoke to Claude as quietly as I had spoken to Mamma then.

"That's it. I want to go to New York right away. I want to get to the point of earning that dollar. I want to hold that dollar in my hand and see how it feels. I realize I don't know anything about theater in America. And probably you don't either. Still you must try your best to launch that play. You owe it to de Filippo and to yourself. As for me, I have to find a job."

Claude reacted in his usual controlled way. The best fights we had during our married life were like fencing, no emotion surfacing. I reminded him of my professor's letter to the president of Columbia. Perhaps Columbia wasn't as famous as Harvard, but it was in New York.

The setting sun skimmed the tops of the birches. It was just us and the dead.

"What do you expect from Columbia?" he asked ironically.

"I don't know what to expect. But I want to get to that point. I mention Columbia *because of the letter....*"

My pride hurt, I finally said what had weighed on me since our arrival in America.

"You have outgrown Schenectady, Claude, as I have outgrown war-weary Italy. I want to help you, if you will help me. I'm offering you a partnership."

He put his long arm around my shoulder. In the dim twilight we leaned down together from the stone bench on which we sat to decipher the inscription on a tombstone. Near the stone like a flower a tiny American flag waved in the evening breeze.

"Strange," I said, "this Henry Rutherford was born on your birthday and died on mine. What do you make of that?"

"He managed, as I did, to come home from the war. That's what the flag says. Here is where I want to be buried."

The next morning, Claude and I took the train from Schenectady to New York.

CHAPTER 17

Manhattan

March 17, 1947 was a cold, windy day in Manhattan. We stored our luggage in a locker at Grand Central and went to a coffee shop to "get some fuel," as Claude put it, "for the long walk ahead of us." The main reason was to study the map. Manhattan looked easier to get around than the cemetery in Schenectady. Avenues and streets. Fifth Avenue cutting the city in two, East and West. Fifth Avenue plus Central Park. Downtown, uptown, and midtown. Claude decided it wasn't necessary to master the subways and buses. We were both good walkers. The day was as clear as it could be and reminded him of the Alps, he said. Our goal was Columbia University because of the letter I kept in my purse next to my passport.

For the moment, Mr. Nicholas Murray Butler was our only reference point in Manhattan. On our map we circled his place, i.e., Columbia, in red. It didn't look difficult to reach. It was uptown on the West Side. We had to go northwest. As we walked briskly north, a freezing wind blew between the skyscrapers. Fortunately I was wearing my gray fur coat with hood and scarf, the one made in Udine by Siora Turon, and I had on heavy shoes and heavy woolen socks. Claude was less protected and he was cold.

We began our trek on flat land, on a large street named Park Avenue. Map in hand, we crossed west to an avenue named Madison — from a famous president who was, I remembered, familiar with the classics and with Europe. We were moving towards Fifth Avenue, the dividing line between east and west when trouble began. We had started our expedition at a brisk pace that kept our body temperature at a reasonable level. Now we were being slowed down by a crowd of people that stood looking at a procession moving up Fifth Avenue. I thought it was a *Carnevale* procession, although it was already Lent; there were costumes and bands, and half-naked girls twirled batons in the air. Claude stopped to admire the show:

"We are damned lucky," he said, "to come to New York on St. Patrick's Day."

And he explained that in America every ethnic group reserved for itself the right to march once a year in a parade up Fifth Avenue. The Irish had the best of it so far. Claude loved the Irish because they were Catholics and three of his sisters were engaged to Irishmen.

I was starving, but Claude said we had to get over to the West side. We finally got there by crossing a beautiful park, and then we allowed ourselves a bite to eat. The wind was so sharp in the open that, for safety's sake, we held on tightly to each other. It was worse than in the Alps, yet between gusts of wind a blue sky smiled at us and we stopped more than once in awe since the park itself was surrounded by a line of towers, gigantic slim blocks shining in the sun, immobile despite the wind.

I was starving, but I knew I had to be patient while Claude looked for a place that was affordable. He finally discovered something called the Automat which, he said, would be a great experience for me. A huge glass facade offered us a myriad of food options. When you inserted a dime and a nickel through a slot, a little door magically opened offering the chosen food on a dish wrapped in cellophane. For a little more than a dollar each of us had soup, a ham sandwich, a piece of exquisite cheesecake, and a cup of coffee with milk and sugar. The place itself was so warm and cozy I would have liked to stay longer, but we were both anxious to reach our destination.

We were already on the West side, according to the map, at 60th Street. The ground was still flat. No climbing.

By the time we reached 72nd Street, I was dragging my feet and Claude was frozen and silent. After a month of ease, we were out of shape. And there was nothing exciting to urge us on.

Broadway unrolled monotonously between two rows of buildings. Now the park, trees, and skyscrapers disappeared from view. With night falling, everything looked hopelessly alike. Even the lights added to the anonymity.

Nose to the map, we decided to turn West simply to break the monotony. A majestic, dark Hudson River on our left and a row of elegant, beautifully lit buildings on our right shook us from our torpor. But gusts of freezing wind forced us back to Broadway.

The only thing that kept us going by now was the slow but steadily climbing number of the streets: 86th, 87th, 88th .... each number preceded by a reassuring W which meant West. We walked for a long time in silence, watching the numbers.

"Do you think Mr. Nicholas Murray Butler lives on the premises?" I asked, not thinking but just to break the silence, but Claude took me seriously. He stopped abruptly and laughed.

"Don't tell me you expected to deliver the letter tonight!"

I was embarrassed because I actually did, but said, "No, I didn't."

At 108th Street I stopped. I was hungry and thirsty. We stumbled in silence into the first luncheonette we saw and fell onto stools at the counter. We were, I noticed after a while, in a place that sold newspapers, cigarettes, and a variety of other items. Claude liked to talk with strangers, a habit he must have developed during his years of interrogating war prisoners. Now in Manhattan, he seemed to be more engaging than usual as he entertained the lady who served us hot soup and some meatballs, a middle-aged lady with a heavily made up fleshy face. She looked tired but happy to discover that Claude was a war veteran and I a war bride. She was divorced, owned the store, and had two cats.

"She is Jewish," Claude explained to me in Italian with an unexpected enthusiasm. "Italians have much in common with Jews, you know, and we're now in a Jewish neighborhood. Everything here is kosher. What you ate was a kosher soup and kosher meatballs."

I did my best to feign interest, though I really didn't care.

"Is the lady's name Primadora?" I asked Claude to make conversation, since that was the name shining in gold over our heads. Everyone around us laughed and I joined them. There wasn't much else I could do.

"You have much to learn!" Claude said, and I agreed. The lady, whose name was Mrs. Goldsmith, turned out, in the coming weeks, to be a goldmine of precious information on the art of living in her neighborhood. She became our first hostess in New York City.

After our meal, Claude indulged in a huge ice cream construction he called an "ice cream sundae." All I longed for was sleep. Mrs. Goldsmith suggested a small hotel within our means at 118th Street and Amsterdam Avenue.

Before Claude, I had admired hotels from the outside. My travels had been limited to a third class train ride from my hometown to the University of Rome and back. Since in Italy the Allies had requisitioned the best hotels, during my two years of marriage I had been spoiled. Manhattan that night set me straight on the matter of ordinary hotels.

On Amsterdam Avenue, without our noticing, the Jewish neighborhood stopped abruptly, and the Black began. A jolly group of Black customers lingered in the cold at the entrance to our hotel. The man at the desk in the weakly lit, dingy entrance hall looked at Claude and inquired with an ironic smile if he really intended to sleep in his hotel. "Why not?" Claude answered, surprised, and we went upstairs, key in hand.

The room assigned us was wide and decorously furnished: an ample bed, an armchair, a table, two chairs. Some paper flowers and heavy velvet curtains made it look pretentious. It smelled of mold and I rushed to open the window. Claude stopped me before I discovered the window could not be opened.

"Are you crazy? Weren't you cold enough during the day?" We took off coats and boots and fell into bed completely dressed, without a word.

In the middle of the night, I woke up sweating.

The room was overheated. I turned on the light, but immediately wished I hadn't. The light revealed that the wall was covered with black insects which now rushed wildly about trying to get out of sight. I screamed in horror, "Bed bugs!" and jumped out of the bed. I was suddenly reminded of the experience I had had a few months after marrying Claude, in a hotel in southern Italy where I had met bed bugs for the first time. Claude had had them destroyed by some Army division with DDT. Now in Manhattan, I screamed in horror to Claude, who tried, but in vain, to explain that the crawling insects were not bed bugs but harmless cockroaches, innocent bugs that thrived all over Manhattan. I clung to the armchair where I had taken refuge, although he was speaking to me fearlessly, lying on the very bed which I had fled.

"Cockroaches stick to the wall. You'll be safe in bed. Manhattan is full of them, Mrs. Goldsmith said."

But nothing he or Mrs. Goldsmith said could persuade me to go back to bed. So he lay quietly in bed at a loss for words. Finally, exhaustion and embarrassment got the better of me. Like a child I threw myself onto the bed and he took me gently in his arms reminding me that it was I and not he who wanted to live in Manhattan.

How true. I got up, washed my face, ignoring the cockroaches, got my purse and took out my passport. Tucked away inside it was Ussani's letter to the president of Columbia. We opened it and reread it carefully together, stopping at every word.

"*Caro amico,*" the letter read, "I think of you often during these last days of my life, days so happy for many, so infinitely sad for me. As you probably know, I dedicated the *Vocabolario di latino medioevale* to Mussolini. Now, I am being punished by the liberators because of what they think was a foolish act on my part. I still stand by my act, but I suffer.... A whole life destroyed.

"The young lady I introduce to you has been my student for many years. She was one of my best students and one of the few devoted workers at that masterpiece, the cause of all my troubles. What counts most is that she has done some exceptional work of her own at the Vatican Library, work that in my opinion she must be allowed to continue because it is promising. And she is so young. I beg you to support her efforts — she can be a precious addition to your Department of Classics. This young lady is very dear to me because she did not abandon me when lightning struck. She and her American husband did much to keep me alive. But, believe me, I would prefer to be dead. With warm greetings, Yours, Vincenzo Ussani."

I folded the letter carefully and put it back in its ivory envelope and in the folds of my passport, issued by the King of Italy before Italy became a republic. Then I joined Claude in bed and fell serenely asleep in his arms. My future would be at Columbia.

CHAPTER 18

Napoli Milionaria

Napoli Milionaria was our main incentive to get to New York in 1947. What attracted us in the play was the redemption of Naples, a city known for its corruption, a city destroyed by bombardment, set against the backdrop of the black market, a tale that de Filippo rendered in his unique language.

In Italy I had seen Claude's dedication to the play and to its author. It was in 1947, when we settled in our first home in New York, that I discovered how intense and how complex his feeling actually was. That discovery left me speechless. *Napoli Milionaria* could be read as the drama of an Italo-American who, forced by circumstance to fight a dirty war in Italy, had suddenly discovered gold under the piles of dross. After he met Eduardo, the deeper reason for his fighting became the conquest of the old home he had lost. In Manhattan, as we reviewed our dealings with de Filippo, some scattered moments surfaced more vividly than ever before.

§ § §

Spring was around the corner. We could smell it and feel it as we sat on College Walk overshadowed by Alma Mater or on a bench in Riverside Park. In Jean Goldsmith's apartment, spring itself didn't make much difference. What made an immense difference was having a place, no matter how small and dark, where we could keep our two suitcases and a huge cardboard box Claude had picked up somewhere to house and protect all the documents he would accumulate from the moment we arrived on this shore. All three pieces were marked with military identifications from the *General Muir*. The box, made out of the sturdiest cardboard available in the army, announced in large letters *Personal Documents* and *Handle with care*.

Claude was by nature and vocation an archivist. He made a copy of every document he handled in the Intelligence Corps and the AMC, and of every letter, personal or other, that he wrote. All of these copies, along with the letters he received during his five years abroad, had found a haven in that sturdy box, his most precious possession. The box contained also all sorts of mementos, from the belt of a German soldier with the motto *Gott mit uns* to invitations to dinners, parties, or great events, especially those collected during our stay in Venezia Giulia.

We were in the first place in America which we could call our own — even though we shared it with Jean Goldsmith — and here Claude gave proof of his strength. In one swoop he lifted this heavy box and settled it neatly on our bed, there to stay, he said with a laugh, at least for the moment. Then he proceeded to break the seals and cut the military cords. When he finally raised the lid, I stood in awe at the display of precious materials before us. Five years of Claude's life overseas were neatly collected there, each labeled by place, subject, and date, and all in chronological order: Africa, Sicily, Italy landings 1, 2, 3, 4, Naples, The Royal Palace of Caserta, Anzio, Montecassino, Rome, Corsica, Rome, Caserta, Florence, Rome, Tarvisio, Latisana, Rome.

Among the bundles defined by subject, there was one labeled *Marriage* and a thick one labeled *de Filippo*. The last bunch of papers was tied with a green, white, and red silk ribbon. It bore the label "Governatore di Latisana." The symbolic colors of the ribbon — the Italian flag — represented the apex of his military career.

Displayed now before us were Claude's five years overseas almost day by day, even at times hour by hour. Touched by the sight, I was about to embrace him, when the doorbell rang twice, impatiently. I hurried to open it.

"What's wrong with you folks? I came twice to deliver these two letters, registered and special delivery. They seem to have

gone around the world — the Army in Europe, Montclair, Schenectady. Didn't you hear me ring the bell?"

Claude, usually so courteous with service people, grabbed the letters, glanced at the name of the sender, and slammed the door in the mailman's face.

"What about signing?" the man yelled.

As I came back after having signed, Claude was standing in the living room, the letters unopened in his hands. He was staring in the void.

"It's Cowan," he blew the name into my face. "Cowan! Doesn't it register, Cowan?"

"Why don't you open the letters?" I cried and grabbed the envelopes.

"How could we be so stupid," Claude mumbled to himself, "as to wander to Montclair and Schenectady, when we had business to do in New York City, when we needed an address, no matter what address, so long as it was in New York."

"We have an address now. Calm down."

I had never seen Claude so upset, not even when Colonel Snapp, his closest friend in the Army, let him know he had been unfairly denied promotion before his discharge.

The letter was from William Cowan of Cowan Associates at the Marvello Trading Corporation, 1199 Broadway, and was dated March 3rd 1947. It was addressed to Lieutenant Claude J. Bové at his AMG detachment in Europe. The envelope contained, besides the letter, two copies of a Dramatic Production Contract, the original dated in pencil by Claude in Rome "January 8, 1947."

"He acknowledges receipt of de Filippo's play, of your translation, of the contract signed by de Filippo that you sent to him," I said slowly.

"And so?"

"And so — 'I read the play,' he writes, 'and found it to have flavor and quality and believe that it has plenty in it to make it a good play. Upon discussion with my director, it was pointed out that the English translation is too formal and the whole play needs to be adapted to the American stage, while maintaining the Italian feeling.'" I ran fast through that sentence.

"An adaptation is what I expected. What else?"

"'I expect to proceed with the adaptation at once,' Cowan adds, 'and as soon as it is ready, to cast and start rehearsals. The play can hardly be ready before May and that is too late in the season for a New York opening. Therefore, it will need to be postponed until September with several weeks' advance showing and try-outs out of town during the summer.'"

We fell into each other's arms without reading any further. Cowan's letter was the crowning of our efforts. It meant, at long last, success after a whole year of very hard work.

Napoli Milionaria, already the most popular play by far in Italy, would be performed on Broadway in September 1947! Eduardo de Filippo, the most successful Italian playwright of our time, would introduce the Naples he had created, an extraordinary Naples of the war years and immediate post-war years, which would show American audiences that the City of Thieves was actually a human community with a big heart.

The play, presenting the radical post-war changes in a family and a city, had been received enthusiastically in Naples, Rome, Milan, and Turin. When I showed it to Claude in December 1945, the strong human message overwhelmed us. Following that first performance, Claude and I met de Filippo. We returned for every performance for a week, each time meeting again with Eduardo. By the end of the week it was clear that we should translate the play and take it to New York.

Now, a year later, here was in broad outline the course the play would take in the American theater, which was as obscure to me as Wall Street. I had come to think of it as a physical theater, where "backers" or "angels" looked on authors with nonchalance, selecting a few from the hundreds offered. These "angels" focused on the potential audience and their potential profit. I had not yet been able to see an actual stage in an American theater. Cowan's letter gave us hope for the dream we had shared, that last year in Europe, of seeing *Millionaire Naples* in an American theater.

Seated together on Jean Goldsmith's bed at 108th Street and Broadway, surrounded by neatly packed documents, we dove into the correspondence between Claude and Cowan, mostly by way of

Lou Lawrence, a New York businessman who acted as intermediary. Apparently, dealings had gone on for a whole year while Claude was translating the play, concluding with Claude's letter to de Filippo announcing that he had sent the complete translation air-mail to New York. When we embraced de Filippo and his American wife in Rome at the end of January 1947, on our way to Livorno, they rejoiced at the news that an English *Napoli Milionaria* was on its way.

Lou Lawrence's last letter to us, which we found together with Cowan's that morning, anticipated Cowan's by a few days. Lou was informing Cowan that we were due to arrive sometime in February to conclude the deal. He warned us, however, that Cowan, though pleased with both play and translation, was disappointed by the delays caused more than once by the changes de Filippo made.

"In fact, Cowan told me," Lou wrote in closing, "that he had turned down an offer to participate in another play to keep himself free in order to concentrate on this play."

It was that warning by Lou that set Claude and me searching through our correspondence to find proof that Cowan was wrong. De Filippo, guided by Claude, had carefully and promptly followed Cowan's instructions.

§ § §

"Yes, Mr. Cowan, no, no I apologize. Of course I am still interested. What do you mean? Yes, of course de Filippo is very much interested. Of course he'll sign. We regret the delay — you know the army.... I agree, I should have called you as soon as we landed... the change from military to civilian life was harder than I expected.... Yes, my wife is with me. She'll be happy to meet with you.... Yes, we agree on the necessity of adaptation.... Yes, she agrees also, and de Filippo of course.... Yes, the contract seems to be fair. I'll send him a draft of the letter he should write to you. Things will move quickly from now on.... I don't know what we can do more than what we are doing.... Tomorrow afternoon? I'll make myself free. I'll be in your office by 3:00 p.m."

When finally Claude put down the receiver, I handed him his sandwich in silence and waited for him to tell me what had transpired with the mysterious Mr. Cowan.

"You heard what I said, you can guess what he told me," Claude said in his usual calm voice.

He needed to prepare for the meeting with Cowan. There was no need for me to come along. It was a business meeting concerning legal issues, mainly money, of which I had no experience.

§   §   §

That afternoon and the next morning, sitting together again on Mrs. Goldsmith's bed, we reviewed carefully the correspondence with Cowan and Lawrence. But as we did —Claude wanted proof that Cowan, not de Filippo, was responsible for the three months' delay in the execution of the contract — I found myself dealing with a new and disturbing feeling. That world was disturbing to me now because it evoked expectations, but also doubts and hesitations which I had overcome during the year Claude and I worked on the project "de Filippo." Once, the count himself had to set me straight, by expressing his faith in the work we could do together in America to improve understanding between Europe and America.

While Claude was meeting with Cowan, I suddenly felt alone. Where had Claude led me? What did he know about theater in America? Until I introduced him to Eduardo de Filippo's <u>Napoli Milionaria</u> in December 1945, Claude was mainly interested in the import-export business, in products such as tires, glass, medicines, building materials, wine and luxuries, for which Italians stood out, to be exchanged for what Italians needed. But *Napoli Milionaria* changed his perspective, giving him a deeper understanding of his own personal connection not just with Italy but especially with Naples, the city from which his parents had emigrated. He moved from business to magic, to the world of theater, though he didn't quite understand the business of theater.

For a year and more, from the first time we saw the play and met de Filippo to the day we left Italy with a contract for a New York production, both Claude and I had lived with that play, a psychological experience that radically influenced our lives. Now finally in New York, I felt strangely excluded from this joint experience. I felt at his mercy, but without the kind of faith that had united us as we worked together in Italy. Claude also seemed to be lost. Paradoxically, at the very moment Cowan's letter opened up "Times Square" to us, we seemed both, for different reasons, blinded by its lights.

I was also angry at the waste of precious time in the attempt to find who caused the delays in the signing of the contract. I was again experiencing some doubts about Claude's ability to carry out a theatrical project. After our visit to Montclair and Schenectady, the long discussion we had of our past together in Italy clarified some things for me. It appeared that I had married a stubborn, even narrow-minded American who thought he had made it in the theater world because he had a contract. On the other hand, I myself was learning that life in Manhattan was much more frightening and humbling than even the ocean had been. I began having doubts about our ability to reach our goal. I was at a loss while Claude seemed to have a simple answer to all questions.

His attitude annoyed and even angered me. But then, I compared the bold American producer who had probably never seen Europe to Claude, who had gone through four landings before meeting de Filippo in Rome, and I was overcome by a sense of sympathy and admiration. I realized that Claude had to make it with this play in order to regain faith in himself and in the message which he wanted to bring from a shattered Europe to America by means of Naples, that much maligned Mediterranean city, victim of both German cruelty and American bombardments.

Everything Claude had done in Italy after the fighting was over had been in view of a change in his future in America. He had to succeed in launching *Millionaire Naples* with Cowan in New York. There was yet another aspect of "America" that angered and energized me. In America, without risking his life, Claude's brother Peter had managed to rise above the crowd to a new level. Claude saw himself as fighting a new war to climb further than Peter. The city to conquer now was Manhattan, the means Eduardo's Naples, the secret the message of the play. It had to be produced and produced well.

That is what we needed to achieve together in New York, fulfilling the dreams we'd had in Italy.

§ § §

When I first met Claude, he was already in love with Italy, like many Italian-American soldiers. Having known discrimination in the States, these Italian-Americans saw the Italian campaign giving them a new kind of identity which they could wear happily back home. They had become proud of their origins. For some, one way to reconnect to that origin would be to go into the import-export business with Italy. Claude and some comrades and his brother Peter in Montclair seriously considered this possibility. Until we met de Filippo I had accepted Claude's interest in business. It looked like a way to revive Italy's dead economy.

But, with his play focused on Naples, Eduardo de Filippo had altered Claude's perspective, first as the perpetrator and later as the victim and heroine of a black market episode. From the title on, the subtle connection between crime and moral values provided depth. *Millionaire Naples* stressed not so much the evil of crime as its coexistence with those moral values that could in the end redeem it. The play's ultimate message was not condemnation but redemption.

Naples' real wealth, its real millions, are to be found in those basic moral values which alone can assure the spiritual revival of a deeply wounded city. The moral lesson is devoid of sentimentality as it emerges in the third act, mainly because of what happens in Act I, where Eduardo allows the warm, deep humanity of the Neapolitans to appear so convincingly that they overwhelm the audience. In this remarkable play, it is the real war which offers the occasion for such a miracle, during one of those violent bombardments which the Allies inflicted on a city before they occupied it.

While Claude was discussing business with Cowan, I studied the photos which Eduardo had sent us to get a clearer sense of what lay ahead. Here was Eduardo himself playing Don Gennaro in Act I sitting at a large dining room table laden with food but not eating while everyone else is happily eating. At the height of a war that Italy could not afford, the lack of food created a flourishing black market, which meant, cruelly, plenty for the few at the expense of the starving many. The photo showed Don Gennaro's wife, Donna Amalia, and her business partner Corrado eating and drinking happily. Next, there was Eduardo on his bed, pretending to be dead, because no Neapolitan would dare touch a corpse. Only as a dead man could he protect the black market goods his wife and her partner had stock-piled and hidden from the police inspector. He was, after all, loyal to his wife, though he disapproved.

As the sirens sound, another photo shows all those at Eduardo's wake running to the shelter; Eduardo and the inspector are left alone as the bombs drop, one playing dead, the other waiting to lay his hands on the booty. They vie with each other fearlessly while the bombs fall all around. Who will give in first? Neither of these two: they are Neapolitans. The last photo shows Don Gennaro in Act III being rewarded for his passive resistance and his heroic loyalty, as he receives from a neighbor — one whom Donna Amalia had once greedily starved — the wonderful gift of penicillin to save her dying child. In the pictures Eduardo is the tall, scrawny, deadly serious, and ironic silent witness of the scene between Donna Amalia and the generous neighbor. When he finally speaks, he will have the courage of his convictions.

Two episodes from our life with the play came to mind. In both cases, the mysteries of "Times Square" and Claude's enthusiasm overcame my hesitations.

December 1947, at the Hotel Ambasciatori in Via Veneto (the most fashionable social area of Rome). The music of "Ama Pola, my pretty Ama Pola," the "Lili Marlene" of the Allies, reached us as Claude and I sat in a corner of the hotel lobby under the palm trees. Sipping rum and coke, we were waiting to meet Lou Lawrence, in Claude's words "a powerhouse in New York's theater world." As Claude's wife, *Mary Bové*, my task was to overwhelm

Lou with the tremendous success of the play in Italy, without dwelling on the identity of author-director-protagonist. Claude as translator would take over from there. An Italian-American, he could attest to the attractions the play would have for Italian-American audiences.

Even before we entered the dining room, Lou seemed fully convinced both of the quality of the play and of its translation into English. In January, Claude and I had reached his posting in the Alps in Venezia Giulia, ready to work at the play with the full support of the author. Three months of silence on the part of Lou and Cowan followed, as we moved from the mountains to the plains of Udine and Latisana on the Adriatic coast.

The second episode surfaced in my memory with stunning vividness, leaving me feeling lonely, lost in the darkness of Jean' bedroom. It was March 24, 1946 — a sparkling day on the estate of our host, the Count Manuel de Asarta. I was sitting under a gigantic magnolia in bloom shedding its fleshy flowers over my books and papers. Lost in my own world, preparing for the forthcoming exam, I didn't hear Claude's jeep approaching nor his steps on the gravel. Triumphantly but without a word, he proudly handed me a telegram that would have moved a mountain:

"INTERESTED PLAY EXCLUSIVE RIGHTS US FILM RADIO AND STAGE WIRE CONDITIONS REQUIRED BY AUTHOR LOU LAWRENCE."

Cold, indifferent, distant, I told Claude that if it took Lou three whole months to get back to us, we certainly had the right to change our minds. De Filippo had caught both of us in his web, but the theater world, theater as a business, was a world unknown to me, even in Italy. I intended to follow my profession and take my state exams.

Claude, seemingly undisturbed, helped me get up and collect my books. Together we walked silently across the meadow towards the count's dining room. He was displeased, not disturbed. He knew me by now, he said later. It was a passing cloud, and he was right. After lunch, I set my books aside. He opened his typewriter and we began deciphering Eduardo's language.

The count solved the problem at lunch, the usual elegant meal with first-rate red wine served in Murano glasses by a waiter wearing white gloves. As soon as we entered, he had sensed that something was wrong between us. Claude handed him the telegram. He glanced at it, then put on his monocle to be sure of what he read.

"*Perbacco* — this calls for a celebration," he proclaimed. "Today we must celebrate," and he raised his glass with a trembling hand. I hope to be able to come to you across the ocean. I've never seen America and have always thought I never would see it. Now, I hope, I believe, I am sure that with your help I can get there."

Then he squeezed my hand and, in a low voice I could hardly make out, he said that during the long evenings we spent together he felt more like a proud father than a friend to us. Very few Italians had had the experience of witnessing close up two worlds, worlds so different from each other, coming together. The magic of the theater had brought this about because we both approached Eduardo's theater with such touching purity and enthusiasm.

He was getting emotional and resented it. It wasn't his style.

"You," he turned to me with a smile, "dream of an ideal bridge across the Atlantic, a bridge through books; Claude aims at it as a tangible reality. If your America will allow you to continue working together at this marvelous project, as you do every night in my library, I feel hopeful that our two worlds — Europe and America — will someday contribute together to some form of peace in our troubled world."

He wiped his eyes with his delicately embroidered napkin and then, smiling at me, he said: "I know how you feel. You fear losing much of what you have believed in and built so far, your books, your way of living, life in Italy, not as you lived it in Rome, but as you live it here in the peace of my villa. Your books you'll take with you and, much more so, your ideas and ideals. As for my park, which you enjoy so much, it is a most precarious reality threatened today more than ever before. There will be chaos before peace, and if peace does come, a different world from this one. Perhaps I'll be too old and tired to reach you in New York."

That night, alone in the count's library, after hours of work together, Claude led me to the balcony overlooking the river. It was a starry, serene night. I asked him to forgive me for my lack of faith. He replied with a faint smile that there was nothing to forgive. I had to take him as he was. I embraced him silently. I did not then understand what he meant. Now, in Jean's basement in March 1947, I did. The discovery left me feeling lonely and troubled.

§ § §

Before Claude was sent to Venezia Giulia, what he had looked forward to after discharge was a radical change of life. Staying in Rome in December 1945 he could make connections. If the play didn't work out, he could turn to the import-export business. De Filippo's play was a means to an end. Now, a year later, in the dim light of Jean's apartment I brought this point to Claude's attention after he returned from Cowan with what seemed like good news. In his effort to create a place for himself back home, I reminded him, his correspondence revealed he was bluffing to Peter about the show business of which he actually knew nothing.

"I am already attempting to market my first Italian successful play here in Rome with the collaboration of Monty Banks — remember him in *A Bell for Adano*? Well, he is here, and I've arranged to see him tomorrow night. I think this play will be a great hit on Broadway."

He looked at me in some dismay, then regained his composure.

"That's the way I am! Take me or leave me. I am not like you, given to fanning delicate feelings and emotions. I keep my feet on the ground.

"You see," he went on, "the poverty you experienced was a kind of, how shall I say, 'noble' poverty, the poverty of those exiled from the world they belong to. Your mother chose a life with books for you, a future in education. Mine was 'vulgar' poverty. Peter led me to Harvard after he had discovered it on his own, depressed by my father's life as a bootlegger. Peter believed in me.

"Fascism was evil, but the Depression we went through in America wasn't a happy alternative. I never knew how hopelessly boring my life was until the Army took me from it. Harvard had let me avoid life in my father's store, but when I came back to Schenectady, I still had to raise Pop's family, and so I felt like a prisoner of the Depot.

"The war freed me from all that. Now all of a sudden the war ends and with it all of my dreams. Except two, you and this play. You yourself were the best part of my dreams. You helped me to dream — though we don't dream the same way. There is something you do not understand about my world, and about America. I wish I could teach you how to stop dreaming in the void. I didn't approach de Filippo's play as a literary masterpiece, like you. I just wanted to try myself out, give myself a chance in show business. What's wrong with that? So I didn't know anything about the theater world in America. I bluffed. But you and I entered that world together, at the Ambassador Hotel in Rome when we first met Monty and then Lou Lawrence. I trusted Lou as much as Eduardo trusted me.

"It was a chain of trust. I wish from the start I had as much artistic sensibility as Lou seemed to have commercial and business acumen. Because this is what we need now. I wish also we two had a flair for publicity. Lou sold us Cowan as if he were the greatest producer in America. But who knows how talented this Cowan is, even if he is ready to disburse as much as $60,000 for production? The Americans look at a play as a business deal. The Italian playwright sees the deal as a marvelous golden bridge across the Atlantic, you see it as an act of redemption for ill-famed Naples. That's what I told Lou in one of my letters.

"The main problem we faced was translation — translation of a language, a dialect, a culture, a historical moment. In my meeting with Cowan today I think I succeeded in impressing on him the point on which you insist: Eduardo is the soul of what on the surface appears to be a cruel, soulless city. Neapolitan dialect, as the Italian press asserts, the language of the soul of Naples, suddenly became through Eduardo the symbol of the redemption of a morally impoverished Italy, physically ruined by the war. The main problem for Cowan, here in New York, where the audience can hardly visualize the experience of war, is to render in English Eduardo's special language, which involves body and soul. For you that language is strictly connected with how Eduardo lived the human expression of theater." And he concluded:

"For me it is the language my parents spoke at home."

As Claude passionately recounted his meeting with Cowan, I understood that *language* had somehow connected Claude to his family roots. Eduardo's language had led him to a new understanding of what the war meant. Four landings in the land of his ancestors, with full awareness of the destruction inflicted by the liberators as well as by the Germans, had left him feeling he had to do something to heal those wounds.

This feeling had grown within him, strangely mixed with a repressed anger, not, as I had expected, against Italians, who had passively accepted the war Mussolini imposed, but against what he saw as a culturally divided America that had exploited the Italian immigrants including his own parents. Thanks to the war, a kind of social justice had finally emerged, and, like many Italian Americans, he planned to take advantage of it. The war had purified him of the social humiliations he had suffered and had cleared him of the debts he had incurred for his studies at Harvard. A wedding in Vatican City, with a Papal blessing, his own beloved Colonel Fisher giving away the Italian bride, and a personal gift to the bride by the first Premier of a democratic Italy had made him feel part of an Italian family so different from, yet firmly connected to, his own. When, after brief stints at Caserta and in Florence, he finally came to Venezia Giulia in the north-eastern corner of the peninsula, with the distinguished Italian title of "Governatore," and tackled the translation of de Filippo's work, Claude felt he had earned sufficient credit both as a kind of savior of Italians and as a respectable public figure at home.

De Filippo's "language" had become for Claude a statement of faith in himself, an American coming face to face with an Italy in ruins. His promotion of de Filippo in New York would generate the monies necessary for us to live in America at the level his newly acquired public reputation called for. The creative spirit of the

Italians, freed from a stifling regime, had proved as contagious to Claude as to Americans who were not of Italian origin. For many of them, an official American reconstruction of Italy seemed to generate an unexpected opportunity to develop what they felt was their newly discovered talent.

His continuing work on *Napoli Milionaria* and his friendship with Eduardo helped him understand the poverty that he had witnessed in post-war Italy, especially in the south. The Neapolitans' down-to-earth yet subtle humor, which triumphs despite misfortune and moral predicaments in de Filippo's language, reminded Claude of his own family's cheerfulness at home and of the life that managed to go on backstage in his father's store. At the same time, there were differences. Eduardo gave voice to a human experience deeper and more significant than Claude's parents had offered their son in Schenectady.

Claude's translation of *Napoli Milionaria* from Neapolitan dialect into the elegant English he had learned in his years at Harvard was a life statement, valid in itself even without the success we hoped the play would have on Broadway.

I recalled that Claude had devoted more energy to promoting Eduardo than to fighting for his own promotion to Captain, even though that promotion was strongly supported by his superiors, Colonel Fisher, Major Hobbes, and especially Colonel Snapp.

Colonel Snapp, who stayed on in Rome after we left, was furious when Claude's promotion was denied "for superior reasons." Claude did not seem to mind. Eduardo came first.

§ § §

Claude spent the whole of the next day with Cowan and Lou Lawrence in meetings in which, he said, I did not belong. In Jean's basement I wanted to support his efforts with all the strength I could master. Yet even now a last cloud lingered.

What worried me was that, suddenly, I did not know where I stood in Claude's dealings with Cowan. Throughout his correspondence with his family, I had always been considered by far the most valuable thing he could have brought home from Italy. In letter after letter, Claude had nagged his sisters to send him the clothes, shoes, or purses essential to my proper appearance. These items were described in detail, in size, color, with an added sketch if necessary: I needed walking shoes for bombed-out roads, unknown items in a country God had preserved from bombs, and a white bathing suit (currently out of stock) for me to show off my swimming talents to his British and South African comrades. As for a purse he specified that it should be leather — not leatherette — with a long shoulder strap, while the black suit should be of the finest wool, and Mademoiselle style — no other style would do — so that he could show me off when we went dancing.

Was I also to become, in America, his expression of a new identity?

This question surfaced here and there in the months that followed as our new sponsors, Lou and Rachel Lawrence, took over the task of connecting us with Cowan's close friends.

At our first dinner meeting with them, Rachel Lawrence was all lips. As she spoke during dinner, I could not stop looking at her lips and wondered what kind of lipstick she was using. I did not at first pay much attention to what she said. A drink Claude had ordered before the meal had made me feel pleasantly hazy. Rachel and Claude spoke most of the time. The two guests were the emissaries of Elia Kazan, the director. Cowan was the main topic of discussion.

Suddenly turning to Claude, the female guest declared: "It must have been hard for you to translate certain expressions of the play. I didn't react to your translation at all."

I silently agreed with her. While Italians recognized in the play Naples as a microcosm of any city in Europe, how could Americans understand Europe after years of brutal war. I did not think the translation captured the intensity of life lived through the war. We would need an adaptation that could convey the power of de Filippo's play. For my part, in any case, how could I discover what Americans were looking for? I had never seen a play in America, I confessed to my dinner mates.

"We'll make sure you see enough American theater to make up your mind about it," Lou replied with a laugh.

They all laughed. I laughed with them, and suddenly I felt at home there, in a restaurant somewhere in midtown Manhattan, surrounded by people I hardly knew. The ice had been broken. Why shouldn't de Filippo stand a chance? The thought gave me a new perspective. We all agreed it was only a question of money, the substantial sum needed for production. And Cowan was ready to pledge it.

That first dinner was followed by other dinners with Lou and Rachel and other allegedly important people in the American theater world. Lou and Rachel took us to the theater and I loved them for it. We remained convinced that a proper adaptation of Eduardo's Naples could indeed make it in New York. Rachel persuaded Claude to buy one of her skunk jackets for me, along with a huge matching skunk hat that dwarfed me. She said it was "in" among theater people. I wore it for our dinners, as late as April, hoping it would help the cause. But actually I was embarrassed by it. I thought it made me look ridiculous.

Notwithstanding the friendly dinners and the skunk coat, I never had the feeling I was a full member of that inner circle where decisions were made. I felt I was being treated as an outsider, someone who couldn't understand how America worked.

Liebling and Wood among others gave a favorable evaluation of the play and Cowan began working on the production. De Filippo was invited to New York; he bought tickets for himself and his wife. He was in seventh heaven. A number of *Life* magazine would introduce the play to the public. Everything would be okay.

Suddenly it was all for real! I could hardly believe it.

On March 8, 1947, de Filippo announced his visit to America in an interview published in *Popolo Nuovo* of Turin. No play — the article read — had filled Italian theaters for such a long time. The President of the Republic himself and de Gasperi had attended it.

§   §   §

Suddenly, one hot, damp summer afternoon, as New York sweltered in heavy smog, there was a frantic call from Lou. He wanted to see Claude immediately. Claude called me up from Lou's office in a calm voice and asked me to join them.

As soon as I entered Lou's office, I knew something had gone wrong. Had Cowan died? Not physically but he had as far as our play was concerned. Cowan's finances were in disarray. He had been offered an opportunity to invest in a new cake called "Babka," less risky than a play. Claude sat expressionless on the sofa in a corner. I tried my best to imitate Claude and not show any emotion. Inside, I felt as if I had swallowed a stone. Lou handed me a glass of water.

Then he said to me gently, "You told me once Mussolini gave you a whole year to accept the idea of a war. I guess life moves more slowly in the old world. Here people in power make quick decisions, not always for good reasons. Sometimes, circumstances do not give them any choice."

Then, perhaps to justify Cowan's sudden desertion, Lou told us that Cowan had been influenced by a very reputable director, Elia Kazan, who had doubts about the play's likely success at this particular time.

"This play," Kazan had declared, "comes to Broadway too late and too early." World War II was being overshadowed by other political developments of more concern to an American audience.

We were facing another kind of war.

We later learned that Kazan, whom Cowan had asked to direct the play, had been accused of being a Communist by the infamous House Un-American Activities Committee (or HUAC), and had left New York. We were the innocent bystanders swept up by the political maelstrom that had hit the theater world. We had barely entered that world when the play, on which Claude had pinned our hopes for a new beginning, fell afoul of a political agenda that neither of us understood. I was to learn quickly, to my cost, that isolationism was a recurring malady in America. Claude tried to explain to Eduardo our feelings of defeat. I myself turned away from the magic of theater which Eduardo's play had shown me. At least for a while. Life is not fair. Maybe deep down I was hoping that America would give Eduardo's Naples another chance.

CHAPTER 19

The Marine Shark

"You must help Eddie and Bona join you in America. The best way for them to enter America, they say, is with a student visa. You must help them get one right away!"

Mamma's letter, addressed to both Claude and me, arrived in July 1947, shortly after the theater debacle. The Italian liner *Giulio Cesare* brought this message as an order. In her imaginative but lapidary style Mamma reminded Claude and me of Eddie's merits as a "liberator of Europe from Hitler," who deserved to be recognized just as much as the "others" (she meant the Americans) for his political activities, to which he had dedicated not just a few years as a soldier but his whole life. She recommended him also for his scholarly merits, which, in her view, were manifest in the way he shaped great events to his purpose, learning. She reminded us in a few dense pages of Eddie's epic story.

A German from Beuten in Upper Silesia, son of a socialist coal miner turned radio-journalist after a debilitating mine accident, Eddie Kostka was about to be imprisoned at eighteen for his anti Nazi activities when his father smuggled him across the Polish border and delivered him to his sister, Otti, fortunately married to a Polish pharmacist in Warsaw. Forced to learn Polish fast so he could get a scholarship to the University of Warsaw, young Eddie was wounded during the German bombardment of Warsaw, but managed to escape the invasion of Poland by once again joining his sister and brother-in law, a Polish Army officer, in a village in eastern Poland. But the Russians didn't trust the Poles and deported him, along with most of his sister's village, to Siberia, where Eddie spent three years, winning a Russian scholarship in "tractorship."

General Anders arranged with the Allies in London to assign Eddie to the new Second Polish Corps. To get to them, Eddie crossed eastern Russia — i.e., east of the Ural Mountains (so Mamma specified) — by whatever means he could find, down through Iran, finally reaching Palestine. The journey took months. Twice he was delayed by illness, first typhus, then diarrhea, and he arrived weakened by lice and lack of food. Recovered, he was trained by the British as an officer of the Second Polish Corps. During that long journey, which General Anders in London had arranged for him and which Mamma interpreted as a "scholarship," Eddie never missed a chance to visit archeological sites. Finally in Egypt he was reunited briefly with his sister Otti, who had escaped from Siberia earlier. In southern Italy, he fought side by side with the British and the Americans, and suffered a shrapnel wound at the battle of Montecassino.

But — and here Mamma tried her best not to offend Claude and the Americans — after Montecassino, Eddie should have entered Rome, just as Claude did, but there was more fighting in the mountains. Only with the utter defeat of the Germans was he granted the scholarship to the University of Rome which he richly deserved. There, in an English literature course, he met his soulmate, my sister Bona. They were married in the Church of Santa Agnese over the catacombs near Via Bolzano, where the family was living in Agostino's apartment at the time.

Mamma's letter ended prophesying that, given an American scholarship, Eddie would make his own story known to the world in a book before America as well as Europe consigned our war to oblivion, i.e., to a history that nobody would read except for a few specialists.

"Who remembers today," she asked pointedly, "the war that I survived, World War I?"

A postscript directed me thus: "Get Bona and Eddie to North America as quickly as possible, so they won't have to go to the only country which will accept them both as a married couple, South Africa. Remember, a student visa and a scholarship. Eddie is an *apolide:* he has no passport.

Eddie lived in Rome as an *apolide,* a stateless or displaced person. This was a new term, often shortened to DP. Before the war, most Italians had never had a passport. Suddenly, a passport became the core of one's identity. An *apolide* was like an orphan who needed to be adopted. The war ended, a breed of *apolidi* sprang up all over the half of Europe liberated by the Allies.

After having seen me sailing off to America, Mamma found it unbearable to think of Bona sailing even further away, into the South, almost at the antipodes of Rome.

Mamma's SOS had the effect that Claude couldn't achieve after Cowan had broken his contract with de Filippo, about our absolute need to find a job. I felt guilty again for leaving Italy. Mamma was just trying to take care of family members who needed help, Bona and Eddie, and she turned to me as she had done in Merano, during our wanderings from villa to villa, or in Rome during the war. She didn't consider the possibility that, a new-comer to America, it would be difficult to make New York the family refuge. The whole world outside this continent looked to me like a world of *apolidi,* while I seemed to be the only proud owner of a visa, which opened the way to an American passport.

But Mamma wasn't begging, she was commanding — commanding me and Claude to pick up where we had left off and help Eddie, who had never lost his love for books or his determination to get an education while fighting a war. Then, since she loved geography, she measured the distance between Rome and New York and between Rome and Johannesburg, calculating the number of days it would take to reach either, and categorically forbade Bona's departure. Bona was the youngest of her four children, the one she had raised alone for some years, the one who needed more support than the others. She didn't realize that twenty-three year old Bona, a blue-eyed beauty with a degree in Roman history, was the toughest of all of us, able to manage on her own anywhere in the world.

Mamma was confident that Claude and I would understand and accept her reasons for ruling out South Africa. She didn't realize that the North American solution we might be able to offer was not easy. In Rome, she had learned to accept the unexpected as part of normal life. Her generous heart took the stateless Eddie into the family with the same warmth with which she had taken Claude in a year and a half earlier. In her generous way, she dreamed that the war's end would unite all of humanity — conquerors and conquered — in a peace without social inequality.

From the start, she saw a relationship. Eddie had fought side by side with Claude at Montecassino. Before that, they had been brothers in arms in the North African campaign, though unknown to each other. They might well have met in Rome in June 1944, but Eddie had ended up at the Gustav Line near Ancona and Ravenna. It was typical of Eddie that he enrolled in a university as soon as the fighting was over. America should certainly honor such a commitment. Mamma was Eddie's fiercest advocate.

In Italy, Claude and I didn't know Eddie well. He was a taciturn, handsome young man with strong Slavic features. Today, he still resembles the last pope. When we visited, he lived at home with Bona, somewhat astonished at our noisy family life. He was German by birth though his name was Polish.

"What is your family fighting about?" he would ask Bona after attending our Easter dinner.

"They are just having fun," Bona would reassure him.

During the summer of 1947, in the void created by the disappearance of de Filippo, Claude took on the cause of Eddie and Bona, perhaps to brighten our lives. It may have been a form of defense. For me, it was something else. For days after Mamma's letter I walked around aimlessly near the Hudson, looking for ships — ships moving out into the ocean. Then one hot morning I took the subway downtown and crossed to the East River to ask about a scholarship from the Institute of International Studies for a war hero who was unfortunately *apolide*. A kind lady listened with genuine interest to my story and said she was sorry but she was not able to rectify this injustice, as I had put it.

"Too late, too late" was her polite response.

I didn't give up. Day after day, I besieged the kind lady who, under pressure, had vaguely promised to look into last-minute withdrawals. She agreed that Eddie was indeed extraordinary. One gray morning in July, the city simmering in its fog, she met me with the kind of smile that, I learned later, only Irish ladies can muster.

"Yes," she whispered, "the University of Kansas in Lawrence, Kansas, in the Middle West has an opening."

"Not far from Cincinnati?" I whispered, trying to hold back my enthusiasm.

"Not too far, not too far. But why Cincinnati?"

"Because of my father — surely I told you about my father."

"Oh yes your father, the American banker," she laughed."

We embraced. That lady knew more about my life than any other person in America.

§ § §

After the Cowan debacle, Claude and I started looking for work. Claude had told me in unequivocal terms that the $10,000.00 in the bank was not to be touched and we needed at least one regular income, preferably two.

"What about the Butler letter?" Claude seemed to be astonished that I hadn't done anything with it so far. "With your sister coming as a student, you should try Columbia University."

I didn't immediately get the connection; she had been accepted as a foreign student at Fordham. But his words brought that letter to mind. I dug it out one morning and read it and reread it. In the end, I thought it wouldn't be so easy to use in the face of a Columbia which looked impenetrable.

The letter was a touching statement of what had befallen a famous man who had tumbled from Olympus. What was so extraordinary about that? So many gods had fallen from Olympus in Italy because of the war and the change of regime. What could Butler, a god on American Olympus, do for this former Accademico d'Italia? (And for me, a little star lost in the myriads here?)

An answer to my question came from a young German Renaissance scholar who had found refuge at Columbia when the war began. He had his office on the sixth floor of a Columbia building on Amsterdam Avenue and 117th Street, an American imitation of a Florentine *palazzo* called *Casa Italian*a. I had been recommended to him by an older Renaissance colleague of mine, Professor Vittore Branca, whom I had met in Florence.

Paul Kristeller received me politely. I brought him a recent article of mine and the draft of my critical edition of Valla's work. Kristeller was so interested in this that he didn't want to talk about anything else. I imagine he was already busy collecting Renaissance manuscripts in Italy and Europe, a project he had started at the Scuola Normale in Pisa under the guidance of the Italian philosopher Giovanni Gentile. Those manuscripts would in me generate a new interpretation of Renaissance Humanism.

He was touched when I told him Gentile had been my philosophy professor in Rome in a course on "The Spirit as Pure Act" and that I had come upon his grave in Florence in 1945. He knew that Gentile, who had created the Italian educational system that stressed the importance of classical studies, had been murdered by an Italian partisan at his home in Fiesole shortly after the Liberation and he knew that Gentile had been involved with Fascism. Gentile, he declared proudly, was a generous and loyal friend. When, as a young Jewish refugee, he escaped the Nazis, Gentile took him under his wing at the Scuola Normale. When Italy also became dangerous, Gentile sent him off to Columbia, where he now had a position in the philosophy department.

Finally, I showed Kristeller Ussani's letter to Butler. He read it attentively. "Unfortunately" — he smiled — "President Butler is in no position to help Professor Ussani, whom I know by reputation. Butler dominated Columbia for thirty years, at first with excellent results. In his last few years, however, everyone has resented him. He is now out for good."

Then he added, "That's the advantage of living in a democracy."

But another smile brightened Kristeller's face, followed by a more serious expression. He now added pragmatically:

"I suggest that you to take some advanced courses in the Department of Classical Philology. They might be useful for your work. At the same time, since you need money, get yourself a job at a private college. You can do that by registering for a small fee in the Teachers' Agency."

Without waiting for my reaction, taking my silence for consent, Kristeller dug out of his desk some Columbia letterhead and typed four letters of recommendation, one after the other — to the Teachers Agency, to Professors Gilbert Highet and Moses Hadas in the Classics Department, and to the head librarian of Butler Library. When the academic year began, I was invited to take the courses of both professors without paying any tuition. Even more, Hadas hired me for a project that included taping Greek tragedy in Greek.

Finally, Kristeller decided it would be useful for me to have library privileges. He gave me a letter of introduction to the head librarian. From then on, the Greek and Latin Reading Room became my refuge whenever I had a break from other daily activities.

Kristeller and his wife Edith remained my dearest friends for life. Through the years, he followed my career at Columbia. His family had been wiped out by the Nazis. But he forgave the Germans, accepting the honorary degrees they offered him when he became famous.

"How can I claim to be a philosopher, if I cannot forgive? he said to me late in his life.

§   §   §

An advertisement in the *Times* under "Import-Export" led Claude to a tiny office in the Bowery where he was immediately employed by two brothers, orthodox Jews who dressed in matching black suits and tails. As their only helper, Claude spent his days behind a huge ancient typewriter. He also answered the phone, especially calls from abroad (except for Palestine) and kept the files in order. All business matters were strictly in the brothers' hands. It didn't seem much better than the Schenectady Depot.

"This is just temporary," I said. "We are in New York. Look around, look upwards."

"For what?" he answered, "the El?"

We laughed.

Claude never cried. That's why I, who understood his silent suffering, felt morally obliged to share his unhappiness. The Marder's Teachers Agency had helped me get a contract to teach German in a Catholic college in New Jersey. While waiting for my college to open in September, I answered an ad in *Il Progresso Italo-Americano*. They were looking for someone fluent in languages who could translate films from French into English for the censors, not in the Village or in Brooklyn but, to my surprise, on Vanderbilt Avenue. A sweet voice invited me to see "the boss."

Just to get there from home on 108th Street and Broadway was an adventure, even apart from the el which seemed to project me into the sky. Nothing, however, surprised me more than the "boss" himself, a statuesque Neapolitan who would have been at home in one of de Filippo's plays, the inscrutable Roman General in the Fascist film "Scipione l'Africano," with a much chewed-up cigar stuck in the corner of his fleshy mouth.

"I am Cesare," he thundered in Neapolitan-accented Italian, as I sat in his spacious office and admired the stunning view of Manhattan. Then he glared at me as if searching for my innermost thoughts, and glanced briefly at the CV carefully devised by Professor Kristeller for more than one purpose. He wanted me to start the next day, he said. I said I would think it over and respond within twenty-four hours.

"Then why did you come to see me?" he thundered, his lips trembling in anger. He was offended. "I know you came because you are aware they take advantage of us. I am here to offer you what they refuse to give you — a decent way of living." There was something strange about this old man.

"I am certainly considering the offer, but need one day to decide," I repeated.

"Typical Italian, incapable of decision. Take it or leave it. This is the rule of the game." He lifted himself painfully, a giant against the skyscrapers in the sunset.

I would have lost this opportunity had it not been for the young lady sitting in the corner on a red velvet sofa. She had silently observed the meeting. Artificially blond and curly, the caricature of a Benozzo Gozzoli angel, huge black eyes circled with blue, her mouth a purple heart, her dress a vivid metallic blue, tight at the waist, Mariangela spoke up firmly.

"Why don't you give her a chance to consider your offer? She can help us also in the future. We agreed that she is overqualified for the job we are offering her now."

I recognized the charming voice on the telephone. Cesare smiled and left without looking at me. Sitting in a coffee shop on Vanderbilt Avenue, Mariangela briefly told me her story with a warmth and a spontaneity that endeared her to me. A Neapolitan who had lost both home and parents to bombs, she had landed in New York the year before, sponsored by some Italian-American relatives who threw her out a month after she arrived. Her story was worthy of a *Napoli Milionaria* in New York.

"That's when Cesare comes on stage," she lowered her voice as if to protect her secret. "He showed me how to see things straight. With so much going on among Italian-Americans in New York, it's easy for us newcomers to misjudge people. I was having dinner one night in an Italian restaurant in Brooklyn — dirt poor, lucky to have found someone who paid for my meal, more than one to be honest — when he showed up, *un vero napoletano tra i mafiosi di Brooklyn* ("a true Neapolitan among the Brooklyn mafiosi"). I swear I could see the difference between him and the others. *Questa la voglio per me!* ("I want this one for myself!"), he thundered with a voice that scared everybody, and he meant it."

She looked for my reaction. Sensing that I was not judging her, she whispered, "It was all very simple. I became his mistress which doesn't mean much because he is old and impotent. He is alone, you know, like you and me, alone among these skyscrapers, playing with money as we play with clothes. He needs the company of another human being. That's what I am for him, a human being who cares for him — and so he cares for me. For the bit I give him he takes care of me better than my father did in Naples." She laughed, "I owe Cesare my America."

We sat in silence for a while as if for a rest during a long hike. Then she walked me to the subway. She liked me, she said, from the moment she saw me.

"Don't worry," she said at the turnstyle, raising her voice above the noise. "Cesare liked you right away. I guess because of that look you had when you came into the room, lost but self-reliant, the look of one who has nothing more to lose. Cesare is good at judging people — that's why he offered you the job then and there. Now don't be stupid. Nothing bad will happen to you. We'll have fun together. Take the job, for God's sake. As for Cesare, you don't have to worry about him. He is mine. I've almost got to the point of loving him. He is mine to take care of. You just do your translations and get paid for them."

I rode home on the IRT at rush hour, as happy as a bird in the woods. Reassured by Mariangela's promise to look out for me, I took the job and from then on sat five days a week at a desk mechanically translating mediocre French film scripts into mediocre English. I didn't know what my translation would be used for and didn't care. Every Friday night I took home a paycheck equal to Claude's, but with extra pay for overtime.

Mariangela had asked me to help her write up four ads for the *Progresso,* a task Cesare had assigned her. She thought my knowledge of classical mythology could provide a special flavor. So we sat side by side on the red velvet sofa in the oppressive heat of a New York August and laughed as we dreamed up ways of alluring customers to buy virgin olive oil flowing from Venus's breasts or Tuscan wine bottled in Bacchus's caves. Every day we added a new stroke of the brush to the picture. And we laughed at ourselves as we laughed at others. I would have liked Claude to share in the fun of our fantastic creations, but he would look at me with a pained expression that made me stop short of telling him how Mariangela had helped me.

Unfortunately, my happy collaboration with Mariangela didn't last long. One important duty she had was to accompany her Old Man wherever he went, to Miami or Palm Beach. With Mariangela gone, all the fun disappeared from the office. What kept me going was the paycheck.

She had never asked me anything about my personal life, why I worked, who took care of me in America. Nor did I ever mention Claude. But Claude had locked himself in his own prison, brooding about I don't know what. He seemed to wake up from a dream when one hot evening in the Park, I told him I needed him. There was nobody I could turn to on this island or this continent. My life hung on ships. And ships took forever to cross that ocean.

"What about having lunch together every working day?"

He laughed. "You at Grand Central and me in the — Bowery one hour lunch? Where? the subway?"

"Why not?" I replied.

So we did. Every day at noon I would rush to the shuttle for Times Square, join the crowd waiting for the IRT, jump into a downtown train, and fling myself into Claude's arms in the lobby of the Woolworth Building. There, in an automat, I would savor a peanut butter sandwich____ lunch for a dollar plus the ten cents for transportation — sitting near the only human being who cared for me this side of the ocean.

That's how Times Square had its revenge on me, or I on Times Square. August 1947 made me a citizen of the New York subway. Gradually, I learned to appreciate in a kind of perverse way getting lost in the crowd beneath Times Square, forgetting there was a city above me and convincing myself that *we,* the people walking together underground, were the real city, as if the other didn't exist — each wrapped up in the impenetrable armor of the self. One day, when I got lost below Times Square, I saw in a flash why New York would never be able to understand de Filippo's subtle and delicate irony. Naples and New York stood as two great cities, but polar opposites. Their languages had nothing in common. They had different souls — the rich and the poor completely apart.

During our weekends in the Park, Claude and I would lie silently side by side for hours among discarded newspapers, looking at the river. Claude checked the *New York Times* for its advertisements; I ignored the paper. We enjoyed what the City allowed us to enjoy after a day of stifling heat — a sunset made more beautiful by the pollution. Claude made fun of me for my obsession with ships — my refusal to face reality —while both of us counted the money we had made during the week. I hoped to place a few precious dollars in the first bank account I had ever had in my life. Claude mocked his employers — they always underpaid him. During those quiet weekends on Riverside Drive, I realized that The Harlem Savings Bank gave me a sense of security. But what good was security if I didn't sense the human warmth that had helped me survive a war?

Here in America, I felt completely alone. As the summer drew to a close, it was in the Greek and Latin Reading Room at Butler Library that I felt somewhat at home. One day, I resigned from my job on Vanderbilt Avenue and from then on spent most of my days at Butler before I had to begin work in New Jersey. I also decided that, as soon as I had enough money in the bank after helping Bona and providing my share for my support, I would enroll in the Department of Classical Philology and pursue the project I had begun in Rome.

§ § §

As the *Marine Shark* slid gracefully into its pier and the passengers began to disembark, I caught sight of Bona and burst into tears. When I held her in my arms, nothing else mattered. What I had missed all along was the warmth of my family. With Bona and Eddie, a solid piece of my family had come to me. We would walk together from now on. Nothing would fail us.

Bona and Eddie's arrival changed both my perspective on life and Claude's. The sense that there was another world over there, where human beings were fighting for survival, was what we needed to readjust our expectations of life in New York. Both Bona and Eddie joined us cheerfully in Jean's basement.

Soon, Eddie left for Kansas, cloaked in the olympic serenity (and silence) which made him — and still makes him today, in his nineties, living on top of one of the Catskill mountains — a mystery to everybody except Bona. He thanked us but soon he would kiss us goodbye. He had crossed the ocean with a clear plan. I could have told him that was a dangerous way to come to America, but I didn't.

As for Bona, at night she and Jean occupied separate corners of our living room, each behind a set of red curtains which made the room look like a stage just before the curtain rises. Our living quarters were tight and dark, but Bona and I kept them spotless and made them unexpectedly quite cheerful as well.

"Nothing to complain about," Bona commented wryly. "No bombs and plenty of food." Then she added, "Of course, nothing and everything, but everything is too much. If you've made it so far, we can make it even better together."

Bona's pragmatic, sunny nature, which had endeared her to me during the war, now overcame what before her arrival had seemed insurmountable barriers to a peaceful life in New York.

"How does one get a job around here?" was her first question after Eddie left. She found a job through the *New York Times* as a file clerk in midtown, so she could earn some money before her courses began. In no time she became an expert on the subways. Her student visa allowed her to pursue a Ph.D. in classics at Fordham University and to work during vacations. Luck helped her to work longer than expected. The art of a file clerk in a huge firm consisted in judging the precise moment at which to insert and extract her fingers from the drawers of file cabinets that opened and closed automatically. She thought she had mastered the art when one day she misjudged and the drawer closed pitilessly on her index finger. The accident provided a long paid leave which she dedicated to an intensive study of Greek tragedy and Horace's satires. In no time, she became the favorite student of a respected Jesuit scholar at Fordham, Father Arbesman.

CHAPTER 20

A Baby and Tuberculosis

While Bona managed her intense program of study at Fordham at the northern tip of Manhattan, I became a regular commuter to New Jersey. By subway, ferry, and Lackawanna Railroad, it took me about three hours from uptown Manhattan to reach Convent Station, between the upscale towns of Madison and Morristown.

For an immigrant who had lived in Manhattan for only six months, the College of St. Elizabeth was Earthly Paradise. It was the oldest women's college in New Jersey, having been founded in 1899, as well as one of the first Catholic colleges in the U.S. A tall, gothic edifice housed a cozy dining room in which the lay faculty could gather, with white tablecloths for lunch prepared and served by nuns. Nearby was the students' dining room, as well as a gym and a music studio with forty-five pianos. From there, a path across the lawn led to the chapel, white brick and stone with a pinnacled tower called "Magdalen," as well as the library and classroom buildings and dormitories. Hundreds of young ladies dedicated themselves to developing the faculties that would "enable them to direct their own lives in such a way as to render service to others and guide them in the choice of a life work."

A green path led finally away from the buildings to a Greek theater on a hillside which overlooked the Passaic River. In semicircular tiers of seats, each year a thousand spectators heard Sophocles' and Euripides' hymns to life and death, against the backdrop of an immense American green valley, while on stage cypress and myrrh evoked the Mediterranean. Not far from the theater, Shakespeare echoed his Greek brothers with a garden reminiscent of his Stratford. For my benefit, St. Elizabeth as a whole was covered in green for half the year. Never had I dreamt of such a place built "to help young ladies to attain the ultimate end of their being."

St. Elizabeth's helped me forget all my worries. Not the enchanted island of Alcina and Armida, where noble warriors forgot their troubles and their responsibilities, this was a kind of Paradise. Here, the angelic Sisters of Charity — forty-four of them – faculty members of the College — flew about as light as butterflies. Their singing in the Gothic Chapel provided the enchanted atmosphere.

During the three years I spent working on this holy ground I had the chance to enjoy the beauty of each season as I had not since leaving Merano. I could teach to my heart's content and earn a decent salary. All in all, with the changing of the seasons, St. Elizabeth offered me a much needed, almost unreal, background for life in Manhattan as our household suddenly grew from two to five members. The nuns simply accepted me as I was, someone they could depend on for what mattered most, the education of their girls. As for the girls, they became good friends, always ready to modify even the sacrosanct schedule when my personal circumstances required it.

I was hired to teach three German courses. Remedial French was added without extra compensation. At the students' request, in my second year I introduced a program in Italian. Latin and Greek loomed in the background. From 1947 on Europe became a living presence for me in my New Jersey paradise.

Claude complained that the nuns were taking advantage of me. I was delighted. Six hours of daily commuting and close to twenty-four hours of weekly teaching were a light load compared to the work I had done before and during the war.

The problem I faced shortly after I started at St. Elizabeth was of a different and unexpected kind.

§ § §

"Don't tell me you are unaware of it," Jeannette Skelton, my daily travel companion, snapped one mid-November morning.

Jeannette was a tiny Greek proudly married to a Princetonian who had never completed his Ph.D. in Religion. He had been excommunicated by his Protestant church when he returned from the war in the Pacific and was now passionately dedicating his life to sociology at the New School for Social Research. His god was now Pareto, and I, as an Italian, was the object of his admiration. Jeannette was bursting with controlled energy, just as I imagined successful American young women would. Everything on her person and around her — from clothing to furniture, jewelry, even food prepared in the most unusual ways — she had created with her own hands. As a lay Professor of Home Economics, the most popular subject at our college, Jeannette had quickly become my trusted guide — which included how to deal with my husband. She knew I was completely in her hands.

As we rode through the woods of New Jersey on a bright November day in 1947, Jeannette declared triumphantly:

"You're expecting, my dear."

Since "expecting" did not produce the desired effect, she insisted, unrelenting:

"Trust me, you little fool, I am better than a doctor. You are several months pregnant. You must take care of yourself. You have to look for a doctor and a hospital — provided, of course, you have insurance to cover the costs."

Registering my confusion and embarrassment as if I had been caught red handed, she went on, "Don't worry. I'm sure your husband has provided."

But I wasn't at all sure, so I asked her how to proceed. She dismissed the matter. I remained silent, embarrassed and angry as if Jeannette was to blame. The poor lady had been trying for three years to get pregnant and could not understand why I was not happy about it. But I was worried about upsetting the delicate equilibrium of life at home.

"First of all," she warned, "as you get bigger and bigger, you must hide your state from the nuns. If they find out they'll fire you."

"Fire me? On what grounds can they fire me?" I was by now shaking from head to foot. "Why? I was married in the Vatican with the blessing of the Pope three years ago."

"This is America, my dear, not the Vatican. Even the Catholics act on their own."

But her only experience in religious matters was the Protestant church that had excommunicated her husband.

The train stopped with a jolt. Climbing the long walkway to the main building we regained our composure.

"Don't worry," she consoled me. "A good snowy winter will take care of it. I'll find the clothes that will keep the nuns guessing until spring." She looked at me confidentially. "Guessing from your condition now, you are safe until April. Then God will take care of it. We can hope that the baby doesn't show up before June."

§ § §

At home that night I discussed the problem with Bona. We carefully examined the college catalogue, searching for something that would explain why the nuns might fire me but found nothing. The Department of Religion, which covered less than half a page in the catalogue — much less than Latin with its two pages — offered, besides a course on "Catholicity in Action," two other courses: "Christian Life and Worship" and "The Catholic Church," and a course on marriage that read:

"Brief review of general notions of ethics and morality. Marriage: natural contract raised to the dignity of a sacrament. The power of state and church over marriage. Prenuptial requirements and general preparation. Discussion of divorce and the whole range of eugenics which will supply arguments and cogent reasons for the Catholic teaching on marriage."

We were relieved by this straightforward official document.

"Let's stop here," Bona declared pragmatically. "We must accept America as it is and act accordingly for our survival."

We spent a good part of the following weekend trying different ways to disguise my change of shape as it would become more apparent. As for Claude, he didn't seem surprised when I told him I was expecting, but said no, we had no insurance and, therefore, I should find a doctor who was not expensive. I should aim low, otherwise all of my salary would be consumed by medical costs. I should follow Jeannette's advice. Home economics was stuff for women not for men. Of course, Bona and Claude did seem happy at the news, Bona especially.

It took me some time to get used to my condition. As months passed, however, a new relationship emerged between me and the little one traveling with me everyday. I reassured myself she or he would be extraordinary in intelligence and the joy of living. Certainly somebody who enjoyed traveling and maybe even teaching far away from home.

By the time word reached the President's office that Mme. Bové was pregnant, I was close to my eighth month. Siora Turon's gray fur coat had beautifully served the purpose with the addition of some picturesque shawls which Jeannette knitted while she prepared my baby's layette. The winter of 1947-48 was fortunately very cold, snowy, and long.

The college president, Sister Marie José Byrne, had been my friend from the moment I first entered her office in July 1947. A Ph.D. in Classical Philology from the University of Chicago and Chairman of the Latin and Greek Department at the College for many years before she was named President, Sister Marie José was an elderly woman of considerable intelligence and charm. She shared with me her love for Homer and Vergil as well as Sappho and Catullus, a love that had lasted for many years. It was as if I had been sent from that very Rome she longed to see into her American paradise. Our first meeting was a dialogue between two souls longing to communicate what each of us thought made life worthwhile.

We had not seen much of each other, when the news of my pregnancy reached her office along with other rumors, which, Jeannette told me, had originated with the German teacher whom I had displaced at the college. In my course on "Deutsche Kulturgeschichte" (German Cultural History) I had more than once mentioned, and had in fact lectured on, Luther, Nietzsche, and even Schopenhauer! But there was more. The rumor was that this new teacher of German was working under the auspices of Columbia on the critical edition of a work by a Renaissance philosopher, Lorenzo Valla, whose books were on the Index. Among other things, Valla had proved that the document establishing the tem-poral power of the Pope was a forgery. He had even argued against the celibacy of the religious orders. Clearly, Martin Luther and Lorenzo Valla had too much in common.

As I walked through a carpet of flowers towards the Gothic administration building, I didn't think that Sister Marie José was concerned about my transgressions. New to America, however, I had followed Bona's advice and carefully prepared my defense. Too, my friend Paul Kristeller at Columbia had done serious research on Lorenzo Valla, whose main works were indeed still on the Index. As for the book I was editing, however, Kristeller discovered a rare edition of the Index that did not include his work on pleasure for a number of years. Kristeller suggested I should bring to the Sisters' attention the fact that Cardinal Mercati, who had been present at my defense, had given me a special dispensation to deal with this particular work, given expanded study in the Vatican of a writer now being "rediscovered." I was not the only one ressuscitating him.

Sister Marie Jose received me with the same warmth with which she had greeted me on my arrival.

"Gossip has it," she said with a smile, "that you are expecting."

When I opened my fur coat her beautiful face darkened for only an instant. Then looking directly at me, she admitted that my condition worried her for more than one reason. A pregnant teacher was unusual on the campus where there were only ten lay faculty. But she was sure the girls would get used to it. Her real worry was about my future. In America, she pointed out, there were no provisions for working mothers. How would I manage my work and a baby? I reassured her, with all the persuasive power I could muster that I could continue. St. Elizabeth was, so far, the only blessing America had shed on my life here. I would not give it up for anything in the world. As for the baby — we smiled together and proclaimed that God would help us.

Encouraged by the God who united us, I quickly moved to the other issue I had expected her to raise: my work on a forbidden book. She listened attentively to my defense, read Kristeller's letter with interest, and made notes. Valla was easily disposed of with the invocation of Cardinal Mercati.

When I was about to leave, she brought up the last issue, the three formidable Germans I brought up in my course: Luther, Nietzsche, and Schopenhauer. She sighed with relief when I told her my reason for allowing them entry to my classrooms. It was better for our students to hear about them while in college than out in the world. Smiling, she whispered, more to herself than to me, "The time has come for our girls to see the world for what it is, not what it should be. I am sure you introduced those Germans with the objectivity called for by your classical training."

She quoted a favorite passage from Ovid's *Ars Amandi* (Art of Love), familiar to us both. We parted with a warm handshake.

§   §   §

In Manhattan, living with Bona was fun most of the time. Intimacy both strengthened and strained our relationship. We were building something together, both foreigners, unaware that there was a basic disjunction because we had entered the country with two different visas. My permanent visa as a GI wife left me free to work. Bona, with her student visa, was allowed to work only under special conditions.

Claude was the happiest one, serving as husband and sponsor respectively. From the start, Bona and I understood that besides the law of the land, we had to take into account Claude's anxiety about falling back into poverty after the war had dug him out of it.

Every Saturday Claude would hand me a copy of a calligraphic masterpiece — the weekly accounting of expenses — so that I could repay him the amount he had put out for my expenses and Bona's, i.e., two-thirds of the household's expenses. Bona and I took Claude as he was, a facet of America we were beginning to understand. We cooked and kept house joyfully.

Together, Bona and I learned at the supermarket — unknown to Italy — how to get the cheapest dinners in New York, cheap but tasty. Claude's appreciation of our efforts came with a gift in style: a pocket cookbook by Elizabeth Woody and the members of the Food Staff of McCalls with a whole page dedication to me as his Muse. Would I, cara mogliettina ("dear little wife"), consider cooking as my subject of research from now on, a subject matching my spiritual as well as my intellectual needs? I was silently furious at the gift: I hated to cook.

Eddie joined us in Jean's apartment for Christmas. Bona and I squeezed a minuscule Christmas tree in the only corner available. We invited Jean to spend Christmas with us and she accepted. We discovered later that Jews celebrate a Christmas of their own, Hanukkah, but the poor woman was so lonely, she was happy to celebrate whatever came her way. We helped her to feel part of the family.

The day Eddie left, it began to snow. It snowed for days and nights on end. Streets became impassable, subways were slowed, the ferry stopped running. The newspapers called it the worst winter in a century. Bona and I greeted the snow with delight at first. It reminded us of our youth in the Alps. It was wonderful to reach Broadway clambering over great mounds of snow. But after a few days, the snow became a problem. 108th Street was blocked. Reaching St. Elizabeth became almost impossible. Yet the college didn't close and I had to do my very best to get there. Bona agreed with me, especially in my condition. Once it took me half a day to get there. The day after, I was allowed to stay home.

Long after the storm ended, the snow was with us, gray and dirty, mixed with garbage, dog poop, and discarded Christmas trees frozen in odd shapes. A disgusting sight and an impediment to traffic. It was during one dark night while we lay peacefully in our beds, our house surrounded by snow, that Jean moaned like a wounded animal from behind her dark red curtain. Bona and I found her in a pool of blood. We worried that she had vomited all her blood. Claude called an ambulance. We accompanied her to St. Luke's Hospital nearby. Her estranged husband appeared while we waited in the emergency with her.

He told us he would take care of her and so we left.

That was the last we ever saw of Jean. She disappeared from our lives as she had entered, like a wraith. She had lived with us for half a year — on tiptoe, never intrusive, always helpful. She appreciated immensely the punctiliousness with which Claude paid her every penny we owed her.

"That's life in Manhattan," Claude commented one evening at dinner after Jean's disappearance. "A lesson for you both."

"For all of us," I corrected him.

It was as if she had died. But she was still alive somewhere, we just didn't know where.

Jean's disappearance from our lives did not come without consequences. Bona began to worry about my health. After much discussion and visits to the hospital where they refused to give us any information on Jean's illness, the two of us concluded that Jean must have tuberculosis. That was the only sickness which, we thought, manifested itself with a sudden outpouring of blood. It had plagued papa's family. Although we had never witnessed the illness itself, we were familiar with it. Merano housed many sanitariums. Horrified, we decided then and there that we must immediately leave the contaminated apartment, before the poor baby I was carrying was infected. I had not yet contacted an obstetrician because of worry about cost.

When, together, we asked Claude to consider helping us to get an apartment of our own, for which, of course, we would pay our own share, just as we were already doing, Claude looked at us as if we were crazy. He even invoked Mamma's authority from across the ocean to knock some sense into our heads. Mamma did not respond.

After a while, under daily pressure, he proposed to look into the possibility of a loan from the Veterans' Administration to buy a little house in Queens. We spent a couple of Sundays looking over little houses in Queens. Bona was almost inclined to reconsider, but I was adamant. Queens looked like a kind of dormitory for Manhattan. True, there were subways connecting Queens to Manhattan. Still, Queens was Queens. I wanted Manhattan and only

Manhattan. Sheer stubbornness on my part, declared Claude, and I agreed. I simply didn't want to move too far from Columbia, I said. Claude laughed.

"Why?" he asked.

"I don't know," I answered.

"I don't know what's wrong with you," he exclaimed in despair.

I didn't argue. I told Bona that, in my opinion, Manhattan was the only place in the whole world that gave us the chance to live all four of us together, all of us commuting to our jobs in different directions.

"That may sound reasonable for us," Bona commented, "not for Claude. Remember he is the only American among us."

Claude didn't budge for weeks. Finally, to push him to act, Bona and I stopped cooking dinner and asked Claude to take us out to a restaurant every night.

§ § §

When Patrick O'Connor, a New York policeman, showed up at Jean's place after Claude had answered his ad in the Times, he looked like every New York policeman: robust, a flat face unimaginable without the hat he never took off, gun and night-stick hanging impressively from his belt. He was courteous and matter of fact. Thrilled to see a New York policeman in our home, both Bona and I stood looking at him in silent awe. He was unreal, a symbol of the power that the city we both loved and feared exercised over violence. The Law Made Flesh. Why didn't Claude ask him to sit down?

He and Claude stood while they discussed the deal. Officer O'Connor wanted to move his family to Queens. He was offering us the opportunity to take over the lease of his apartment in uptown Manhattan, if we paid him the sum of $800.00 for the furniture he was leaving behind. Sturdy furniture, he said, that had outlived a generation of Irishmen.

"Peanuts," he kept repeating. As he spoke, he looked around Jean's living room to corroborate this sad fact: a city as big a Manhattan without a single apartment for rent.

Though Bona and I didn't understand what "peanuts" had to do with the money he wanted, we agreed with him. Here was Officer O'Connor of the New York Police giving a veteran hero and two poor immigrants the unheard-of chance to take over an apartment in Manhattan for a modest outlay of $800.

Claude was tense as if in a supreme act of concentration, his lips trembling, his eyes shining behind his thick lenses, tiny drops of perspiration visible on his forehead. He seemed an animal caught in a trap. A painful thought flickered through my mind: an interrogator of prisoners of war, a respected governor of a province in Venezia Giulia, a veteran of four landings, paying off a policeman to get a miserable apartment in New York? Bona and I, who had seen entire apartment buildings crumble under Allied bombs, were now pushing the liberator of Rome into a humiliating deal. I was about to tell Claude, "Don't bother, we can do without it," when officer O'Connor turned to Claude.

"I know what you're thinking," he said. "At first, I didn't want to tell you why I decided to move to Queens, but I'll tell you anyway. My wound bothers me. I don't know how long I can continue on active duty in Manhattan. At thirty-five, I have to prepare for retirement. Queens is my first step."

He took off his hat. A huge scar disfigured the left side of his head. The muscles of Claude's face relaxed. Patrick O'Connor, a former sailor, was a veteran like Claude. He had spent two years in the Japanese theater.

"Sit down," Claude mumbled. "Let's have a cup of coffee."

Two weeks later we entered Officer O'Connor's apartment at Bennett Avenue and took possession of its furniture. We had paid just $500.00 for the furniture; I had happily agreed to give Claude, in installments, half that amount.

§ § §

The vacuum cleaner was the most precious item we inherited. It was a powerful machine that worked miracles. Bona and I stood in awe as Claude put it together and followed it from room to room. There were five rooms, two bedrooms overlooking a courtyard, a bathroom, a kitchen, a dining room, and a living room, with plenty of sun all around.

After a full day of vacuuming, scrubbing, and dusting, apartment 62 at 31 Bennett Avenue made the city real for us. That Hoover was our passport to Manhattan citizenship. Seen from the vantage point of 31 Bennett Avenue, Times Square and the whole of downtown and midtown lay somewhere far off. Claude stowed the box with de Filippo's play and the precious war documents under our bed. The best corner of our bedroom we reserved for the crib to receive little Claudia.

Bennett Avenue runs down the hill near Fort Tryon Park and the Cloisters. Parallel to Broadway, it ends at 181st Street. For the next eight years, we found there all that we needed for our daily lives: supermarket, Harlem Savings Bank, hardware store, baby store, bakery, barber shop, and Catholic Church built by an Italian woman, a saint who had cared for the poor of the city.

It was a comforting thought, for me at least, that the Broadway we could see from our back windows was the same Broadway that ran past the Woolworth building — the first skyscraper I had ever seen — and along Columbia University, the first reference point I had had in the city.

People in our building dressed up every Saturday mostly in black, moved together down the avenue, and lit candles on five-branch candelabra. They spoke English with a German accent; among themselves, they spoke a German dialect that Bona and I could almost understand. They were orthodox Jews, Claude said, like his bosses at the office. They ate kosher just as Jean had. On the sixth floor where we lived there was also a Greek orthodox family, the Alexandropoulos family, with three children.

Down on the second floor there was a French family from the Pyrenees: five *garçons* (waiters) who worked in restaurants, all called Junqua. Madame Junqua, the wife of one of them, kept house for all.

Maithè was the family's child. We made friends with the Junquas, a happy tribe, ready to laugh and to cry as they told their stories. They were also the only family, with us, who didn't own or co-own a store. Most of the Jews were in the jewelry or fur business. The Greeks owned a vegetable store. Most of them were longtime American citizens; they had landed in New York before the war. They all remembered, the Jews especially, the ship that brought them to this blessed land.

During our eight years at 31 Bennett Avenue we lived happily together, respecting each other's privacy, but always ready to help one another.

§ § §

The winter of 1948 was dreary and interminable. Snow piled up on Bennett Avenue and Broadway, slowing down traffic at times to a standstill. New Jersey was worse. Wrapped in Jeannette's shawls over my Italian fur coat, I traveled early every weekday morning by way of the A train, the tube, and the Lackawanna railroad to Santa Maria Hall. Every night, Bona looked from our living room window for me to appear at the corner of 181st and Bennett Avenue. That was an old habit from our childhood. We would wait for our mother late at night. When I did not show up one evening at the usual time or even three hours later, Bona appealed to Claude for reassurance. He was reading the paper in a corner of the living room. Hardly raising his head, he mumbled that I was capable of overcoming all sorts of difficulties.

When I finally appeared late that night, Claude was asleep in his armchair. Bona, weeping, fell into my arms.

"We didn't eat dinner," she said. "That wicked man, he got what he deserved. He wasn't worried at all."

No, Claude wasn't wicked. He was matter-of-fact, as he had always been, with no place for emotion.

Bona called me from the kitchen where she was warming up some soup. While we ate, the two of us alone, I told Bona my adventure. By four that afternoon the Lackawanna railroad had stopped running. The nuns suggested I spend the night at the college. I wanted to go home, I said, because my family would worry, and I asked a male colleague to take me along in his car. He warned me that the car was old, small, and in bad condition. That didn't bother me; I wanted to go. He thought I must be tough because I had survived a war. When we were a short distance from campus, in the middle of nowhere, we got stuck in the deep snow. He asked me to get out and help him push the car out of a ditch, I did my best until I felt a sharp pain. "I am pregnant," I confessed. But he shouldn't tell the nuns. "It is a secret."

"A secret?" He was furious, as if had confessed to a murder.

He finally agreed to keep the secret and, suddenly gentle, led me on foot to a highway. It took us over an hour to reach it. Deep in the night we stood side by side —as we used to during the war outside Rome when we were in search of food — my colleague waving his white scarf and hollering "Emergency."

A truck-driver took me on board. The father of five children, he took my pregnancy as a matter of course.

"A first child is trouble," he said. "But don't let it get you. By the time you get to the third you learn to take them as a gift of God. By the way, where is your husband, what is he doing? Is he unemployed?" he asked.

I told him he worked in the Bowery. He laughed, for no obvious reason, and we parted laughing, like old friends.

§ § §

Spring did not arrive until late May, with lots of flowers in Fort Tryon Park and at St. Elizabeth's. Bona and I discovered the art of shopping, something totally and absolutely new in our lives: you dive into a huge store among thousands of dresses, arranged like books in a library, and you get lost among them. We discovered Klein's at 114th Street, which was cheap compared to anything downtown. There we bought a dress for Bona and my first and only maternity dress: ten dollars in all, on sale. We didn't know such dresses existed.

At home we lived happily. Claude and I were employed. Eddie, in Kansas, was about to finish his exams; he got top grades. He would soon come home to write his Master's thesis. Every night was an occasion to celebrate with a big dinner, flowers in the middle of the table, and Italian wine which we thought would give me strength. Since I wasn't insured, Jeannette helped us find an inexpensive doctor. He saw me once and pronounced me in excellent health. He told me that the baby would be born after final exams. He had spent years in China, he told me, where women give birth in the fields. I was lucky to be in America, with its excellent hospitals. I should phone him if I was in pain. That settled the matter of childbirth to everybody's satisfaction. I never saw him until after childbirth; I had no money for a check-up.

§   §   §

"Stop walking around! This is a hospital not your home! You're upsetting the whole ward. Go back to your bed, I said, or—"

The nurse who had stopped me in my tracks was a blonde Valkyrie, more fit to be a prison guard than a nurse.

Maybe she was right. I didn't know what a hospital was, since I had never been in one, except to bring food to our men in hiding during the war. But I was in no mood to comply and I called her bluff: "I'll stop walking around when you bring me my baby!"

On June 16, 1948, a chilly wind was blowing across the Hudson. We could feel it in our bones even at Bennett Avenue, several blocks from the river. But who cared? After having graded the last paper and filled out the grade sheets, Bona and I were content.

"We've made it! The baby will be born free."

We meant free of academic obligations.

Then Bona pushed me into the bathtub with her blessings: "Now a good warm bath and you'll enter the hospital as clean as when you entered the world!"

Neither of us had the faintest idea, until late in adolescence, of how we entered the world. Much of it was still a mystery, though America was making us aware of what we'd missed so far.

It happened as I was relaxing in the hot water. A pain darted through my whole body like lightning. I jumped out of the bathtub, and as I stood naked in the middle of the bathroom, I felt a gush of lukewarm water flowing down between my legs.

"*Le acque*! The waters!" Bona screamed in alarm and vanished to get a taxi.

The taxi driver was a blessing. All this commotion for a baby? I wasn't the first woman to give birth in his taxi. He was well equipped. We kept control of our nerves in time to put up a vigorous fight in the reception room of the hospital — a thin slice of a building between two tall apartment houses somewhere on Central Park West. We had never seen the building before.

I was now in great pain, but Bona was not. "No is NO!" the nurse shouted at Bona. The middle-aged, impeccably dressed receptionist followed her "NO" with a cascade of words. Rules are rules. No one was allowed to be with the patient but her mother or husband. Was she one of them? A sister didn't count. Ah, we were immigrants, that explained it. Where did we come from, Poland perhaps? She should have guessed —but what could one expect from a name like Kostka!

Bona was screaming at the top of her lungs as they wheeled me upstairs. The last I heard from Bona was "Get the doctor fast!" Then I fell into a deep sleep that lasted almost twelve hours. I found out days later that, since the doctor was too busy to come to the hospital, he had ordered the nurses to give me an injection to retard childbirth. I woke up close to midnight, a sweaty face over mine.

"Bona?" I whispered, incredulous.

"I am about to give you an anesthetic to help you," a sugary voice murmured.

"What's that? I want my sister. Where is she?"

"Now you don't need anybody but me. Don't you see, I am your doctor."

Everything clicked in my mind.

"Please," I pleaded, "don't make my baby be born on the 17th. It will bring her bad luck." Then I passed out.

When I woke up vomiting, I searched around all over my bed.

"Where is IT?" I cried.

"Your IT is a beautiful little girl," said a black nurse's aide with a reassuring smile. She was holding a pan under my chin.

For an entire day I waited, longing to see that little girl. Finally I lost my patience and got out of the bed and went in search of the nursery. (I remembered from the General Muir that Americans confine newborn babies to nurseries for hygienic reasons.) That is when the Valkyrie saw me, pushed me back into bed, and made me swallow a bunch of pills. They were meant to stop my milk, she told me. I was horrified.

"Doctor's orders! Didn't you tell your doctor you planned to go back to work after childbirth?" was the nurse's matter-of-fact explanation.

"And so what?" replied.

"And so your baby will be fed on formula like most American babies! You now live in a civilized country, you know. The rate of infant mortality..."

"Who cares about civilization?" I cried. "Give me my baby!"

The Valkyrie filled the whole space between my bed and the window. I had looked all day at that window as my way out of prison. I wished she would get out of the way and told her so.

"I hope you realize," she said calmly, "that you are the most unpleasant patient in this ward."

She was right. Humbled, I buried my head in the pillow. Towards evening, my Valkyrie reappeared.

"Here is your husband!" she said sweetly, as Claude entered with a bouquet of daisies. As soon as he handed it to me, I hurled it with all my strength at the open window. I missed the target. Claude picked up the flowers, and I burst into tears of shame. (I knew the Valkyrie had witnessed the scene discreetly from the hall.) We made peace.

Claude's boss had told him that very day, on June 17, 1948, that he was fired. Despite my request, the doctor had put down June 17 as Claudia's official date of birth, although I was told she had actually been born two minutes before midnight on June 16th.

Why did everything have to happen to me?

After Claude left, the kind nurse's aide brought me a soft white bundle. Hidden under protective veils, like tender leaves, my rose was opening its petals, vivified by the morning dew. A perfect little face. Two immense dark eyes with long lashes. I warmed her ice cold little feet against my aching swollen breast.

§ § §

Hansel entered the household shortly after Claudia: a little bird Eddie bought to keep him company while he wrote his Master's thesis on German literature for the University of Kansas. Eddie and Hansel were waiting when Bona and I brought home little Claudia.

There was one big difference between Hansel and Claudia. Eddie cleaned Hansel's cage every day and then carried it to wherever he would sit to read. Hansel sang its happy song from morning till night. When Eddie covered the cage with a cloth at night, little Hansel fell into a sweet silence. Hansel lived to make Eddie happy. With Claudia, it was just the opposite. She dominated the household — except for Eddie and Hansel — day and night, for three months, precisely until I left Bennett Avenue again for the College of Saint Elizabeth on September 17th, 1948.

The summer of 1948 in New York was a nightmare. For weeks on end, the temperature went up over 90 degrees. Smog and high humidity covered the city like a heavy blanket. Our top-floor apartment retained the heat and humidity. Overwhelmed by lack of sleep, Bona and I lost our points of reference. Summers in Rome were hot, but we could get relief by opening the windows at night to catch the breeze from the sea. But Bennett Avenue was in a valley, so there rarely was a breeze.

We regained some equilibrium when we discovered the advantages of open air. Towards the end of July, Bona and I began spending our days and most of our nights in Fort Tryon Park. We slept but were always ready to give Claudia her bottle or rock her back to sleep.

Eddie and Claude did not join us. Prisoners of the apartment, they stoically put up with the stultifying combination of heat, humidity, and smog that upset little Claudia and was driving Bona and me crazy. Sometimes, Eddie would place Hansel's cage on the fire escape for the night, joining Claudia's bassinette. In the mornings, Bona and I would wheel Claudia to the park in her carriage. When we returned home one night, Hansel lay stiff in his cage, victim of sunstroke. Eddie buried the little bird in the park.

§ § §

Claudia's unhappiness was surely due to our inability to communicate with her — so said Dr. Spock in our Bible. As little Claudia lay for the first time naked on my bed, we stood like the Three Magi, looking at her in awe. Here was a miracle we had never dreamt of, a creature perfect and beautiful, yet small and tender and so fragile and helpless we were reluctant to touch her, until she cried.

With Dr. Spock's backing, Claudia made clear what she needed or wanted or did not want. Being born into a family that earned its living by teaching languages, she must have decided to force us to add another language, hers. Dr. Spock agreed with her most of the time and made gentle fun of us. Her way of communicating seemed contrary to her miraculous, serene beauty. She communicated with us during the first three months of her life in an imperious way, mainly through heartbreaking, piercing cries which we tried desperately to interpret. Dr. Spock confirmed that we had to learn her language — that was the law of nature.

Formula did not agree with Claudia. Bona and I realized that one night, after Claude had reread aloud the pages which directed new mothers to the language of their babies' delicate digestive system. (He didn't seem to understand it either.) Our new doctor, who lived next door, a former parachutist of the Normandy landings, tried again and again to modify the hospital's formula, while I, in a moment of despair, attempted to breastfeed the baby. (I had stopped taking the pills when I left the hospital.) Claudia's response was a firm "No!" When she took her formula she refused to burp, so we kept her endlessly on our shoulders, a rite which we carried out with devotion. Jeannette Skelton, who came to our aid, scolded us for overdressing her. Didn't we notice that she had a heat rash? We kept her naked from then on and, on Jeannette's advice, gave her brief sunbaths in the park, followed by sponge baths with cool water from a fountain.

The park, near the Hudson, agreed with her better than the apartment did. That was the only clear message from our little princess. So, most of the time we let her feel the cool breeze from the river. Sadly, we had run out of ways to interpret Claudia's language. I was at my wits' end. I had lost twenty pounds, and could hardly eat or sleep, not even when she herself was asleep. It was a terrible time.

More than once, towards the end of that summer, as I wheeled the carriage up Bennett Avenue, I was exhausted to the point of being barely able to stand. I yearned for an end to my physical and mental exhaustion. I wished I could be flown home with my baby, home to Italy. I looked now with an envy I'd never felt before, at the ships sailing toward the open sea. If only I had enough money to pay for a trip back to Europe.

Things changed miraculously on September 17. I arrived at 31 Bennett Avenue, at 5:00 p.m. Bona assured me that little Claudia had behaved normally. Greatly relieved, we bathed her and put her to bed. She slept through the night from that day on.

By now all four of us were students. Taking advantage of the GI Bill, Claude had decided to work towards an M.A. in Economics, Eddie was going for a Ph.D. in Comparative Literature (German/Russian), I was in Classical Philology, planning to work towards publication of the Valla book. Bona continued her studies at Fordham.

Even though I was the only one with a full-time job, under Claude's leadership we succeeded in running a well-balanced household in which nobody owed any money to anybody. Claude paid for his own support and half of Claudia's. I contributed my own support, half of Claudia's, and a weekly rate for the furniture we used. I also paid Bona weekly to take care of Claudia while I was working. Eddie learned that he was allowed to work part-time and got a part-time position teaching German at Adelphi Academy in Brooklyn, and thus also contributed.

Weekly messages from Mamma brought her blessings together with some vague plans for other members of the family to join us. We were still hoping for a united family in America. I wished God had allowed us to continue as we had started. But He didn't. (The fault was only partially His.)

"*Carissime!*" Mamma's letter, received after Christmas, made me laugh and cry. She could not believe we had fallen so low as to leave our baby each morning with some French waiters. What she implied was that she, alone and penniless after Papa's death, had succeeded in supporting the four of us at home, while we here in America, the land of plenty, were parking a six-month-old baby in a neighbor's apartment every morning.

It took more than one letter to get her to understand. At the same time, I had the feeling that the "Other Shore" was fading. Mamma, of course, sympathized but couldn't afford to come. Was I forgetting that my people were fighting for survival — survival with dignity, as Mamma put it? She wouldn't ask for money, although the dollar was much stronger than the lira. And even if she had asked, I didn't have enough to pay for her crossing.

One mild evening in late November Eddie came home from Brooklyn shivering like the last leaf of autumn. Dr. Marcus, our GP, sat on his bed angry and swearing. Finally, he told us it was viral pneumonia. We were dumbfounded. What was that? He did not explain, he just kept cursing. Why did Eddie, after all he'd been through, fall victim to an epidemic, in New York City for God's sake? Why Eddie and not somebody who had suffered less and was less deserving? For Christ's sake! Wasn't there any justice in this world?

We silently applauded the doctor's generous heart and helped as much as we could as he took care of Eddie for months. The illness lingered much longer than anyone expected. When, late in January, Eddie got back on his feet, he could hardly walk and kept on coughing a dry hollow cough that seemed to come from the bottom of his soul. He would have been a miserable sight, had he not been Eddie. In bed or in an armchair, being Eddie, he smiled but was silent. He kept a pile of books by his side and continued to prepare for his Ph.D. exams.

At Christmas, Bona and I decorated a huge tree and built a manger so big it could have housed Claudia. We roasted a turkey and drank Chianti. A huge box of German sweets came from Eddie's sisters, Otti and Gerda, now reunited in West Berlin.

As the illness lingered, Eddie's employer, Adelphi Academy, proposed that Bona replace him. She accepted. This raised the question of care for Claudia while I was teaching. This drove home the obvious: while we had all shared so far in the joys and pains, the responsibility for Claudia was mine and mine alone. Bona's help, great as it was, was a gift on her part. We had to look elsewhere for help. I felt now for the first time the brunt of Sister Marie José's warning, when she learned about my pregnancy, that in America there are no facilities to help working mothers.

Bona and I considered, and discarded, various options. Claude did not offer to help with either time or money. But had he offered, I was sure, he wouldn't be much help. What he liked most was his sleep, his freedom, and his financial independence. We had no car for me to take the baby with me to New Jersey where the nuns would have been happy to care for her while I was in class. I could not afford a regular babysitter. One possibility was the neighbors to whom we felt close.

One evening, as Bona and I sat in their dingy and dark but cheery kitchen, drinking a glass of superb wine from their village, together with Madame Junqua and Tonton, the world changed. While they talked and laughed and sang, that dingy kitchen suddenly seemed to include the whole Pyrenees — snow-covered mountains, and cozy villages in their lush valley. As Tonton spoke about his village in his heavily-accented Southern French, we could hear the farmers whistling and the dogs barking at the moon. Then he sang.

The four able men — there were five brothers, one of them married to Madame — were out working nights in a downtown restaurant. Madame worked there part-time when her daughter Maithe was not home. Maithe was a cute six-year-old with a big red ribbon in her hair that made her look like a butterfly. Tonton kept the household going. He was limping so badly he could hardly walk. Around the house he limped merrily along while doing the chores better than any woman could.

Take care of little Claudia? Why not? With pleasure! Provided I brought her down to their home by 8:00 am and picked her up no later than 3:00 pm. The cost was minimal, something I could afford. They weren't doing it for the money, they said.

The arrangement required ingenuity all around. With the help of my students, I was able to rearrange my schedule so that I would teach from 8:00 am to 1:00, which meant having to leave home at 5:00 a.m. Then I could take Claudia out into the fresh air of Fort Tryon Park for a couple of hours. I would then give her a bath, prepare dinner, feed her, and put her to bed. Bona would bring Claudia to the Junquas and also help me as much as she could at night. The two men were left to their own devices. Eddie was trying to regain his strength so he could return to the university. Claude slept most of the day, then read the newspaper without even opening the blinds. The effect on his studies was disastrous. He couldn't get the grade of B-minus that would allow him to continue.

Claudia became the darling of Madame J. and especially of Tonton, who spent hours singing French songs to her. The first words she could mumble were in French. Everyone in the building knew of Claudia's miracle and was invited to the show. When, however, it was time to leave the park, she would kick and scream. Naturally. She had always loved the river. It took all my strength to strap her in the carriage and wheel her home. Getting her out of the bathtub at night, Bona and I wore raincoats. Yet, most of the time, neither Bona nor I took her tantrums seriously. Claudia's reactions were funny and different from anything one would expect. She was curious about life around her. Dr. Spock would probably have agreed with her, except that he had been dismissed; Claudia herself had taken his place. We were learning her language fast.

§ § §

The Junquas' kitchen had the aroma of open fields, Bona said one night after we had spent a couple of hours around their oak table. Although it actually smelled of garlic, we both agreed that that kitchen evoked the skies, the grass, the brooks, and the flowers of our childhood. The kitchen gave off odors that had the kind of color and texture, for which we both yearned.

Bona and I had sworn we would never spend another summer in New York if we could help it. Madame J. and Tonton showed us how. What we needed first was a car. Not owning a car, we were missing the best of America. An old jalopy would do, provided it could hold the road. The highway would provide our way to freedom.

Then, of course, we needed a place to go with that car, a place as far as possible from New York.

At this point, there was an intense exchange in French dialect between Madame and Tonton, until they agreed to tell us the secret of the Paradise of the "Pyrenean *garçons*": a huddle of cottages in the Berkshires. The area was unbelievably beautiful — all green and blue, with a lake. A lake? Bona and I couldn't believe our ears. Yes, a real lake, not an artificial one, with boats on it. We'd have a boat available if we rented the cottage. The cottage stood among apple trees. Yes, we could pick the apples late in the summer.

Neither Bona nor I bothered to ask about the cottages themselves; Madame, however, warned us that they were very basic, just a roof over your head. But then, Tonton added, wasn't the reason for leaving the city to be in Nature? We had a beautiful apartment in New York. Wasn't that enough? The owners of the colony were an old retired couple, the Sterns. They were so old they were all wrinkles and could hardly stand. Still they kept the place going. Of course, one had to reserve well in advance because the price was so modest.

Bona and I kept this secret until we needed Claude's support. He responded by immediately beginning to search for a car, and I agreed to pay half, in weekly installments. He chose an old, cheap

Oldsmobile. On an April weekend, we tried it out, all except Eddie, who was still too weak. After twelve hours of huffing and puffing, we reached Lake Pantoussec; Claude was such an expert mechanic he could have made a living at that. He thought so too, and at times we wondered why he wasn't a mechanic.

The cottages were near the lake, wooden skeletons with shaky steps. We didn't enter any of them for fear of being disappointed and thus ruining our deal with the Sterns. We spent our time instead admiring the apple trees and the grass and the lake shimmering in the sun. We felt for the old couple leaning on canes and shuffling between cottages. Their wrinkled faces resembled a map. But their eyes sparkled like the lake itself. If they could manage, we surely could too. Claude got the price reduced and advanced the payment. The old woman embraced us. We were the first, she said. She would give us the best.

Spring flew by, as we went about our work waiting patiently for summer. The car opened America to us. We went to Washington and Monticello, to Princeton, to Montauk Point on Long Island, always delighted.

At graduation time, Claude drove us to the college. We reveled in the lilacs and linden trees, and in the nuns who took turns carrying little Claudia — "the jewel of our campus," Sister Annunciata proudly proclaimed.

Amid dazzling floral displays, I experienced my first graduation in cap and gown, holding little Claudia in my arms, with Bona and Eddie standing guard near us in every picture, and always some smiling nuns around us. For the occasion, both Bona and I wore colorful peasant skirts and blouses that made us look like Alpine villagers, in contrast to the severe black and white of the nuns. Jeannette Skelton matched our worldliness with an equally multicolored ample skirt. She was flanked by her sinful husband who insisted on talking with me about Pareto and his avant-garde ideas, while I — ignorant of Pareto or sociology in general — was busy admiring the flowers of my paradise. Ken Skelton then turned to Claude, who didn't know anything about Pareto either but pretended to. He was an expert at that.

The crowning event of that graduation on a glorious June day was the Greek Theater. The students recited Euripides, while Claudia played with the veil of the nun who was holding her.

Pantoussec was a miracle, much better than we expected. In letter after letter, I tried in vain to convey to the family in Rome the exhilarating feeling of "open spaces."

"Wide spaces and spacious skies" were something new to them and so they could hardly understand our delight in our total freedom, having never experienced a hot New York summer. But it was more than that, Bona said. They hadn't crossed the ocean.

For Mamma in postwar Rome, not open spaces but plain survival made America attractive. We had work, the secret not only of survival but of growth. So we, who had made it here, had the moral obligation to find openings for the families left behind. How could we waste precious time camping around wild apple trees when we could put our energy to work in the heart of New York City? Mamma did not understand our happiness. But she was able to admit to herself that we needed a rest, which we surely did.

The trip from New York to the Berkshires in late June 1949 was an adventure. The car was overloaded, much against Claude's advice, especially with what we might need for Claudia: crib, carriages, playpen, a bathtub, diapers, as well as covers and sleeping bags, and what we'd need for cooking outdoors; with a tent in case the cottage collapsed, which it did; with sheets, towels, pillows, blankets; with plenty of tools for the men to cut the grass and stack wood for the fire — all to make the cottage livable. Our Oldsmobile looked more like a covered wagon than a car. So it broke down regularly, every fifty miles or so. Each time, we women camped on the side of the road while the two men fixed things. Twice we took shelter in a garage. We reached our destination after twenty hours on the road. A record, Claude stated with pride, under the circumstances. The two men were exhausted, but, war veterans that they were, they didn't complain.

We reached the cottage at dawn, too tired to clean it. We hauled in all our stuff and then camped under an apple tree. We made the cottage livable a little at a time. It was a roof over our heads. Luckily, it rained very little that summer.

For the next three months, that apple tree was the center of our lives. We mowed the grass, trimmed bushes, learned how to use sickle and scythe, hammer and saw. When the hut collapsed in mid-July, we reinforced our tent and our fireplace, where we prepared all our meals. Our neighbors kindly helped us, as we helped them. Our child lived with their children, all of us learning from each other.

Since one-year old Jimmy Jones was walking, Bona and I attached Claudia with a rope to our apple tree and helped her learn to walk. She balked at first but then became the center of attention. Soon, she could run freely. We had to keep her tied most of the time because she was just too adventuresome for our peace of mind. She knew no fear.

We walked in the Berkshires and followed the Appalachian trail to the top of Greylock Mountain with its wonderful views. We went on the lake in our leaky row boat, two rowing, two baling water. On an occasional moonlit night, Claude would strum his mandolin and teach us American folk songs.

One night in late August, we woke up to an overpowering smell, which, Claude told us, emanated from a skunk under our cottage. In the morning, the Joneses offered to help us dislodge it. It took a week. By that time, we were busy picking apples. We had worked out the art of climbing a tree carrying Claudia. Since apples were so common in the Alps, Bona and I taught the Americans how to manage them. We picked enough apples to take boxes of them back to New York.

But Pantoussec was just an oasis; life had to move on. And that meant returning to New York.

§ § §

Like his comrades in the Second Polish Corps, Eddie learned that he was entitled to a permanent U.S. visa. In the Fall of 1949, just as Eddie and Bona engaged a lawyer for the purpose, his head-master at Adelphi told him that the results of his X-rays (obligatory for every teacher in a New York school) showed spots on his lungs. Further examinations confirmed their fears: Eddie had tuberculosis.

Claude and Eddie stoically accepted the bad news. Bona and I could not. We had grown up with all the old terrors of TB. We believed it was an inherited illness. Convalescing from TB, Papa had left Cincinnati to visit his mother in the Austrian Alps. Mamma told us about his showing up in his mother's rose garden; she was pale and shaking. And there were cousins who died from it, Graziella at thirty and Antonia, a stunning twenty-year-old beauty, both daughters of Papa's sister Gemma, as well as handsome cousin Renzo, son of Uncle Tullio.

In the sanatoria of Merano, rich patients lay all day long half-naked on sunny balconies, reading books, sipping milk and eating ice creams and oranges. Many, after months or years of treatment, seemed to be cured, but they were subject to relapses. Mamma tutored some of those patients, mostly artists and writers. Bona and I had met some of them. They looked healthy and cheerful but we were required to wash our hands thoroughly after being with them.

The sanatoria were only for those who could afford them, such as Papa's family, but even so they didn't provide much help. In any event, the poor, like our family, had to avoid catching the disease. Mamma emphasized good diet and fresh air. She made us study in the open, even in the cold of winter. Our rosy cheeks made us seem the very picture of health in the land of sanatoria. And we felt proud of having won the battle.

Now, we thought, in spite of Pantoussec, Eddie had lost the battle for a visa. America rejected immigrants who showed any sign of TB. In 1890, shortly after arriving in New York, Papa had written to his mother, the Baroness, that immigrants climbing the winding staircase at Ellis Island, took care not to seem out of breath or to cough. Those who showed any symptoms had to undergo a thorough examination and eventually they would be sent back home; others would go to an isolation ward, to die.

A TB specialist told us about a new wonder drug, penicillin, fortunately available under Eddie's insurance plan. Eddie's physician, one Dr. Markus, prescribed absolute bed rest. A nurse came every other day to inject him with penicillin. Because he now needed special care from morning till night, Bona became his daily nurse.

This went on for two months until penicillin finally beat the disease. Then he was sent to a sanatorium in Otisville in the Catskills, to live there until his x-rays showed no sign of TB.

With Bona home and able to keep an eye on Claudia, my problems would have been simplified, had Claude helped out, but he said he needed his time and energy for study. So did we all, I responded. I was stuck at that time on an essay for Professor von Fritz in the Greek and Latin department at Columbia. My subject was "Education in Quintilian's Institutiones," which I tried to put together on the train. Bona had to prepare an essay on Sophocles' Ajax, which I also composed on the train, because, nursing Eddie, she was overwhelmed.

§ § §

"Why can't you get a damned B?" I asked Claude one night. Keeping silent for a while, Claude then replied: "Because I am what I am. You haven't realized as yet that you married ME and not someone else."

I knew he meant every word; he always took things at face value, unable or unwilling to look beyond them. But I was taken aback by that plainly articulated statement and by his implied reproach. I gave the obvious answer — I'd never thought I could change him. I took Claude as I took America, as it was.

The issue was not raised again for a couple of years. But from that night on, my sense of his unwillingness to change kept eroding my faith in him, especially when I was overtired. It had troubled me especially after Claudia was born. Clearly, Claudia needed a father more than I a husband. I insisted that he should act like a father. We locked horns more than once. I pressed him to recognize that she was growing up in a multilingual world. I wanted her to be fluent in Italian, French, and German.

Then there was the problem of our television set. Having introduced it into our household, Claude would let little Claudia watch it for as long as she wanted. I wanted Claudia to play outside. But I would come home after hours of teaching and commuting and find him asleep while Claudia was watching television or playing in a neighbor's dark kitchen. This infuriated me.

Though we did not consider living apart, we began to see things differently. Bona and I also found ourselves bickering for silly reasons. TB, I thought, was taking its toll on the household. For the first time, we saw Christmas 1949 as a storm to weather, not a wonderful feast to enjoy. Of course, we put up a tree in the living room, but only Claudia enjoyed it. Bona spent her days mostly in Eddie's room, caring for him in her own special way. She would sit and he would wrap his arm around her as if to protect her against the evils of the world, both of them a little forlorn. Bona had cut her hair short, Joan of Arc style, Eddie's hairline was receding, making his forehead look even wider than it was.

Claudia was the only member of the family who kept her good humor, loving everyone. She moved easily from home to the Junquas' apartment, where she would sing in French with Tonton. Or she would go to the Alexandropoulos apartment. She was beautiful to look at and challenging to live with.

By the end of the winter of 1950 Eddie had moved to Otisville. Visiting him gave us the opportunity to explore the Hudson valley. Route 17 revealed beauties easily comparable to those of Pantoussec. But now we were living on edge, anxious about the future, longing for some kind of security. Eddie's sanatorium was a compound of neat cabins, each equipped for several patients. There was plenty of milk and orange juice and ice cream available. He had his books and his own internal resources.

By the end of the spring he was discharged. Home had not been the same without him.

We were also learning that America could offer many possibilities to those who had imagination and the will to overcome obstacles. But you could take nothing for granted.

CHAPTER 21

Rome: Lost and Reconquered

In odd moments of my daily life — on the train, in the evening as I tried to bathe Claudia, or as I dragged my overloaded shopping cart up Bennett Avenue, or lay in bed — I discovered that my longing for home had not diminished. It was like a thin but sturdy disturbance. The situation in Rome contributed to it.

Mamma's weekly letters brought us both rays of Roman sunshine and news of unemployment, corruption, and political instability. At the same time, our family situation seemed to be in trouble. Each part of the family was in a precarious financial and emotional state. Proposals to move to America became less frequent. My family in Rome was still struggling to emerge from the rubble of the war. At times, I envied them, though I could hardly say why. Most of the time, I felt a need to see what was happening with my own eyes.

The thought of a peacefully united family in Rome, such as I had experienced during the war, had so far been a basis for my survival in America. Now that unity seemed to be undermined in an Italian society adapting to democracy. Nepotism and plain corruption weakened a government already torn by the conflict between the Italian Communist party — now the strongest in Europe but ready to collaborate in a democracy — and the non-Communists dominated by the Demo-Christians, headed by de Gasperi. During the past year, Mamma's letters kept hinting at a split in the family, mostly between the left and the right. Bona and I speculated: it really meant between the successful survivors and the unsuccessful.

Francesca was the headmistress of a very large school in Trastevere, the most troubled section of Rome, a grim contrast to my idyllic St. Elizabeth. I admired Francesca, who was as resourceful as her husband Bruno, now a history professor in a liceo; Bruno was tutoring and editing for extra income. He seemed to have made his political choice with the Communists. My brother Neri, an independent thinker, gregarious, witty, and handsome, was not, in the view of Bruno and Francesca, aggressive enough to take his place in the sun.

The heroes of the day were Palmiro Togliatti, head of the Communist party, and Alcide de Gasperi, head of the Christian Democrats; they would soon be replaced by Enrico Berlinguer and Giulio Andreotti.

Neri seemed to stay free of politics at a time when everyone breathed politics. Francesca and Bruno argued that Neri was a victim. Born to use words like a lawyer or a professor, he was persuaded at the onset of the war by cousin Agostino to study engineering with the promise of employment. But now Agostino was dead and Neri was stuck. Machines were not his strength, and he had been blocked by an exam commonly called *"macchinette"* — mathematics applied to machines. He kept taking the exam and failing. According to Bruno, the reason was political. He should have turned left. Meanwhile, he depended on Mamma, living off her small pension and sleeping in her room.

I loved Neri and in my letters I strongly supported him and Mamma, though I could not help either one financially. However, the time had come for me to live their life for a while. Instead of judging them in their disputes from a distance, I had to restore my connection to myself-at-home. We could see from photos that Francesca, Bruno, and Neri had gotten very fat, while Bona and I were as thin as models. Nobody could explain why. At any rate, the plan for a summer visit grew slowly, almost unnoticeably, while I was doing my best to juggle motherhood, teaching, classes at Columbia, Claude's puzzling indolence, Eddie's illnesses, and the problems of permanent visas for him and Bona.

But Eddie overcame tuberculosis. By 1950 he was back teaching German at Adelphi Academy while taking courses in Russian and German literature at Columbia, Bona was attending Fordham and working part-time at a high school. Claude and I tried to help them in their struggle with the immigration authorities. Once, at his attorney's suggestion, Eddie and Bona went off to Canada, despite the risk that they might not be allowed to come back.

By the late Fall of 1949, I was aware that something within me was crumbling. My mentor on family matters, Jeannette Skelton, told me so one morning as we rode towards our Convent. Next to notice the phenomenon were my two friends at Columbia, Gilbert Highet and Moses Hadas, the two pillars of the Department of Latin and Greek. They had taken me under their wing even before I registered. One night, after I fell asleep in his course, Hadas called me to his office and insisted I stop paying Columbia for his course. I could attend it if I wished, at no charge. In the meanwhile, he offered me again the possibility of taping Greek tragedy in Greek. I did as he suggested. I set aside the income from that for the best possible use — a trip to Europe with husband and child.

A California agency that went by the seductive name of "Youth Argosy" offered a crossing by plane to Luxembourg at a price I could afford. Claudia at two (free of charge) was the first Youth Argosy child to cross the Atlantic.

The hardest and most painful moment was the separation from Bona. She accompanied us to Idlewild Airport, turned back with us to Manhattan after we learned that the plane needed some repairs, took us back to Idlewild, and saw us off. Claudia was inconsolable until she discovered our fellow travelers, young boys from California. We stopped for half a day in Newfoundland for more repairs and for another four hours in Ireland. Most of us were deadly sick at every landing, except Claudia. She played, ate, and slept like a seasoned traveler.

When we landed in Luxembourg, she was given a diploma and a medal as the youngest member of the Youth Argosy group. The flight had lasted twenty hours. When finally, on a sunny Sunday afternoon, the three of us sat at a cafe in Luxembourg, in the heart of Europe, I was so overwhelmed by the feeling of home I could barely refrain from kissing the ground. My home from that moment on would be Europe, the whole of Europe.

We traveled to Paris by train and visited the City of Lights in a trance, despite squabbling about who paid for what and who had to carry Claudia, since she refused to walk as soon as we were on European soil. She also refused to sleep or to eat anything but potato chips. (Once in a restaurant in the Latin Quarter she shared some of her potato chips with Orson Welles at a nearby table, whom she had approached on her own.)

Twenty-four hours by train took us to Rome, as many hours as had taken to cross the Atlantic by plane. On the train were Italian immigrants returning home from the mines of Belgium. Claudia and Claude slept for long stretches. I was tirelessly exchanging news with my traveling companions. Europe had changed, but it was still home for me. What made it home was Mamma and Rome.

When the Roman aqueducts appeared, I woke up Claude and Claudia to share the excitement of homecoming. The whole family was waiting at Stazione Termini: Francesca with young Paolo in her arms, Antonella, Bruno, and Neri, Bruno's father and Zia Rina his wife, and our Poldina, who had endured the battle of Rome with us. Poldina was hiding behind a huge bouquet of roses, which she threw into my arms the moment I set foot on Roman soil.

In the intensity of that instant we were united again. We embraced as if I had just come home after work. Francesca told me what Paolo had eaten that morning while I tried to push Claudia into her arms. Claudia resisted and hid her face on my shoulder, whispering in my ear "What language are they speaking?" Then she added softly: "Where is Bona? Why don't we go back home?"

The three months of my Roman summer flew by. The airy apartment on Via Bolzano in the familiar environment of Via Nomentana and near the Church and Catacombs of Sant'Agnese received me as if I had never left. It took Claudia just one day to fall in with the family, mainly through the children Antonella and Paolo. Within a week she was speaking fluent Italian with Antonella's Roman accent, mimicking Paolo's baby talk. Claude didn't object.

After a week in Rome, Francesca and Bruno invited us to be their guests in an apartment they had rented in Anzio, an old town on the sea, rebuilt after having been the base of the Allied landing in 1943. The rooms, all on the ground floor, opened onto a sandy courtyard where the children could play. But we spent our days under an umbrella on a crowded beach or strolling around the old city of

Anzio, Claudia and Paolo huddled together in Paolo's baby carriage which Antonella pushed. Claudia would pinch poor Paolo to get his attention.

There was nothing extraordinary that summer. It was a simple life — an over-crowded, dirty beach; a colorful umbrella, one of hundreds; women, men, and children dressed in old-fashioned bathing suits. From America, it might have looked cheap and grey, but above it shone an amazing blue sky.

It was life in the bosom of the family. We took pleasure in simple entertainments, jokes around the dinner table, children romping around and dogs baying at the moon. Life was sipping a vermouth together at dusk — adults and children alike — in a crowded cafe on the Piazza del Duomo, while Vespas noisily passed the sitting customers, in a world taken over by ebullient and indolent "*bulli*" or "*Vitelloni*," as Fellini had christened them. Rome and the surrounding beach-towns were teeming with them. Francesca, Neri, Bruno, and I enjoyed making fun of them, of everything else, mainly of ourselves. We laughed at the Italian political scene though we really should have cried because it had worsened so much.

The miracle of that summer was that Francesca, Neri, Bruno, and I were able to recapture the joy of our lives before and even during the war. For a brief time, we lived the impossible: the past as present. Like acrobats, we walked a tightrope, enjoying the challenge. We had to seize the moment: a summer in 1950 on a crowded Italian beach.

Claude was completely one of us that whole summer. Unlike our people in the Alps, who are as hard as steel, he had the gift of being able to adapt, probably inherited from his Southern Italian ancestors. Claude could be, when he chose, as flexible as a bulrush.

I told him we didn't owe anything to anybody. We were guests of my family. Claude was happy to accept and limited himself to occasionally offering wine for dinners. As for me, I was proud of the generosity of my family. I even boasted about it to Claude. But lightly.

I began feeling the pangs of separation days before we were to leave. I would wake up early and count the days remaining.

"Ridiculous!" Francesca reproached me, although she agreed she also couldn't bear the idea of separating again. Neither of us could understand why, yet the pain was very real. It was much harder than I had expected. It wasn't only separating from the family. It was separating from Rome. The taste of the food, the wine, the water, the sight of the buildings against the sky, the color of the sky, the color of the air around ancient churches and buildings, the familiar ancient fountains, the chatter in cafés — everything about Rome had become as dear to me as my family. And yet I knew deep down that I had lost it forever.

During that summer dream, Rome became my city as it never had been before, and I loved it as my city, in its disorder and its corruption. My Rome was at the threshold of democratic life. I understand now, years later, that I loved Rome as I left it as you love an old flame you are unwillingly about to leave forever.

When we separated at the train, we were exhausted emotionally. This time I was leaving with no dreams or illusions. My America was a country of harsh realities. As I left Rome, I was aware of another harsh reality: America was out of bounds for my European family. To come and visit would be too expensive. Our current finances would hardly allow us even the pleasure of each other's voices on the telephone.

Bad news at Luxembourg: The government needed all the planes for the war in Korea, on the other side of the world. I was pleased by the delay. A week in this quaint European city smoothed our transition back to New York. As I walked the quiet streets, I wondered how I could pick up life again at home. However I did it, from now on, I had to take America as it was and make the best of it. Europe was over.

When we finally arrived, Bona had been waiting for five hours at LaGuardia. Claudia fell into her arms, laughing and crying. They spoke Italian together, as did Claude.

Everybody at the college awaited my return, a pilgrim from the Holy City. I was offered all sorts of opportunities — lectures to alumnae in the affluent towns surrounding Convent Station: Morristown, Madison, Montclair. I reveled in the enthusiasm of the matrons who came to hear about the conditions of the beloved peninsula. I enjoyed answering their naïve questions. They were inevitable among these successful people, whose parents, I was reminded, had come from Europe like me searching for a better life. But I must add that I wished sometimes that my hostess wouldn't knit while I talked.

I was also invited by the Italians to give radio talks on American history. With the help of Neri and especially Francesca, I put the best of my students in radio-contact with Italian students in Rome. The American students surprised Francesca's with their cheerful determination to do good. The broadcasts became so popular that registration in our newly-created Italian Department soared. My name, much to the satisfaction of the nuns, appeared in the local newspapers.

I shared the college's excitement and quickly arranged to offer a special course, "Italy Today: Society and Literature," which included theater, film, the arts, and daily life. The course was the first in what developed into an "area studies" program. For "daily life," I had to sugarcoat the hard reality I'd seen there. When the nuns produced a movie projector to show 16mm films, these had to be chosen with special care lest they conflict with the ethos of the college. I am sure St. Elizabeth showed the first neo-realistic films in America.

§   §   §

Meanwhile, Eddie and Bona were working again, part-time. In this relaxed atmosphere, Claude agreed to help with the costs of a regular baby-sitter for Claudia; Mrs. McMullen was precisely what Claudia needed. A statuesque Jamaican woman in her sixties, she took over Claudia and the household magisterially. She opened our bedroom windows wide, without regard that Claude was still asleep, gave Claudia a hearty breakfast, and then took her to the park. By evening, Claudia was ready for bed. She and Mrs. Mc Mullen got on wonderfully. Mrs. McMullen was a pillar of our household for two years, when suddenly Claudia one day told her she didn't need her anymore; she was ready to go to school. Mrs. McMullen passed the message on to me. We parted on good terms. I never saw her again.

On weekends, we were able to escape New York's polluted air. Claude pointed out that TB was a genetic trait we all had to put up with, but everybody needed a break. So we drove out, Claudia nestled between Bona and Eddie, exacting story after story from Eddie, focusing mainly on Wilhelm Tell and Germanic folklore, with which he was dealing in his doctoral courses. But he never tried to teach her German, as he later did his own children.

Eventually, I learned to drive. My European license, issued by the AMG out of regard for Claude, was set aside and I had to submit to intensive training by Claude, who insulted and humiliated me — quite rightly — even threatening once to stop and abandon the car. On another occasion, he had to kick me to save us from a crash. I finally did get a license. I passed the exam on my second try, but I took comfort in the assurance that New York was tougher on these exams than any other city in the country.

CHAPTER 22

Theater at Barnard

In order to cope with my growing workload at the College, I stopped taking courses at Columbia. I was the first in our family to abandon student status. Claude remained a student for many years, Eddie until he finished his Ph.D., Bona when she got her permanent visa. At the same time, I was proud to be the only family member with a full-time job. Too, no more embarrassment because of falling asleep during class. Instead, I could now work on my critical edition, with the help of colleagues at Columbia.

In mid-winter, Claude decided that we would go to Schenectady to celebrate both our wedding anniversary February 12 and the anniversary of our arrival in the States. There was more than one reason for celebration. Claude's sister Laura, a well-regarded teacher of high-school Spanish, was about to marry a gentleman from La Mancha who taught at a college in upstate New York. The marriage was celebrated without fanfare because Xavier had just been through a difficult divorce from a colleague in the French Department. Subsequently, that marriage was annulled. For a time, Xavier's ex-wife and children were not well disposed towards him or Laura. Things would change in time, Claude's family assured me. We were all, especially Xavier, practicing Catholics hoping that God looked more kindly on human frailty than an ecclesiastical law did.

The whole family, including the Montclair contingent, was at 8 Eagle Street for the usual noisy welcome. Claudia disappeared amid the welter of her cousins. We donned our Ohrbach's garments for the ceremonial dinner. Like all the Bové girls, Laura was charming and intelligent, thoughtful, delicate but also sturdy. Claude and I agreed that Xavier had made an excellent choice.

Professor Xavier Fernandez was an old-school gentleman with a wide forehead and large hazel eyes that gently smiled at the world while observing it keenly. We were both European, he said with gentle irony during his brief address, smiling at those who surrounded us, but with one major difference. Spain had managed to keep out of the war, while Italy.... we all knew what had happened to Italy.

Then Claude intoned his usual paean to me as an Italian war bride, an exceptional one at that, with European degrees and now about to get yet another degree from Columbia. Claude stopped at the arrival of a cake, which was properly applauded. Among its adornments was a small American flag. America never ceased to surprise me in its abundant use of the flag.

During the dinner, at which I was given the place of honor next to the professor, Xavier broached the subject of my career. It was a thorny issue. I had to confess that, despite my proud degree in Classical Philology with the great Vincenzo Ussani, I had descended to teaching Modern Languages in an unknown college.

"St. Elizabeth —" I began, but he cut me short.

"Don't tell me you are still buried in that Catholic college in New Jersey? Laura told me about it."

He started off slowly and in a low voice so that at first I could hardly make out what he was saying. He was not aggressive, a sweet gentleman with a keen sense of humor well schooled in the ways of the American academic world. He led me into that world more deftly than anyone else could have. I got the feeling that a career in Modern Languages was as risky as a career in the State Department.

"It is absolutely clear," he concluded, "that a university as internationally concerned as Columbia would welcome you, simply because it needs you!"

I listened speechless, wishing Paul Kristeller could have sat in on our conversation. Xavier ridiculed the Teachers' Agency which Kristeller had praised three years before. Kristeller had approached the matter of my career with a different kind of pragmatism than Xavier. Xavier advised me carefully. I was right to stop paying Columbia for courses. On the other hand, I should see this as the moment to work on my book. Was I aware of the situation in their Italian Department? He had heard from colleagues that the head of the Italian Department at Barnard had died suddenly after a stomach operation while vacationing in Italy. This looked like a good opportunity for a young Italian with my qualification.

The next day, Xavier helped me draft a letter of application for the chairmanship of the Italian department at Barnard. While we tried to compose a document concise and to the point, he dispelled the last cloud. Was I fit for the job? I had no degree in Italian and had never taught Italian until I introduced the subject at St. Elizabeth. I didn't feel qualified for it.

"Nonsense!" he kept on repeating. "Nonsense! You seem to forget how much Europeans like us are needed in America after four years of war. Hitler's gift to America, the Jews have made Americans aware of what they lack. A young scholar like you, with such an academic background, is God's gift to Columbia."

He also pointed out that the study of modern languages was believed to have no practical use. It lacked the prestige of Philosophy, English Literature, or the Classics. For practical reason Spanish was an exception to the rule. I listened without asking questions.

Thanks to Xavier, I left Schenectady with a new sense of myself as well as boundless admiration for him. Through the years that followed I regretted we didn't live near each other. He was that rare combination: a true scholar and a practical man.

In March 1951, I mailed my application to Barnard College and waited. I waited and waited. Months passed without any response.

§ § §

The Thursday before Memorial Day weekend 1951 was a mild but sunny day at St. Elizabeth. All the students in my Italian classes gathered around me in a meadow amid scatterings of periwinkles and daisies. We were reading Petrarch and Sappho.

Da' be' rami scendea
(dolce ne la memoria)
una pioggia di fior' sovra 'l suo grembo;
ed ella si sedea
umile in tanta gloria
coverta già de l'amoroso nembo....

Petrarch's lines raining petals on Laura mingled with the passionate prayer of Sappho to the Goddess of Love (which I translated from the Greek for the benefit of my students):

Poikilothron, athanath'Aphrodites....
Aphrodite, Goddess of the flowers, Goddess of deceit, daughter of Zeus, do not taint with bitterness and deceit this heart of mine.

The harmony of these images was such that we had to think of the two worlds as one, and one with our own world. I told my students about Xavier. Xavier, I told them, was aware of the miracle we were experiencing at that moment: a resurrection of European poetry. Only a gentleman from La Mancha could perceive with clarity such a simple truth!

§ § §

"Tomorrow you have an interview!" Bona yelled breathlessly as I entered our apartment. "They called — the Search Committee is waiting for you — call them right away!"

At that she stopped, maybe afraid that she had gone too far in her enthusiasm. But I was already on the telephone, agreeing to see them now, yes, now not tomorrow, but now, in a half-hour. Yes, no later than a half-hour, just time to wash my hands and collect my thoughts.

Instead of collecting thoughts, Bona and I discussed what I should wear. Half an hour later, wearing an elegant close-fitting black and white checkered woolen suit, half-price at Klein's 14th Street, I was in the Milbank Hall office of Dean Thomas Peardon. My outfit was topped by a straw hat with a tiny red ribbon. To match the ensemble, I had borrowed Bona's black patent leather shoes, a bit too big for my feet, and her black patent leather purse.

The search committee consisted of the Dean of the Faculty and the chairmen of modern and ancient languages. All middle-aged men except for one woman, all pleasant to look at. Señora Amelia del Rio was a stunning Puerto Rican Aphrodite.

Each chairman introduced himself to me in the language he taught: Hofferr in French, Herr Pucket in German, Señora Del Rio in Spanish, a language I understood but could not speak. Only Professor Day of Latin and Greek, whose face looked like an ancient parchment, and the chairman, Professor Peardon, Dean of the Faculty, addressed me in plain English. I answered each of them in the chosen language and we engaged with gusto in a pleasant concerto of individual instruments. Dean Peardon, a diplomatic gentleman who taught Political Science at Barnard and Columbia, put a masterful end to the display by asking me if indeed the subjects in which I was trained were Latin and Greek. Professor Day at that point entered the arena, saving me the embarrassment of an answer I hesitated to give.

"How would you choose to present Euripides to your students? I mean what plays would you choose, what passages and from what perspective?"

I silently thanked Papa in Heaven, whose support I had invoked as I entered the room. This was indeed the kind of question I loved to answer because I had taught Euripides in Rome for four years, and I had recently recorded some of his plays for Professor Hadas. So the question gave me the opportunity to demonstrate that I could speak English fluently. I was also aware that I should limit myself to the essentials, because they might otherwise conclude that I was at my best teaching Greek, for which they had no openings. I gave them the facts unadorned.

By this time, I was feeling at ease. The chairmen's friendliness had won me over. Soon, I was answering their questions about St. Elizabeth, but these questions became irrelevant.

"I have the feeling you love that college so much you might regret leaving it," said Dean Peardon with a smile. I retraced my steps precipitously.

"I love it, yes; it was the best I was able to find here, but...."

My cause was lost. I was miserably groping for an appropriate response, when a truth I had not admitted even to myself saved me.

"— but from the first moment I arrived in Manhattan there was one and only one place where I wanted to work, Columbia."

In one breath I told them the story of my arrival in Manhattan with Claude on March 17, 1947, of our long trek through the Irish parade to reach 116th Street, led by the guiding spirit to whom Professor Ussani had addressed his letter, our play on Naples and the Cowan affair, and finally of Paul Kristeller's advice. St. Elizabeth was recommended by the Marder Teachers Agency. The rest they knew.

When I stopped, there was a moment of silence. Then Dean Peardon asked me if I still had the letter Ussani had written to President Nicholas Murray Butler. It was of interest to him, he added, since he had known President Butler.

"I have it here" I answered and dug it out of Bona's purse, together with the letter Kristeller had written for me in March 1947. Dean Peardon looked through Professor Ussani's letter, then passed it to M. Hofferr who in turn passed it to Señora Del Rio, who passed it on to Herr Pucket. Finally the letter landed in the hands of Professor Day. Nobody could make out what it said because nobody understood Italian.

"By the way," Dean Peardon concluded the interview with a smile, "how can you prove you are fluent in Italian, which is the only subject you'll be expected to teach at Barnard?"

I said I could prove it by translating the letter which I did.

"And now to our final question. What would you expect as a salary?" asked Dean Peardon as we stood near the door. "We can do better than St. Elizabeth but not much better."

A salary? My enthusiasm knew no limits. Did he say a salary? I repeated the word to myself.

"I am not concerned about a salary," I answered, without trying to hide my delight. "A salary is for me of limited interest. All I want now is to put an end to my commuting."

We shook hands like old friends. I had already reached the main door of the building when I heard M. Hofferr's voice behind me: "*Madame, vous avez oublié votre sac*" ("Madam, you forgot your purse"). He didn't know that the only contents were the two letters which I had given to Dean Peardon.

Bona met me and cried out, "Dean McIntosh just called, she wants to see you immediately. They'll pay for a taxi!"

Dean Millicent McIntosh wanted to congratulate me. The Search Committee had reported to her that I was the candidate they had chosen after a year of search. I was the last candidate they had interviewed. Would I accept? They needed an immediate answer because they intended to conclude their work before Memorial Day weekend. I felt like embracing her, but remembered what Claude told me about Anglo-Saxon restraint.

"You can tell the Committee," I heard myself saying in a calm, almost preternatural voice, "that I am happy to accept their offer."

§ § §

During two years taking courses in Classical Philology at Columbia, I had not had any connection with the Italian Department or any interest in its center, the *Casa Italiana*. The *Casa* was a pseudo-Florentine building on 117th Street and Amsterdam Avenue, amid old brownstones — *Deutsches Haus, Casa Hispanica,* and *Maison Française. Casa Italiana* was much larger than the others. Inside, however, it felt lugubrious until, one day, I met, courtesy of Paul Kristeller, an elderly Italian gentleman who had had an office in that building most of his adult life. Thanks to him, I began to see the Casa in a different light.

Professor Dino Bigongiari was a legendary figure at Columbia. Over the years, he had taught fascinating courses on Dante which students flocked to. Bigongiari had no degrees and had not published a single book. He was now retired. Part of the legend was that all the lending slips for library books on medieval civilization bore Bigongiari's signature.

Bigongiari was a born-again Catholic, one who had discovered a new sense of the old religion he had inherited. He believed in Christian forgiveness not of the sins we commit against society, which are up to God to forgive, but of all the sins society commits against us.

Sometime before my meeting at Barnard, he had introduced me to the Men's Faculty Club at Columbia, a building closed to women unless they were accompanied by a male professor. After Memorial Day, he phoned and invited me to lunch at the Faculty Club. I was already living in such a state of bliss that nothing could make me happier short of a guarantee of eternal salvation. I accepted Bigongiari's invitation as a side benefit of my new status.

However, from the moment Bigongiari met me in front of the Ladies Parlor to escort me upstairs, I sensed there was something unusual about his invitation. The mystery was revealed before dessert, after we had both sipped enough white wine to feel relaxed.

"There is a war going on," the old professor said slowly, just as I was about to begin on my ice-cream cake, "a bloody war between Barnard and Columbia."

Before he continued, Bigongiari asked for my solemn promise both to forgive the person he was about to name and, more, to forget, at least for the time being, the whole episode. It was sad enough to make everybody involved wish it had never happened. The reason he had decided to speak to me about it was that he believed I was the right person to help put an end to the ferocious struggle between the two departments of Italian, a war which my predecessor, a little round bundle of fat on fire, had promoted.

He stopped, as if expecting a question from me, but I was so taken aback by the drama he hinted at that I forgot that I might be involved in it. That would be unpleasant, indeed frightening. On Sunday evening of that memorable weekend, Professor Bigongiari had received in his sunny apartment on Morningside Drive the totally unexpected and unannounced visit of three respected colleagues: Professors Pucket, Hofferr, and Peardon.

They were all three rightly embarrassed — he said with some satisfaction – for intruding on him, but they felt they had to ask for his help, as the senior professor of Italian, on an important problem.

The news of the choice of a new head of the Italian department at Barnard, though still unofficial, had spread through the campus and reached the office of the head of Italian in Columbia's School of General Studies. It went further. Through the chairman of the History Department, it reached the Italian department at Hunter College, where a faculty member, who was to remain anonymous, had expected to get it. The surprising choice of the search committee hit her very hard. Related by marriage to a Columbia professor, she had had a long discussion with Professor Marraro of General Studies.

They decided that Marraro should point out to the Dean of Barnard, the Quaker Millicent McIntosh, the moral danger in such a choice. "The lady from Hunter" had met the woman chosen by the committee and could testify that she was indeed a charmer, a typical product of a sad war that not only had seen so many young Americans die on foreign soil but was now importing Communism into our vulnerable society. The academic credentials of this woman were covering up her social background. She could, however, assure Barnard that the candidate chosen was "*la figlia di nessuno*" (nobody's daughter). Married to an American war hero, she had come to America with thousands of soldiers and a sprinkling of war brides on a military ship. How could she be trusted?

"I stopped Hofferr short at this point," Bigongiari proudly declared, "and told the three that if they came to me as ambassadors for such a cause they were wasting their time. They should please get up and leave. I wasn't willing to sacrifice the serenity of my Memorial Day weekend to vulgar gossip."

Dean Peardon, however, who had kept silent so far, intervened with a sad note. He said that Marraro had called Millicent McIntosh and persuaded her to annul the choice of the search committee. Unless someone at Columbia intervened immediately, someone whose authority and credibility McIntosh respected, Barnard would lose the opportunity to put an end to the maneuvers of the warring parties, the two departments of Italian.

At this point, Herr Pucket reminded Peardon that the whole search committee had threatened to resign if their choice was vetoed. They had worked hard and objectively for a whole year on behalf of both the college and the university. Enough was enough.

Bigongiari congratulated the search committee for its stand and then phoned McIntosh. He couldn't believe, he said, that the administration was taking this business seriously. He held the work of the search committee in high esteem and approved of the choice they had made. He personally knew the candidate and could guarantee her academic and personal standards. McIntosh apologized and assured him she would happily accept the decision of the search committee.

I sighed with relief. Now, however, Bigongiari reminded me of my promise. Though he had tried his best not to reveal the name of the lady from Hunter, he had said enough for me to guess. I had to solemnly promise that I would both forget the whole sad episode and, much more difficult, would forgive. I could reveal it — he added with a laugh — when it was history.

§   §   §

After a quiet summer, I settled down to work at Barnard. Sister Marie José had welcomed Eddie as my replacement teaching German, French, and Italian. This was a real blessing. After he signed his contract, they sponsored his admission to the U.S. as a desirable, indeed indispensable, alien. Eddie proposed to introduce Russian into the college curriculum, as I had done with Italian.

A mild day in October 1951 was coming to a close — a very different day from any other I had lived so far in America. My life, I thought, was about to change. Yes, change, but how? My mind wandered lazily, like a bee in the spring, from flower to flower, as I sat in the office of my deceased predecessor, filled with books, papers, posters, announcements, and pamphlets of all kinds.

I had never before had an office of my own and was asking myself what I could do with it. From her books and papers, I was tempted to try to discover what my deceased predecessor was like. But there was an immense amount of material of no interest to me. I set it aside. What I longed for was to teach and to work on the critical edition of Valla's *On Pleasure*. I had not published a word since my two articles of 1943 and 1944 that had produced the contract for the critical edition.

A discreet, almost timid, knock at my door woke me as from a dream. It was my next-door neighbor, Professor LeRoy Breunig, a recent arrival from Harvard, the successor of M. Hofferr, the retiring chairman of French. He sat down and said in French that he was taking advantage of the fact that we were both recent recruits in Barnard's army. How did he know that I spoke French? A mathematician who attended my classes had told him, he said with a smile. Why did he speak of the army?

He freed a chair from its papers and books and sat down close to me, like a comrade in arms.

"Should we speak French or English?" he asked. We agreed on French. Roy, slightly older than me, was a Midwestern gentleman, courteous, witty, charming. His smile was captivating, his laughter contagious.

He had spent the war in the Navy and ended up stationed in Athens for two years. There he married a young Greek woman named Ersi, which in modern Greek means Dawn. He was delighted when he found that I was a war bride. Athens and Rome. What a marvelous combination. Better still was Athens and Naples, Naples as the colony of Athens, *Nea Polis,* the New City.

Roy's specialty was theater. We discussed Euripides, Greek tragedy, theater in general. As he spoke of the rise and fall of Athens in contrast to the immortality of its theater, my thoughts moved from the Mediterranean to West 108th Street and I asked myself while he spoke, what had happened to the gentle Jean Goldstein, my first mentor on theatrical matters in Manhattan. Was she still alive? Perhaps she was right when she innocently suggested that de Filippo's *Millionaire Naples,* the play we wanted to launch from her apartment, would have had a good chance as a musical comedy.

I told Roy about Jean and mostly about the dream Claude and I cherished, of producing de Filippo's play on Broadway. I told him of Eduardo's extraordinary success in conveying to an Italian audience the fall and rise of Naples, of how he had put full trust in Claude and me. I told him of the letters, the great expectations, and our bitter disappointment when the project collapsed.

It was as if I was talking to myself about this painful subject for the first time after a long silence. I felt relieved to finally be able to speak out about it. I told Roy how Cowan's sudden withdrawal had depressed Claude deeply, an Italian-American veteran who, in translating the play, had identified with Naples, the city of his ancestors. His withdrawal had driven me back to my books, though theater was still my passion.

Roy was dumbfounded. A fascinating story, he said. But why, why in God's name did I give up? Why did I not pursue the original plan? Why did I not try to find the cause for its failure? His relentless questioning, far from humiliating me, forced me to look into my own behavior following Cowan's withdrawal, and to try to discover finally where I, not Claude, had failed de Filippo.

"I don't know," I answered at first. But then: "Money," I said finally. "Money."

"What do you mean, money? You didn't invest a cent of your own. Why did you not search for another producer?"

"We needed money to survive in America, that is to pay for my support. In order to induce Claude to give up his job at the Depot in Schenectady and launch Eduardo on Broadway, I had agreed to support myself. And then there was the *Marine Shark* about to show up in New York."

"A shark?" Roy asked in surprise.

"Yes, my sister and her stateless war-hero husband were about to arrive from Italy on the *Marine Shark* and come live with us. Claude sponsored them for my sake, and I had sworn they would never be a burden."

He laughed, and as he asked me how many pledges I had made to Claude, it dawned upon me that I had perhaps made one too many, given my limited possibilities as an immigrant. But, I thought to myself, how could I do otherwise? What could I do, alone in Manhattan, to pursue a theatrical venture on my own without his full support? Claude was the key to my life in America, not just in the de Filippo affair. My only point of reference was a letter my old professor in Rome had written to the President of Columbia. I had introduced de Filippo to Claude and had helped Claude deal with him and the play. After the defeat, I intended to pursue my own career.

"Was that the letter you gave to Dean Reardon?" he asked.

"How did you know about that?" I asked.

"Gossip spreads fast," he said.

We both laughed as I mimicked parts of my interview and he mimicked parts of his to me. We compared notes.

"I understand now, I understand."

I didn't understand what he understood. But it was clear that we were kindred spirits.

Years later — after Roy and I had embarked together in a theatrical career of Barnard professors on the stage of the Casa Italiana — Roy confessed to me that he didn't understand a lot of what was going on between Claude and me on the de Filippo project. Nonetheless, he saw that I really loved the theater and guessed that I had a hard life with my husband, a veteran like him. He didn't dare tell me that at first, for fear of hurting my feelings. Perhaps he didn't even go as far as thinking that. All he thought during that first meeting was that being in the next office would be great fun for him. He was looking forward to it. And so was I.

It was getting late. My watch warned me that Mrs. McMullen was about to leave Claudia. Before parting, however, Roy warned me that Barnard had employed —together with us — a new director of the theater, a veteran like Claude, who had been shot down over Sicily. His name was Dolph Sweet, an activist and innovator in the world of theater who sooner or later would wind up in Hollywood. Why didn't I show Claude's translation of *Millionaire Naples* to him? I should keep in mind that the entrance to the Barnard Theater was on Broadway!

Dolph Sweet's office was not far from mine in the basement of Milbank. As I walked there the next day with Eduardo's play in hand, I thought, with a mixture of pain, anger, and resentment, about

Cowan's failure. I felt then as I had never felt before the shame of having failed an Italian friend whom I esteemed and loved more and more as the years passed.

Dolph was rehearsing with some students. Delighted to meet me, he said, and clearly he meant it. He listened to what I had to tell him about de Filippo's play with genuine interest of a kind no one else had shown. We sat at length in his rehearsal room discussing ways to present *Napoli Milionaria* to the faculty and the administration on a special occasion, perhaps an evening in honor of Dean McIntosh.

We agreed to limit our production to the first act, which was self-contained. I wanted it to be in Italian and recited by the faculty. Roy Breunig was to have a prominent role in it. We could choose the rest of the cast together. No, he said, the choice of actors was up to me. He didn't know any faculty members and didn't want to take any risks.

"That's your job as producer," Dolph laughed, "I can only take on the direction of this play. That's enough, believe me." We were now partners in a challenging enterprise.

Dolph Sweet was a robust young man of about my age. He had a square face, square shoulders, and powerful muscles — an American gladiator of Irish-French extraction.

"I love the Italians," he said as we parted, with a twinkle in his eyes. "I think that their shooting down my plane in Sicily in 1942 gave them the only chance to boast of victory against us. I was their first. I fear there wasn't any other."

His laughter lit up his face.

Dolph had spent the rest of the war in prison camps, first Italian then German. He survived the German camps by organizing playgroups among the prisoners. Directing the Barnard Theater was the first job he held as a civilian in the U.S.

During the next month, *Napoli Milionaria* was finally performed by members of the faculty, literally near Broadway and on a kind of symbolic Broadway — in the James Room in Barnard Hall. We intended it to be enjoyed mainly by the Barnard community, after an Italian-style dinner in honor of Millicent McIntosh.

The first scene takes place at a dining room table loaded with pasta and wine. At the center sat Donna Amalia, surrounded by men involved in her black-market activities during the final year of the German occupation. All outlaws, Donna Amalia's clan mocked her husband, the mild, melancholy, odd-looking Don Gennaro, the hero, a man committed to moral principles but without the strength to fight for them. He wanted Donna Amalia to give up her trade, but at the same time he knew that her trade provided the family's support. At the end of our version of this part of the play, Don Gennaro has an unexpected revenge.

The last scene of our adaptation focuses on two Neapolitans, Neapolitans to the core, outsmarting each other at this dangerous time in their lives for they were tempting death. Don Gennaro, plagued by his wife's dealings, nonetheless lies silently on his bed; he has agreed to fake death in order to conceal the black market merchandise Amalia and company had collected. During dinner, warned that a police officer was coming, Donna Amalia and her supporters loudly mourn Don Gennaro's death. No Neapolitan, they know, would ever dare to touch a corpse. The policeman — *il maresciallo* — is suspicious and places himself right at the foot of the bed. But he is too much a Neapolitan to touch the corpse — even though he doubts that it is a corpse.

It might be.

A siren shrieks, announcing a raid. We all knew the Americans bombarded Naples every night for weeks before the Salerno landing, killing innocent people by the hundreds. The bombs are already falling indiscriminately over the *bassi* where people try to live, family on top of family.

The shrieking siren drowns out the thunder of crashing walls.

Everyone runs for shelter, leaving the *maresciallo* and Don Gennaro alone. It is a striking ballet, each stubbornly trying to persuade the other to give up. The policeman goads Don Gennaro to quit this farce so they can both avoid the bombs; Don Gennaro's mortal silence challenges the *maresciallo*. Don Gennaro rises from the dead only after the *maresciallo* has admitted defeat and announced that he will not arrest him. The two then leave the room together as friends, joining the family in the shelter.

Our adaptation stressed the moral message, to be elaborated in Act III. When they faced the real trial, the bombs, Don Gennaro proved as courageous as the *maresciallo*. Both of them come out more courageous than Donna Amalia and her clan, who had all run away and abandoned Don Gennaro. Innocent, he stood up to the representative of the law, risking his life to protect the guilty. Thus, Don Gennaro wins the respect and admiration of the *maresciallo*, symbol of the law.

Eduardo's play subtly reveals the Janus-like nature of his city. But it seemed too hard to convey that to an American audience. Dolph solved the problem by doing just the first act. Another problem he had to deal with: a cast of non-professionals who could hardly speak Italian, the agreed-upon language of the performance. As always, Dolph decided to improvise. He wanted his cast to share the enjoyment he felt in this production. He asked me to work with him; I would lead the actors, he would serve as offstage director as well as lead actor.

"Listen, friends," he said as he sat among us in his rehearsal room, a thermos of black coffee always within reach, "remember that this is entertainment. You have to enjoy it yourselves if you want your colleagues to enjoy it. You have to be willing to laugh at yourselves, which is not easy in your profession."

I admired him for saying this because he knew that, like me, he was an outsider talking to tenured professors.

He divided his play into two scenes, leaving to Donna Amalia the task of smoothly running the first, the longer and more difficult because it was all dialogue in Italian. My choice for the role of Donna Amelia fell on Amelia Del Rio, chair of Spanish, who annually presented a Spanish play in the Barnard Theater with colleagues from her department as actors; Marguerita Dacal, Eugenio Florit, Francisco and Laura Garcia Lorca. At the time, they were rehearsing a play by Federico Garcia Lorca, Francisco's brother. Dolph, however, cordially insisted that I couldn't sneak out of my job — making the actors feel easy in their roles. And I myself had to take on the role of Donna Amalia.

Among the actors surrounding Donna Amalia at the dining room table, besides of course Roy Breunig, was Barry Ulanov, a rising star in the English Department, writing a doctoral dissertation on an Italian Renaissance subject. Well known for his book on jazz, Barry played Amalia's main partner and lover. Joe Brennan, chair of the Philosophy Department, was Donna Amalia's closest friend. Like Claude a veteran of the Mediterranean campaign, he had a basic knowledge of Italian.

Eugenio Florit, poet laureate from Cuba, who knew Castro before he became famous, was assigned the most important role after Don Gennaro and Donna Amalia, that of *maresciallo*, the policeman who uncovers the plot and has a standoff with Don Gennaro. Florit, a Spaniard and a good actor, sailed well in Neapolitan waters. During rehearsal, Don Eugenio, as we called him, was impressive as an actor and thus inspired and helped his colleagues. Yet, during the performance itself Don Eugenio trusted himself too much as an actor since he was hard of hearing. So on the day of the performance our most capable actor risked destroying the delicate balance among the other actors by entering before his cue. Bona, who regulated the traffic backstage, did her best, she said to me later, to hold him back, but he had shut off his hearing aid.

Each player learned his own lines by heart, without bothering to understand the lines of the others. They all depended on cues. When Florit came on prematurely, the crew looked at me in despair. I got up, shook hands with Florit / Eugenio, and asked him, in a loud English voice, to come back later. My crew was visibly relieved, but Florit looked at me in dismay. As he exited, there was a stunned silence on stage and in the audience. When, on cue, Florit came back later, he was welcomed by applause and friendly laughter.

Dolph, playing Don Gennaro, was our hero, not, however, for his diligence in learning his role by heart; all the other actors had excelled in that. But Dolph never learned his lines by heart, no matter how much Roy and Barry and I insisted he should, as an example to the others.

"You don't seem to understand," he said as I complained, "that language is secondary in a play such as this. That's why we can do what we are doing. Eduardo might shudder at us, but it is his magic, his theatrical energy that keeps our play going, not his language. No wonder Cowan balked at producing it. This play is a living example of *commedia dell'arte*! It calls for some improvisation. Why do you want to spoil my efforts as I pay homage to your great Master with my modest ability as director?"

For the first part of his role — the dialogue around the table — Dolph built a cubicle on one side of the stage, intended as a bathroom. In this cubicle he rapidly read his Italian lines; they hung on a wall, handwritten on long sheets of paper. Exiting with razor in hand, he spoke his lines as if he was reciting the *Divine Comedy,* while he shaved in front of the audience. While a different interpretation from Eduardo's, it had great effect. The only lines he learned by heart were those in the final dialogue with the policeman.

"I am not Eduardo, and we are not his troupe!" he said laughing when I protested mildly. We are not in Naples, we're in New York, to be precise, we are at Barnard College on the Columbia campus. But we are working in the spirit of Eduardo's script. He is with us from beginning to end."

Dolph was a veritable fountain of ideas; at the same time, he was very demanding in what he required of us.

"The first scene runs smoothly, a real *commedia dell'arte*, full of fun," he said the night before the performance, singling out Florit's Don Eugenio for praise.

"But the second scene leaves me perplexed. The policeman and Don Gennaro, before and especially after the alarm, are alone on stage. Fortunately Don Gennaro is mute until the end."

As Roy protested that they had all done their best, he smiled. "That has nothing to do with you; the problem is my reading and directing of the play. De Filippo has two more acts to drive home his message. We have just the first act. What did we get out of that final scene today? Nothing, absolutely nothing! The message stayed hidden."

He opened his thermos and poured himself a full mug of coffee. As he sipped it, we all sat in expectant silence.

"You see,'" he began as if talking to himself, "here we have two faces of Naples within one family. The scene around the table communicates the sense of deceit for which Neapolitans are famous. That first scene works well in our version, but the second? What do you get from that? Nothing! The policeman speaks and Don Gennaro is silent. And his family has abandoned him. And so what?"

He was by now standing tall like a Roman soldier among us talking at the top of his voice. He was clearly upset, not at us but at himself, for having waited until the last rehearsal to figure out the weak point in his direction. Then he sat down and placed the mug in the middle of the table.

"Here we are," he said pointing to the mug. "This is Naples during the German occupation. The Allies are advancing rapidly from the South. Naples is the first big city they encounter. Night after night, powerful aircraft fly over this mass of buildings, houses so close to one another you can hardly walk side by side down the alleys between them." And he turned the mug upside down.

"Within its old walls every building conceals hundreds of people, miserable human beings who have been starving for months, waiting to be liberated. They are starving. Except Donna Amalia and her friends, of course. But now even they are caught. The policeman, a Neapolitan like them, has discovered their misdeeds. Only God can save the family now, and God, in his infinite generosity, is Don Gennaro, Donna Amalia's husband, whom Donna Amalia's clan scorns because he stands for law while at the same time eating their food.

But God is a Neapolitan like Don Gennaro and the policeman. He knows how to contrive solutions you don't expect. And God at this point works through our aircraft. I flew in one of those monsters, over cities like Naples. After I was shot down I could hear them from my cell, and I felt so powerless that I was wishing I didn't exist. You shudder as the sirens shatter the night and you run as fast as you can to the nearest shelter. It was a strange experience for me in my prison to hear our planes."

He stopped and looked away and there was silence.

"Yes," he continued, "it is a strange feeling when you hear those sirens and you are locked up in a room and cannot run away like the others and you wait for bombs to come down like rain."

"Now here we are." He pointed to the mug. "This is Naples. And the sirens tell us the thundering monsters are approaching — you can hear them coming — and you run for your life. Everyone runs from that bed on which Don Gennaro lies mimicking death while trying to protect his wife's booty. Everyone runs except Don Gennaro and the policeman. They could run away too, but they don't. Here is the key to the drama: *They do not run away when everybody else does."*

He paused again and then he turned to us with a commanding voice. "I want our audience to feel what these two Neapolitans must feel when they decide to stay despite those sirens."

We looked at him at a loss.

"I want to shock our audience, to get them away from this cozy campus, to blast them into another dimension, the one those of us who fought in Europe knew well. I want a frightened audience. I need some real sirens, the most powerful ones you can find. We must have them by tomorrow night."

Looking directly at us, he said, "You have done your part very well so far, but the play depends on that final scene. You cannot shock the audience with words. We need action. The play evokes the tragedy of the war. *I want the audience to feel it!"*

He pronounced his final plea like Caesar addressing his army on the banks of the Rubicon, first standing, erect and tall and strong, then pacing with vigorous steps as on a battlefield. Fully aware that he was addressing an audience of timid professors, who, except for Florit, had had no stage experience, he was trying to prod us into action:

"We must lead our American audience into the very heart of Naples in that one dark night."

We listened in silence. In silence, we moved out of the rehearsal room. It was just two days before the performance.

The next morning, Dolph received a call from a nearby fire station. They required more information about installing two sirens in Barnard Hall. A little later, the member of our troupe who provided the piano accompaniment showed up in Dolph's theater with two firemen. He hoped we didn't mind inviting his collaborators from the fire department to attend the performance. He didn't trust himself to work the sirens alone.

That night, to Dolph's complete satisfaction, the whole of Barnard Hall shook so powerfully that the audience was about to jump up and rush out. Only the voices of the two firemen could reassure them.

Dolph had succeeded. The evening was a wonderful success.

Epilogue

The performance produced an army of admirers of de Filippo, of Dolph Sweet, and of the professors who performed. The following day, over a cup of coffee, Dolph whispered to me what I already knew. The firemen had been contacted by a Columbia professor, the chairman of the Mathematics Department at Barnard, a mysterious figure who, it was rumored, had worked on the Manhattan project.

That happened to be the professor whom I had agreed to admit to my Advanced Italian class, although with some reluctance. There, although he didn't know a word of Italian at first, he quickly became one of my best students. I feared at first that he might be a spy for the College. Dolph laughed at my naïveté. I confessed to him also that the mathematician did not do his homework like the other students. Instead, he left me funny personal notes in Italian which I corrected and returned to him.

At the end of our next class in Advanced Italian, I thanked the math professor for his contribution to the play, the key to the play's success. He smiled, then added in French, so as to distance himself from the students around him: "It was the least I could do for you. You deserve much more. I hope I can do much more for you in the future" — and he looked at me with such intensity that I blushed and hurried out of the room.

His notes continued for months, signed always simply *ERL*. Then the notes became letters, 352 of them in all.

The acronym *ERL* stood for *Edgar Raymond Lorch*.

A Personal Note

Beyond Gibraltar may be read simply as the memoir of a woman in America reviewing her European past, with the history in the background, and exploring connections between the Old and the New World. I have laid out my story within my family between two world wars, from my childhood to the middle of my life. I have relived the story half a century and more later.

Memoir or what the French call récit? If the distinction matters, perhaps récit because the characters of *Beyond Gibraltar,* as soon as they feel comfortable, live as they feel like living, obeying only the law of their own lives. I "lived" joyfully with them, precious fragments of my own life.

The moments I have relived are those in which we experienced as our actual life what is now history. Smelling the hay in Mamma's village and warming up close to my siblings' bodies in the bed we shared for years, admiring gentle Mamma with gun in hand ready to shoot, dreaming of a beautiful Rome from the familiar Russian colony of Villa Moskau made Mussolini's dreams of empire merely secondary to our lives, though Hitler, after the *Anschluss,* hovered threateningly.

Il Duce's dreams became a nightmare for us after he shook hands with der Führer. Only then did we experience the deadly reality of war. The World War was a labyrinth which Il Duce entered without Ariadne's thread. At home, we saw it as a terrifying sequence of wars. Albania, a modest little country across the Adriatic, is suddenly subjected to our King. The Black Shirts bring to Rome the throne of emperors from an African country that now becomes part of an empire "due" to us by Destiny. Zeus thunders from Olympus attacked by our regular army, while thousands of Italian soldiers die in North Africa fighting alongside our German allies against the British. Suddenly — Radio Moscow tells us — a strange army from beyond Gibraltar lands in Sicily to fight alongside the British. Inch by inch they conquer the peninsula fighting our King's army. After a harsh bombardment of Rome and an Armistice, our army suddenly vanishes into the void, joining the rebels known as *partigiani*.

Rome falls to our quondam ally, now our enemy. One hot September day, we stand horrified in front of the body of a blond German boy-soldier killed on our doorstep, at the historic Porta Metronia. He is as blond as Corradino di Svevia of the thirteenth century, the last descendant of the Swabian dynasty of Holy Roman emperors. As traitors, we then brace ourselves for a year of harsh military treatment by General Albert Kesselring, now in charge of all operations in Italy. Two women of the family end up in prison, as they try to save their men. Finally, with a sense of relief, I hear myself repeating aloud again and again my first words of English, a language I love at first sight.

I cross Gibraltar.

What can four years of America offer to a survivor of that war? Plenty of healthy, radically new experiences which I face both as an explorer full of bright dreams and as an immigrant struggling in a land that has itself harshly suffered war.

As an escape from the laws that govern the story from above, *Beyond Gibraltar* became a reminder of how consequential Chance is in our lives. Chance is a powerful player in the unexpected developments of the story. ERL, the mathematician who became the companion of my life, told me shortly before he died that he would have liked to make my life the subject of a story because it was "so much more chancy" than his.

Beyond Gibraltar offers its protagonists the fulfillment of a dream of America that World War I had denied the protagonists of the preceding volume, *Mamma in her Village*. World War II leads me, the eldest daughter, to America. Yet, as I overcome the first hurdles of life in my adopted country by clinging to what had kept me alive back home, I delay the process of assimilation. By nature prone to dreams, I take longer than a down-to-earth immigrant to adapt to my new country. I make it only at the end of the story.

My behavior reminds me that today *Beyond Gibraltar* is a stage in a long-standing project. Originally planned during the early 1980s and the 1990s as a historical novel of explorers in the wake of Dante's

Ulysses (at that time a regular subject of my lectures), it has become, following the glorious celebrations in 1992 of the Columbus quincentenary, a story of immigrants going beyond Gibraltar.

The common inspiration of all my past attempts is my own long-standing fascination with the idea of ocean. As a child and adolescent, I dreamt of the ocean as what lies "beyond the beyond," beyond chains of high mountains that, because of family and political circumstances, held me in my village during my early years. I finally saw the ocean for the first time at seventeen at the mouth of the Tiber.

My first crossing of Gibraltar as a war bride on a Liberty ship in 1947 lives in my memory as a two-week struggle with high seas, during which the ocean became a more dangerous obstacle to the "beyond" of my dreams than the mountains that had kept me prisoner for too long. I survived that crossing trying to envision America in long debates with my disillusioned companions, faithfully reporting my experience in long letters to Mamma. I promised that I would call her and the others to America as soon as I had taken my first steps on the blessed land. But that would be after my husband and I had presented the play he had begun to translate while fighting the first Communists of the Cold War in Venezia Giulia.

In contrast to my maiden crossing in 1947, the trips to and from Europe — seventeen between the 1960s and the 1990s with my second husband and my new American family — evoke today an indescribable experience of nights with myriads of stars falling on me from a sky I could almost touch, and my husband trying in vain to give me an education in astronomy. They evoke the joyous experience of running through the crowded ship in search of a lost child — one of many — whom I would always find fully occupied in a new discovery.

Just as important as my life-long fascination with the ocean for *Beyond Gibraltar* was my many years of reading Dante to American audiences, both on and off the Columbia campus, from the perspective of Dante's Ulysses. Born to be an explorer, as an old man Ulysses abandons wife and family in his beloved Ithaca, dragging with him beyond Gibraltar the few survivors of his past adventures with a bewitching speech that every child in Italy had to learn by heart. With those old sailors, after six months of navigation, Dante's Ulysses is shipwrecked, like many explorers in Dante's time, much, I believe, to Dante's deep regret.

The book could not have developed into what it is today if, as I wrote it, I had not weathered on my own skin, over sixty years ago, the ups and downs of my adopted country from a New York that had become, for me and for my life-companion, our privileged balcony. The miracle happened slowly at first, then suddenly after 1970 — after the chronological limits *of Beyond Gibraltar* — with unexpected speed, mainly thanks to the many scholars who crisscrossed the ocean between Europe and America, meeting in New York, Rome, or Paris with the support of Barnard and Columbia. Those years, the happiest of my life, will, I hope, come alive again in a forthcoming work.

Chronology

Rosengarten: 1920-25 — Villa Soell in Gries
(Bolzano/Bozen): From Villa to Villa in Merano: 1925–1928
Villa Dolomitenblick: 1928–33
Villa Fontana: 1933–36
Villa Moskau: 1936–40
The Dream of Rome 1936–40
War at Porta Metronia: 1940–1945
A Vatican Marriage: February 1945 — February 1947
America: February 1947 — Fall 1951

Chronology of Events Related to the Story
Fascism: October 27, 1922 — July 25, 1943
June 10, 1924: Murder of last opposition leader, the Socialist Matteotti
Neo-Fascism: September 1943 — May 1945
Hitler in Power: 1933-1945
World War II in Europe: September 1939 — May 1945

Particular Events (Italy and Germany)
October 1935 — May 1936: Abyssinian war
October 1936: Axis Alliance Germany-Italy
March 1938: *Anschluss*: Germany annexes Austria (Tyrol's fears and hopes)
1939: Pact of Steel between Hitler and Mussolini
April 1939: Italy occupies Albania
October 1940-41: Italy occupies Greece. Greek resistance forces Italy to ask Germany for help.
April 1940-42: Axis North Africa campaign ends with defeat at El Alamein
July 19, 1943: exceptionally destructive bombardment of Rome
July 25, 1943: Mussolini, demoted by his own Party's Gran Consiglio, is detained by the King — first on the island of Ponza then on top of the Gran Sasso.
July 25 — September 8, 1943: King Victor Emanuel III governs Italy with General Badoglio as Prime Minister

September 8, 1943: Victor Emanuel III and General Badoglio flee Rome to join Allies at Brindisi, in the South. They sign an armistice with the Allies, effectively abandoning the Italian Army and two-thirds of Italy to German revenge.

September 9, 1943 — June 5, 1944: General Albert Kesselring — "smiling Albert" Commander of the German Army in Italy, having captured Rome after a brief resistance by isolated contingents, holds for nine months under his iron rule, while the Allies, who had landed at Anzio in January 1944, fight hard to reach the city, goal of the whole Mediterranean Campaign.

September 11, 1943: A German parachutist frees Benito Mussolini from the top of Gran Sasso. Mussolini creates the NeoFascist Republic of Italy, North of Rome. South of Rome, under Allied protection, the legitimate Kingdom of Italy survives with its King and Prime Minister.

June 5, 1944: General Clark ("Marcus Aurelius Clarcus") and his Fifth Army are the first Allied contingent to enter Rome, while exhausted German soldiers cross the city just ahead of them.

June 1944 — May 18, 1945: The Allies continue fighting north of Rome to the Gothic Line (north of Bologna) and beyond it to the Brenner Pass, the border between Italy and Austria. Allied Landings (Morocco and Algiers, Sicily, Salerno, Anzio): Amphibious landings in the Mediterranean, the first experiments in a new daring military strategy.

November 1942 — June 1943: With landings in Morocco and Algiers, the North African Campaign ends victoriously with the capture of Bizerte.

July 10, 1943 — August 17, 1943: Operation Husky: from Gela on the southeastern shore of the island, to Messina on the northeast, the occupation of Sicily, which had begun with a chaotic landing in Gela, ends successfully, observed by Supreme Commander Dwight Eisenhower from the island of Malta. (Operation Husky is distorted by the official Roman press; the event is taken most seriously by Kesselring. From Radio Moskau, Romans know that the Germans are preparing a resistance against further landings. The Russians are relieved: less pressure on their front.)

September 9-14, 1943. Operation Avalanche, landing in the Bay of Salerno with serious losses and occupation of Naples after heavy bombardments. Following the landing, the Allies fight for months during a cold winter first on the river Volturno between the region of Lazio (Rome) and Campania (Naples), and then in the area of Cassino. They bomb the Abbey of Montecassino — with no German inside — and are incapable of stopping atrocities committed by French Moroccan soldiers against the local population. (Their actions are covered superficially by the Roman press. The Romans get their news from couriers who leave the starving city regularly to get food or simply for relief from the protracted siege. Nothing stops the black-marketeers, among others, from freely moving north and south almost to the front line. Chewing gum and chocolate bars reach the Romans regularly. During brief leaves, German soldiers visit the city as tourists with guide books and cameras.)

January 22-31, 1944: With a landing at Anzio and Lav n o, c.100 miles from Rome, Operation Shingle (so named by Churchill) centers on General Clark and the Fifth Army. They advance very slowly. Poor preparation (Allies were busy preparing for Normandy) results in heavy losses.

June 5, 1944: The day before the landings in Normandy, the Allies reach Rome.

June 6, 1944 — May 18, 1945: Fighting continues north of Rome up to the Gothic Line (in Apennine Mountains above Bologna) and beyond, until Allies reach the Brenner Pass. (The Tyrol had been occupied by the Germans early in the War and Merano used as a hospital town.)

About the Author

Born and educated in a classical school in the Alto Adige –Sudtirol between the two world wars, Maristella de Panizza Lorch earned a doctorate in classical philology in 1942 at the University of Rome with the Accademico d'Italia Professor Vincenzo Ussani, Sr.

After fifty years of teaching, she is Professor Emerita of Italian and Medieval and Renaissance Studies at Barnard and Columbia. Among her books: the critical edition of Lorenzo Valla's De Voluptate (1431-44), its English translation On Pleasure, the edition of Ziliolo Zilioli's Michaelida (1431), A Defense of Life (a study of Renaissance Epicureanism) and, with the philosopher Ernesto Grassi, Folly and Insanity in Renaissance Literature, an interpretation of humanistic literature and chivalric poetry. Albert Rabil's four volume collection of essays on Renaissance Humanism was dedicated to her in recognition of her promotion of Medieval and Renaissance Studies in America.

Maristella Lorch is known at Columbia for her courses on Dante, Petrarch, Renaissance Humanism, Renaissance Theatre, Machiavelli and Ariosto; in Europe, particularly Italy and France, as an active promoter of international exchanges. She founded and directed the Center for Medieval and Renaissance Studies, the Center for Italian Studies, the Center for International Scholarly Exchange, and the Italian Academy for Advanced Studies in America (1991). She founded La Scuola New York Guglielmo Marconi, was member of the Advisory Board of the Lycee Français de New York, Vice-President of EPIC (the fellowship of Emeriti Professors in Columbia), and a teaching faculty member in the M.A. in Liberal Arts Program at Columbia's Graduate School of Arts and Sciences.

Since 1996, as Founding Director Emerita of the Academy for Advanced Studies, she worked at the trilogy Beyond Gibraltar, a fictionalized memoir or *récit d'initiation*, based on her Euro-American identity, while at the same time offering courses for adults on Dante, Homer, Virgil, and Ovid. The first volume of that trilogy, Mamma in her Village, was first published by Ruder Finn Press, N.Y., in 2005 and republished by TBR Books in 2020. The second volume, Beyond

Gibraltar, was first published in 2013 by Pegasus Press and republished by TBR Books in 2020. Finally, The Other Shore was originally published by TBR Books in 2019.

Maristella Lorch is the mother of three daughters and the widow of the mathematician Edgar Raymond Lorch. She divides her time between her homes in New York City and in Napanoch, N.Y.

About TBR Books

A Program of The Center for the Advancement of Languages, Education, and Communities (CALEC)

TBR Books is a program of the Center for the Advancement of Languages, Education, and Communities. We publish researchers and practitioners who seek to engage diverse communities on topics related to education, languages, cultural history, and social initiatives. We translate our books in a variety of languages to further expand our impact. Become a member of TBR Books and receive complimentary access to all our books.

Our Books in English

Immigrant Dreams By Barbara Goldowsky

Rainbows, Masks, and Ice Cream By Deana Sobel Lederman

Can We Agree to Disagree? By Agathe Laurent and Sabine Landolt

Salsa Dancing in Gym Shoes: Developing Cultural Competence to Foster Latino Student Success by Tammy Oberg de la Garza and Alyson Leah Lavigne

Mamma in her Village by Maristella de Panniza Lorch

The Other Shore by Maristella de Panniza Lorch

The Clarks of Willsborough Point: A Journey through Childhood by Darcey Hale

Beyond Gibraltar by Maristella de Panniza Lorch

The Gift of Languages: Paradigm Shift in U.S. Foreign Language Education by Fabrice Jaumont and Kathleen Stein-Smith

Two Centuries of French Education in New York: The Role of Schools in Cultural Diplomacy by Jane Flatau Ross

The Clarks of Willsborough Point: The Long Trek North by Darcey Hale

The Bilingual Revolution: The Future of Education is in Two Languages by Fabrice Jaumont

Our Books in Translation

Rainbows, Masks, and Ice Cream By Deana Sobel Lederman is available in 7 languages.

Can We Agree to Disagree? By Agathe Laurent and Sabine Landolt is available in 2 languages.

The Bilingual Revolution by Fabrice Jaumont is available in 11 languages.

The Gift of Languages by Fabrice Jaumont and Kathleen Stein-Smith is available in 3 languages.

Our books are available on our website and on all major online bookstores as paperback and e-book. Some of our books have been translated in Arabic, Chinese, English, French, German, Hebrew, Italian, Japanese, Polish, Russian, Spanish. For a listing of all books published by TBR Books, information on our series, or for our submission guidelines for authors, visit our website at

http://www.tbr-books.org

About CALEC

The Center for the Advancement of Languages, Education, and Communities is a nonprofit organization with a focus on multilingualism, cross-cultural understanding, and the dissemination of ideas. Our mission is to transform lives by helping linguistic communities create innovative programs, and by supporting parents and educators through research, publications, mentoring, and connections.

We have served multiple communities through our flagship programs which include:

- TBR Books, our publishing arm; which publishes research, essays, and case studies with a focus on innovative ideas for education, languages, and cultural development;

- Our online platform provides information, coaching, support to multilingual families seeking to create dual-language programs in schools;

- NewYorkinFrench.net, an online platform which provides collaborative tools to support New York's Francophone community and the diversity of people who speak French.

We also support parents and educators interested in advancing languages, education, and communities. We participate in events and conferences that promote multilingualism and cultural development. We provide consulting for school leaders and educators who implement multilingual programs in their school. For more information and ways, you can support our mission, visit

http://www.calec.org

www.ingramcontent.com/pod-product-compliance
Lightning Source LLC
Chambersburg PA
CBHW072000150426
43194CB00008B/940